DEVELOPING MANAGERIAL INFORMATION SYSTEMS

Developing Managerial Information Systems

Andrew M. McCosh, Mawdudur Rahman and
Michael J. Earl

First edition 1981
Reprinted 1982

Published by
THE MACMILLAN PRESS LTD
London and Basingstoke
Companies and representatives
throughout the world

Printed in Hong Kong

British Library Cataloguing in Publication Data

McCosh, Andrew M.
　　Developing managerial information systems
　　1. Management information systems
　　I. Title　　II. Rahman, Mawdudur
　　III. Earl, Michael J.
　　658.4′03　　　　T58.6

ISBN 0–333–23374–3

55, 306

To Anne, Rasheeda and Alison

Contents

Preface

Organisations are investing more and more in management information systems (MIS). The uncertainty of the business environment, the complexity of the management tasks, and the rapid advances which have occurred in information technology have all contributed to this growing investment. The scale of the investment has caused managers of many organisations to seek to ensure that the information systems are efficient and effective. The size of the MIS industry has stimulated researchers to explore and seek to understand information processing in organisations. There has been a considerable growth in interest from managers, MIS professionals and business students in the overall task of 'managing information'.

We believe this book will be of value and interest to (1) managers with responsibility for, or experience of, information systems, (2) MIS professionals who wish to understand the managerial and organisational interfaces which any information system must have if it is to be valuable to the organisation, and (3) management and business students who recognise the importance of MIS and are studying the subject at an advanced level. We expect that each of these groups will use the book in a different manner from the others.

The book is structured around two themes. First, we use Anthony's established framework for planning and control systems. This has influenced a great deal of MIS thinking and has provided a useful classification scheme for viewing the different management roles which information systems can fulfil. In Part II of this book, we examine operational control systems; Part III is devoted to management control systems; and Part IV is concerned with strategic planning.

Secondly, within each of these managerial role levels, we have considered three broad topics. At each level we discuss (1) the management context, (2) the technical issues involved, including the principles of systems design, and (3) the vital behavioural issues involved in the use of information.

Before beginning our discussions of these topics, however, we believe it essential to introduce certain principles, both technical and behavioural, which seem to us to apply to all kinds of MIS. These are discussed in Part I of the book. Finally, two chapters are somewhat independent of this structure: Chapter 6 examines database management which is critical in operational control but is relevant to all levels of MIS; and Chapter 11 discusses systems performance measurement, with particular reference to both operational control and management control.

Every user will doubtless have his own way of using this book. However, we have given thought to the diversity of possible users and believe there are three approaches to this book which will be sufficiently widely used to be worth recording here as a matter of guidance. Two of these are very obvious ones. The first is to read the book through from beginning to end, which we would suggest for those who seek a comprehensive appreciation of the subject. The second would be for managers and practitioners who have particular and circumstantial needs for parts of the book. For example, a manager confronted with a management control problem would proceed directly to Part III, whereas someone interested in strategic planning could go straight to Part IV. We would remind readers choosing this approach that Part I is (at least in our opinion) essential background for the proper understanding of each of the later sections.

The third approach to the book would be as material for a business or management course. A course divided into eight modules may be offered following the structure given in the table, especially if the book is supplemented by case analysis or project work.

Module	Sessions recommended	Chapters	Topic
1	1	1	The Nature of Information
2	1	2	Information in Use
3	1	3	MIS Design
4	1–3	4,5,7	Operational Control MIS
5	1	6	Database Management
6	1–3	8–10	Management Control MIS
7	1	11	MIS Performance Measurement
8	2–4	12–15	Strategic Planning MIS

Our objective has been to be practical. Accordingly the ideas, framework and principles presented in this book are derived from proven experience (often our own), applied research and conceptual frameworks which have been found workable in practice. However, at the strategic level in which experience of MIS is as yet limited, we have allowed ourselves a certain amount of speculation. Proven techniques are not sufficiently numerous in this area for us to be sure of the choices.

Such is the breadth of MIS as a subject that we have drawn on many disciplines. Inevitably, we may have excluded some work which others might have emphasised. However, we believe that this book reflects the mainstream of MIS thought and experience at this time. Any errors obviously remain our own responsibility.

We are grateful for the patience and care with which secretarial assistance was provided by Mary Heath, Wynne Waterworth and Md. Alauddin. We also are grateful for the sustained encouragement received while this book was being written from our wives, Anne, Rasheeda and Alison.

Manchester, Dacca and Oxford, 1979   ANDREW M. McCOSH
                                                      MAWDUDUR RAHMAN
                                                      MICHAEL J. EARL

Part I Introduction

1 The Need to be Informed

We have written this book in the hope of helping to promote professionalism in the design, construction, and use of management information systems. A management information system, if it is going to be effective, must be congruent with the decisions to be taken by managers in their evolving roles, must make use of technological developments in systems, accounting, and computation that are just sufficiently advanced to ensure that no major opportunities are missed, and must fit the style of the organisation and of its people. To make a system fit all of the specifications of the last sentence is a very tall order indeed. But that is what being professional entails. And that is our objective.

Concepts and techniques have been drawn from many disciplines to create the 'state of the art' in MIS as it stands at present. No doubt other disciplines will be drawn upon in the future, and no doubt also the existing disciplines will be drawn upon for further concepts as the needs of managers and of designers evolve and our understanding of these needs grows. But at the present, that is, early in 1978, it seems to us reasonable to draw upon the theory base of six disciplines in addition to the slowly growing theory base of MIS itself. These are corporate strategy, management control, accountancy, sociology, social psychology, and computer methods. Even this shortened list of parent disciplines offers a formidable breadth of knowledge.

It is not uncommon for a manager to have training in accountancy or in management control, and he will have a practical understanding of corporate strategy. Many specialists in information systems have a thorough knowledge of computing systems. Many managers and a small proportion of the computer specialists have a practical knowledge of behavioural matters, though neither group has, usually, any training in either psychology or sociology. We therefore have a possible problem of communication. Not only do the principal parties involved in the design, construction, and use of information systems tend to have knowledge of different segments of the total body of knowledge that MIS involves, but also they often have a very different orientation toward the topic. The manager sees himself as an executive for whom an effective MIS is a

3

desirable tool. The systems specialist may see himself as a guardian of his own original discipline's interests, the accountant guarding the integrity of the accounting mechanism, the computer man promoting the use of advanced technical methods, and so on. The complete breadth of coverage required for professionalism as a user, a designer, or a builder of an information system is not easily found in one place.

Logically, one can try to solve this problem in several ways. One could help managers learn about computing and the behavioural sciences. Or one could give the accountants a better understanding of strategy and behavioural science so that they could communicate these items to the computer people. Or one could try to help each of the groups to learn about each subject.

Or, as we have sought to achieve in this present volume, one could assist all the parties in learning more about management from each other's point of view. We regard the management task as paramount in the design, construction, and use of any MIS, and we look upon all the other disciplines as useful but subordinate.

We shall, therefore, be looking at the contribution each discipline can make to the solution of various kinds of management problem. It is our hope that this orientation will help managers, accountants, computer specialists, and all others involved to produce more useful systems and to employ them to better effect.

THE DILEMMA OF SYSTEM DESIGN

A perennial issue in the area of system design, whether the system be for accounting, for planning, or for control, is the choice of designer. At one extreme, the end user of the system output might be seen as the best designer. At the other extreme the professional in systems design will produce and operate the system after consulting the user group. Although the extremes are very rare indeed, the normal firm has to decide where to place itself on that spectrum.

If the user group decide to design the system themselves, and if the firm does not have a central systems staff, they may hire outsiders to do the work. The consultants will then retire from the scene, leaving only any required technical help behind. Such systems tend to be very clearly aimed at managers' perceived problems and requirements. Each manager, or group of managers, can obtain the reporting system he wants. And he can change it at once when the need arises. But the system will tend to be technically primitive, poorly documented and maintained, incomplete, and may well miss many of the opportunities created by new technical developments in both computation and accountancy.

The central headquarters approach involves the use of a team of highly trained specialists who will consult the user group carefully, and will then design, implement, and operate the resulting system for the users. A system devised according to this plan will normally be comprehensive, integrated, and will make good use of recent developments in the technologies concerned. It will normally also respond well to the needs of the users at the time of initial design, and will be maintained and documented in accordance with the best practice. But such systems have tended to be rather slow to respond to changes in the needs of managers, and have often failed to meet the idiosyncratic requirements of particular executives' styles.

Where, then, should an entity position itself on the spectrum? It is our contention that the decision should depend upon the level of managerial awareness possessed by the entity's information specialists. The more fully this group can understand the managerial issues, and the better their understanding of the essence of the managers' tasks, the greater will be the justification for entrusting the bulk of the design and implementation work to the central group. Conversely, if the central group is technically talented but is not equipped by inclination, experience, and formal training to cope with the management issues, the users ought to be encouraged to do-it-themselves. Our hope is that this book will contribute to increased understanding, on the part of the technically able specialist, of the essence of management. At the same time, we hope that the manager will be assisted in seeing the issues which are of concern to him in a new light, by studying them from the viewpoint of the several specialisms discussed earlier.

THE TWO FACTS ABOUT SYSTEMS DESIGN

For many years, it has been known that top management support and user involvement were crucial to systems design success. A series of studies of systems and their effectiveness have been made, and all, without exception, have identified these two elements as critical. The very early work of Garrity, Taylor and Dean, and McKinsey each came to the same conclusion. Ginzberg, in a far-reaching survey of similar studies, reinforced their view. We can take it as a fact that the close personal support of the highest levels of manager in an enterprise is crucial to systems success. We can also take it as a fact that any system which is designed without the active support and involvement of the people who have to use its output will either fail or, at best, be mediocre.

A major airline, for example, obtained a computer in 1969 to carry out detailed analysis of statistical information. The staff of the chief executive thought the top man would want these data in due course, but did not obtain his approval in advance. It was still analysing the statistics in 1975. And they were still expecting him to start using the results shortly.

A chain of food shops in the north of England put in a computerised stock reordering system in 1972. As the system had been used for some years in a very similar chain store in the south-west, no need was felt for consultation with the store managers and buyers, except to get their agreement that such a system would be a good idea in principle. Unfortunately, the buyers in the south-west had much more discretion, and the managers much less, than had been the practice in the northern chain. Two of the northern buyers left and one suffered a nervous breakdown, because of the unaccustomed stress. The managers were upset for the opposite reason, and condoned carelessness in feeding data that they would never have allowed in their shop operations. The system reached its planned level of impact on operations only in 1977, three traumatic years late.

The above anecdotes could be replicated a hundred times over. The early history of computerised information systems saw far too many violations of the two basic rules.

There do not, however, seem to be any other facts which are so incontrovertible or of such universal applicability. All the other concepts and theories and rules-of-thumb seem to have exceptions. In the present volume we shall try to identify some of these concepts and to indicate the circumstances in which they are relevant. These concepts are drawn from each of the six disciplines mentioned before, and will be discussed in the section to which they relate most closely.

THE ORGANISATION OF THE BOOK

Throughout the book we have drawn upon the framework for analysis first put forward by Robert N. Anthony. This framework has proved very worthwhile and helpful in the analysis of control systems for nearly two decades. He divides the topic into three parts. The first of these, operational control, is concerned with getting an assigned job done efficiently. Operational control systems are intended to measure performance against a clearly defined target. Such systems are characterised by large volumes of repetitive data, by reasonably clear-cut operating rules, and by fairly high degrees of automation.

The second category is management control. This includes the process of designing an organisation which will carry out policies and also entails the measurement of the performance of groups of people, including managers. The task in this case is usually defined only in broad terms and the management control system design issue includes the selection of a procedure for carrying the tasks out.

The third category in Anthony's framework, strategic planning, is the least precise. It is concerned with the problem of deciding what goals the organisation should strive for. It is concerned with selecting broad methods of approach which can later be worked out in detail as part of the management control process. The information systems required to support strategic planning are, necessarily, vaguer, more forward-looking, and longer-term, than those required for the support of management decisions and operational decisions.

The three principal segments of this book are devoted to the study of operational planning and control systems, management planning and control systems, and strategic planning systems, respectively. The kind of systems which are needed to support the different managerial activities are themselves different. The operational control and information systems can normally be very precise, can normally be measured with accuracy, and normally include a relatively small number of dimensions, each of which can be measured with some assurance on a numerical scale. For strategic planning the reverse is true on all of these fronts. The data are vague. They are nearly all imprecise as to definition and certainly as to measurement. The questions which have to be asked are themselves of an unstructured kind. The answers may be in numerical form, but are more commonly in the form of tentative verbal descriptions. It is relatively easy to say that a product is selling better than, or not as well as, the operational plan had suggested. It is quite another matter to evaluate the prospects of a move into a different industrial sphere, perhaps involving a corporate acquisition. The latter problem is not only larger in scale and of greater financial importance, it also has more dimensions, and is therefore more difficult to solve. Information systems to support this kind of strategic decision are normally as different from operational systems as the decisions themselves differ.

Before we move into discussions of these three kinds of planning and control systems in Parts II, III and IV of the book, we must set forth a number of basic principles in the rest of Part I. The rest of this chapter will be concerned with the nature of the basic commodity with which the designer, the implementer, and the user of any system must be concerned, information itself.

Then, in Chapters 2 and 3 we will introduce a number of behavioural and computational concepts which will be applicable in all three of the major segments of the work.

ON THE NATURE OF INFORMATION

If it were possible to provide a workable definition of the term 'information', which would be applicable in all, or substantially all situations, then the many problems which have been associated with the design, development, and use of information delivery systems, should be rendered simpler.

If we could, further, produce a procedure for valuing information, we would have guidance as to how much money it was appropriate to spend on an information delivery system of a particular design. Obviously by reference to our definitions it would be possible to separate information from non-information in any particular situation, and concentrate on designing the information delivery system so that it generated the information and only the information.

Attention has been directed towards the nature of information from many sources and for many years, though it should be said that much of that attention has been a peripheral aspect of the study of some other topic. The literatures of communication theory (sometimes called information theory), of educational psychology, of management control, and of philosophy all have contributions to make towards a useful definition. It is not surprising that these diverse disciplines, tending to emphasise different things, are to some extent in conflict in what they have to say about information. It may therefore turn out that the investigation will prove lengthy, and no guarantee of results can be made. Nevertheless, if we are ever going to get a definition, we have to start somewhere.

It is difficult to discuss information. What we can say with assurance and certainty is trite. What we would really like to know about is ill-defined, imprecise. In the present chapter, we shall try to set forth a preliminary intuitive model of the process by means of which an individual becomes informed. We shall see that the state of 'being informed' is a function of the psychological traits of the individual, as well as of the system for delivering data to the users.

WHAT IS INFORMATION?

We could begin by considering the possible opinion that information is identical to knowledge. Obviously the two words can be used synonymously, but it is useful to distinguish between the two in the sense that information systems are not the same as the mechanisms used for the extension of knowledge. After all, it is at least arguably true that knowledge is eternal in character and that it need have no specific purpose. Indeed, it is an article of faith on the part of many workers in the field of philosophy that the growth of knowledge is beneficial by its very character, without regard to the ultimate purpose to which that knowledge may be devoted— this is certainly no place to enter into that controversy. Information seems, however, to have a materially different character. It is undoubtedly a selection from the totality of knowledge and shares its characteristics to that extent, but it has a variety of additional characteristics.[1]

The literature of philosophy is full of references to the general question: what does it mean to 'know something'? Some of the results obtained in these analyses are rather startling for the non-philosopher. The criteria used to decide whether knowledge exists are not universally agreed. Some argue that it is not possible to have direct knowledge of anything at all; others that we can best be 'acquainted' with a proposition. There seems to be some agreement that one cannot know anything if it is not *true*, and there seems to be some further agreement that the *subject* (the person who is the knower or the one who is to be informed) *must believe* the proposition before he can be said to know it. In addition, it has been pointed out that the belief must be founded on some *reasonable base* before it can be said that the proposition is known.

Such grounds are insufficient for it to be possible to say that the subject is 'informed' by that proposition. Instead it is necessary that he be able to *alter his behaviour* because the proposition has come before him.[2] The alteration in behaviour may be in any of its more obvious forms, but we would specifically include the decision to do nothing different from what he would have done before, provided the proposition either strengthens or weakens his belief in the validity of his previously chosen course.[3]

For example, I may know that an atom contains electrons, protons and neutrons, but if I am not a physicist, my behaviour is not going to be altered by that knowledge. I may know, by reading its destination board, the name of the place a bus is going to. If my current purpose is to board a bus, I will be informed by that destination board that the bus is or is not the one I am waiting for. On the other hand, if my reading of the destination board was accidental, and I have no intention of getting on a bus at all, my knowledge of its destination cannot inform me; I will go on walking whatever the board says. Of course, if the destination was, in fact, where I wanted to go, but I had not previously intended to go by bus, the reading is also informative; my current purpose, in such a case, would be to get to X. This facet of information is often of the greatest importance in a hierarchic organisation. The various roles played by each level in the hierarchy are, obviously, different. These differences imply similar differences between the perceptual 'filters' through which the various role-occupants absorb data. One person may therefore not regard as information a message which another person at a different level in the same organisation might regard as vital. The 'filters' by means of which data are brought into the entity must be carefully tuned to the role-levels they aim to service.

The *passage of time* is another factor which determines whether information exists. It is quite conceivable for a proposition to be known by the subject for some considerable time, without his being informed by it. Later the proposition may assume the characteristics of information to the subject because of outside events, and it may later revert to the status of knowledge again. For example, a subject may possess geographical knowledge which may become converted into information when he visits the area and has to navigate in it. His change in circumstances, that is his move into the area, converts the pre-existing knowledge into information without any change occurring in the knowledge itself. Or again, a piece of military intelligence may possess the attribute of potential information when it is first obtained by an agent. However, it may lose that attribute before it is delivered to the field commander, who may get the news too late to change his behaviour or that of his army. Clearly it is a function of an information delivery system to try to avoid problems of that sort. Knowledge must be conveyed to the subject before or during its currency as information, for obvious reasons.

A further feature that characterises the word information deals with its *probabilistic nature*. This feature of information has been most fully explored by the communications theorists, who tend to be more concerned with the problems of transmitting a message along a 'noisy' channel with a given required probability of success than with the broader problem of information meaning and relevance with which we are here concerned. Nonetheless, the concept that information and entropy are essentially equivalent is an important idea which should be taken into account in our analysis.[4] The basic idea behind this concept is that the less we know about a given situation, the more we would expect to learn from a message which told us about that situation. The entropy, the uncertainty associated with the source of the message, has a very specific and clearly defined meaning in the communication theory literature, and this contrasts importantly with the much vaguer idea of ignorance described in the previous sentence. This distinction has made it very difficult indeed to apply the methods of communication theory to the broader problem. It is doubtful if we can say more, at the present stage, than that the information definition ultimately reached should not be inconsistent with the intuitively attractive ideas of the communications theory literature. The prior state of knowledge of the subject about the topic should be a determinant of the value of propositions he receives about that topic. Some experimental work has already been done on this matter, to try to quantify various aspects of the relationship; more is undoubtedly required.

Some further light on the nature of information may be cast by the science of pragmatism. Peirce, for example, said 'consider what effects, that might conceivably have practical bearings, we conceive the object of our conception to have. Then our conception of these effects is the whole of our conception of the object'.[5] In this maxim Peirce implicitly classes as meaningless anything (including any message) that has no effect on practical affairs. William James put the same point slightly differently when he said 'what difference would it practically make to anyone if this notion rather than that notion were true? If no practical difference whatever can be traced, then the alternatives mean practically the same thing, and all dispute is idle'.[6]

If the reader has by this point concluded that the concept of information is an elusive one, we are very willing to agree. It is a difficult concept. As a philosophical question, it may even be unanswerable, though perhaps we should leave it to the philosophers to deal with that point. But we must have some kind of operational definition of information if we are going to talk about information systems and their management and use at a professional standard. Until a logically complete definition is obtained, therefore, we shall have to be content with the simpler and more usable definition with which we end this chapter. We have not found its logical circularity to be a practical obstacle to its use, although clearly it would be difficult to justify theoretically.

We define information to be any piece of knowledge which may rationally be applied to a decision by a person who has the authority and responsibility to take that decision.

In Parts II, III and IV of this book we shall look at a range of levels in enterprises, and at a range of decisions, to see how information may be systematically generated and effectively used.

NOTES

1. Peter Drucker, in his 1964 book *Managing for Results*, suggests that the ability to *use* knowledge is the distinctive characteristic of an organisation: the knowledge itself is not a business resource but a resource of society (Heinemann, p. 5).
2. See C. Cherry, *On Human Communication*. Cambridge, Mass.: MIT Press, 1966, p. 228 *et seq.*
3. See Shannon, C. E. and Weaver, W., *The Mathematical Theory of Communication*. Urbana, Illinois: University of Illinois Press, 1964, p. 5.
4. See Pierce, J. R. *Symbols, Signals and Noise*. London: Hutchinson, 1962.
5. Peirce, C. S., *The Collected Papers of Charles Sanders Peirce*. Vol. V, para. 2, (1878).
6. James, W., *Pragmatism*. London: Longmans Green, 1908, p. 45.

BIBLIOGRAPHY

Anthony, R. N., *Planning and Control Systems, A Framework for Analysis.* Harvard Business School, Division of Research, 1964.
Cherry, C., *On Human Communication*. Cambridge, Mass.: MIT Press, 1966.
Drucker, P., *Managing for Results*. London, Heinemann, 1964.
Garrity, J. T., 'Top Management and Computer Profits', *Harvard Business Review*, July/August 1963.
Ginzberg, M. J., *Implementation As A Process of Change: Framework and Empirical Study*. Cambridge, Mass.: Centre for Information Systems Research, 1975.
James, W., *Pragmatism*. London: Longmans Green, 1908.
Peirce, C. S., *Collected Papers*, Vol. V, ed. C. Hartshawe and O. P. Weiss. Cambridge, Mass.: Harvard University Press, 1878.
Pierce, J. R., *Symbols, Signals and Noise*. London: Hutchinson, 1962.
Shannon, C. E. and Weaver, W., *The Mathematical Theory of Communication*. Urbana, Illinois: University of Illinois Press, 1964.
Taylor, J. W. and Dean, N. J., 'Managing to Manage the Computer', *Harvard Business Review*, September/October 1966.

2 Behavioural Principles of Systems Design

If a management information system is designed with social and behavioural design principles in mind, it is more likely to be effective and to be adaptable than if only technical principles are considered. This chapter seeks to acquaint systems designers and users with some of these social and behavioural principles.

All systems design work is carried on against an organisational background. The goals of the organisation, its structure, its controls, and its environment all affect the systems designers' work. There is little point in designing, say, an accounting system that is technically perfect if it assumes a hierarchical structure, whereas the firm actually operates as a cooperative.

ENVIRONMENTAL ANALYSIS

As a first step, the designer must learn about the environment of the business, both internal and external. Some of the elements of each are listed in Table 2.1.

TABLE 2.1. Environmental context of an MIS

Internal context	External context
Organisational functions, purposes, structures, control strategies, resources and constraints; individual members and groups; styles, needs and motives of the individuals; group norms, pressures and controls.	Social, economic and political factors, technological aspects (level of technology) level of economic achievement and aspiration of people, cultural values and norms, information market and technology.

The external environment provides the boundaries for operation of the firm. The firm devises its goals, plans, and controls in the light of local social values, cultural norms, and economic opportunities. The society regulates the organisation by means of a range of social control processes. Each society devises its own system for controlling organisations and influencing people, and they can be very different. For instance:

Two groups of operatives from two different societies worked on a joint project. At the end of each day, workers from the society characterised by the free economic system used to carry their tools back with them. The work supervisor had to count them all, and enter in the tool inventory and close the book. Nothing like this happened with the other group coming from the controlled economy. They used to leave behind their tools at the work place. They did this to save the time and energy which was needed to bring the tools and take them back every day. Both the systems worked very well in their respective social-economic systems.

It is worth noting that private tool ownership was not allowed in the controlled economy. Nevertheless, the very considerable differences in control systems between cultures is illustrated by this simple example.

As the organisational design depends on the external environment, the MIS design remains contingent on it. Many of the organisational control systems have interfaces with the outside environments. An organisation needs to commit a portion of its resources in the boundary management activity due to the pressure and purpose of the environment. An MIS has a definite role to play in this area. Examples of organisational investments in boundary management activities may be advertising and other promotional activities, new investments, public relations and R&D activities.

The relationship between organisation, MIS and the environment is expressed by Figure 2.1.

FIGURE 2.1. Environment and organisation interface

An organisation seeks to maintain its interface relationships with the environment through its information system. Nevertheless, communication can occur outside the formal MIS. If the MIS is inadequate or ineffective, these informal means maintain the vital links between the environment and the organisation. However, even if the MIS is excellent, it is not possible for the MIS to capture the entire panorama of the environment needed for the organisation. Both the environment and the organisation are dynamic. The continuous monitoring and control of environmental inputs is not enough: periodic reviews of the systems are also essential.

The economic system offers constraints and resources for an organisation. The firm cannot plan to operate beyond what the economic system can accommodate. Again, it cannot lag much behind the need of the system. Its management style, products and production technology and marketing strategies are influenced by the external economic environment. For example, the success of a product depends on its market acceptability. Among other things, the organisation seeks to provide a product of appropriate quality at a reasonable price. The two relevant control aspects are quality control systems and the cost control system. These systems need market information to formulate their goals. An MIS establishes a link between the market and the specific control systems and makes relevant information available. Pharmaceutical companies operating in a large number of countries with varied economic and social conditions are found to vary their information systems among countries.

In a dynamic economy, changes continuously threaten growth. Setting up an organisational system in such an environment requires an information system which is advanced and able to maintain viability through adequate information monitoring, control and feedback. In contrast, in a slower-moving, traditional economy the threat from change is low. In such a situation an MIS is used more to maintain the existing condition than to monitor and manage change information.

THE ORGANISATIONAL PERSPECTIVE

An organisation is a consciously created artefact with a set of rules and goals which may change. It possesses a pattern of relationships. It often seeks to effect changes in social relationships.

Many theorists have worked on the design of organisations. The earliest concepts were mechanistic, and sought to design organisational rules which could last for long periods and which were often quite rigid. More recent work has emphasised the need for fluidity in organisational design, if the organisation is to continue to meet the needs of its evolving environments. We shall look first at the mechanistic theories, upon which many enterprises are still designed, and then look at more recent organisation theory work on structures and management systems.

MECHANISTIC APPROACHES

Mechanistic approaches to organisations are primarily based on traditional views which are mainly concerned with the stable characteristics of the organisation. Readers familiar with these aspects of the organisation may prefer to give this section only a quick review. This section provides a brief description of management functions and organisational aspects based on such traditional views.

The traditional approach to organising focuses on work division and work combination. First, the work is broken down into components and then the components are combined into meaningful clusters on the basis of products, customers, functions, processes, territories, and time. Within each of these departments, managers are involved in management functions, which include planning, organising, staffing, directing and control.

The basic steps involved in the process of organising, following traditional approaches are as follows:

(1) Defining the objectives of the organisation. In this concept a limited number of objectives are considered. These objectives are related primarily to economic efficiency, e.g. profit earning.
(2) The necessary activities are derived from the objectives. The activities are broken down into components. These components are regrouped into workable units. This process involves work division and work combination.

Task performance requires defining duties and assigning responsibilities to qualified or trainable personnel. Then, the different task positions are linked by formal rules and procedures to coordinate the activities of different positions. The tasks to be done are divided among departments. The key factors which are considered in departmentalisation are:

(1) Specialisation—the people in each department can specialise in a certain kind of work, which may help them become very good at it.
(2) Facilitate control—division and subdivision of tasks makes control of tasks easier. Tasks may be separated in such a way as to provide internal check, as for example inventory control, control of cash receipts and disbursement.

(3) Aid coordination—departments need hierarchical control. Coordination among different tasks and functions is achieved primarily through the hierarchical relationships.

(4) Cost effectiveness—one objective of the organisation is to improve performance efficiency by being cost-effective. Creation of additional departments increases costs. Benefits from additional departments must justify the additional costs.

(5) Consideration of human aspects—within each department attention to human needs and values can become easier.

The most common departmental organisation on a functional basis follows the following divisions:

(1) Finance—activities of providing funds and ensuring their effective use.

(2) Supply—procurement of raw materials and other inputs for production.

(3) Production—providing and maintaining facilities to convert raw materials into the finished products and controlling the production operation.

(4) Sales—marketing the products.

(5) Personnel—providing people for operation.

Another common kind of functional organisation is the following:

(1) Marketing—a broader term than sales, includes distribution, channel selection, promotion, and sales.

(2) Production—providing and maintaining facilities to convert raw materials into the finished products and controlling the production operation.

(3) Accounting and finance—accounting for utilisation of resources and providing resources and assuring their effective and efficient use.

(4) Research and development—to develop new products or modify existing products.

In most functional organisation designs, the structure is hierarchical. There are organisational links between the top management, the middle management and the first line managers. The inputs to the structure, which give it its linking strength, are in the form of policies, functions, responsibilities, authority levels, and status. Some examples are shown in Figures 2.2, 2.3 and 2.4.

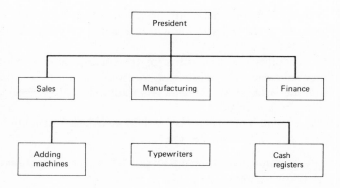

FIGURE 2.2. A line organisation with manufacturing departments divided on a product basis

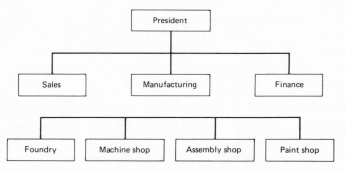

FIGURE 2.3. A line organisation with manufacturing departments divided on an operational basis

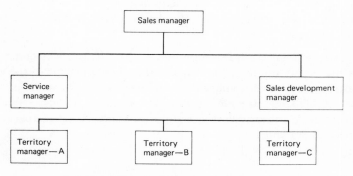

FIGURE 2.4. Example of sales organisation at territory level

FIVE BASIC PRINCIPLES

Five basic principles are used to manage task performance, departmentalisation and structuring of activities in a functional organisation. These tenets are the scalar principle, unity of command, span of control, organisational specialisation and parity of authority and responsibility. The scalar principle defines the hierarchical relationship between the top management and subordinates. It emphasises the need for the flow of authority and responsibility from top to bottom in an unbroken chain through delegation.

Unity of command has the goal of avoiding dual subordination on specific tasks. No member should receive orders from more than one boss.

Span of control sets the limit on the number of men one should effectively supervise. The limits specified by theorists vary from three at the top of the firm to six at the bottom. At the higher level, where responsibility is heavy the span should be small, and at the lower level where activities are repetitive the span may be large.

Organisational specialisation assumes that the task can be divided and performed efficiently. Specialisation occurs through division of labour. The tasks of each department are grouped around some common base, e.g. products, process, functions, etc. Parity of authority and responsibility recognises that if a manager is assigned responsibility for task achievement, he needs to be given, or earn, matching authority.

It must be remembered that the management and organisation perspective based on the traditional principles largely failed to consider the behavioural and other dynamic aspects of organisation.

LINE AND STAFF ORGANISATION

Line and staff organisations are very important concepts associated with the traditional hierarchical organisation. Line organisation establishes direct line relationships of the lower supervisory positions with the higher supervisory positions. Authority flows from the topmost executive to the subordinate at lowest level in a straight line relationship.

Staff organisations are created to make up the deficiencies of line type organisation. They primarily serve advisory functions. However, line positions of one function may fulfil staff roles for other functions. For example, factory accountants have line relationships with the head office accounting organisation and a staff relationship with the factory management.

FUNCTIONS OF MANAGERS

From the viewpoint of designers of management information systems, the functional tasks of managers are outlined below. The functional focus is based on an analysis of what managers do. The five fundamental functions of management are: planning; organising; staffing; directing; control.

PLANNING

Planning precedes all managerial actions. It involves development of alternatives, selection of goals, defining of policies, and developing procedures and programmes to achieve organisational and departmental goals.

ORGANISING

Organising involves task identification, definition, grouping and distribution among subordinates, fixing of responsibility and authority and also ensuring coordination between different activities and efforts.

STAFFING

Staffing involves the process of fulfilling the personnel requirements of the organisation. It covers such functions as recruiting, selecting, training and hiring personnel to man the organisation to perform its tasks.

DIRECTING

Directing involves leading, guiding, supervising and motivating subordinates in the organisation. It is essentially a leadership function and is concerned with people.

CONTROL

Controlling is ensuring the performance of events to conform to plans. It involves (1) setting a standard, (2) measurement of performance, (3) comparisons against standard, and (4) corrective actions.

Here we have drawn the attention of the students of system design to a few basic things, such as departmentalisation, management tasks and line and staff functions. These essential bases are necessary for the system designer:

(1) to develop the hierarchical view of the organisation; (2) to understand the functional, line, and staff relationships; (3) to comprehend the authority/subordinate relationships; and (4) to realise the managerial tasks involved in each position.

From here we proceed to more complex but also more relevant aspects of the organisational system. So far, we have ignored two things: (1) human and behavioural aspects, and (2) the dynamic nature of the organisation, which are so relevant for organisational systems.

STRUCTURE AND MANAGEMENT SYSTEMS

The interest of the MIS designer lies in understanding the relevant variables necessary to predict decision-making behaviour of managers within an organisation. 'Human behaviour is seldom a direct response to objective reality, but is rather a response to individual's perception of that reality.' The ultimate job of a system designer is to influence human behaviour through the MIS. Furthermore, the MIS pervades all aspects of an organisational system, its structure, rules, roles, purposes, etc.

We shall observe that any organisational analysis necessarily includes both situational and behavioural variables. Thus, the necessity for explanations of human behaviour to take account of both the 'situation' and individual orientations towards it held by the people concerned must be emphasised. Organisation structure and individual interaction results in behaviour.

organisation structure × individual (human personality
and its needs) ⎯⎯⎯⎯→ resulting behaviour

Our focus in this section will be on understanding the organisation structure while in the next section we shall concentrate on motivation and managerial behaviour.

PERSPECTIVE FOR ORGANISATIONAL STRUCTURE

Structure defines the organisational form. For a useful organisational analysis, structure should be broadly conceived. The modern concept of 'structure' incorporates the properties of stable characteristics of the organisation and also of the social and psychological aspects of the members of the organisation. This, in other words, is a 'behaviour structure' of the organisation in interaction with the environment. It is a combination of organisational rules and procedures, roles of the members of the organisation and the relationships that exist between the members and also between the systems and subsystems of the organisation. The structure is to be conceived as being composed of social and non-social factors. The social factors are due to individuals and groups, while non-social factors are the results of organisational rules and procedures, technology and product–market interactions. This conception of structure sharply deviates from the traditional, mechanistic concepts, where only the stable and non-social factors were considered.

CLASSIFICATION OF ORGANISATIONAL SYSTEMS

Under traditional approaches all organisations are treated similarly. Recent developments focus on the differences in organisational systems based on such major aspects as environment, tasks and technology. These provide the basis for classifications of organisations which are very useful for analysis and design of systems. These newer studies help us to develop different systems frameworks for different types of organisations, and to identify both what is common to the groups and the differences between them.

CLASSIFICATION DUE TO ENVIRONMENTAL VARIABILITY

Organisations can be classified as mechanistic or organismic[1] on the basis of their adaptation to their environment. The firm's environment may be highly stable and certain or highly variable and uncertain. The nature of the management systems within the organisations vary accordingly. Different properties of mechanistic and organismic systems are given in Table 2.2.

TABLE 2.2

Mechanistic	*Organismic*
High functional specialisation possible	Low functional specialisation predominant
Rate of innovation slow	Rapid rate of innovation
Detailed differentiation of duties and responsibilities possible	Management is more consultative and less structured
Environment is stable, characterised by high certainty and predictability	Condition of uncertainty is high and thus predictability is low

The traditional industries, which experience a slower rate of innovation, are of the mechanistic type where management controls and information systems are based on elaborate rules and procedures, e.g. the textile industry. In contrast, pharmaceutical industries are facing constant threats of new inventions and innovations, which force them to develop systems of management conducive to the rapidly changing nature of the industry. In this situation management control and information systems serve a relatively uncertain and unstructured situation, and the system designer must be innovative.

TECHNOLOGY AND ORGANISATION

Technology provides the next major consideration for classification. We can usefully distinguish organisations as to technology for developing effective management control and information systems. For example, the same type of management control system will not be equally effective in mass production and unit production technologies.

Woodward[2] observed that many organisational characteristics have direct relationships with the technological systems. Things like length of line of command, span of control and system of management have direct relationships with technology. Organisations can be differentiated on the basis of the technology as (1) small batch or individual units production system, (2) large batch or mass production system, and (3) continuous process production systems.

The distinctions between the firms employing these technologies are shown in Table 2.3. The distinctive features outlined highlight the similarities and differences between different technologies. A system designer must not overlook these differences. His experience in one technology or his programme of system study for one technology is not all relevant for another technology. He will require to modify his programme of study and the framework of design utilising the characteristics listed below. For example, in unit and small batch production, management is more by intimate personal relationship with fewer rules and less paperwork. This suggests that management control systems and information systems should be flexible and less elaborate. Here, introduction of controls by rules and documents may frustrate the designers. On the other hand in mass production the system is more rule-oriented, and elaborate controls through impersonal rules and procedures tend to be highly effective.

TABLE 2.3

	Unit or small batch production	Mass production	Process production
Length of the level of management	Short	Medium	Long
Span of control, top management	Low	Medium	Large
Span of control, middle management	Board based	Medium	Large
Span of control of the first line supervisor	Small	Large	Small
Ratio of managerial and supervising personnel	Low	Medium	High
Relationship between personnel	Intimate and personal	Impersonal	Personal
Flexible organisation with objectives of authority and responsibility	Fewer rules	Clear-cut definition of authority and responsibility—more rules	As in small batch—fewer rules
Organismic system	Predominant	Mechanistic system predominant	Organismic system predominant
Amount of paperwork	Small	Large	Small
Communication tends to be	Verbal	Written	Verbal
Power of functional areas	Engineering and development	Production	Marketing

TASK DIFFERENTIATION AND ORGANISATION

Task differentiation is another important way of viewing the organisational system. This draws our attention from organisational levels to functional levels. The important thing to note here is that different functional management needs different control systems and control information. For example, the control system which is suitable for production management is not applicable to research management. Control through budget is a highly successful system for production management, but for research management the limitations of budgetary control far exceed its usefulness. These distinctions between functional areas are due to (1) the peculiarities of the functions, (2) the influence of the environment, and (3) the orientations of the people involved.

The functional area differences on the basis of the managerial orientations are outlined in Table 2.4.[3] Structure mainly refers to formality

TABLE 2.4

	Production	Sales	Research
Structure	High	Medium	Low
Time orientation	Short	Medium	Long
Goal orientation	Techno-economic	Market	Scientific and techno-economic
Interpersonal orientation	High task motivated	Socially oriented	Low task motivated

through rules, procedures and hierarchy; time orientation is the managerial expectation about the required time to produce results from their effort; goal orientation is the main concern of the functional area; and interpersonal orientation refers to managers' motivation towards establishing relationships or task performance.

The organisation sub-units' environment differs because each sub-unit is engaged in different types of activities and has interfaces with different segments of the environment (see Table 2.5).

TABLE 2.5. Sub-unit environment

Production	Marketing	Research
Certainty high	Moderately uncertain	High uncertainty

The functional management sub-units can be differentiated on the basis of four characteristics mentioned before which can be measured as managerial orientations.[4] These measures were validated in subsequent studies also. One of the present authors also validated these measures, which are structural orientation, time orientation, goal orientation and interpersonal orientation.

Another important aspect is to integrate the activities of these sub-units. In a predictable environment, such as the container industry, integration is achieved through management hierarchy and rules and procedures, budget and schedules. In an uncertain environment, essential direct links must be set up between sales and research and between research and production, with a moderate use of administrative control. The MIS also has integrative value.

MOTIVATIONAL ASPECTS

In our discussion of the organisational aspects of systems design so far, we have left aside the aspects of human behaviour and motivation. Organisational controls seek to influence the behaviour of individuals and groups within the organisation in desired directions.

The importance of individual and group characteristics in organisational controls is always acknowledged by industrial psychologists and behavioural scientists. It may be noted that an organisation attempts to influence the behaviour of its members through its MIS. The system designer's interest in the motivational system emerges from this consideration.

What people will do within a firm is a function of the needs they may have at the time. They will also be influenced by their prior expectations and by the steps taken by managers to lead and to influence. Different researchers studied various aspects of organisational behaviour at different times. The needs of people, whether in organisations or not, were studied by Maslow. The styles of managers were studied by Likert and Fiedler, and the factors which motivate people to act were studied by Herzberg. Although many others have also studied these topics, we will attempt a brief review of a few important viewpoints. Interested readers are referred to the readings in this area suggested at the end of this chapter.

The needs of an individual at any moment are said to be hierarchical (Maslow). The physiological needs are at the top of the needs hierarchy. Once the physiological needs are satisfied (though not fully) an individual attends to his other lower order needs such as affiliation and self-esteem. Maslow's arrangement of needs in order is:

(1) Physiological needs—satisfaction of physical needs, such as hunger.
(2) Security needs—protection against threat and danger.
(3) Affiliation needs—need for love and affection and association with others.
(4) Esteem needs—self-respect and recognition from others.
(5) Self-actualisation—need to achieve self-fulfilment.

This arrangement of needs is very close to one's perception of reality. It is an extensively discussed and an important point of departure for motivational analysis.

When one need is more or less satisfied for an individual, other needs become dominant. However, there are also specific variations from this order of need satisfaction. While Maslow's need hierarchy has relevance to organisational subsystems (e.g. incentive systems) design, contributions to the analysis of organisational motivation by others are helpful.

Herzberg developed motivation-hygiene theory to explain behaviour in the work situation. Hygiene factors of money, fringe benefit, and human relation in supervision are of immediate concern and have short-term perspective for the organisation. Hygiene factors are not considered as intrinsic to the job.

The satisfying factors in the job are considered as motivators. When a job contains factors involving feeling of achievement, professional growth, recognition, challenge in the job, and increased responsibility, the job is potentially providing motivators.

Herzberg contends that hygiene factors provide no growth in employees' output capacity but do maintain it. Motivators provide job satisfaction and are necessary to the achievement of increased output (see Table 2.6). Modern managers keep their focus on both for short-run operating effectiveness and long-run growth. Hygiene factors maintain production and motivators induce increase in output in the long run.

TABLE 2.6

Hygiene factors	Motivators
Policies and administration	Achievement
Supervision	Challenge in the job
Working conditions	Increased responsibility
Money	Growth and development
Job security	Recognition
Status	
Interpersonal relations	

Seemingly, there are some differences in approaches provided by Maslow and Herzberg. Nevertheless, they tend to assert that the individual's needs in the job can be classified as basic needs, for maintaining performance, and higher-order needs, for improving performance.

Furthermore, individual behaviour in the organisation also depends on the leadership behaviour. Any organisational analysis must focus on leadership behaviour which highlights the individual differences among managers within an organisation.

So an analysis of individual leadership characteristics is essential in MIS design consideration. Two recent research works [5] have produced evidence in this direction. The available evidence from these works justifies the consideration of leadership styles in systems design. Implications for systems design from these studies will be discussed in later chapters. Of the available leadership style research, by far the most frequently used is Fielder's contingency model,[6] which shows that effective leadership is a function of individual style and environment. His measures divide managerial styles into task orientation and relationship orientation. Task orientation is motivating towards successful task performance and relationship orientation is motivating towards establishing interpersonal relation. A task-oriented manager's needs for formal information are higher than a relationship-oriented manager's. Another similar way of defining the leadership behaviour dimension is initiation of structure and consideration. High initiation of structure is task oriented and high consideration is relationship oriented.[7]

We shall observe in later chapters that different leadership styles and managerial traits have different needs for management control information.

This brief review indicates that a system designer needs to develop appropriate assumptions about the environment, the organisation and leadership and individual behaviour if he is to produce an adaptive and effective system.

ORGANISATIONAL PRINCIPLES

1. Different organisations face different types of environment. Different segments of environment have different rates of change. In a stable and placid environment, mechanistic type information systems are effective. In such situations relationships between variables are stable and inputs and outputs requirements are well defined. Whereas, in a turbulent environment, information inputs and outputs requirements cannot be rigidly defined and an organic type of system is effective.

2. An organisation may have a placid or a dynamic and turbulent environment. Organisations respond to a placid environment through a structured and mechanistic form of control; there is a need for more formal information output. In such a situation of less uncertainty the use of formal information is high because these are directly relevant to control situations. However, where uncertainty is high, where the environment is turbulent and dynamic, more information processing is necessary to produce effective control and planning information.

3. The technology of a firm influences its structure and so also information processing. In general, high technology methods such as a mass production system permit a broader span of control for supervisors at the expense of a

lot of paperwork. Process production permits closer supervision at the lower level and requires less paperwork but has a tall management structure and needs an information system with strong vertical chains.

4. Within the organisation, functional sub-units are different on measurable dimensions, so that information need and use also vary among functional sub-units. Production management systems can use rigid controls and information structure is definitive. The research management systems have high uncertainty in inputs and outputs; controls and information for control are not rigidly definable. Marketing management systems, in terms of uncertainty and information processing, lie in between production management and research management.

5. Hierarchical levels in the management systems differ in information needs. Managers at different levels should be fed with information commensurate with their needs. At the upper hierarchical level more formal information is used than at the operating levels.

BEHAVIOURAL PRINCIPLES

1. Leadership behaviour styles are different. Information production and processing should match individual leadership style. Task-oriented leaders use more formal information than relationship-oriented leaders for operating decisions and subordinate evaluation.

2. Individual personality influences information use. Effective use can be ensured by matching personality types and MIS design. For example, low conceptual level managers need more information than high conceptual level managers.

3. Subordinates experience different types of psychological emotions with different types of use of formal information. Rigid use of formal information for subordinate evaluation creates tensions and dissatisfaction and flexible use of formal information assures long-term benefits.

4. Formal information is perceived as both a role prescription device and as a role perception system. Information should match individual users' and the subordinates' orientations. Employees' authorities and responsibilities, their achievements and failures, their hopes and aspirations are enmeshed in the formal information systems.

5. Managers are participants in, manipulators as well as observers of, the information system. It affects managers' psychological universes.

Information and control systems should be less in conflict with managers' maintenance of 'boundaries' and self-respect. An information system designed without consideration of this aspect may be in conflict with managers' psychological universes.

Finally, MIS design expertise should include: (1) technical expertise, (2) social psychological expertise, and (3) management expertise. An effective MIS is technically perfect, behaviourally conducive and managerially efficient. As there are different ways of designing effective organisations, so also are there different designs for effective management information systems.

CHAPTER 2—PROJECTS

1. International Incorporated was invited to act as the consultants in an industry sector of publicly owned enterprises of a developing country. The economic and political conditions there are similar to most other developing countries. The primary job was to introduce an MIS so as to make the individual units operate economically and efficiently. Managers and decision-makers in developing countries very often act as disbelievers, because they find results which in most occasions frustrate their expectations.

Though trained management specialists were available, in small numbers, use of them was seldom made. International Incorporated knew that an assignment like this involved reputation, challenge and also good return. At the same time, experience has shown that a high percentage of the advisory and counselling work done by foreign consultants fails to work. Local consultants were available but their credibility was low. International Incorporated had been doing good business at home but lately keen competition had compelled them to seek new opportunities.

The Executive Vice-President of International Incorporated has asked you to prepare a preliminary report, which must include a reasonable framework to analyse the potential for a possible assignment.

2. You are a partner in charge of management services in a medium-sized accounting and consulting firm. The firm has the policy of using pre-printed systems design programmes. The materials in the present chapter appeared new to you. You wanted to incorporate some new sub-programmes to reflect some of the aspects discussed in this chapter. Your partners agreed and asked you to develop a draft sub-programme to be reviewed at the next board meeting. Prepare the sub-programme and add any necessary comments as an annex.

NOTES

1. Burns, T. and Stalker, G. U., *The Management of Innovation*. London: Tavistock Publications, 1961.
2. Woodward, J., *Industrial Organisation: Theory and Practice*. London: Oxford University Press, 1965.
3. Lawrence, P. R., and Lorsch, J. W., *Organisation and Environment Managing Differentiation and Integration*. Boston: Harvard University Press, 1957.
4. See Lawrence and Lorsch, *ibid*.
5. Rahman, M., 'An Empirical Investigation into Management Use of Accounting Information', unpublished Ph.D. thesis, Manchester University, 1976. Hopwood, A. G., *An Accounting System and Managerial Behaviour*. Farnborough, England: Saxon House, 1973.
6. Fielder, P. E., *A Theory of Leadership Effectiveness*. New York: McGraw-Hill, 1967.
7. Ohio State University, *Leadership Behaviour Description Questionnaires*.

BIBLIOGRAPHY

Allen III, S. A., 'Managing Organisational Diversity: A Comparative Study of Corporate Divisional Relations', Thesis abstract. Boston, Mass., Harvard Business School, 1968.

Alvero, Elbing, *Behavioural Decisions in Organisations*, Glenview, Illinois: Scott, Foresman and Co., 1970.

Argyris, C., *Personality and Organisation*. New York: Harper and Row, 1970.

Barnard, C. I., *The Functions of the Executive*. Cambridge, Mass.: Harvard University Press, 1938.

Blau, P. M., and Schoenherr, R. A., *The Structure of Organisations*. New York, Basic Books, 1971.

Bonini and others, *Management Control: New Directions in Basic Research*. New York: McGraw-Hill, 1964.

Burns, T., and Stalker, G. U., *The Management of Innovation*. London: Tavistock Publications, 1961.

Caplan, E. G., *Management Accounting and Behavioural Science*. Reading, Mass., Addison-Wesley, 1971.

Chandler, A. D. Jr, *Strategy and Structure*. Cambridge, Mass.: MIT Press, 1962.

Dalton, M., *Men Who Manage*. New York: Wiley, 1959.

Fielder, P. E., *A Theory of Leadership Effectiveness*. New York: McGraw-Hill, 1967.

Gross Neal, M., Ward, S., and McEchern, A. W., *Exploration in Role Analysis*, New York: Wiley, 1958.

Haire, M., Ghiselli, E. E., and Porter, L. W., *Managerial Thinking: An International Study*. New York: Wiley, 1966.

Herzberg, F. *et al.*, *The Motivation to Work*. New York: Wiley, 1959.

Hill, W. A., and Egan, D., *Readings in Organisation Theory: A Behavioural Approach*. Boston: Allyn and Bacon, 1968.

Homans, C. G., *Social Behaviour, its Elementary Forms*. New York: Harcourt, Brace and World, 1961.

Hopwood, A. G., *An Accounting System and Managerial Behaviour*. Farnborough, England: Saxon House, 1973.

Kahn, R. L. *et al.*, *Organisational Stress*. New York: Wiley, 1964.

Korman, A. H., *Industrial and Organisational Psychology*. New York: Prentice-Hall, 1971.

Lawrence, P. R., and Lorsch, J. W., 'Differentiation and Integration in Complex Organisation', *Administrative Science Quarterly*, 12 (1967), 2–47.

March, J. G., and Simon, H. A., *Organisations*. New York: Wiley, 1958.

Miner, J. B., *Personnel Psychology*. London, Macmillan, 1969.

Porter, L. W., and Lawler, E. E., *Managerial Attitude and Performance*. Homewood, Ill., Richard D. Irwin, 1968.

Pugh, D., Hickson, D., Hinings, C. R., and Turner, C., 'The Context of Organisational Structure', *Administrative Science Quarterly*, 14 (1969), 91–114.

Pugh, S. D., 'Modern Organisation Theory: A Psychological and Sociological Study', *Psychological Bulletin*, 66, No. 4 (1966).

Silverman, David, *The Theory of Organisations: A Sociological Framework*. London: Heinemann, 1970.

Tannenbaum, A. S., 'Control in Organisations: Individual and Organisational Performance', *Administrative Science Quarterly*, 7 (1962), 236–57.

Woodward, J., *Industrial Organisation: Theory and Practice*. London: Oxford University Press, 1965.

3 Technical Principles of Systems Design

It is clear from both the research literature and from discussions with managers that the reality of management information systems has been disappointing. Often MIS fail to meet their intended objectives, especially it seems where they are computer-based. On examination of the cause, it is frequently found that the MIS has addressed a wrong or irrelevant problem, that behavioural factors have been overlooked, or that management support has been lacking. Indeed many systems have not been *designed* at all, being the result of automating or improving existing systems so that it is fortuitous if management's real needs are satisfied.[1] Furthermore such systems tend to evolve through their own momentum, but with little explicit attention to design decisions, so that alternatives and trade-offs are not considered and critical questions rarely asked. Nor are 'greenfield' systems necessarily any better. Both Diebold[2] and McKinsey discovered that commonly both the goals and the structure of MIS were decided and guided, not by management or the users, but by the technical specialists themselves. Thus technically feasible systems were built, but by those who had little appreciation of business or of wider design issues.

The MIS design process therefore is often inadequate. This chapter accordingly develops some technical principles of design which research and experience suggest can increase MIS effectiveness. By technical principles, however, we do not mean techniques or technology. Techniques imply procedures and tools which can be applied in any situation, guaranteeing success. We have learnt that needs, situations and organisations differ too much for such universal solutions. Technology implies computing, but computers are only one possible component of MIS and MIS design. Instead the search for design principles is a search for a methodology or approach which can be adopted independently of the particular characteristics of different applications and situations.

In reality, a firm methodology is not yet proven. We prefer to develop some conceptual frameworks, which, by being a robust mix of theory and of pragmatic constructs, have proved valuable in practice. The MIS design problem is not the pursuit of technical sophistication, nor even the prevention of technical errors. It is the need to combine all relevant knowledge, experience and skills and to learn in the process. The aim of these conceptual frameworks is to help both specialists and users understand and communicate about MIS, and thus improve the design process. Four sets of concepts are relevant. In Chapter 1, information was defined as knowledge of use in decision-making. So decision concepts will be explored. Secondly, since many MIS are computer-based, computer concepts are relevant. Managers who are involved in systems design, systems use and systems decisions need at least some basic understanding of computers and computation. Thirdly, in developing and operating MIS, 'systems thinking' has proved useful. Indeed many MIS design principles have evolved out of the 'systems approach'. So systems concepts are introduced. Finally most design problems are management problems; how to manage the technology, how to manage a creative process, how to cross boundaries and how to protect values. Simplistic procedures and mechanistic structures cannot cope with such complexity. Instead we have to bring the specialist and manager together, to develop an understanding of information management, and to ensure design principles adapt to new demands. Process rather than procedure, processes rather than structures, hold more promise. So process concepts are examined.

DECISION CONCEPTS

DECISION TYPES

The structure of this book is founded on Anthony's taxonomy of planning and control systems, which we described in Chapter 1. This classification of management processes was based on decision types as follows:

(1) Strategic planning — where decisions are non-repetitive are made under uncertainty, and largely depend on prediction and creativity. Typically, time-frames are long, considerable resources are at risk and data are scarce.
(2) Management control — where decisions again often are made under uncertainty, require judgement and are implemented through others. Typically, management control is concerned with effective and efficient use of resources, seeks goal congruence and depends on interpersonal skills.
(3) Operational control — where decisions are repetitive, generally programmable and unambiguous. Typically concerned with day-to-day

operations, tasks and resources are clearly delineated, fewer resources are at risk, time-frames are short and data are abundant.

Anthony's distinctive decision types in turn require different supporting information. Gorry and Scott-Morton attempted to predict these information differences as shown in Table 3.1. Whilst these decisions and information types lie on a continuum, rather than being discrete categories, they nevertheless are significant in their implications for MIS design. Operational control systems process historical and internal data, very often in some detail such as individual pieceparts, items on an invoice, or inventory receipts and issues. These systems are transaction-based and often processed in real-time, producing highly structured and accurate information. Strategic information systems conversely tend to process predictive and external data, very often in aggregate, producing information trends and alternatives in looser, less structured form. Management control information systems tend to process a mix of data, internal as well as external, historical and predictive and producing summary and regular reports as well as enquiry and more detailed analyses.

TABLE 3.1. Decision types and information characteristics

Characteristics of information	Operational control	Management control	Strategic planning
Source	Largely internal	⟶	External
Scope	Well-defined, narrow	⟶	Very wide
Level of aggregation	Detailed	⟶	Aggregate
Time horizon	Historical	⟶	Future
Currency	Highly current	⟶	Quite old
Required accuracy	High	⟶	Low
Frequency of use	Very frequent	⟶	Infrequent

Use of this framework can help systems designers avoid providing inappropriate information for decision-making, and warns us against trying to develop the multi-purpose MIS. Simon's classification of decisions into programmed and non-programmed decisions is a similar reminder. He suggested that

Decisions are programmed to the extent that they are repetitive and routine, to the extent that a definite procedure has been worked out for handling them so that they don't have to be treated *de novo* each time they occur. Decisions are non-programmed to the extend that they are novel, unstructured and consequential. There is no cut or dried method for handling the problem because its precise nature and structure are elusive and complex, or because it is so important that it deserves a custom-tailored treatment.

Simon's programmed decisions thus imply that the required information processing can be well defined. They can be formalised or automated since rules exist and any exceptions can be specified and handled. Typical examples are inventory re-ordering or credit control. Non-programmed decisions imply that information requirements are unpredictable, that processing logic is not clearly defined and that criteria for solution and evaluation are absent or arguable. Formalisation or automation may only be feasible each time the decision occurs.

Thus MIS for programmed decisions are likely to be quite different in design from those supporting non-programmed decisions. Established models, for example standard techniques of management science, may be available for the former. For non-programmed decisions, models may have to be formulated and developed each time, with the decision-maker being the major source.

DECISION-MAKING

Simon also suggests a series of descriptive phases for decision-making which help in understanding MIS design. These are:

(1) Intelligence — the searching of the environment for conditions calling for decisions.
(2) Design — identifying possible alternative courses of action.
(3) Choice — selecting the 'best' course of action from the alternatives available.

He might also have added a fourth phase, implementation, in which we ensure the solution is effected.

MIS designers have concentrated largely on the choice phase, developing computer-based models and analysis systems, and on the implementation phase by constructing feedback and reporting systems. Simon's intelligence phase reminds us that MIS are also concerned with scanning, in both systematic and ad hoc mode. His design phase emphasises how MIS should also aid exploration and experimentation so that decision-making is not overly constrained by inadequate information processing.

Gorry and Scott-Morton have synthesised the work of Anthony and Simon into a framework for MIS. Firstly they substitute the terms 'structured' and 'unstructured' for Simon's programmed and non-programmed decisions so as to imply less dependence on the computer and more on the basic character of the problem. A fully structured decision is one where all three phases of intelligence, design and choice are structured. Conversely an unstructured problem is unstructured in all phases, whilst a problem with both structured and unstructured phases is semi-structured. This classification is then matched with Anthony's three management processes to produce the MIS framework in Table 3.2.

TABLE 3.2. Framework for MIS

Classification	Operational control	Management control	Strategic planning
Structured	Accounts receivable Order entry Inventory control	Budget analysis Engineered costs	Tanker fleet mix Warehouse and factory location
Semi-structured	Production scheduling Cash management	Variance analysis Budget preparation	Mergers and acquisitions New product planning
Unstructured	PERT/COST	Sales and production	R&D planning

This framework emphasises two important points. First, structured decisions are not confined to operational control. Different degrees of structure exist in each of Anthony's management processes. Indeed the boundary between what is structured and what is not is forever moving. Not long ago, inventory re-ordering decisions were extraordinarily difficult, involving not only much computation but also considerable management expertise and judgement; today such decisions are often taken by computer program. As our decision-making ability and computational aids improve, so the boundaries of structure move. Yet unstructured problems do not reduce in number, for in an increasingly uncertain and complex world new challenges arise.

Secondly it appears that most MIS development has been in the structured and operational control cell. These applications are similar in many organisations, are more easily understood, are easier to mechanise, are more readily cost-justified and are fundamental to business. Yet perhaps greater contributions to organisational effectiveness can be gained by developing MIS in the other cells.

DECISION FOCUS

The frameworks derived from studies of decision types and decision-making could be viewed purely as appealing and convenient constructs. However they provide further benefits in understanding MIS and in avoiding some of the pitfalls of earlier eras. At least six major implications can be drawn.

First, whilst, as Chapter 1 emphasised, the concept of information is as yet imperfectly understood, the decision focus provides useful insights. We can measure information value by the change in decision behaviour caused by the information, less the cost of supplying it. It is value in decision-making which distinguishes information from data; information has value, data has cost. Data is the raw material of information; information is the raw material of decision-making. The MIS therefore processes data into information and ultimately into decisions. Clearly management information systems are of a different order than data processing systems.

The MIS becomes a more complex entity. Mason and Mitroff[3] suggest that 'an information system consists of, at least, a *person* of a certain *psychological type* who faces a *problem* within some *organisational context* for which he needs *evidence* to arrive at a solution, where the evidence is made available through some *mode of presentation*'. Such a definition emphasises why, as Chapter 2 explained, behavioural studies of decision-making and human information processing are so relevant to MIS design. For example, designers may assume all users adopt one cognitive style in decision-making, yet some managers favour analytic or systematic approaches and others prefer heuristic or intuitive methods. Likewise, most MIS produce impersonalistic outputs of tabulations, displays and reports, yet many managers may prefer, or respond better to personalistic outputs such as interactive devices, vocal media or more informal means. Weaver[4] in his companion work with Shannon on communication theory realised that information was more complex than data. He viewed communication at three levels:

(1) Technical level or the accuracy of transmission.
(2) Semantic level or the precision with which the transmitted symbols convey the desired meaning.
(3) Effectiveness level or the suitability of the message in motivating and influencing human action.

The value of Mason and Mitroff's definition of MIS in system design is in focusing on the semantic and effectiveness levels.

Thirdly, the decision focus provides a corrective to some shibboleths of management information. As the power of computers grew, and associated technologies of integrated systems, databases and real-time processing evolved, demands were made for more accurate, available, timely and finally relevant information. These attributes are not unimportant, but they became dogma because they were seen as absolutes. The decision focus helps ensure that they become relative—relative to decision-making and decision type.

Also some myths of MIS design are exploded, myths which Ackoff[5] suggested create management *misinformation* systems. For instance the claim that 'the manager needs the information he wants' overlooks the fact that a manager is seldom aware of each type of decision he should make and rarely has an adequate model of each. Asked what information he wants, he consequently tends to seek more information, hoping for illumination or requesting it 'just in case'. Preferably MIS design should start by explicating, testing and then trying to improve models of decision processes. Systems analysis—analysing decision-making and specifying informaion requirements—should precede the more data-oriented phase of systems design. This may seem obvious, but too many ineffective MIS exist which have been designed on contrary principles.

Even then, better information does not guarantee better decision-making. MIS design is also concerned with developing managers in the use of information and with supplying feedback for learning from subsequent action. This task, together with the need for decision as well as information analysis, thus emphasises that MIS design is not the responsibility of the specialist alone. The decision focus reminds us that if the manager is to interact optimally with the MIS to produce decisions, he must select and decide what issues and problems the system addresses, and be involved both with developing the initial model and agreeing on the information requirements it specifies.

The decision focus also provides a framework for information systems planning. Frequent claims have been made that MIS have had little impact on decision-making. In particular it has been suggested by McKinsey, Zani[6] and others that instead of developing systems function by function, reacting to the demands of the strongest managers, solving the latest crisis or satisfying the objectives of the technical specialists, MIS should attack the critical tasks, key result areas and vital decisions of an organisation. The alternatives to this decision-oriented MIS strategy speak for themselves. The 'integrated systems' approach was obviously data-oriented, being centred on data flows rather than the different needs of different decision processes. The 'total system' objective of centralised processing of a tighly-knit data network has not only proved unworkable and too rigid but has ignored the information differences that Anthony's and Simon's frameworks imply. The 'database'approach of building one integrated data foundation has similar flaws and readily produces data at the expense of information.

Finally the decision focus demonstrates the dangers of standard systems design and of universal design techniques. Information design depends on decision type and decision-making behaviour. These in turn will be influenced by an organisation's particular environment, strategy, structure and technology. In other words MIS design, and design processes, will be contingent upon situational variables. Our belief in *contingency theory*, that there is no one best MIS design, or design process, is the major reason for developing conceptual frameworks for systems design.

COMPUTER CONCEPTS

Many MIS are computer-based and therefore if managers are to be involved in planning, designing and using them, they can benefit from understanding some basic computing concepts. This section is an *introductory* description of computers which many managers and students have found useful, but which experienced computer users may ignore without loss. The subsequent sections on computability and on man-machines systems, however, are fundamental since they develop two frameworks for understanding the role and nature of *computer-based* MIS.

COMPUTERS

Computer science is a rapidly growing field in its own right, so that this introduction to computers is inevitably deficient, and runs the risk of over-simplification. Furthermore, so rapid is the rate of technological change that it is diffcult to give typical specifications with confidence. So readers who wish to understand computers and computation more thoroughly should consult a more specialised text.

What is clear is that we can no longer talk about a computer, for there is a spectrum of diffrent shapes and sizes, for example from micro-computer costing £500 through a mini-computer costing £5000 to mainframe computers which can cost over £3m.[7] By computer is meant a 'kit' of computing equipment selected to perform the following five essential functions:

(1) Accept data input.
(2) Process data by manipulation and arithmetic.
(3) Store data.
(4) Produce data output.
(5) Control its own processing.

—all with speed, accuracy and reliability. It is, however, a tool, and no more, for it can only perform whatever we know how to do and can instruct it to do. Yet it is a powerful tool, for example doing as much arithmetic in one second as a man could do in his working life—and cheaply and reliably.

By computer is generally meant digital computer, the general-purpose machine of common usage and parlance. Analogue computers—used mainly in science and engineering—instead of representing digits by seperate indicators, produce output based on continuous input of physical analogies such as electrical or mechanical quantities, and thus are less accurate and provide limited storage.

Viewing computing as a 'black box', three elements can be distinguished:

(1) Hardware—comprising the physical and visible components of the computer, namely the central processing unit, the input/output devices or peripherals, and the data communication links.
(2) Software—comprising the programs, or instructions, which drive and use the computer.
(3) Liveware—the euphemism describing the systems analysts and programmers who design and create the computer system, and the operators and ancillaries who run the computer and its associated equipment.

This section is concerned only with hardware and software, which is diagrammatically represented in Figure 3.1 and described below.

Hardware
The heart of the computer is the *central processing unit*, or CPU, which comprises three elements, namely the control unit, the arithmetic unit and the main store. The control unit is the computer's 'command centre' which is directed by program and initiates whatever action is required in all parts of the computer. The arithmetic unit is the 'workshop', but is directed by the control unit. It can perform the basic arithmetic functions of add, subtract, multiply and divide, but also manipulates data by logical operations such as comparison.

The program, current data and current results are held in the main store.

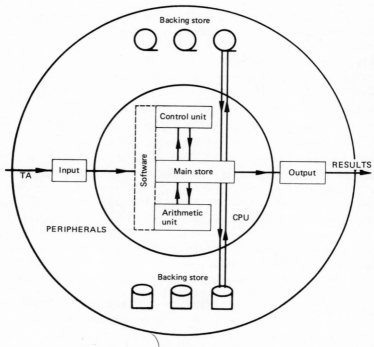

FIGURE 3.1. The computer

Data is represented in binary form in computers, not decimal, because it is much easier to design electronic equipment to discriminate reliably between only two levels of current—on and off—than, say, ten levels. Thus until recently the main store contained many thousands of rings or cores of magnetic material threaded on grids of wires; the presence of a pulse represented 1, absence equalled zero. Thus one core can store one bit. It takes eight bits, commonly called a byte, to represent any character, although four bits can represent any numerical character. Typical main stores range from 4000 to 10,000,000 bytes (commonly expressed as 4 kilobytes to 10 megabytes), with access times to one byte ranging from $2 \mu s$ to $0 \cdot 2 \mu s$ (where μs = microseconds or $1/1,000,000$ second). Today the ferrite cores of main storage are being replaced by solid state or integrated circuits which operate at higher speed and lower cost. The speed of the main store sets the speed of the computer.

The computer's input/output devices and secondary storage are described as *peripherals*. The most familiar input device is the punched card containing 80 columns, holes in which are interpreted by electric eyes into characters at speeds of 600 to 2000 cards per minute. Punched cards have been the dominant input medium, but are declining. They can also be manipulated (sorting, counting, merging, listing, and tabulating) on ancillary Hollerith machinery.

Card punching, however, is error-prone, despite verification through a second pass, and card reading is slow, thereby reducing efficiency of the faster CPU. Consequently card data is often read onto faster devices, such as magnetic tape, and then read into the computer at speeds up to 5,000,000 bits per second—a process called spooling. Alternatively data is punched via keyboards direct to special magnetic tape or disk through error-vetting hardware and software. This increases productivity through error elimination, but the special tapes or disks may still have to be copied to conventional tapes or disk to speed up computer processing.

Paper tape sometimes replaces the punched card since it is a simple, cheap and neat medium for data collection at source, often produced by office or shop-floor terminals. Again rows of holes across the tape are electrically read, at up to 1000 characters per second. However, this is relatively slow and can be unreliable.

If source documents can be read electronically, intermediary data preparation is avoided. For example, clock cards or cash register tapes can be input directly. Alternatively optical character recognition (OCR) can be employed for document input. Here photoelectric cells convert variations in reflected light into pulses. Magnetic ink character recognition (MICR) is a similar technique, whereby characters in magnetic ink are electronically read. Bank cheques are processed by MICR.

The visual display unit, or VDU, is a popular input device. Comprising a keyboard and cathode ray tube, it not only accepts data but displays it so that content and format can be checked. VDUs also are used as output devices, especially for enquiry systems and interactive processing.

An alternative output terminal is the electric typewriter, or teletype, which displays results as typed output, but is slow and noisy and generally operates at ten characters per second. However, for interactive work they are effective devices.

The conventional printer for volume output is the lineprinter, producing the common print-out or tabulation at speeds up to 2000 lines per minute. Non-impact printers can operate at speeds up to 20,000 lines per minute, but duplicate copies cannot be produced. Where high volumes of output are required for archival access, then computer-output microfilm (COM) can replace lineprinters. COM converts magnetic tape output to microfilm for subsequent reading through a viewer.

Magnetic tape is the commonest form of secondary or backing store. Since main store is expensive, secondary forms of storage are required to hold data not in current use. Magnetic tape is equivalent to tape-recording whereby an iron oxide coating records data written and read as spots by electromagnetic heads at speeds up to 320,000 bytes per second. Each 2400-foot-long tape can hold up to 30 megabytes and can be read in four to five minutes. Its major disadvantage is that such speeds are only exploited by serial processing. In other words, it can take just as long to find one record towards the end of the tape as to process the whole tape.

It is when records are required at random that disks are advantageous. These look like a series of gramophone records on a spindle with moving arms of magnetic read/write heads in between. Each 'record' surface has tracks divided into sections, and the average access time for one record is half the revolution time of the disk plus the time to locate the record through the track and sector index, and can be as rapid as 30 milliseconds. Thus disk storage is suitable for enquiry, timesharing or low input systems. The data transfer rate can be up to 806 kilobytes per second and the capacity to 200 megabytes. The drum is a quicker access device but has lower capacity and operates at higher cost. This, as it sounds, is a cylinder under a battery of read/write heads.

All these storage devices are designed on similar physical principles, but differ in access time, capacity and cost. It is on these storage devices that the permanent and temporary data of computer systems is held as files. These are organised according to the demands of the MIS and may be permanently on-line to the computer, or stored until needed in a secure area nearby. File design and database organisation is discussed in Chapter 6.

Discussion of peripherals so far has assumed that they are connected directly to the CPU. Increasingly we need to collect, store, or receive data at a distance from the principal central processor— perhaps at the other end of a factory or maybe on another continent. Data communication between computer and computer, or peripheral and computer, is achieved by telecommunication using telephone lines, wideband circuits or even satellite transmission. In the U.K., Post Office lines can transmit data at speeds up to 5000 bits per second. Interface mechanisms are required, in particular modems or acoustic couplers, to convert characters into telephonic tones at each end. In a timesharing system where there are many terminals, a multiplexer directs messages in and out of the computer, constantly polling the 'air' for business.

Software

Software comprises the programs which 'drive' and use the computer. Resident in the main store and directing the control unit is the control or *executive program*. Usually provided by the hardware supplier, this directs the operations of the computer from moment to moment—since the activity is too complex and rapid for the computer operators. The executive program controls the input/output process, the data network and the peripherals and handles the requests and interrupts. It logs failures, monitors all processing and provides recovery procedures, besides allocating all jobs in order of priority. Where it manages many types of processing, it is frequently called the operating system.

Application programs are the sets of instructions which users or programmers write to execute their own tasks. Often such programs are written in assembler language, which is a language supplied with the computer, and is based on mnemonics and English language statements. However, the computer does not understand assembler language until it has been translated into its own machine language. The assembler or source coding is translated into the machine or object coding by a compiler which is part of the executive program or operating system.

Higher-level languages make the computer easier to program and thus more accessible to users. Examples are FORTRAN, designed for more mathematical work, COBOL which is business-oriented, and BASIC designed for both business and educational use. These languages are more like English, or are more problem-oriented, and generally can be based on many makes of computer. Also there are special-purpose languages such as SPSS used for statistical work in the social sciences, or APL which is used for interactive business problem-solving and modelling.

Utility programs are usually supplied with the computer and are software routines which execute basic data processing functions which application programs use all the time. Examples include sorting, file-creation, filehandling, copying and various testing and diagnosis facilities.

Computer manufacturers and software houses may also supply *package programs*. These fall into two categories. Firstly standard 'off the shelf' application programs and systems can be bought or leased. Generally they perform the more uniform data processing applications such as payroll, PERT or basic ledgers, and provide proven, available, maintained and efficient computer systems at low cost. Their advantages and disadvantages are examined in detail in Chapter 5. Secondly, specialised system software, such as data-communication systems or database management systems are generally bought in package form, because they are complex and expensive to develop alone and because they need not be sensitive to local needs.

PROCESSING

The conventional mode of computer operation is *batch processing*. Typically input data is collected into batches and then processed when ready or at a particular time. Because batch processing has to be scheduled it is insensitive to timeliness. In return, however, it is highly efficient and thus is suitable and preferable for high volume data applications. Batch processing is illustrated in Figure 3.2, where it is also shown incorporating multi-programming or the ability to run several, perhaps four, jobs at once. Multi-programming is achieved by segmenting the core storage, or by flexible allocation of core by operating system software. Priorities are set for each core segment, and thus each job, so that for example the slower input/output tasks of some jobs are performed alongside faster central processing of other jobs.

It is the batch processing mode within which a typical computer system

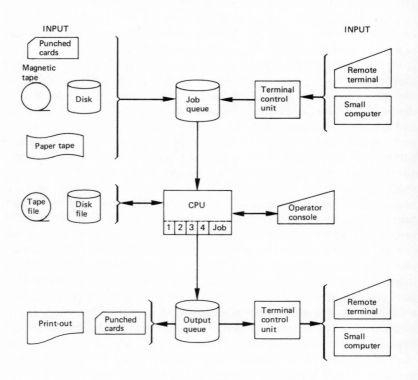

FIGURE 3.2. Batch processing with multi-programming

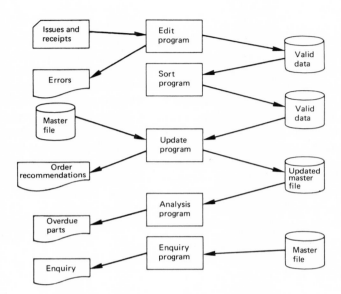

FIGURE 3.3. A typical computer system

can be described. A stock recording system is illustrated in Figure 3.3. Here each part number stocked has a record, identified by part number or code, on the master file. This record of several bytes length also contains the part's description, store number, quantity in stock, reorder level, reorder quantity and other relevant data. Each day perhaps, all stores issues and receipts are recorded on dockets, cards or a data collection device and then batched and input to the computer. They are edited for syntax, any errors being rejected and reported to the user. Valid data is then sorted into part number order and processed sequentially against the master file. The stock quantities are updated with issues and receipts and if the re-order level is reached as a result, order recommendations are printed. Any input/file mismatches are reported to the user. Subsequently file analyses may be performed producing lists say of parts on order and overdue, or parts of surplus stock. Between this run and the next, individual items may be interrogated through an enquiry and program, accessing the disk master file randomly.

In contrast to batch processing, *real-time processing* accepts data as events occur and can produce results in time for immediate action. Real-time systems are thus transaction-driven and require peripherals to be on-line continuously and the CPU to be available almost immediately. A distinction has to be made between on-line and real-time systems. Martin[8] defines an on-line system as 'one in which the input data enters the computer directly from the point of origination and/or the output data are transmitted directly to where they are used'. A real-time system is one 'which controls an environment by receiving the data, processing them and taking action' or returning results sufficiently quickly to affect the functioning of the environment at time'.

The typical real-time system, say an airline reservation system, is triggered by an input from a remote terminal. The data is then stored in an input buffer, processed and the results returned to the terminal within say two minutes. The user expects to observe action or receive some response at the terminal within three seconds—the computer's real-time processing is therefore 'virtual' rather than true. It requires rapid access hardware, accessible file storage, a supervisory program to poll, allocate and control activity, and terminals to match data load, task pattern and user ability. Above all, careful and adequate capacity planning is needed to ensure real-time performance.

Timesharing is on-line but not necessarily real-time. It is a logical progression from multi-programming whereby, instead of handling a few jobs at the same time, a large number of jobs are processed at once. Each user is given as much core as required for a very short time, thereby apparently having a 'virtual machine' available in continual mode in pace with his own thought. With a terminal connected by telephone line, interactive computing becomes possible. Thus the principal elements of a timesharing system are a user, a terminal, a telephone line and a computer, as illustrated in Figure 3.4. Advantages include speed of response, error checking ability and the flexibility of interaction. In short, timesharing

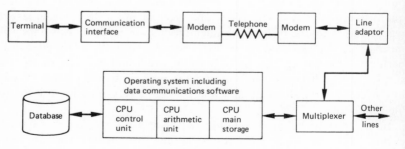

FIGURE 3.4. Timesharing

allows the ideas, experience and judgement of users to be combined with the power of the computer. The cost, besides the hardware and system software, is the skilful database design and careful input/output design which it requires. Increasingly today the value outweighs the cost.

Timesharing is one of the pressures which is behind the trend of *distributed processing.* This allows that part of computing which is better handled at the user-end to be decentralised through a hierarchy of smaller computers, mini-computers and terminals, with only major or special tasks executed on the central or mainframe, computer. One survey[9] suggests that distributed processing is growing as a means of relieving loads and reducing two-way data communication costs. Also, advantages are reported of increased flexibility, local data responsibility, quicker systems development and user sovereignty.

The arrival of the *mini-computer* has helped in distributing computing. Having been used in process control and similar applications for some time, they are now bursting into information systems. A typical minicomputer[10] costs £5000 and comprises up to 32 kilobytes main store, a 150-character-per-second printer, perhaps a VDU, and floppy disk or cassette tape file storage. Minis can sit on desk-tops and require no special environment such as air-conditioning. Their attraction, besides being cheap, is that they are programmable in high-level languages such as COBOL or BASIC, are easy to use, and are compatible with larger-scale computers. Furthermore mini-systems design uses the same principles as mainframe systems design so that new users need not relearn when, or if, they upgrade their computer. Application packages are also being developed for minis.

Silicon chip, or 'semiconductor', technology has led to the development of *micro-computers.* Distinction between minis and micros is not always clear, and probably any definitions are directly tied to the time period in which they are formulated. The key element of micro-computers is the microprocessor which is founded on the silicon chip. A microprocessor can be as small as 1 cm^2, is flat and is made of silicon. It can contain power which in the early days of computing would have required a roomful of computing equipment comprising extensive wiring and vacuum tubes. A microprocessor can be produced for under 50p and can incorporate, by miniaturised circuiting, all the functions of the computer.

A micro-computer kit comprising 32K storage, a VDU and cassette tape storage can be purchased for £500. At the time of writing, a 'do-it-yourself' computer is about to be announced costing £150. Software appears to lag behind hardware development, micro-computer programs having to be compiled first on mini- or mainframe computers. However, high-level and assembler languages for micro-computers are being developed, as are application program packages.

Mini- and micro-computers bring new opportunities in MIS. They also pose threats to security and control and complicate corporate MIS planning. It seems likely that the impetus they provide for user involvement and control will outweigh any disadvantages.

COMPUTABILITY

The study of management information is not about the use of computers. Much information should not be automated at all. Equally despite many organisations' heavy investment in computing, potential management information exists and still lies unused. Finally technology no longer is a real barrier to MIS progress.

However, it is important to know when computers should be used in information processing and when they should not. The full potential of technology should be enlisted, but with discretion. This partly depends on a sense of computability, that is the ability to recognise when the strength of the computer matches the needs of the MIS.

Computers execute the data processing functions of input, processing, storage and output with speed and reliability. They are good at rapid and accurate calculation, manipulation and retrieval, but bad at either unexpected or qualitative work. Computers thus enhance the efficiency of data processing and extend its frontiers, but with limitations. Dearden and McFarlan[11] suggests that a computer can be used to best advantage in processing information which has the following general attributes: a number of interacting variables; presence of reasonably accurate values; speed an important factor; operations to be repetitive; accuracy to matter; large amounts of data to exist.

This simple matching of attributes provides a guide to computability. If computers are regarded as any more sophisticated, their use is likely to be extravagant. By matching these attributes with decision types, borrowing from the frameworks of Anthony and Gorry and Scott-Morton, a computability matrix can be constructed as shown in Table 3.3. Here it is seen that operational control's demand for information currency, detail, accuracy and frequency processed from abundant data can be met by the computer's speed, capacity, accuracy and reliability. In strategic planning such qualities are less relevant, but the computer's power of storage, retrieval and iteration may be of potential. Management control may require a mix of the two extremes.

The picture may be recast into the computability profile of Figure 3.5.

TABLE 3.3. Computability matrix

Computability tests	Operational control	Management control	Strategic planning
Interacting variables	Often	⟶	Always
Data accuracy	High	⟶	Low
Speed important	Generally	⟶	Rarely
Operations repetitive	Generally	⟶	Rarely
Accuracy matters	Always	⟶	Never
Data volumes	High	⟶	Low

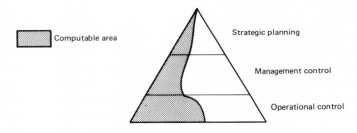

FIGURE 3.5. Computability profile

Here the unshaded area represents the problem space which is predominantly the domain of man and not the machine, where problems are generally unstructured. So operational control decisions tend to be more computable than management control problems, whilst strategic planning is even less computable. However, one small computer application in strategic planning may well contribute far more to organisational effectiveness than a major computer system in operational control. Equally important, computability is only a test of technical feasibility; it does not help in assessing whether an application is economically or operationally viable.

The computability matrix is a simple yet powerful framework. Use of it can help avoid dysfunctional computing in MIS. Also the framework can be exploited further. For example, the attributes of real-time or timeshared computing can be matched against decision type. Dearden[12] adopted a similar approach in pleading for caution when the 'disease' of unthinking real-time applications was rife. Where speed of input, update, processing, output or access is critical, then real-time processing is of value. Otherwise it is a luxury, 'right-time', often being more relevant than 'real-time'. Likewise timesharing suits decision-making which requires man–machine conversation and iterative and corrective facilities. Otherwise it also can become an extravagance.

MAN–MACHINE SYSTEMS

The computability matrix suggests where computers are most likely to be beneficial. However, it does not imply that MIS are only either manual or machine systems. Very often a mix is required; indeed in its richest sense, as discussed earlier, the MIS is rarely a machine system alone. Thus the concept of man–machine systems is very relevant to MIS design.

Cleland and King developed Mason's[13] earlier model of the information-decision process into the MIS flow diagram of Figure 3.6. This can be used to describe the concept of man–machine systems. It shows a data source which provides potential information to a database. The data are then used in predictive models[14] and optimisation models before action is taken. Predictive models are those used to predict future events, whereas optimisation models serve also to evaluate and select the best course of action on the basis of predictions in the future. Thus a formal predictive model might result in sales forecasts, whilst a linear programming refinery model which produces the best production plan is an optimisation model.

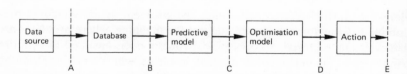

FIGURE 3.6. Man–machine systems

Each dashed line in Figure 3.6 represents a possible man–machine interface. Thus if the interface is at A, the machine system purely collects data whilst all the data and models used in the decision process are stored by the manager, often in his mind. At B, the machanised system also includes a database providing reports which aggregate and summarise basic information for the decision-maker. At C the manager is provided with predictions upon which to apply his judgement. At D he is presented with the recommended course of action which he evaluates in the light of his knowledge of the model and of those things which the model omits. At E all the information processing and decision-making have been automated.

This view of man–machine systems is of value in MIS design in at least three ways.

(1) It emphasises that MIS differ in man–machine mix along a continuum of interfaces from A to E.

(2) It reminds us that the MIS may contain more than one man–machine interface.

(3) It stresses the importance of, and provides an aid to, carefully defining the crucial interface between man and machine.

Each of these points needs expansion.

First, designers and managers alike can perceive MIS differently, building up their expectations and agreeing on procedures only to find they are talking of two different things. This man–machine framework emphasises that MIS do differ in scope; indeed it can be used to explicate and resolve different designer–user perceptions. For example, the computer system may only collect data for subsequent processing by the user. This is a common, necessary and viable application. The database system goes further, observing, classifying and storing data in a single pool that is keyed to the lowest common denominator of detail required for each decision-making application. The user then requests and interprets data from the database, relevant to his decision need. Such an approach is sensible for many problems, especially in management control where the decision-maker has to consider many complex and uncertain interdependencies and interactions which the computer system cannot handle.

Where the predicted outcomes may be evaluated and calculated, or where the decision-maker requires aid and tuition, then a predictive model can be built into the computer system. Such systems draw interfaces and make predictions as well as collect and store data. The simulation model is an obvious example, allowing the manager to ask 'what if' questions and providing predictions under different sets of his assumptions, to which he can then apply his own judgement. Such predictive computer systems are beneficial in semi-structured problem-solving.

Where the organisation's goals and decision criteria are unambiguous, an optimising (or perhaps satisficing) model can be incorporated into the computer system. Such decision-making information systems provide the manager with a recommended course of action which he may veto or modify, but often will accept and implement. For example, a linear program operating on data from the production database might be used in production scheduling. Where there is both general agreement on the objective function and confidence in the model's results, the MIS may be totally computer-based. Examples of such decision-taking systems are computerised process control or inventory ordering applications.

The MIS however may contain more than one man–machine interface, or indeed comprise partial interfaces. For example a predictive system may be converted into a partial decision-taking system, whereby 'normal' events are automated but 'exceptions' reported to the user for special attention. Alternatively where automated decision-taking is possible, but the manager must first formulate the decision rules, the computer could output information at interface C for user-processing and re-input at interface D. In other cases inputs at interfaces A, B, C or D can be a mix of computer and user data where management intervention is required.

In short, in MIS design there may be several man–machine interfaces; to seek one ultimate interface may be sub-optimal in that opportunities are overlooked. The computability profile can therefore be recast as shown in Figure 3.7 into a man–machine profile. Computer-based data processing needs manual support to become a management information system. Computer-based information processing needs no manual intervention. The remaining problem space is totally man's domain.

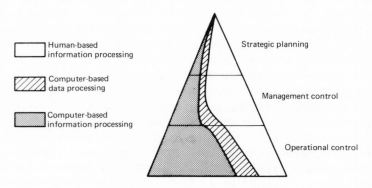

FIGURE 3.7. Man–machine profile

Finally, many of the problems of MIS design and operation arise from inadequate attention to the man–machine interface. The decision focus should force designers to seek the best point of interface, the point where the manager's intuition, experience and judgement need to supplement, or take over from the computer. Yet this may be too narrow a view.

Behavioural considerations may require a different view, maybe a retreat along the continuum, or perhaps a partial rather than total man–machine interface. Research suggests that computer systems design and implementation are far from neutral in their impact on human behaviour.[15] Despite designers' stated intentions, MIS may well impair job satisfaction or ride roughshod over the social system in other ways. Therefore the interface may have to be modified or shifted to seek a congruent match between man and machine, perhaps by reallocating tasks or by simpler adjustments such as output design.

The man–machine framework reminds us that in developing MIS we are designing socio-technical systems,[16] seeking a match between technology and social behaviour. By caring for both the social and technical systems, the ultimate MIS will probably be more effective.

SYSTEMS CONCEPTS

SYSTEMS

Many of the principles and practices of MIS design have evolved out of systems thinking. Justice cannot be done to 'systems theory' (or its controversies) in one section of one chapter, but the conceptual frameworks it provides can be distilled. A system may be defined as a regularly interacting or interdependent group of items forming a whole. The key concepts of a 'system' for MIS design are its delineation, its subsystems, its interaction and interdependence, and its holism.

The general model of a system is input, processor and output, the MIS being an example transforming data into information as in Figure 3.8. The features which delineate a system form its boundary, beyond which is its environment. The system is inside the boundary. The environment therefore is a set of elements outside the boundary. The substantial environment comprises those external elements a change in which affects the state of the system. Distinguishing the system boundary is an important aspect of MIS design. Often the original locus of the problem is too narrow and hasty delineation can lead to important variables being excluded.

Systems are composed of subsystems which in turn are made up of other subsystems, each delineated by its boundary. Thus systems are hierarchical. For example, a data processing system may be a subsystem of an information system which in turn is a subsystem of a planning and control system which is a subsystem of the organisation. To design a system without examining its role within its hierarchy may be dysfunctional.

TABLE 3.4. System attributes

System attribute	Description or definition	Implications for MIS design
Open and closed system	A closed system does not interact with its environment An open system exchanges inputs and outputs with its environment	Some MIS are closed, working as controllers, as in process control or credit control Many MIS must be open to ensure the organisation adapts to its environment. External data are often required, so is manual intervention
Socio-technical systems	An organisation is viewed not simply as a social or technical system. Rather the technology is designed to fit the social system	MIS depend on people. Unless people are designed into MIS, both the users and the MIS will be impaired
Contrived systems	Organisations are made of people and thus are imperfect and unpredictable. They cannot be designed exactly like physical or biological systems	MIS comprise people as well as information and technology. MIS design has to take into account social attitudes, values, perceptions, motivations etc.
Adaptive systems	Mechanistic systems do not learn and never change. Adaptive systems can change objectives, can adjust subsystem relationships and can adapt to environmental change	Few MIS exist in stable conditions. Most must adapt by using loose coupling, being regularly reviewed or being designed as open systems
Purposeful and purposive systems	A purposeful system can change goals under constant conditions A purposive system can pursue different goals but not change them	MIS may be designed as purposive systems. Users can treat them as purposeful systems by using them for different purposes

Negentropy	Entropy is a system's movement towards disorder. Its prevention—negentropy—depends on supply of new resources	MIS have a life cycle and die. To preserve life, new resources are required. System amendments enhancements or new technology are examples
Homeostasis	A system's subsystems have to be balanced in their relationships and forces to ensure a steady state, or homeostasis	Balance in MIS is achieved through design attention to interfaces, slack or tight coupling and use of slack resources such as ensuring spare capacity
Equifinality	In open systems, results can be achieved in different ways	There is no one best MIS design. What suits one organisation or manager may not suit another.
Feedback	The process of feedback is the flow of information to correct action or change objectives	Most MIS in control applications adopt feedback principles. Both corrective and adaptive feedback is often required. Feedback on MIS by audit is also beneficial

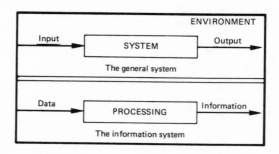

FIGURE 3.8. The system model

However, to render the design task manageable, we sometimes have to treat subordinate and superior systems as a 'black box'. That is, we concentrate on their input and output but ignore their processing. MIS designers adopt the same principle when they break down a system into modules or subsystems to aid systems development.

Systems and subsystems interact and are interdependent. Thus not only must superior and subordinate systems be designed congruently, but so must 'peer systems'. For example, to design an inventory control system independently of a provisioning or purchasing system would be folly. The interfaces between interacting and interdependent systems are the inputs and outputs, where the coupling may be tight or loose. For example the coupling between payroll and personnel records subsystems may need to be tight to ensure data consistency. Conversely the coupling between a raw materials system and an assembly production system may be slack, using manual interfaces to overcome uncertainty.

Perhaps the most pervasive influence of systems thinking is holism, that is seeing the system as a whole, where the whole is greater than the sum of the parts. Effective system performance depends on congruence between subsystems. It also depends on those subsystems working towards the goal of their higher or meta-system. Thus in management systems, if subsystems such as decentralised units pursue optimisation within their local boundaries, the total or corporate system may be sub-optimised. The MIS designer seeks to minimise sub-optimisation.

Theorists have identified and described many attributes of systems, most of which have implications for MIS design. Table 3.4 summarises and interprets them in practical terms. It is important, however, to realise that systems and their structure, behaviour and attributes are conceptual so that their use varies with the need.

SYSTEMS DEVELOPMENT LIFE CYCLE

Systematic procedure is one element of the systems approach. The system development life cycle provides such a procedure for MIS design. It is based on the premise that every system should be planned, developed and implemented through the same process. Neglect of any one phase in the life cycle is liable to result in ultimate system failure, although the relative importance of each phase will depend on the nature of the particular application and on its man–machine orientation. In short, the systems development life cycle is a structural framework to bring discipline into a creative process. Indeed it often provides the structure for MIS project planning and control.

Essentially the life cycle comprises six phases, although different authorities may have marginally different views. The six phases and their component tasks are:

(1) Feasibility study—problem definition, preliminary analysis and design, cost–benefit study.
(2) Systems analysis—confirmation of objectives, analysis of existing system, information requirements analysis.
(3) Systems design—design of alternatives, design selection, system specification and plan.
(4) Programming and testing—programming, program and subsystem testing, procedures and documentation.
(5) Conversion and implementation—final testing, training, file and data conversion, implementation.
(6) Operation and review—operation, maintenance and adaptation, audit and review, enhancement.

An approximate distribution of elapsed time and development effort in the life cycle is shown in Table 3.5. However, each project is different and often there is hidden effort and cost. What is clear is that whilst the production phases of programming and testing and of conversion and implementation, are labour intensive, the design phases require nearly as much elapsed time. Management pressures for system delivery often constrain design effort with dysfunctional results. The operation and review phase is not included in the table since it is a separate and ongoing activity.

TABLE 3.5. Life cycle balance

Phase	Elapsed time (%)	Development effort (%)
Feasibility study	12·5	5
Systems analysis	15·0	19
Systems design	12·5	15
Programming and testing	40·0	50
Conversion and implementation	20·0	20
Operation and review	—	—
	100	100

Four points arise out of the life cycle framework. Firstly, as a checklist of design activities, it can be followed too rigidly. It has most universal application in the development of computer-based, transaction-based MIS. It is therefore examined more fully in Chapter 5, for it has evolved largely out of operational control system design. It is not quite so proven in management control and strategic planning applications. Secondly, the life cycle can be interpreted and employed as a sequential list of design activities. However, MIS design is rarely so simple and structured. The complexity of management problems and the creativity which design requires, demand that the life cycle be iterative (Figure 3.9). Each phase

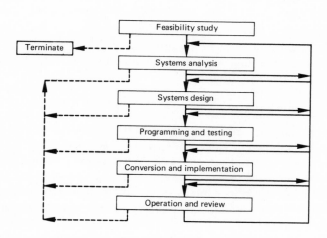

FIGURE 3.9. The iterative life cycle

may be reviewed and if necessary an earlier phase re-entered, or possibly the entire project terminated.

Thirdly, the life cycle's phases emphasise the technical tasks of MIS design, implying perhaps that it is the technical specialists' procedure. However, all phases depend on user involvement, and the cycle very often benefits from user control. So the relationships or processes of MIS design are examined later in the chapter. Finally the emphasis on a systematic approach may dominate systemic thinking. Many practitioners view the life cycle as a description of *systems analysis*. In so doing, many of the original concepts of systems analysis—examined below—may be lost.

SYSTEMS ANALYSIS

The methodology of systems analysis recognises that most systems behaviour is complex and uncertain and thus difficult to control. Systems analysis grew out of military decision-making, but is just as relevant to MIS and organisational design, where complexity and uncertainty abound. Since 'complexity and uncertainty' have become management cliches, Table 3.6 attempts to expand them in systems terms, by borrowing from Beer.[17]

TABLE 3.6. Complexity and uncertainty

Complexity	
Innate complexity	The complexity of management problems themselves
External complexity	The complexity of the system's environment
Internal complexity	The complexity of internal connectivity

Uncertainty	
Uncertainty of mishap	Systems and subsystems go wrong
Uncertainty of probability	Many outcomes are probabilistic or risky
Uncertainty of indeterminacy	Many outcomes are unpredictable and our knowledge lacking

The essence of systems analysis is that it focuses on the entire problem, concentrates on objectives and explores alternatives in a systematic way. Advocates claim that the methodology also recognises that systems and decision-making cannot always be optimised, that objectives may conflict, and that intuition and judgement may be as valid as reason and analysis.

Therefore it must be seen as a conceptual, but pragmatic framework for complex problem-solving, such as MIS design.

Quade[18] and others suggest there are five elements in the systems analysis methodology. These are explained in the MIS context below:

(1) Determination of objectives—establishing what are or should be the MIS objectives.

(2) Seeking alternatives—examining alternative system designs to meet the MIS objectives.

(3) Cost–benefit analysis—establishing the costs and benefits of the MIS, both tangible and intangible.

(4) Constructing an explanatory model—creating or explicating a model to organise thinking in the MIS design and to determine how well the design meets the MIS objectives and at what cost.

(5) Selecting criteria—defining criteria which help relate often incommensurate MIS costs and benefits, so as to select or rank preferred designs and audit the MIS subsequently.

MIS design is seldom so tidy that these steps can be followed in a neat progression. Objectives can be obscure or may well conflict, criteria of both effectiveness and efficiency may be vague, and costs and benefits may initially elude quantification. Therefore systems analysis has to be iterative and the designer may enter the cycle at any stage, very often selecting the most promising starting point.

Six implications for MIS design arise out of this framework. Firstly, the need to determine MIS objectives and address the 'right' problem is emphasised. In particular the designers need time to think about the problem, exploring its full breadth and trying to discover appropriate objectives and relevant criteria. Often terms of reference are biased, stated objectives obscure or conflicting, and the sponsor's assumptions invalid. Time spent on examining and re-examining objectives can help prevent development of extravagant, unrealistic or irrelevant systems.

Secondly, the search for criteria can help in refining vague or fuzzy objectives. It also provides a frame of reference for cost–benefit analysis and post-implementation review.

The emphasis on seeking alternatives can also bring more creative–constructive and critical approaches to MIS design. Commonly system alternatives are not explored and trade-offs not examined. Experimental design, combining different solutions, and adopting an iterative approach are all ways of creating alternatives.

A central element of systems analysis is the construction of models. Models are abstract representations of reality, scaled down or simplified, to help organise our thinking, prescribe information requirements and test and evaluate alternatives. The concept of models is examined further in the next section.

Systems analysis assesses uncertainty through the model. Initially certainty is assumed and then relaxed as questions are asked of the model. These might include the effect of a program error, potential user errors or manipulations, possible disturbances between subsystems and sensitivity to different values and assumptions. Risk management, sensitivity analysis and contingency planning are all relevant to MIS design.

Finally the framework emphasises cost–benefit analysis, which is discussed in detail in Chapter 5. Few MIS escape economic assessment today, but the systems analysis approach by linking together cost–benefit analysis with formulation of objectives and specification of criteria provides a wider dimension and a methodology.

MODELS

A model is an abstract representation of reality. It reduces or simplifies real-world complexity by leaving some things out and concentrating on critical components, processes and relationships. Thus the model helps us describe, understand and predict the system we are designing. Examples of models are simplified physical miniatures, games, mathematical equations, flowcharts or even 'back of an envelope' diagrams and verbal descriptions.

Management scientists classify models according to their construction:

(1) Iconic models, or simple scale transformations of real-world systems.
(2) Analogue models, or the use of one property to represent another.
(3) Symbolic models, or the use of symbols to represent properties.

When these models become formalised into the MIS itself, management scientists then classify them along other dimensions such as descriptive or normative, deterministic or probabilistic, predictive or optimising. These are discussed further in Chapter 11.

However, the type is irrelevant to the MIS design process. The critical task is to explicate the implicit models which exist throughout organisations in decision-makers minds, to construct a conceptual model and translate it into an operational device for specifying information requirements. A more useful classification therefore might be into verbal (e.g. descriptive), analytical (e.g. flowchart) and mathematical (i.e. numerical), representing a continuum of increased understanding or structure. In other words the model is used to describe the decision system, then to understand it and finally to prescribe information requirements.

Cleland and King suggest that models provide four major benefits in systems design. The model's predictive variables—the variables which influence the decision—serve to specify the predictors and measures which will be used to assess information requirements. The model's criterion—the decision-making objectives—indicate the particular quantities, measurement bases and qualities which the information flows should contain. For example, a merger and acquisition model might concentrate on price-earnings ratios, earnings per share and asset values, or perhaps include a qualitative assessment of good or bad stock-market image. The model's solution helps refine the form of information required, whilst the model's sensitivity can be used to assess uncertainty and the effect of various input data or estimates. A fifth benefit is that models help in creating and assessing alternative designs, since alternative models can be evaluated in terms of accuracy, utility, and cost of development and operation. Thus models help in evaluating information.

Models also can be a catalyst to joint user–analyst MIS design. They provide a means of joint understanding and development, for the user becomes the source upon which the analyst draws. The manager can better ask questions of the proposed design, satisfy himself of its relevance, and then improve his use of the information, develop his decision-making ability, and improve the MIS once it is available. The analyst may have to acquire new social skills, becoming a 'systems catalyst' as much as an analyst. In return, however, he has a device which provides a precise structure and terminology, aids dialogue and understanding, can incorporate the role of managerial intuition and judgement, focuses on the man–machine interface, and, above all perhaps, is a learning medium for both parties. In short the model is not so much a design tool, or a technique, as might be the models of operations research. The model central to systems analysis is of a higher order: it is more a *process* device, Process concepts are examined in the next section.

PROCESS CONCEPTS

PROCESS AND STRUCTURE

Researchers and practitioners have recognised a set of MIS problems which confront organisations. Frequently MIS fail to meet intended objectives, design is undervalued, impact on decision-making is disappointing, social considerations are lacking and management support and involvement is inadequate. In response to these impediments, new techniques, procedures and structures are adopted. The disciplines of the systems development life cycle are introduced, top management steering committees are devised, rigorous project controls are applied and interface roles, bridging the specialists and the users, are developed. Yet still managers are heard to say '*They're* designing a new system', '*it* will never work', 'it was not what *I expected*', and '*what* consultation?'. In other words investment in structures and procedures may have brought some improvement, but MIS design and operation often seem remote from the user. This phenomenon, that the actual behaviour of one group of people to another bears only limited relation to how the formal organisational structure and procedures says they should behave, has led to development of concepts of process rather than structure.

Structure can be seen as comprising the organisational chart, the reporting relationships, the formal committees, and the defined spans of control which are often used to describe organisations. The emphasis on structure is understandable because it is a search for stability, and a necessary prescription of roles and relationships. However, organisations are also networks of people with processes always occurring between them. Process concepts are a way of understanding and harnessing the informal relationships, traditions and culture which surrounds the structure. Only if these relationships work smoothly can organisational effectiveness be ensured. Thus in MIS design, process concepts concerned with analyst–user relationships are very relevant.

Furthermore attention to processes may be more effective because they can be extrapolated more reliably than the behaviours they generate, since they are more versatile and inertial.[19] Processes, and their design, will adapt to most variations in an organisation's capabilities, internal politics, or environmental constraints and opportunities. In other words whereas it is difficult to prescribe MIS design structures and procedures which fit comfortably into all organisations, MIS design processes can be described with more confidence because they are more readily designed to fit the situation and are likely to adapt naturally as circumstances change. Process designs enhance an organisation's flexibility and responsiveness. Systematic procedures and rational structures offer weaker protection against unpredictability and change.

JOINT DESIGN

Many of the conventional wisdoms of MIS design still are oriented towards structure and technique and consequently are inadequate. As an antidote, this chapter focuses on frameworks and processes which perhaps hold more promise. A particular fault of earlier wisdoms has been their specialist-orientation. Yet, whilst specialists may provide 'sophisticated' information, it is the users who have to employ it and we have learnt that provision of information does not guarantee use. Users therefore must be involved in the design process, not only ensuring systems are usable, but also providing critical know-how, ensuring the important minutiae of detail and exception are not overlooked and learning how the MIS will affect them.

Users therefore should design their own systems, or more realistically, MIS design should be a joint process between the analyst with his specialist skills and the user with his managerial and business knowledge. The arguments for user involvement in design thus include:

(1) Contribution of local knowledge and business expertise.

(2) Attention to behavioural issues especially concerned with the man–machine interface.

(3) Reduction of power-conflict problems between information providers and information users. [20]

(4) Retention of user control over information processing.

(5) Pursuit of a common goal of developing and implementing a workable and relevant system.

(6) An aid to organisational learning.

(7) Help in breaking down language and jargon barriers to communication.

(8) Greater understanding of system interactions and interdependencies.

(9) Explication, and perhaps resolution, of different value systems.

(10) Contribution of management experience from users' own unofficial and private MIS that they inevitably will have developed.

Thus the driving rationale behind joint design is to encourage joint MIS ownership, common loyalty to system objectives and shared commitment to successful operation and continual adaptation. Certainly, one researcher[21] found that user involvement in design led to greater appreciation of the MIS and thus greater use.

However, joint design is not a panacea, for problems do arise. These include:

(1) Raised user expectations.

(2) User alienation.

(3) Time and cost pressures.

(4) Systems analyst attitudes.

(5) Form of joint design.

For example Neergaard[22] has found that if users have a bad experience in joint design, they are far less willing to participate again. Also if those users involved in design are not fully representative of their wider population, alienation is likely. Then systems analysts may regard participative design as threatening, and may not possess the necessary social skills. Some helpful participative processes are examined below. Finally, managers often find it difficult to devote time to MIS design or regard any major user involvement as indulgent. Recognising this particular problem, Orlicky[23] called for full-time user secondment, which is frequently the only practical approach. However, as discussed later, different forms of involvement or participation exist and may suit different situations.

It is likely that meaningful user involvement will lead to different views of system success. Sophistication may be measured in terms of system use and benefits, rather than 'advance' in design, and a broader view of optimality may evolve. For example participative design may help overcome the problems that Hedberg and Mumford[24] have discovered, namely over-mechanistic systems designed by technically oriented specialists. They found that whilst systems analysts have a Theory Y view of both of themselves and the users, the eventual system designs tend to be Theory X on impact. Participation may thus allow users to shout out that 'we are not as you think we are!'. Furthermore, not only may resistance to change be avoided and more effective management information be designed, but opportunities can also be seized to improve job satisfaction by designing the system and its interfaces to meet users' knowledge needs, psychological needs, control support needs and task needs.[25] Likewise, user involvement may influence design so that different user psychologies, methods of evidence generation or modes of information presentation are adopted, much as Mason and Mitroff have suggested. Certainly there is the possibility of designing information which managers understand and thus may use more readily.

Such aims however depend on systems analysts behaving more as catalysts or *process consultants*, providing process skills of diagnosis and prognosis rather than problem skills. Schein[26] suggests some assumptions which underlie process consultation including:

(1) Managers often do not know what is wrong and need help in diagnosis.
(2) Managers need help in seeking what help to seek.
(3) Managers want improvements but need help in identifying what to improve and how.
(4) Most organisations can be more effective if they learn how to diagnose their own strengths and weaknesses

(5) The process consultant cannot learn enough about the culture of an organisation.

(6) The manager must learn to see the problem for himself, share in diagnosis and be actively involved in generating a remedy.

(7) The process consultant must be expert at diagnosis and in establishing effective helping relationships with managers.

(8) The process consultant is expert on individual, interpersonal and intergroup processes.

If we substitute user for manager and systems analyst for process consultant in the above statements, we see at once the rationale, relevant skills and requisite roles of joint design.

There are, however, alternative forms of joint design. There is also the danger both of pseudo-participation and of excessive, ill-suited or unthinking participation. A continuum of joint design processes exists, as shown in Figure 3.10. 'Consultation ex-post' is characterised by training, induction and familiarisation at the implementation stage, but with little involvement earlier. 'Consultation during' is typified by systems analysts discussing system needs and alternatives with users in the analysis, design and testing phases. 'User representatives' are typically individuals appointed by user functions or departments as liaison officers. 'Working parties' are temporary analyst–user task forces or committees formed to monitor a project's development or tackle a particular problem. 'Interface roles' include user-analysts, information analysts and the like created to bridge the gap between specialist and user. 'User designers' are users seconded to a design team for the duration of the project. 'Democratic design', an example of which is described later, is the involvement of all 'stakeholders' in the MIS.

It is not yet clear that one form of joint design is always more effective than another. 'Consultation ex-post' is generally inadequate, but equally

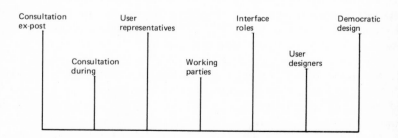

FIGURE 3.10 Joint design continuum

'democratic design' may be too ambitious in some situations. The contingent factors which might be examined to determine the most suitable form of joint design include:

(1) The nature of the decision problem: whether it is structured or unstructured.
(2) The technology available; for example, timesharing, mini-computing or mainframe computing may demand different approaches or offer different opportunities.
(3) The organisation structure; perhaps organic rather than mechanistic organisations favour joint design.
(4) User and analyst skills; the process skills required of analysts and technical skills required of users for some forms of participation may have to be developed.
(5) The stage of MIS evolution in the organisation; experience may be a crucial factor.

So, whilst lack of user involvement has caused many MIS failures, selection of the appropriate form of participation may be critical.

One experiment in democratic design is described by Land.[27] In designing a real-time system for a bank, it was recognised that there were several different 'stakeholders'. Goal, value and information conflicts seemed inevitable, and a technique for reconciling design requirements and evaluating system benefits was devised. Although complex and perhaps too involved for wide practice, the process framework it provides is valuable.

A group is formed of the major stakeholders and the system objectives they seek are identified. If a stakeholder is unavailable, someone role-plays the part. General objectives are formulated as in Figure 3.11 and then factored into sub-goals which have objectively measurable properties, or to which the stakeholder can attach a meaningful value (Figure 3.12). By

FIGURE 3.11. System stakeholders and goals

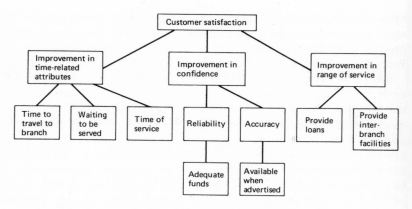

FIGURE 3.12. Customer stakeholder sub-goals

consultation and discussion among the stakeholders, weights are attached to each stakeholder goal group, and a 'collective bargain' is sought. Then each stakeholder group, by investigation, attaches values to its own sub-goals.

A computer program can then be used to reconcile values and weights and to calculate weighted values of each sub-goal. Then the alternative system designs created in the systems analysis can be scored as to how they satisfy each goal. Ranking and sensitivity analysis can then be applied. The computations may well be less important than the opportunity to explicate the different, and perhaps hidden, values of organisations and to provide an arena for negotiation. This stakeholder approach is perhaps best viewed as a systematic and explicit attempt to recognise and incorporate different claims on MIS design. It is more a process framework than a technique. Joint design, to be practicable, needs such process-enablers; another is described in the next section.

PROTOTYPE SYSTEMS[28]

Successful joint design depends on users and systems analysts learning together. Argyris[29] suggests that the majority of organisational learning is single loop, namely the identification and correction of errors so that the job gets done and action remains within stated policy guidelines. As long as objectives, competences and loyalties are not questioned, this single loop learning occurs. However, joint design depends on such questions being raised, discussed and resolved—double loop learning—which Argyris finds most organisational behaviour inhibits. Therefore he calls for design processes which focus on learning and on individual theories in use. Prototype systems are one possible response to this need.

Prototype systems are cheap, flexible and simplified systems used for exploration and experimentation in an operational environment, before the 'production' system is developed. They are designed and written quickly and thus may be crude, and rough and ready. Prototypes test alternative designs through live operation and so are continually amended, growing in complexity over time, with reliability perhaps sacrificed for flexibility. Once the prototype has served its experimental purpose, it will be replaced by a robust, viable system. A prototype is the ultimate version of the model and in engineering is the accepted methodology; engineers prefer to try out new designs before inflicting them on unsuspecting environments. Prototypes aim to reduce the risks of MIS design, by providing experimentation in a live environment. A prototype is also a *process-enabler* whose rationale is based on eight arguments:

(1) Systems are expensive. Because MIS design represents a considerable investment in time and cost, management pressures often constrain the phases of systems analysis and design with dysfunctional consequences. Likewise, post-implementation maintenance and enhancement is minimised as newer projects gain momentum. The prototype approach provides an early system to satisfy immediate demands, but also provides an opportunity for users to influence system design experimentally and derive tried and tested design which is then re-developed into the final, robust MIS.

(2) Participation is painful. Effective user involvement in MIS design is not easy. Often through lack of technical knowledge, users become hostages of the design team because they refrain from asking 'silly questions'. Then if they acquire specialist knowledge, they become indoctrinated and no longer truly represent their user group.[30] Prototype systems provide a participative vehicle because users cannot opt out so easily. They are expected to derive a system that works, by trial and error. The live state of the prototype may induce the pain and pleasure which learning requires.

(3) Models are abstract. The concept of the model is valuable, but can be limited because models often are abstract. Users do not necessarily think in models and good models are difficult to find and develop. However, managers usually welcome and grasp a physical reality. Given a simple

working model, such as the prototype, they will fill in the gaps, criticise it and then extend its scope.[31]

(4) Organisations are complex. The interface between man and machine, and between MIS and organisation, is complex and difficult to predict. A prototype system allows the impact at the interface to be studied, tested and varied in an experimental way so as to derive a more acceptable and viable system.

(5) Information is a process. Satisfying information needs does not automatically improve decision-making. Managers may require new methods to understand and process information. Prototypes provide a vehicle for management and organisational development alongside MIS design.

(6) Users are 'perverse'. Users abuse, misuse, ignore, adapt and manipulate information. Often such behaviours represent realistic, adaptive or creative responses to inadequate MIS design. If we fail to consider and study MIS use, opportunities for improvement will be missed. Prototype systems afford opportunity to observe and jointly examine information use.

(7) Modelling has a message. Several surveys report that computer-based modelling has succeeded where managers are given a simple and available system first, and then develop it with experience. The prototype approach is founded on the same premise.

(8) Systems must learn. If systems are too rigid and robust, they may not adapt to changing circumstances. Thus MIS design itself can constrain organisational adaptation and survival. Prototype systems may, by being experimental, create a culture of change, adaptation and learning.

The prototype approach ideally fits into the systems analysis and systems design phases of the development life cycle. It condenses much of the normal iteration of MIS design into these two phases. However, it is critical that the prototype does not live for too long without review; like all systems it may need to be killed if it turns out to be non-viable. Furthermore many formal MIS cannot survive in prototype mode since they need to be robust, reliable and efficient. So it may be necessary to declare the prototype's life span in advance and to monitor it closely.

Arguments have been raised against prototype systems. Some critics suggest they are costly. However, many less evolutionary approaches have failed and proved more expensive in the long run. Also prototypes can satisfy immediate needs and are becoming more feasible to develop as software improves. Secondly, concern is expressed that prototypes may cause disruption and conflict. This may be true but may also be necessary to generate real learning and stimulate the search for alternatives. Thirdly, simulation approaches to design could be adopted instead. However, they do not produce the live environment which is so essential for many aspects of MIS design. Nor are they so valuable a process device. Finally, concern is expressed that the prototype approach demands special skills. Undoubtedly process skills are beneficial, but prototypes may be a 'natural' process device in that they use conventional systems structure and techniques, but through experimentation and incrementalism.

PROCESS CONTROL

MIS development is no different from any other organisational activity: it must be controlled. Concepts of management control, project management and the systems approach are all relevant to control of the MIS design process. Planning and control techniques such as project budgets, network analysis, GANTT charts and periodic reporting are commonly employed, generally within the framework of the systems development life cycle since it provides a set of identifiable tasks and phases. Systems thinking is often adopted by factoring large systems into manageable subsystems or modules for development, and by employing a project manager or leader to ensure subsystems are integrated and to oversee all development tasks, specialist and user, as a whole.

Managements rightly have been concerned to avoid some of the early experiences of MIS design, such as out-of-control expenditure and repeated failure to meet completion dates. So cost budgets and time/effort schedules have been encouraged. MIS designers, however, have learnt how to meet such targets, often to the detriment of the MIS. Initial objectives and time scales are rigidly followed, uncertainties and complexities ignored or removed and change or adaptation constrained. The milestone approach[32] can provide a more balanced framework. Here each phase of the life cycle represents a milestone and when reported as complete, senior management ensures that all component tasks have been achieved to the satisfaction of all parties; otherwise the next phase cannot commence. Also the MIS must still be viable in economic, operational and technical terms; otherwise the project is killed. In this way, outstanding tasks, new challenges, changing requirements or need for reiteration are not subordinated to time and cost targets. Nor do marginal projects survive by stays of execution (as costs-to-date are written off as sunk costs and future benefits become even more magnetic) because milestones are potential kill-points.

However, Dickson and Powers[33] found no correlation between use of formal planning and control techniques and eventual MIS success. Alloway[34] likewise found no correlation between achievement of time and cost targets and project success. Both research studies led to suggestions that, rather than apply universal techniques and 'laws', project control should adapt to the nature of each project and its environment. Alloway went on to construct a practical framework for this contingency approach.

He sees the MIS design project as a temporary management system, each project being unique.

> This is why managers create a temporary management organisation or team of multi-departmental, multi-disciplinary personnel to create a [management information system]. The uncertainties and complexities of managing a temporary task and succeeding the first and only time require a management approach which is flexible, responsive and has a variety of the probably necessary skills. The luxury of iterative improvements found in repetitive task management simply does not exist for the temporary task of creating (MIS).

In other words Alloway is concerned with *process control* rather than project control.

Alloway's research results showed that project management should be designed according to the nature of the task and the organisational context. The key factors of the task are uncertainty and complexity of both MIS objectives and appropriate skills. The greater the uncertainty and complexity, the higher the task index and the less likely is success. The managerial and technical skills of the project team must match the task index 'correspondence'. The representativeness of the user participants in the team and the perceived relevance of the MIS to their needs must also match the task index 'interdependence'. If necessary, the task should be modified to increase perception of relevance.

The key factors of organisational context are differentiation among user departments, measured by their number and organisational span, and the degree of compensating integration, such as existence of integrative mechanisms, previous cooperation or common reporting relationships. The greater the uncompensated differentiation, the higher is the context index and the less likely is success. Balance between the project and the context is achieved by good interdependence, that is representative participation and strong perceived relevance, and good coupling, that is shared perception of appropriate problem-solving mode and open channels of communication for information flow, conflict resolution and control of the project by the context.

If both the task and context indices are high or low, separate decisions on correspondence and coupling will be compatible. If, however, the task index is high and the context is low, most project teams satisfy the context at the expense of the task, by concentrating on meeting efficiency targets rather than MIS effectiveness. Communication channels in this case are vital, so that information about the project's objectives flows to the context, and progress on these objectives flows back in return. Good conflict resolution devices are also required.

Alloway, then, sees four factors as the key to project success:

(1) A mix of managerial and technical skills which corresponds in diversity and depth to the uncertainty and complexity of the task.
(2) Clearly established behavioural expectations for roles, role incumbents and problem-solving mode.
(3) Integration within the project team, adequate to overcome team differentiation due to skill diversity and divided organisational loyalties.
(4) Use of planning and control techniques, both within the project and for reporting progress to the context, which are compatiable with the particular project approach.

He makes two further important points. The project team structure should be changed as both task and context themselves change; it should be adaptive. Secondly, use of project planning and control techniques influences the approach (and thus design process) of the team, the way reports are made to the context, and the integration of the team. Precise and rigid techniques like PERT thus only suit projects with a low task index. More flexible techniques are required when the task is uncertain and complex.

Such a contingency framework for 'process control' is preferable to universal solutions. Otherwise organisations are liable to design ineffective MIS for the more difficult problem areas, and perhaps will consequently confine their developments to one class of system. Furthermore it is apparent that both design of MIS, and its control, is a joint specialist–user responsibility.

SUMMARY

There is no one best way to design an MIS. Needs, situations and organisations differ too much for such universal solutions. Thus principles of system design are better seen as frameworks, the following having proved valuable in practice.

(1) Management information needs and characteristics can be determined by studying decision types and decision-making. MIS can be classified and described in this way.

(2) The decision focus provides useful insights into the value of information, the components of MIS, information requirements analysis, the MIS design process and information systems planning.

(3) Whilst MIS increasingly are computer-based, optimal use of computers requires a sense of 'computability'. A computability framework can be constructed by studying decision types and computer attributes.

(4) MIS are rarely machine systems alone. The concept of man–machine systems is valuable since it focuses on interfaces, stresses that MIS can differ in scope considerably along the man–machine continuum, and reminds us that MIS are socio-technical systems.

(5) 'Systems thinking' is useful in MIS design since it emphasises systems boundaries, systems interaction and interdependence, systems hierachies, holism and systems behaviour.

(6) The systems development life cycle can be seen as one example of the systems approach. It provides a systematic, iterative and modular approach to MIS design.

(7) The concept of systems analysis is valuable since it stresses the need for objectives, the search for alternatives, the importance of criteria, the contribution of models and the importance of cost–benefit analysis.

(8) The model is central to systems design since it helps organise thinking, specify information requirements, assess uncertainty and create user–specialist dialogue.

(9) The concept of process is important in MIS design because it emphasises user–specialist relationships, the need for flexibility and the importance of adaptation.

(10) MIS design is a joint process between specialist and user. Joint design is essential because it is the users who will employ the system, because they provide crucial know-how and because it is they who will be affected by the MIS.

(11) Joint design may lead to different views of MIS sophistication and optimality. Also systems analysts may need to be systems catalysts or process consultants.

(12) Different forms of joint design are possible and should be designed to fit the circumstances. Joint design or participation are in need of process-enabling devices. One is the stakeholder approach.

(13) Another methodology is the prototype system which not only aims to reduce the risks of MIS design but facilitate user–specialist cooperation. (14) MIS should be controlled, but a balance between discipline and creativity and between control and flexibility should be ensured. One approach is to analyse the design task and its organisational context and match the controls accordingly.

(15) Such contingency frameworks offer most promise for MIS design. The design process, methodology, techniques and controls should fit the task and the context.

CHAPTER 3—PROJECTS

1. A recent textbook suggested '. . . an advanced management information system should be computer based, integrated with all subsystems, accessible through a common databank or database, utilise input terminals on site and at remote locations, timely through use of communications capability, and interactive between the user and the information available'. Do you agree?

2. Assess one of the following situations being considered for the application of computers and suggest one potential application area, giving reasons:

(a) Production control in an engineering company.
(b) Ground services at an airport.
(c) Town and country planning in a local government authority.
(d) Administration in a university.
(e) Running a mail-order business.

3. Figure 3.6 portrays the information–decision process in terms of man–machine interfaces. Assess the following information systems in the light of this continuum and discuss the implications:

(a) A bank branch accounting system.
(b) A process control system in a paper mill.
(c) A capital investment appraisal modelling system.
(d) A stock recording system.
(e) A personnel records system.
(f) A linear programming oil refinery production mix model.

4. 'At the heart of every information system is a model.' Discuss.

5. How might an effective project control system differ for each of the following MIS design projects?

(a) A credit control system.

(b) A financial control system in a hospital.

(c) A machine shop scheduling system.

NOTES

1. Zani, W. N., 'Blueprint for MIS', *Harvard Business Review*, November–December 1970.
2. Diebold, J., 'Bad Decisions on Computer Use', *Harvard Business Review*, January–February 1969.
3. Mason, R. O., and Mitroff, I. M., 'A Program for Research in Management Information Systems', *Management Science*, January 1973.
4. Shannon, C. E., and Weaver, W., *The Mathematical Theory of Communication*. Urbana, Ill.: The University of Illinois Press, 1962.
5. Ackoff, R. L., 'Management Misinformation Systems', *Management Science*, December 1967.
6. Zani, W. M., 'Blueprint for MIS', *Harvard Business Review*, November–December 1970.
7. These figures were derived in early 1978.
8. Martin, J., *Design of Real Time Computer Systems*. Englewood Cliffs, N.J.: Prentice-Hall, 1969.
9. Down, P. J., and Taylor, F. E., *Why Distributed Computing?* National Computing Centre Ltd, 1976.
10. Specifications of mini- and micro-computers relate to early 1978.
11. Dearden, J., and McFarlan, W. F., *Management Information Systems*. Homewood, Ill.: Irwin, 1966.
12. Dearden, J., 'Myth of Real-Time Management Information', *Harvard Business Review*, May–June 1966.
13. Mason, R. O. Jr., 'Basic Concepts for Designing Management Information Systems', AIS Research Paper No. 8, Graduate School of Business Administration, University of California, Los Angeles, October 1969.
14. Models are defined and explained later in the chapter.
15. Hedberg, B., and Mumford, E., 'The Design of Computer Systems', in Mumford, E., and Sackman, H. (eds.), *Human Choice and Computers*. Amsterdam: North-Holland Publishing Co., 1975.
16. The concept of socio-technical systems can be explored further in Emery, F. E., and Trist, E. L., 'Socio-technical Systems', in Churchman, C., and Cerhulst, M. (eds.), *Management Sciences: Models and Techniques*. New York: Pergamon Press, 1960.
17. Beer, S., *Decision and Control*. London: Wiley, 1966.
18. Quade, E. S., 'Systems Analysis Techniques for Planning, Programming, Budgeting', Report 3322, The Rand Corporation, March 1966.
19. Hedberg, B., Nystrom, P., and Starbuck, W., 'Camping on Seesaws:

Prescriptions for a Self-designing Organisation', *Administrative Science Quarterly*, 21 (1976).

20. Edstrom and De Brabander suggest conflicts are inevitable in joint design, because of power asymmetries between the parties. They therefore suggest use of third party arbitrators or catalysts. See De Brabander B., and Edstrom, A., 'A Theory of Success of Information System Development Projects', European Institute for Advanced Studies in Management, Working Paper 76–45, 1976.

21. Burton, Swanson E., 'MIS Appreciation and Involvement', *Management Science*, 2, October 1974.

22. Neergaard, P., 'Some Research Results on Participative Design', European Institute for Advanced Studies in Management, Working Paper, 1977.

23. Orlicky, J., *The Successful Computer System*. New York: McGraw-Hill, 1969.

24. Hedberg, B., and Mumford, E., 'The Design of Computer Systems', in Mumford, E., and Sackman, H. (eds.), *Computers and Human Choice*. New York: American Elsevier, 1975.

25. Mumford, E., 'Industrial Democracy and Systems Design', *Manchester Business School Review*, 1976.

26. Schein, E., *Process Consultation: Its Role in Organisation Development*. Reading, Mass.: Addison-Wesley, 1969.

27. Land, F. F., 'Evaluation of Systems Goals in Determining a Design Strategy for CBIS', *The Computer Journal*, November 1976.

28. Earl, M. J., 'Prototype Systems for Accounting Information and Control', *Accounting, Organisations and Society*, 3, No. 2 (1978).

29. Argyris, C., 'Organisational Learning and Management Information Systems', *Accounting, Organisations and Society*, 2, No. 2 (1977).

30. Hedberg, B., 'Computer Systems to Support Industrial Democracy, in Mumford, E., and Sackman, H. (eds.), *Computers and Human Choice*. New York: American Elsevier, 1975.

31. Gorry, G. A., 'The Development of Managerial Models', *Sloan Management Review*, Fall 1971.

32. Charman, J., 'Effective Project Costing and Killing Techniques', in McFarlan, F. W., Nolan, R. L., and Norton, D. P. (eds.), *Information Systems Administration*, New York: Holt, Rinehart and Winston, 1973.

33. Dickson, G. W., and Powers, R. F., 'MIS Project Management: Myths, Opinion and Reality', Working Paper 71–01, MIS Research Centre, University of Minnesota, May 1971.

34. Alloway, R. M., 'Temporary Management Systems: Application of a Contingency Model to the Creation of Computer-Based Information Systems', Executive Summary, Stockholm School of Economics, November 1976.

BIBLIOGRAPHY

Anthony, R. N., 'Planning and Control Systems. A Framework for Analysis', Harvard Business School, Division of Research, 1964.

Beishon, J., and Peters, G., *Systems Behaviour*. Milton Keynes: The Open University Press, 1976.

Cleland, D. I. and King, W. R., *Systems Analysis and Project Management*. New York: McGraw-Hill, 1975.

Forrester, J., *Industrial Dynamics*. New York: Wiley, 1961.

Gorry, G. A., and Scott-Morton, M. S., 'A Framework for Management Information Systems', *Sloan Management Review*, Fall 1971.

McFarlan, F. W., Nolan, R. L., and Norton, D. P., *Information Systems Administration*. New York: Holt, Rinehart and Winston, 1973.

Nolan, R. L. (ed.), *Managing the Data Resource Function*. St. Paul, Minn., West Publishing Company, 1974.

Simon, H. A., *The New Science of Management Decision*. Englewood Cliffs, N.J.: Prentice-Hall, 1977.

Part II Operational Control Systems

4 Characteristics of Operational Control Systems

In this present part of the book, Part II, we are concerned with operational control systems. These systems are devoted to the job of ensuring that specific organisational tasks are carried out effectively and efficiently. In this chapter we shall be examining the overall characteristics of such systems. We shall then move, in later chapters, to a more detailed discussion of how they can be made effective, efficient, cost-effective and technically advantageous.

The operational control system of an organisation functions where the organisation's basic work is done. It is the system, or series of systems, with which all the operating personnel interact on a daily basis. The operational control system should help all these personnel fulfil their assignments in a manner that will meet the firm's goals. Ideally, it should also help them to ensure that their own personal targets are achieved, insofar as these may be job-related.

An operational control system therefore exists to monitor and measure live, current data concerning the daily work of the firm. It must, therefore, be automatic in its working, and must be set up to function systematically with little or no intervention from the managers.

CHARACTERISTICS OF OPERATING CONTROLS

TASKS AND TRANSACTIONS

A task may be defined as the smallest portion of a function which is managerially meaningful. Although it can be subdivided further in clerical terms, it is neither natural, nor efficient, nor effective to subdivide that task in organisational terms. A transaction, on the other hand, may involve work for more than one organisational unit. Table 4.1 gives examples that illustrate the difference between tasks and subtasks.

TABLE 4.1

Tasks	Subtasks
Receiving job application	Performed on the basis of some rules or predetermined standards, the subtasks are (a) receiving, (b) checking, (c) sorting, (d) filing, and (e) despatching to the next department
Stock issue	Receiving requisition, verification, recording, preparing documents for physical transfer, balancing
Timekeeping	Completing time cards, computing actual time, idle time, overtime, informing accounts and personnel

A transaction may involve several departments or sections. It initiates a chain of actions in those departments. For example, the issue of purchase order to vendor is associated with a number of transactions, most of them involving information transmittal (see Figure 4.1). Actions are taken on these files or in these departments to complete the purchase transaction.

FIGURE 4.1. Purchase order transaction

Tasks or transactions are subdivisions of the organisation functions or functional tasks. In Chapter 2, we discussed functional task classifications. Usual classifications of functional task include (1) marketing, (2) production, (3) logistics, (4) personnel, (5) finance, (6) information processing, and (7) top management. However, the basic functions are (1) production, (2) marketing, and (3) logistics (purchasing, inventory and distribution). Accounting and finance integrate these functions in economic terms. For example, credit terms are marketing instruments, while the control of credit is an accounting or finance function. Production scheduling is a logistic operation, while production costing is an accounting operation. Later in this chapter we will discuss the specific operational control subsystems and some aspects of functional controls.

OPERATING CONTROLS AND CONTROL DATA

Operational control data are generated close to the points of use, and tend to be exact and real-time. Operational control data are specific to the task or situation. Various units of measurement are used for operating data, e.g. man-hour, machine-hour, counts, inches, etc. In other types of control such as management or strategic control, measurement is limited to monetary measurements.

The data in operational control systems are specific, detailed, and (usually) unabridged. The subsystems generate data in large volumes, and do so with precision and speed. Most operational control systems involve the use of formal, systematic, and structured models, which may be quite complicated but which tend to be mathematically or logically certain.

Operational control systems are most heavily involved at the lower levels of the organisation. Their actions are measured in quantitative and mechanical terms, and there is a high premium on unambiguous, clear and relevant data. If the data are not precise, it becomes very hard to maintain control over the work.

Managerial interventions in operational control systems are few, and should be. Many of these systems are automated and some are computerised. The computer is now routinely used to set re-order points for stock, to evaluate credit ratings of customers, and to process personnel files, using predetermined decision rules. At the design stage, considerable technical skill is needed. The relevant discipline must be available to the system designer. The personnel system must be designed with the help of an industrial psychologist, the stock recorder system with the aid of an operational research worker, and so on.

Operating controls are by their nature repetitive. The system designer should examine the decision-taking and operating situation very carefully at the early stages, to make sure that the procedures really are repetitive and predictable. If they are not, and if there are regular violations of the rules, it may be impossible to treat a control system as though it were genuinely repetitive. Different procedures, of the kind discussed in Part III of this book, must then be invoked.

Furthermore, our experience shows that the same task (e.g. customer billing) in different situations requires different control models.

In a cosmetics company, salesmen used to be rotated between different locations. For a given department the rule was that an employee must be rotated after he had completed one year serving in a particular location. On this principle salesmen's rotation could be programmed. However, decision in actual practice was also influenced by such other variables, as (a) salesmen's preference, (b) personal influence, and (c) executive evaluation of effectiveness. This task was repetitive only to the extent that after the end of one year the relocation question was to be considered. Actual action involved judgement and management decision. Therefore, in such a situation no programmed decision was effective. The problem was more a management control problem than an operating control problem.

If, during the task performance, operators face situations which call for frequent deviations from the rules and the defined structure, then the task loses its repetitive nature. Frequent management interventions, which are liable to change the parameters, disrupts the repetitive characteristics of the operation. In such a situation decisions given by algorithm are ineffective.

The characteristics of operating controls can be classified as: (a) control-related, and (b) data-related. Table 4.2 summarises the operating control characteristics.

STEPS IN OPERATING CONTROLS DESIGN AND EVALUATION

A systematic approach towards operating control analyses should be adopted. Generally, six steps are identified as useful in the design and evaluation of operating controls. These are:

(1) Task definition and delimiting the task boundary.
(2) Developing an appropriate model.
(3) Identifying the variables that are to be manipulated.
(4) Developing mathematical or logical formulae for variable manipulation.
(5) Data inputs into the model.
(6) Actions or decisions.

TABLE 4.2. Characteristics of operating controls

Control-related traits	Data-related traits
1. Control system is a rational system	1. Data used for control are real time and current (or on line)
2. A set of logical rules is relied upon	2. Data are exact and accurate
3. It focuses on a single task or transaction	3. Units of measurement are monetary and non-monetary
4. Basic disciplines employed are economics and physical sciences	4. Data are collected and reported daily, hourly, etc.
5. Scope is precise and narrow	5. Data are internally generated
6. Guided by pre-established procedures and decision rules	6. Data are detailed and less aggregate
7. It often uses mathematical models	7. Cost data are engineered
8. Decisions are not judgement-based, though decision rules are	8. Other measurements are mechanical or technical
9. Control is repetitive	9. Reports are in the nature of 'attention directing' and 'score card'*
10. Control is stable, predictable and prescribed	
11. Short-run current perspective is predominant	

* Simon, H. A., *et al., Centralisation vs Decentralisation.* New York, Controllership Foundation Inc., 1954, p. 34.

Task definition is the first step. Drawing an appropriate task boundary is very often difficult. Nevertheless, it is crucial. A clear understanding of the problem helps to evolve a comprehensive task definition. Task definition is necessary to separate one task from another and also to provide for appropriate coordination between different tasks.

Models are essential in systems problem-solving. Models may be diagrams, pictures, statements or mathematical formulations. Models integrate between tasks and subtasks. Models help to identify variables and variable-relations. Mathematical or logical models are then applied to carry out the control action. Sometimes this can be done without making the model explicit. The feeding of data to the model is often the most resource demanding and error-prone part of an operational control system, but it is obviously the step which brings the system to life and results in action.

SPECIFIC OPERATIONAL CONTROL SUBSYSTEMS

Operational control subsystems are numerous. These subsystems are constituent parts of functional controls.

Operational controls are based on functional division and subdivision of tasks. Some major functions and their related subtasks are listed below:

(1) Sales—operational controls which are related to sales include order-processing, shipping, invoicing, collection, packaging, delivery, warehousing, inventory controls, etc.

(2) Production—production operating controls, for example, include re-order, control of procurement, work scheduling, control of jobs, processes or operations, variance analysis, quality control, stores control, etc.

(3) Personnel—personnel functional controls include such tasks as staffing, appraisal, bonus, leave, safety, security, timekeeping, payroll, etc.

(4) Accounting—accounting operations include journaling transactions, ledger entry, accounts receivable, accounts payable, cash, payroll, credit, etc.

However, the different functions are linked through operating control information systems. For example, the production, personnel and accounting functions are related through the payroll tasks. Data for payroll are generated from production records, personnel department records and accounting records. Ultimately, these data are manipulated at the accounting department for pay computation and ledger entries.

A typical order processing example is given below:

An order for purchases is initiated outside the purchasing department, at a place where something is needed, usually through a purchase requisition. Request for purchase determines what is needed in the form of a purchase requisition. A simple calculation, or a sophisticated computer or mathematical model is employed to determine the items and the quantity. It embraces such concepts as economic order quantity (EOQ).[1] Requisition is compared with the established standards and specifications. The next step is to select a vendor on precise procedures about price and related information such as distance of shipments, delivery date, etc. After these standard tasks of the purchase department are completed, a purchase order is issued. The purchase order initiates the remaining chain of work associated with the procurement.

INFORMATION PROCESSING

The operating control information system processes information for different purposes. Generally, operating control information processing can be of three types: (1) transaction processing, (2) processing for control reports, and (3) inquiry processing.[2] Outputs from transaction processing are transaction reports and permanent records. It involves transaction inputs, processing and interaction with files, and transaction reports. Operational control reports are regular periodic reports. These periodic reports are produced through operational control processing procedures and the use of files. The value of these reports rests on their timely presentation. They do not need external inputs to the processing system. Enquiry processing is initiated through an external enquiry. Enquiry response outputs are produced through enquiry processing of the files data. The following examples will explain the three types of processing.

1. A purchase transaction produces several transaction documents. These documents (purchase requisition, purchase order, invoices, receiving reports, etc.) initiate several actions, e.g. updating inventory record, recording accounts payable. These actions may be completed mechanically or through human interventions.

2. Routine reporting is done periodically. These reports are the performance reports of operational controls. Reports on inventory levels, time record, wastage, etc. are some of this type of reports. Operational control reports are mainly routine reports. Transaction processing precedes routine reporting.

3. An enquiry to an inventory record describes the inventory level of a particular item, e.g. a report includes item specifications, prices, quality, vendors and quantity last produced. This is often programmed in a computerised system. Enquiry reporting systems are designed to report on the current status of the operating situation.

FUNCTIONAL OPERATING CONTROLS

We observed that operating controls in different functional areas exist in large numbers. In this section we will outline some of the controls in four of the main business functions, production, sales, purchasing and accounting. At operational levels for effective performance, these functions depend on elaborate procedures. Procedures are important in operational controls. They relate the progress of work to the standards. The facts are provided for analysis and action through procedures. Discussions of individual procedures are beyond the limited scope of this book. Furthermore, we will restrict our attention to the outlines of the aspects of controls and will not attempt to elaborate them. Analysts are recommended to review the references provided for more detailed discussions.

PRODUCTION OPERATIONAL CONTROL ASPECTS

In manufacturing concerns production operations occupy a major position. The nature of the production system determines the complexity of the controls. High technology industrial operations need sophisticated controls. Production operational controls include activities and elements involved in production. There are seven elements and activities:[3]

(1) Activities control—involves release of production orders, despatching and setting plans in motion.
(2) Materials control—checks on material, on planned and actual time of delivery, on issue of materials and movement of materials within shops.
(3) Tooling control—checks on progress of tool design, on tool manufacturing and tool purchase and on issue of tools to the shops.
(4) Production time control—checks on machine loading, delays and stoppages of work assigned to each machine.
(5) Quality and quantity control—checks at predetermined stages of production to monitor (a) production of right quantity and (b) right quality of output.
(6) Replacement control—checks on the quantity of raw materials and work-in-progress and arranging replacements for them.
(7) Material handling control—checks on the movements of work between departments by cranes, trucks, etc.

These controls are developed through operating procedures, rules and manuals. Most of these controls are divided and subdivided into numerous small tasks and transactions.

Production activities are performed through a system of authorisation and action. The four stages associated with it are:

(1) Manufacturing or production order—an authorisation of work. It initiates one set of subsidiary orders.
(2) Routing order—determines where the work is to be done. It assures production according to design or plan.
(3) Scheduling order—the timetable for the job.
(4) Despatching—sets the productive activities in motion. Route sheets and loading schedules show planned times and sequences. In accordance with them despatching releases orders and instruction to generate actions. All these activities involve a number of tasks. For example, despatching includes the following main tasks: (a) movement of materials, (b) issue of tools orders, (c) issue of job orders, (d) issue of time tickets, (e) issue of inspection orders, (f) clean-up on the job: (i) collecting time tickets, (ii)

recovering blueprints and instructions charts, (iii) sending the documents to the production department, (g) forwarding the work to the next department, storeroom or stockroom, (h) recording time required, and forwarding it to the payroll department, and (i) recording and reporting idle time.

Operating controls in production lie at the point of execution of these tasks. Schedules, rules, procedures and algorithms are combined to control each task.

MARKETING AND SALES FUNCTIONS

Though the end of production sets in motion the marketing operation, in practice marketing functions start long before production. It may be observed that controls in production are more rational, but marketing functions have a mixture of judgemental and rational controls. Nevertheless, the basic operating levels retain the characteristics of operating controls.

Operating controls in marketing function can be analysed into three broad categories:[4]

(1) Merchandising functions—(a) functions of buying, (b) functions of selling.
(2) Supplying functions—(a) transportation, (b) storage.
(3) Auxiliary facilities functions—(a) marketing finance, (b) risk bearing, (c) market information, (d) standardisation and grading.

These functions are composed of a number of tasks. These tasks are related to product planning, improvement and development, packaging, service policing, pricing, selling, advertising, sales promotion, public relations, distribution channels and costs, market research and budgeting.

As an example, the sales functions of a firm can be broken down as follows:[5] (1) daily, weekly, monthly, sales calls; (2) inventories taking; (3) display set up; (4) stock rearrangement; (5) literature distribution; (6) sales demonstration; (7) sample distribution; (8) sales meetings; (9) attending calls books; (10) orders taking.

Information reports that are needed to monitor sales operation include: (1) sales expense report, (2) report on calls made and results obtained, (3) credit information report, (4) market information report, (5) competitive condition, (6) lost orders, (7) reports on customers inventories, and (8) service and complained reports.

PURCHASING FUNCTIONS

Following Aljian[6], purchasing functions responsibilities can be grouped as direct responsibilities and shared responsibilities. Direct responsibilities include the following functions: (1) obtaining prices, (2) selecting vendors, (3) awarding purchase orders, (4) following-up on delivery promises, (5) adjusting and settling complaints, (6) selecting training of purchasing personnel, and (7) vendor relations.

Usually the following tasks are performed in operations of purchasing functions: (1) obtaining the preliminary information, specifications and prices; (2) routing of requisition to proper buyer; (3) editing the requisition and assignment of suppliers; (4) obtaining competitive bids; (5) typing of purchase orders and distribution of copies; (6) expediting if necessary; (7) receiving of materials; (8) price checking; (9) approval of invoice for payment; and (10) providing records and information for data processing system.

Purchase departments share responsibilities with other departments with respect to the following tasks: (1) obtaining technical information and advice; (2) receiving sales presentations and arranging for sales opportunities; (3) establishing specifications; (4) scheduling orders and delivery; (5) specifying delivery method and routing; (6) inspecting; (7) expediting; (8) purchase accounting; (9) purchasing research; (10) warehousing control, (11) forward buying and hedging procedures; (12) construction contracting; (13) service contracts and agreements; (14) sales of scrap, salvage and surplus; (15) purchasing for employees; (16) contracting for machines and equipment; (17) development of specifications; (18) consideration of quantity or limiting on planning deliveries; (19) transportation traffic; (20) make or buy decisions; (21) customs; and (22) other functions.

ACCOUNTING FUNCTIONS

The accounting system is a system of integrated procedures. The system functions can be broadly divided into two parts: (1) transactions recording and (2) results reporting. Transaction processing involves primarily the following:

(1) Operation of books of accounts
  (a) Cash books recording
  (b) Ledgers
  (c) Vouchers
  (d) Posting

    (e) Coding plan
    (f) Accumulation of costs in cost centres
    (g) Allocation of cost among cost centres
    (h) Monthly closing of cost centres
(2) Reporting
  (a) (i) Monthly balance sheet and movement of fund
     (ii) Bank reconciliation statement
     (iii) Head Office current account statement
  (b) (i) Income statement
     (ii) Schedules of sales, non-operating income and recoveries
     (iii) Cost of sales statement
     (iv) Statement of inventory changes
     (v) Statement of administrative expenses
     (vi) Statement of selling and distribution expenses
  (c) (i) Cost sheets of individual cost centres
     (ii) Distribution of service expenses
     (iii) Distribution of general expenses
  (d) Responsibility reporting

Heckert[7] included the tasks shown in Table 4.3 within the accounting category. These tasks are performed on the basis of rules and procedures. They integrate the different functions in an organisation, in money terms.

Accounting is used to integrate the activities of different functions in economic terms. Table 4.4 provides an accounting view of information processing which covers purchase, production and sales functions.

The functional subtasks described in this chapter could be amplified in volumes. Most of these functions relate to our everyday business experience. We suggest that, if a system analyst is not conversant with the detail of operations of any function, he should seek expert advice.

TABLE 4.3

Sales	Purchasing	Overhead
Sales analysis	Receiving	Factory costs
Shipping and delivery	Accounts payable	Non-factory costs
Billing	Cash disbursement	End-period summarising and closing
Accounts receivable	Timekeeping	Plant and equipment
Credit collection	Payroll	Production control
Cash receipts	Inventory	Tax
Insurance		

TABLE 4.4. A summarised view of business functions and MIS support

Functions	Documents needed for information generation	Information contexts	Data distribution
Purchase	Requisition; purchase order; receiving report; vouchers	Quantity needed; received; payments; supplier's nature; price; quality; grades; etc.	Accounts payable; inventory record (quantity, price, grades); cash disbursements
Production	Requisition; time ticket; cost distribution; record for each kind of product	Material consumed for each kind of product; time for each kind of product; work-in-process; overtime; wastages; factory overhead	Payrolls; cost to process; cost to finished goods; inventory record; overhead distribution
Sales	Sales order; invoice; tickets of shipment, delivery, credit approval	Sales by broker, salesmen, product, price, discounts, customs returns, allowances, date	Accounts receivable; general ledger for total sales; finished goods inventory; salesmen's records; other selling expenses

CONCLUSION

Operating controls are numerous. Operations consist of tasks and subtasks. We have developed an appropriate understanding of the operating controls characteristics, tasks involved and their functional relevance. Moreover, we have provided lists of the aspects of functional operations. Operating controls have many virtues. Repetitiveness and stability are two of the most important. Appropriate information systems are needed for effective operational controls. The following peculiarities of operating control make an *efficient* information system highly desirable:

(1) These controls are numerous and a constant flow of data is needed to establish coordination among them.

(2) Constant monitoring needs real-time data which are precise and direct.

(3) A large volume of data handling is needed. These data are summarised and condensed to be used as inputs to the MIS.

To achieve control of operations, a considerable amount of control information must be produced and used. In this regard, a systems analyst has immense scope to contribute to making controls effective.

CHAPTER 4—PROJECT

1. A manufacturing firm currently is reviewing its tasks procedures and operating controls. The purchasing function processes 500 purchase requisitions, 400 purchase orders, 300 receiving tickets and 300 vendor invoices a day.

The receiving function involves inspecting, counting, transferring and reporting. Outline an information processing model for receiving functions which will fulfil transaction processing, reporting and control requirements.

2. The Royal Stationery was a small company producing office stationery. Its annual sales amounting to £800,000. Mr Tootal, the managing director of the company, was concerned about a recent complaint regarding the finished goods inventory.

Mr Howell, administrative assistant of the managing director, was assigned to look into the problem. Mr Howell talked to the production foreman, personnel foreman, inventory clerk and the accountant. Mr Howell was to prepare a proposal for inventory control which would help to maintain adequate inventory, customer's service and forecast sales and inventory level.

(1) Explain, step-by-step, how Mr Howell should cope with the managing director's request.
(2) Prepare a one-page report suggesting the possible controls that should be included in Mr Howell's proposal.

NOTES

1. Economic Order Quantity (EOQ), determines the order-size and the number of orders which is the most economic for the enterprise.
2. Davis, Gordon, *Management Information System*, New York: McGraw-Hill, 1974.
3. See Carson, G. B. (ed.), *Production Handbook*. New York: Ronald Press, 1964.
4. Frey, A. W., and Albaum, S., *Marketing Handbook*. New York: Ronald Press, 1965.
5. Aspley, J. C., and Harkness, J. C., *Sales Managers Handbook*. London, The Dawtwell Corporation, 1966.

6. Aljian, G. W., *Purchasing Handbook*. New York: McGraw-Hill, 1966.
7. Heckert, J. B., and Kerrigen, H. D., *Accounting Systems, Design and Installation*. New York: Ronald Press, 1967.

BIBLIOGRAPHY

Anderson, D. R., Schmidt, L. A., and McCosh, A. M., *Practical Controllership*. Homewood, Ill.: Richard D. Irwin, 1973.

Anthony, Robert N., *Planning and Control System: A Framework for Analysis*. Boston: Graduate School of Business Administration, Harvard University, 1965.

Blumenthal, S. C., *Management Information Systems: A Framework for Planning and Development*. Englewood Cliffs, N.J.: Prentice-Hall, 1969.

Davis, G., *Management Information System*. New York: McGraw-Hill, 1974.

Demming, R. H., *Characteristics of an Effective Control*. Boston: Graduate School of Business Administration, Harvard University, 1968.

Heckert, J. B., and Kerrigan, H. D., *Accounting Systems: Design and Installation*. New York: Ronald Press, 1967.

O'Brien, James, *Management Information System*. New York: Van Nostrand, Reinhold, 1970.

Prince, T. R., *Information System for Management Planning and Control*. Homewood, Ill.: Richard D. Irwin, 1966.

5 Design of Operational Control Information Systems

The process of operational control is highly dependent upon formal MIS. Efficient and effective information processing is essential since controls are typically numerous, data is voluminous, monitoring is constant and response is frequently real-time. Consequently operational control information systems are often computer-based. However, they may lie anywhere along the man–machine systems continuum, and may well incorporate a range of man–machine interfaces. Many MIS address such structured problems that they are full decision-taking systems. Most at least are mechanised in their data-collection and database functions, because operational control MIS are essentially routine, transaction-intensive, file processing systems.

The immediacy of operational control demands reliability, the data-intensity demands efficiency and the scale demands controls and disciplines. Technical professionalism and systems standards are therefore important. Operational control applications are often well structured and thus many of the standard decision-making models and algorithms are relevant, for example stock control formulae or optimising techniques. These characteristics, together with similarities of task and context in many operational control applications have made the systems development life cycle an appropriate structural framework for systems design. Thus the first three sections of this chapter describe the design process in the form of a life cycle, as depicted in Table 5.1. Indeed it is in operational control systems design that the systems development life cycle is generally adopted in its purest form.

Implicit throughout this chapter are the design concepts introduced in Chapter 3, particularly the need for joint design. Where operational control problems are semi-structured, computer-based modelling has proved valuable. This is not described here, but left over until Chapter 11 since modelling is especially relevant to management control systems. There are,

TABLE 5.1. The system development life cycle

Phase	Tasks	Major outputs
DESIGN		

Feasibility study	— problem definition
	— preliminary analysis
	  + design
	— cost–benefit analysis
		— feasibility report for
		  management approv

Systems analysis	— define/confirm
	  objectives
	— analysis of existing
	  system
	— information
	  requirements analysis
		— merges into system
		  design as an iterativ
		  process

Systems design	— design formal system
	  alternatives
	— design modules and
	  interfaces
	— project planning
		— system specification
		
		— project plan

IMPLEMENTATION		

Programming and testing	— programming
	— suite and system
	  testing
	— procedures
	  + documentation
		— project reports
		— complete system
		  documentation
		— tested system

Conversion and implementation	— final testing — training — file + data conversion — implementation	— system acceptance

Operation and review	— project review
	— maintenance and
	  adaptation
	— post-implementation
	  audit
	— later modules
		— systems development
		— project report
		
		— post-implementation
		
		— audit report

however, other design issues in operational control, for example development of integrated systems, standard systems or application packages, and these are discussed in the fourth section of this chapter. Finally a section is devoted to controls, since operational control has proved to be very dependent upon disciplines, procedures and standards.

FEASIBILITY STUDY

The feasibility study is the most critical phase of the systems development life cycle. It is here where 'management' truly can be put into systems design—by careful definition of system objectives and rigorous examination of systems feasibility. The aim is, through investigation of an identified need or opportunity, to present a proposal which management can accept, reject, or accelerate.

The study defines functional requirements rather than system design or architecture. It clarifies system objectives, assesses the probable impact, identifies constraints and indicates likely interfaces. Feasibility is evaluated on three criteria: economic, technical and operational. The study is therefore a joint user–specialist process. The resultant feasibility report is primarily in user terminology and, if approved, becomes a communication device, continuously updated, throughout the development life cycle.

PROBLEM DEFINITION

In order to provide a focus for subsequent system analysis and design, the original, identified need or opportunity is redefined into precise MIS objectives. As the system evolves, objectives and functional requirements may be modified, but an initial statement is required to ensure that direction is not lost and to prevent data processing values submerging information needs. Formulation of objectives is often a difficult, fuzzy and intuitive process, but the aim is to state clearly what the MIS is for. It is sufficient to express objectives in overall terms, such as reduced inventory levels, improved quality control or whatever, as they can be divided into subgoals in the next phase.

System boundaries are defined in terms of system scope, functional impact, man–machine interfaces and system/subsystem interactions. These also may evolve as system design progresses, but if they are not examined at the outset, potential benefits as well as important impacts may be overlooked. This is particularly important in operational control because of its scale and immediacy. A written document then provides a vehicle for discussion, and a checkpoint as the MIS takes shape.

PRELIMINARY ANALYSIS AND DESIGN

The overall system objectives are now translated into functional subgoals and requirements, to the extent necessary for management approval. The systems analysts and users explore the application area, firstly to identify the subgoals the system must support if overall objectives are to be met, and secondly to translate these into broad information requirements. The systems analyst often benefits from an induction period in the application area to understand the business and develop a feel for its culture. This is because preliminary analysis and design is from the users' perspective, in user terms and formulated in user language. The emphasis is on what the system is to achieve and not how.

The problem definition provides the initial direction and sets the ideal goals. Early background investigation seeks an ideal system, perhaps drawing on conventional management science models for guidance. Joint development and agreement of a simple process flowchart may, by comparison with the ideal, indicate a possible design. Further dialogue and functional management review will reorient this model towards a probable and feasible design.

Although this feasible design is presented in user terms, some technical analysis is necessary. Hardware and processing are specified in outline form, and data volumes, frequencies, response times and controls defined. Also the database, or master-files, will be specified in embryonic form, as they are the hub of operational control systems with major implications for users and technical specialists alike. Finally any interfaces or relationships with other MIS are examined to aid systems, database and implementation planning.

COST–BENEFIT ANALYSIS

Cost–benefit analysis is concerned with assessing the system's economic, technical and operational feasibility. It is a global, but nonetheless rigorous, assessment required for the following reasons:

(1) To assess the system's viability on all fronts.
(2) To help determine systems development priorities where resources are scarce.
(3) To provide a standard for later system performance measurement.
(4) To provide standards for system development project control.
(5) To rank alternative system designs (albeit in outline form).
(6) To stimulate MIS awareness and commitment.

Economic assessment aims to test whether the system's financial benefits outweigh the costs, or more precisely whether future returns justify initial investment. Costs are generally easier to derive than benefits. Table 5.2 summarises the relevant costs and reminds us that there are user costs as well as 'technical' costs. Especially in operational control where a new MIS

TABLE 5.2. Cost analysis

	TECHNICAL COSTS	USER COSTS
DEVELOPMENT COSTS	—hardware and software purchase —hardware and software use —systems analysis and programming —professional training	—user design effort —implementation and conversion —training —data collection —displacement costs
OPERATION COSTS	—hardware and software use —data preparation —supplies —maintenance	—support staff —data collection and control —data distribution —maintenance

often replaces an earlier version, it is important to remember that relevant costs are differential costs. Once the relevant costs are identified, estimation is rarely difficult. Purchase and rental costs are easily obtained, development costs can be obtained from project commitments, and most remaining costs can be determined by experience and reasoned prediction.

Benefits are more difficult to determine and can be classified into cost displacement, improved performance and intangibles. Cost displacement savings arise from straightforward automation, replacement or rationalisation. Often manpower savings, they are easily calculated and tend to increase over time as activity levels increase.

Improved economic performance includes such benefits as improvements in stock control, quality control, delivery performance or response to customer enquiries. It is not sufficient to state such benefits in nebulous terms, or even as operational targets or ratios. Financial justification is sought, for example translating reduced stock levels into working capital savings, or improved delivery performance into extra sales revenue.

Intangible benefits do not really exist, being essentially those benefits which are difficult or impossible to measure in advance. Examples are 'improved data control', 'better customer service', or 'byproduct management information'. Experience suggests that at the operational control level it is frequently only disinclination which prevents quantification of most 'intangibles'. For example, *expected values* can be derived. Instead of asking users to give single point estimates of benefits, they are asked to assign probability values to them. The systems analyst may have to help the user, for example querying how certain are the benefits or pointing out the implications of their predictions and seeking revisions or ranges. An alternative approach, is to ask managers how much they would pay for a system, facility or piece of information—especially if asked would they pay less than, or more than, the cost of its provision. Often more effective is to determine the cost of *not* developing the MIS, for example in terms of inefficient use of resources or lower service levels.

Economic appraisal is a joint exercise. The technical specialists can supply many of the costs and can suggest possible benefits. However, their views of benefits can be optimistic, or alternatively may be laced with invalid assumptions or important qualifications. Since it is the users who will achieve the benefits, it is they who should predict them. Furthermore, if their predictions are built into future responsibility budgets, users may then be committed to successful system development and operation. Users directly at the system interface can often identify and quantify MIS benefits, in operational terms, better than their more remote superiors. Senior management can then translate such judgements into financial terms, perhaps providing a check or balance to undue optimism or pessimism. Double checks can be made by seeking different views from users in similar or related functions. This horizontal and vertical cross-sectional analysis may be time-consuming, but such persistence and participation has proved to be a reliable methodology.

Once costs and benefits have been determined, economic assessment becomes a matter of capital investment appraisal to see whether future returns justify the initial investment. Some organisations use the accounting rate of return method, although setting a hurdle rate may be difficult. Calculation of project net present value recognises the time value of money over the system's life, commonly reported as three to five years for operational control applications. This method can also incorporate sensitivity analysis which helps managers assess risk, helps identify the major pay-offs, and highlights key result variables needing management support.

However, such 'sophistication' may be inappropriate. MIS appraisal is more than usually dependent upon the quality of cost–benefit estimates. Moreover, the commitment and capability to achieve the benefits is as important as finesse of quantification. Explicit economic assessment is certainly vital, not least to create MIS awareness and aid MIS learning; the method of calculation, however, is less important. Finally economic appraisal is only one factor. Operational and technical feasibility can be equally, or more, important. Many an apparently viable system from an economic viewpoint has failed because the technology has been too advanced, or because data or human problems have been ignored. Equally technical operational or social opportunities may be overlooked. So the framework of cost–benefit analysis must be widened. Technical feasibility involves questions such as the following:

(1) Is the requisite technology available and proven?
(2) Are the relevant technical skills available to exploit it?
(3) Does the proposed system impose undue technical demands?
(4) Does the proposed system depend on constructing other systems not yet available?
(5) Can the system be combined with other developments, or should interfaces be built in?

Thus all technical exposures are assessed and implications defined—partly to prevent the pursuit of technical goals for their own sake. Equally, opportunities should be examined, since advances in MIS have often derived from technological innovation. Organisations have to learn new skills and new technologies need to be tried and tested. Therefore, if opportunities for innovation exist without undue risk, the project may deserve support. Finally the interrelatedness of operational control systems often brings opportunities for combined development of system modules, or construction of interfaces for later exploitation.

Operational feasibility is primarily concerned with data, procedures and people. Questions to be asked include the following:

(1) Is the base-data available and reliable?
(2) Do supporting procedures and disciplines exist?
(3) Will there be resistance to implementation?
(4) Does the MIS impose undue demands on people?
(5) Will the MIS have management support?
(6) Does the project offer opportunities for reorganisation?
(7) Does the project offer opportunities for work re-design and job improvement?

The first five questions should be assessed rigorously. It may be best to postpone MIS development until a sound operational environment and foundation have been built. Also MIS can harm the social environment, to the detriment of the system as much as of people. The remaining questions remind us that MIS design, especially at the operational control level, provide opportunities for experiments or advances in job enhancement, ergonomics or participation.

How these three feasibility criteria are measured is not as important as the recognition of their validity and their reasoned explication. Once evaluated they become inputs to the project approval decision. Thus a framework, such as the matrix in Table 5.3 can be a catalyst to discussion, negotiation, and resolution. Each criterion is described in terms of viability, risks and opportunities. Economic viability can be entered quantitatively, or like operational and technical viability, be graded as high, medium or low. Some workers have tried to break down the criteria further and to introduce relative weighting. Such efforts probably only confuse, and may hinder management discussion. Furthermore the risk and opportunity columns help ensure key issues and relativities are not overlooked.

TABLE 5.3. Cost–benefit framework

SYSTEM *Personnel records*	VIABILITY	RISK	OPPORTUNITY
ECONOMIC	High	Dependent upon employee growth	Could extend into manpower planning
TECHNICAL	High	First use of on-line terminals	Chance to develop non-financial, non-production system
OPERATIONAL	Medium	Major data exercise required; trade union cautious	Enhance clerical jobs; learn about security and privacy

The prime purpose of this matrix is to encourage a wider cost–benefit perspective. It is also a learning device whereby top management can not only probe the MIS but also understand all its implications, and give relevant support. Finally it may contribute to better allocation of MIS resources. With such a multi-dimensional approach, top management can select a portfolio of projects which spreads risk. For instance, a project of high economic potential but also high technical risk might be sponsored alongside 'safer' projects.

FEASIBILITY REPORT

The feasibility report summarises the findings of the feasibility study. It is a user–analyst production from which senior management makes the following decisions:

(1) Approves or rejects the proposal, or seeks more information.
(2) Assigns priority to the system against competing claims on scarce resources, recognising opportunities for common parallel or integrated development.
(3) Redefines the project team, and project planning and control techniques, the nature of the task and the organisational context.
(4) Approves the project plan.
(5) Decides on the level of management support required.

Thus the feasibility report should in user terms outline the system's objectives, describe the current facilities, describe the proposed system in black-box form, provide a cost–benefit analysis, recommend the project organisation and management system, and detail the project plan. Since it is a document for top management action, the report should also provide a summary of the study's conclusions and recommendations.

SYSTEMS ANALYSIS AND DESIGN

The systems analysis phase adds precision to black-box design, by investigating in depth the information needs of the operational control application. Systems analysis should not be rushed in order to enter the design phase and formulate the system architecture. Design is comparatively easy: it is the analysis which is demanding.

Traditionally the systems analysis phase begins with analysis of the existing system in order to understand and refine functional requirements. Critics sometimes argue that this biases the design towards existing data flows rather than towards real information needs. They insist that information requirements analysis, studying and modelling the decision system, is the correct approach. However, in operational control applications, both approaches are usually necessary, since to achieve efficient task execution current procedures must be analysed, whilst to ensure effectiveness decision and information analysis is required. Thus the two approaches tend to merge together through iteration.

Once a viable system has been *defined* by systems analysis, it is converted into a man–machine system in the design phase. This is primarily a technical task where the precise architecture of the system's input, processing and output is specified. The end result is a system specification.

ANALYSIS OF EXISTING SYSTEM

The existing system is examined to assess how well it meets the objectives set by the feasibility study and to seek improvements. It is a joint user–analyst exercise, the results of which should be approved by functional management since any operational control MIS is likely to have considerable impact on the functions for which they are responsible.

A descriptive model of the current operational control process is constructed by interview, observation and data collection, usually producing a system flowchart. This describes the input, processing and output of the operational control system and will also record data statistics. Flowcharting is generally essential to comprehension of any complex process. Data and information processing performance is then assessed in terms of timeliness, accuracy, utility, efficiency, necessity, complexity, reliability and responsibility—all relative to the decisions being made and their internal environment. It often helps to compare performance between functions, against established models or with systems in use elsewhere.

The end-result of this analysis is not only an efficiency audit, but also an inventory of ideas to feed into the subsequent information requirements analysis.

INFORMATION REQUIREMENTS ANALYSIS

Methodologies for information requirements analysis were described in some depth in Chapter 3. Two of those frameworks, the decision focus and the concept of the model, are especially relevant. Firstly, operational efficiency and effectiveness can be improved through better decision-making, exploiting automation, new decision models, or new techniques, and/or using better information. Secondly, model development is fundamental to understanding how these can be achieved.

Therefore a *normative model* of how the operational functions should be accomplished is initially constructed. Any sources of ideas are exploited, for example users, analysts, senior management, consultants, journals or other organisations. This is a creative process using any available wisdom or experience. This ideal model is then reduced to a *feasible model* by discussion with all relevant parties, and by comparison against the *descriptive model* developed from analysis of the existing system. Gaps are closed, differences examined, practical considerations recognised and resolved and alternatives investigated.

The eventual viable model is finally tested against original objectives, its sensitivity explored and its costs and benefits (plus those of derivatives) analysed. The acid test of the model is to assess its likely effect on the quality of operational performance. Then the model's solution, variables, criterion and sensitivity—as described in Chapter 3—prescribe the information requirements. The shape of the MIS is defined by using the model to specify where the system should lie on the man–machine continuum, to delineate the interfaces and to determine critical data processing requirements, such as real-time computing or timesharing. A user specification is then written and agreed and becomes the input to the system design phase.

TECHNIQUES

Inadequate information requirements analysis often stems from inadequate models, in particular from poor conceptualisation, in attention to alternatives, rigid boundary-setting and lack of sensitivity analysis. One technique developed to try and overcome some of these problems is *industrial dynamics*. Initiated by Forrester,[1] this technique has become well-known and probably has proved most effective at the operational control level. Essentially it is the use of computer-based simulation to develop a model from which a viable MIS is designed. Its advocate claim that it explicitly incorporates elements of empirically proven system theory and thus is more than simulation alone. Since simulation modelling is described in Chapter 9, it is an overview of industrial dynamics which is provided here.

Industrial dynamics is the study of the information feedback characteristics of organisational activity designed to show how organisational structure, amplification in policies, and time delays in decisions and actions interact to influence the success of the enterprise. The organisation is seen as a system of flows and levels controlled by an interrelated set of decisions. The flows include funds, orders and goods, whilst levels could be investment, deposits or employment. The systems analyst prepares an industrial dynamics model by drawing a flowchart of flows and levels that constitute the system, and of the information flows and decisions upon which they depend. Equations describing these relationships are written and then manipulated using a simulation language called DYNAMO. The simulation model thereby helps explore interactions and interdependencies between systems, so that boundaries are not too narrowly delineated and so that causes rather than symptoms are addressed. It also aids examination of alternatives by testing their system consequences—especially in terms of information parameters such as quality, delay, frequency and redundancy. The classical operational control example is the study of relationships between production and distribution, in which the impact of sales rates on production levels is studied by examining the intervening information delays and amplifications.

Simulation modelling in general is useful in understanding complex business systems and thus in helping to prescribe information requirements. However it is approached—and industrial dynamics is similar to most methods—it is a practicable and cheap form of experimental design suited to many operational control problems. Users can 'play' with such models, learning games can be devised, and still more 'artistic' techniques used[2] to explore and understand often implicit, misunderstood or previously unknown relationships.

Other techniques used in systems analysis include flowcharting processes, decision tables and 'systems algebra'. Flow charting and other data-gathering techniques are well described elsewhere.[3] Decision tables can help both systems analysis and systems design since they force consideration of all possible condition–response combinations, provide a useful visual model and provide a shorthand specification for subsequent programming. Basically they are matrix representations of relationships between decision conditions and decision actions. An example is shown in Table 5.4. Systems algebra is derived from linear graphy theory and matrix arithmetic and has been developed primarily by Langefors.[4] In essence, sets of data elements required for decision or computation processes are formulated, from which the algebra derives preferred data organisations, procedures and outputs. The technique perhaps is oriented more towards systems design, but may help is exploration of alternatives during analysis.

In the structured and semi-structured area of operational control, there

TABLE 5.4. Decision table format

Credit control	Rule 1	Rule 2	Rule 3	Decision table header
Value is	£50	£25–£50	£25	Condition
Approve			x	
Seek authorisation		x		Actions
Reject	x			

is opportunity for use of operations research techniques and models. Many applications call for optimising techniques such as linear programming in production-mix problems, or forecasting techniques, such as exponential smoothing in inventory control. Standard formulae and algorithms, like economic order quantities or credit rules, have application in production and financial systems, whilst simulators have been built into many operations planning systems like steel furnace programming, job shop scheduling or maintenance planning. Thus normative or near-normative models exist[5] which not only provide tools for analysis, but can become core routines in the eventual MIS themselves. It is for this reason that the concept of a *model-base* has meaning. MIS can draw on a foundation of readily available management science models, during development and operation, analogous to new application programs exploiting a database. However, there is a danger of fitting problems to the model—or even of models searching for an application! It is therefore essential that information requirements analysis precedes the use of models, and that standard models are adapted to fit the circumstances, especially as many computer-based models available from software suppliers contain assumptions which are not universally sound.

SYSTEMS DESIGN

The viable system defined by systems analysis is now converted into a technical specification from which computer programs are written and manual procedures devised. This systems specification prescribes in detail the input, processing and output functions of the MIS. The design goal is to produce a system which is efficient, reliable, easy to maintain and adapt, is capable of growth and is compatible with other systems.

Operational control systems, whether manual or computerised, are file-processing systems. Their input comprises operational transactions and their outputs are primarily reports, action documents and enquiry facilities. Typically they satisfy most tests of computability, so that relevant design skills are those of computer science. A major design question which therefore arises is selection of computer processing mode. The computability frameworks of Chapter 3, matching characteristics of information requirements to computing attributes, are therefore relevant.

Many operational control MIS, being transaction-based and file-processing intensive, are batch-processing systems. Where data volumes are high, data processing efficiency is important and periodic reporting is sufficient, batch processing is, and will continue to be, most appropriate. Furthermore, on-line enquiry and data-entry facilities can be provided using the last batch-updated master files or awaiting the next update run.

However, operational control activities may often be real-time in that the time-span of control is almost immediate, or rapid response is essential. The following conditions indicate the need for real-time computing:

(1) On demand service; e.g. reservation systems.
(2) Short time-span of control; e.g. foreign exchange dealings.
(3) Short activity lifecycle; e.g. distribution of perishables.
(4) Interrogative style; e.g. stock issuing.
(5) Data validation critical; e.g. shopfloor data collection.
(6) Continuous process; e.g. steel rolling mill control.

The nature of real-time processing imposes stringent demands on design. First the system should be reliable. Being essentially transaction-driven, the system must cope with all conditions and contingencies. Then in the event of failure, recovery procedures must be built in, so that logging of all inputs, processing and output plus the ability to reconstruct data and files are essential. Secondly efficiency is crucial, for if the system responds slowly it ceases to contribute. Thus careful capacity planning is required, as is efficient programming. These twin demands of reliability (imposing processing overheads) and of efficiency (to ensure responsiveness), require sophisticated software which is often purchased from computer manufacturers or software houses.

Timesharing has less application in operational control than elsewhere since it is best suited to interactive decision-making typical of less structured problems. However, if users' own data are relevant, managerial judgement required, and man–machine interaction beneficial then timesharing is appropriate. Production planning modelling is an example.

Hardware decisions may be necessary in systems design. Input/output devices often are selected to meet particular needs, especially where remote terminals are required. Increasingly as mini- and micro-computers develop, a choice exists between local and global processing. If local processing seems beneficial, no longer need data processing be centralised at the mainframe computer. For example, data validation may be more rigorous or responsive on a local basis, and output be more timely or flexible. Likewise operational control decisions may be specialised or local and therefore better devolved. Perhaps information processing is better managed and controlled when decentralised. Certainly data communication costs can be reduced by distributed processing. Thus the systems designers now can choose to incorporate mini- and micro-computing in the MIS architecture.

Conversely operational control often has to be global. Production planning may cover several plants, distribution may involve several depots, and orders may be processed from many collection points. Equally optimisation may be a global concept coordinating many factories, machines or activities. Thus much operational control information processing will be a mix of global and local information systems and of centralised and decentralised data processing.

Galbraith[6] has classified information systems according to uncertainty and coordination. Task uncertainty tends to demand real-time processing; task coordination demands global processing. This typology is reproduced in Table 5.5 and suggests how small computing (mini- and micro-computers) will be used alongside mainframe computing in operational control. Independent small computers may provide local periodic systems for application's whose uncertainty and interdependence is low. Global periodic systems demand central processing with unintelligent terminals for input/output, or limited intelligence for data validation. Local real-time applications can be satisfied by intelligent terminals or dedicated small computers, Global real-time applications demand mainframe computers with either intelligent or unintelligent terminals, perhaps accompanied by small computers for essentially local tasks.

TABLE 5.5. Information system typology

	PERIODIC (low uncertainty)	CONTINUOUS (high uncertainty)
LOCAL (low task coordination)	Local periodic MIS; e.g. weekly order entry and stock control in warehouses	Local real-time MIS; e.g. interactive scheduling system for job-shop
GLOBAL (high task coordination)	Global periodic MIS; e.g. batch-processed factory production scheduling	e.g. Global real-time MIS; networked airline; airline reservation system

If hardware has to be acquired for the MIS, the following criteria are relevant to selection: purchase cost, running cost, reliability, performance, ergonomics, software support, compatibility, manufacturer support, manufacturer experience, enhancement potential, standards, rate of technological advance. Benchmark tests, trial runs and discussion with users already using the hardware can be useful in making these judgements.

File design is another key task of system design. Indeed it is critical because data definition and organisation affect system reliability and flexibility. Chapter 6 is therefore devoted to this topic. File design is very much a function of output requirements, and to a lesser degree of inputs, so that the definitions derived by systems analysis generally provide the initial specification. However, file design should not be rushed; many systems have proved to be inefficient through inattention to data organisation, inflexible through lack of vision, and unreliable through poor data definition.

Input/output design also should not be undervalued. Input design affects system reliability, efficiency and potential. Reliability is a function of data disciplines and controls which are examined later. Efficiency is dependent upon input media, for which the options have been described in Chapter 3. Potential is often a matter of creative and astute data definition and coding, allowing for expansion, new codes, later applications and skilful manipulation.

Output design influences system effectiveness. The different media were described in Chapter 3, but it is output format and design which can be crucial. Much formal information lies unused, and many potential applications remain untapped, because output design is myopic. Designers must appreciate that users prefer and need clear tabulations and displays, English language rather than codes and hieroglyphics, sub-totals as well as totals—in short, normal standards of visual presentation. Output design may seem trival to the specialist, it is vital to the user. For this reason in particular, users should be involved in output design. Indeed, where they have designed their own interfaces, not only is system effectiveness improved, but working methods are more successfully integrated into the MIS, and job design opportunities may be seized. Finally moves towards simpler, user-controlled, output programming are to be encouraged, for they can be a catalyst to participative design, facilitate tailor-made outputs, enhance flexibility and may lead to add-on facilities.

The end-product of the system analysis and design phases is the system specification, from which computer programs are written, manual procedures are developed, and implementation is planned. It is primarily a technical document, with some managerial sections to aid project control and review. Table 5.6 summarises its contents. Since in operational control systems, typically more than 50 per cent of project time and effort is still to follow, the system specification is a vital report and discipline.

IMPLEMENTATION

Implementation comprises the three 'production' phases which translate the system specification into a 'live' system, namely programming and testing, conversion and implementation, and operation and review.

TABLE 5.6. The system specification

Section	Content
System objectives	Original objectives, modifications and how to be met
System outline	Summary of system's functions, shape and with flowcharts
System interfaces	Delineation of man–machine interfaces and relationships with other MIS
System inputs	Specification of input formats, media and contents
System outputs	Specification of output formats, media and contents
System database	Specification of files, their form, organisation and content
System processing	Outline of computer programs
System procedures	Outline of manual procedures
System statistics	Data volumes and growth: run frequency and timings
System hardware and software	Hardware and software requirements
System testing	Testing plan, specification and responsibilities
Conversion and implementation	Data foundations required, file conversion plans, training needs, implementation plan
Final cost–benefit analysis	Updated cost–benefit analysis
System controls	System, file and data controls; internal controls and auditing requirements
Management supports	Vital training, personnel, organisation, data needs
Project plan	Detailed effort and time budget with review points and responsibilities
Performance criteria	Criteria by which systems operation should be judged
Management summary	A managerial summary

PROGRAMMING AND TESTING

The system specification is now broken down into program specifications by the systems analysts and into procedure specifications by analyst–user teamwork. Program specifications, from which programmers write programs, should define input, processing and output in conformity with the agreed system specification. Any amendments must be agreed by the users. Program design and development are matters of data processing technology and are subject to local standards and thus outside the scope of this book. However, certain principles of sound programming exist, including:

(1) Simplicity—contrary to many programmers' preferences, simplicity pays in the long run.
(2) Maintainability—system changes and errors are inevitable and therefore ease of maintenance is essential.

(3) Testability—programs, and overall system design, should be structured to aid testing.

(4) Standards—programming standards are essential for compatibility, maintainability and control.

(5) Expansion—programs should cater for future growth in activity.

(6) Stability—any functions which require frequent amendment, such as cost codes or tax codes should be stored outside the program.

(7) Documentation—future reference to programs depends on sound documentation, namely a specification, flowchart, up-to-date listing and test results.

In parallel with programming, manual procedures are designed. Many of the same principles apply whilst techniques of organisation and methods are relevant. Of particular importance are forms design, which can help or hinder data integrity, and internal controls (see later), which provide a fabric of security around both manual and machine systems. Formal disciplines, procedures and operating instructions are also written at this stage.

Training is begun here in readiness for effective system testing and subsequent conversion and implementation. Firstly, users at the operational level—data preparation teams, clerks, shop-floor personnel and the like—are given detailed training on the functions and procedures they are to perform in the total man–machine system. Secondly, together with those who will be influenced by the MIS, they will probably benefit form appreciation or familiarity training, explaining the aims of the system, its structure and likely course of implementation.

Testing is a crucial, and often ill-planned, phase in systems development. As deadlines approach, pressures can easily lead to short-cuts, only to bring disaster and disillusion in system conversion or early operation. There are five levels of testing:

(1) Program specification testing—desk checking by the systems analyst to verify design logic and create test data for subsequent program testing.

(2) Initial program testing—desk checking by the programmer against the specification to verify program logic, followed by syntax testing until a clean compilation is achieved, followed by rudimentary logic testing with simple data.

(3) Final program testing—testing by the systems analyst and programmer using the former's test data to check data validation, program logic, output formats and exception handling.

(4) Suite and system testing—by the systems analyst and users to ensure programs fit together and that user requirements are met.

(5) Parallel run testing—by the systems analyst and all users (see next section).

In program testing, there is often reluctance to use testing aids such as execution monitors, file comparison utilities and core dumps. Whilst such automation may reduce human diligence and be costly, the goal of system reliability is paramount and any aid is invaluable. In real-time system testing, where programs are transaction-driven and other tasks are executed in parallel, such devices are essential.

System testing first uses analysts' data to test all conditions, the data being preserved for testing of subsequent system changes. Then user data is employed, not only as a check and balance but also to test user data collection and understanding. It is as important to test system abnormality, especially recovery procedures, as much as normality. The users' role is to test the system 'to destruction' until there is complete confidence in its reliability. Only then can the next phase begin.

CONVERSION AND IMPLEMENTATION

The aim of this phase is to gain user acceptance of the MIS with minimal disruption. Caution, anticipation and attention to detail are thus imperative.

The tasks of data preparation and file creation are often underestimated. New data may have to be gathered and old data re-analysed and re-formatted, the repercussions of which can be formidable. Consider, for example, the problems of introducing new cost codes, clock numbers or part numbers into an organisation. File creation can be equally difficult, especially if an existing file is being converted, since discrepancies can have a severe impact. There is no substitute, however costly and time-consuming, in these tasks for assiduous monitoring, diligent testing and contingency plans, such as parallel file maintenance.

Implementation from a technical viewpoint is largely a matter of risk reduction, in which four approaches are helpful. Firstly implementation can be phased, for example installing the file creation and update subsystem first, so that other subsystems or programs do not access the master files until they are proven. Phasing by organisational boundaries, by geography or by operational functions are alternative mechanisms. Secondly, parallel running against the old system can reduce risk, by providing a standby system aiding comparison and allowing a calmer implementation. Where this is not feasible, for example in completely new operational control functions, where organisation has changed or where timing is critical, then 'straight turnover' is required. Here phasing is even more desirable, together with the third approach of contingency planning. All participants, the designers, users and managers, should be clear as to what is to be done if the system fails. Such decisions taken in haste often compound earlier problems. Finally MIS implementation should not proceed if any doubts exist. The system is not implemented until all its functions—occasional facilities included—have been successfully executed, not only in their initial state, but in their ongoing condition as well.

However, despite such discipline, a system may fail on implementation for behavioural reasons, notably through resistance to change. Implementation is about managing change. Mumford[7] suggests four variables are relevant:

(1) The degree of stability in the user system or the extent to which operations and systems meet users' internal and external needs. If needs are fulfilled there is stability and thus no internal dynamic for change. Consequently positive attitudes to change will have to be fostered. Conversely instability, where user needs are unfulfilled, may create a receptive climate since change presents opportunity. Unfortunately the instability may alternatively create hostility if the change is perceived as posing still more threats.

(2) User perception of change, or how the departments believe the new system will affect them. These perceptions can be quite unrealistic.

(3) Strategy for change, or how the innovating group introduces change, especially what 'levers' it selects.

(4) Role perception of the innovating group, or how the innovating group perceives its own role and how this affects their models of man and their strategies for change.

The first variable is a given, whilst the remainder can be manipulated using approaches such as the following:

(1) Communication to users of system aims, plans and impacts well before implementation.

(2) Participation of users throughout MIS design.

(3) Ensuring the MIS is operationally feasible during the feasibility study, and identifying social threats and opportunities.

(4) Involving personnel management, especially where sensitive issues such as redundancy are involved.

(5) Designing the system from a social as well as technical viewpoint.

(6) Training of user departments before implementation.

(7) Exposing systems analysts to the behavioural sciences, to help in

management of change and in developing socio-technical views of organisations.

(8) Creating a climate and history of successful implementations.

Clearly, therefore, implementation should not be seen as just one phase of the system development life cycle. Successful implementation depends on sound and sensitive design, especially joint design. Implementation also carries on beyond initial system acceptance. The 'shakedown' period may last as long as a year and should be stringently monitored. Any problem should be investigated—user queries, unusual conditions, peculiar or repeated error listings, suspicious operations logs or any untoward event—for the smallest oddity may be a symptom of a more serious disorder. Also records of such events should be maintained, not only to stimulate and document corrections, but because history may help solve later problems.

OPERATION AND REVIEW

System maintenance also should not be under-resourced. Both change and errors are inevitable and thus development time and effort should be budgeted to handle the three types of maintenance required:

(1) Error correction which has to be provided as required.

(2) Adaptation which has to be provided, but perhaps in phases or alongside error correction where opportune.

(3) Further facilities which can become a separate project, perhaps including some adaptive measures.

The importance of this classifications is to better organise technical maintenance in a more job-satisfying manner, to avoid disrupting development priorities, to ensure maintenance (other than error correction) is subject to cost–benefit analysis, and to minimise frequency of change for users.

Finally, system review, discussed in detail in Chapter 11, is part of the implementation process. Two types of review are beneficial:

(1) Process review—an audit of the MIS project shortly after system installation to learn from any mistakes or successes, thereby strengthening methodology for subsequent projects. Since MIS projects are temporary systems, each generally differing in task and context from another, such learning is essential.

(2) Product review—a post-installation audit of the MIS to investigate whether objectives have been met. The cost–benefit framework described earlier in the chapter, can be applied, and becomes simpler ex-post. Any

variances from expectations are analysed, recommending corrective action and communicating any 'lessons'. System controls should be examined, whilst any informal design adaptations may repay study since they may indicate potential enhancements.

DESIGN QUESTIONS

As operational control MIS have evolved over time, certain design questions recur. These include the concept of integrated systems, the policy of standard systems development, the use of application packages and the contribution of 'control theories'.

INTEGRATED SYSTEMS

Some years ago, the concept of the integrated MIS or the 'total information system' was rife in the literature and also in popular parlance. This concept has now been discredited. There is no reason why all MIS should be integrated and there are many reasons why they should not, for example differences in decision types and information characteristics, the rigidity of tight coupling and the operational problems of too much interdependence. In addition the total system concept was always nebulous, and in particular was dangerous in suggesting that one formal MIS could satisfy all information needs. Finally the fully integrated system or total MIS has never been implemented.

However, especially at the operational control level, there are data interdependencies between applications or functional systems. Furthermore, critical information sometimes transcends application boundaries, so that, say, production data may need to be combined with sales data. Thus some measure of integration can be valid. Reasons include:

(1) Use of a common database or master file, e.g. production control and product costing systems.
(2) Dependence on common data collection, e.g. personnel and payroll systems.
(3) Existence of functional interfaces, e.g. sales order processing and production planning.
(4) Information requirement linkages, e.g. customer enquiries and production control.

A more practical framework for integration was devised by Blumenthal. He called for modularity in MIS design and developed a general taxonomy of modules in operational control which could be constructed to an integrated blueprint, but relevant to particular needs and with different degrees of coupling. His arguments for modularity include the following:

(1) Modules provide units for MIS planning.
(2) Modules reduce complexity in MIS design.
(3) Modules aid project management and control.
(4) Modules simplify error correction and maintenance.
(5) Modules eliminate processing and development redundancy.
(6) Modules allow stable system components to be isolated from those which are more volatile.

The last argument is particularly valid in operational control, for there do seem to be subsystems which form a relatively stable core, for example file creation and maintenance or basic transaction processing, and others which are more volatile. Sources of change are changes in the business environment, changes in the internal organisation and changes in information processing technology. Since MIS are expensive to develop and maintain, and yet adaptation is essential for organisational survival, any design framework which simplifies the problem of change is valuable. Thus Blumenthal saw modules as ways of grouping together information processing functions according to classes of change, so that modifications could be made without disturbing the remainder of the system. Future modules could also be defined, which would be subsystems likely to be developed, for which an interface could be provided. The modular concept can be employed to build a *dynamic system* whose components gradually change and to which new subsystems are added, but whose identity persists over time.

STANDARD SYSTEMS

Another issue is the design of standard systems in operational control, that is the development of one MIS for the same application across multiple sites, divisions or companies within one corporate organisation. The arguments for standard systems can be considerable, including: (a) minimisation of redundancy in MIS development; (b) minimisation of redundancy, conflict and ambiguity in basic operational processes; (c) enforcement of common standards, procedures, techniques and terminology in basic operational functions; (d) economies in data processing; (e) the need to use common facilities or integrated functions, for example group-wide distribution or order processing; (f) encouragement to integrate information and cross boundaries; (g) facilitation of job and management mobility.

In practice, however there are some dangers. Factories, divisions and companies are not always alike and the needs and styles of one application may differ among them, because their external and internal environments are different. Most organisations recognise this fact, but standard systems policies readily become exaggerated in the hands of the technical specialists. Standardisation, uniformity and rationalisation become their goals, rather than satisfaction of real information requirements and user needs. Clearly standard systems policies can be appropriate; it is their interpretation which is difficult. It is therefore important to recognise where standardisation fits and where it does not. Some MIS can be more standard than others. There are three types of non-conformity: Type 1—differences which can be resolved by a common denominator solution; Type 2—differences which can only be met by special optional subsystems or modules; Type 3—differences which need special stand-alone solutions. It is the responsibility of the project team, and ultimately of its conflict resolution mechanisms such as a top management steering committee, to ensure such differences are explicated and realistically resolved.

APPLICATION PACKAGES

Since many operational control applications have universal features, and because MIS development can be expensive, computer manufactures and software houses supply packaged systems for users to customise to their own requirements. Examples include payroll, inventory control, production scheduling, network analysis and nominal ledger systems. Application packages have many advantages. For example, they can save MIS development time and cost, they can be a source of ideas and a learning device, they can solve short-term needs and generally they are technically proven. Conversely there are potential problems and the following questions are usually relevant:

(1) Does the package satisfy information requirements?
(2) Does the package conform to local standards?
(3) What level of maintenance and service is provided?
(4) Is training provided, especially on implementation?
(5) What documentation is provided?
(6) Can the package be modified by user coding?
(7) How efficient is the package in view of its universality?
(8) Is the package compatible with other systems?

(9) What personalisation is necessary?
(10) What performance constraints are there?
(11) What assumptions, especially in models and algorithms, are built in?
(12) Who else uses the package?
(13) What hidden costs are there?

Despite this portentous list of questions, application packages are useful for experimentation, for urgent needs and in the more universal applications. Organisations with common requirements have also combined to sponsor package development in order to reduce development costs.

CONTROL THEORIES

Many disciplines, subject-areas and fields of practice are concerned with control and have developed concepts which can be transplanted elsewhere. Industrial dynamics, described earlier, has borrowed terminology from control engineering whilst organisation theory has adopted concepts from general systems theory. Indeed management, essentially a pragmatic endeavour, *should* be eclectic and employ any control theories or ideas which seem useful and relevant. A further source is cybernetics, which Beer calls the science of control. It is probably premature to describe this set of ideas as a science, but three cybernetic 'laws' have application in MIS design, especially at the operational control level.

Firstly, in order for a system of inputs, process and output to achieve regulation or control, it requires a *feedback* loop. Basically feedback is the comparison of actual outputs of the system against a desired output or standard, such that any difference initiates corrective action. In operational control systems most feedback processes are negative, whereby any fluctuations around the norm or standard are reduced, dampened or brought into line. For example, many process control applications are deemed to be in control if inputs of material and energy are being converted into production outputs by use of a standard amount of material and energy, and if the outputs fall within certain limits or tolerances. Figure 5.1 depicts a negative feedback control system, where it is clear that control is dependent upon (a) being able to measure the level or some other characteristic of output; (b) having a sensor or measurement process to do this; (c) having a control unit or device which compares the measured outputs with a standard for the level or characteristic; (d) having an activating unit which initiates a corrective input signal.

Such feedback systems are closed, in that they do not interact with their environment, and mechanistic, in that the standard does not change.

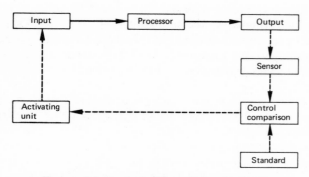

FIGURE 5.1. System with negative feedback

Where the environment is unpredictable or turbulent, an open feedback system is achieved by allowing for manual intervention, that is designing a man–machine system. Adaptive feedback can also be achieved in this way, or by allowing the activating unit to alter the standard when regular or extreme variances are detected.

Finally, positive feedback can be designed where the need is to reinforce the direction in which the system is moving. For example, variances from standard may be favourable and should be encouraged. Here open feedback systems often are required, and tend to be more relevant in management control applications.

A second 'law' of cybernetics is the law of *requisite variety*, which states that control depends on the existence of enough control actions to match all possible control conditions. This clearly requires considerable information processing. In simple and structured applications, closed feedback systems may suffice. In more complex and uncertain applications, open feedback systems, especially man–machine solutions, are more appropriate. MIS strategies for requisite variety include: (a) construction of decision rules and algorithms to cover all conditions; (b) design of exception routines for manual intervention; (c) design of slack resources into systems to handle or absorb the unexpected; (d) filtering of decision conditions to reduce variety, for example factoring down the application into specialised subsystems; (e) filtering of channels, for example reducing noisy or rogue input data or limiting outputs using management by exception techniques; (f) emphasis on testing the model's sensitivity during MIS design.

The theorem or law of *recursion* is the third cybernetic principle of relevance, namely that each viable system nests within a higher level system. This reminds us that exceptions or conflicts within an operational control system can generally be resolved by a higher level system. Thus operational control MIS should be designed with interfaces to management control systems. Likewise if local MIS are designed in complete isolation from global MIS, discontinuities conflicts and sub-optimisation are likely.

SYSTEM CONTROLS

MIS serve to plan and control the business. System reliability is therefore of paramount importance, especially in the immediacy of operational control. System reliability can be defined as the ability to withstand deliberate or unwitting attack. To ensure reliability controls are required both in MIS development and operation. Three sets of controls are relevant: (1) data controls; (2) processing controls; (3) standards. The body of knowledge on systems controls is substantial and detail can be sought in specialised texts listed in this chapter's bibliography. The fundamentals are discussed below.

DATA CONTROLS

Data controls are concerned with quality control of MIS input and output. Input control seeks to ensure that data is clean on entry to the system. Output control seeks to ensure output is to specification and reaches its intended users.

Input controls include the following:

(1) Edit tests—program tests to verify the syntax, range reasonableness and content of captured data.
(2) Validity tests—program tests against the database to ensure input conforms to master-file specification and processing logic.
(3) Batch controls—clerical/computer input totalling to ensure data has not been lost or subverted.
(4) Check-digit verification—arithmetic tests on key data elements to ensure codes or keys are valid.
(5) Prenumbering and precoding—use of preprinted input documents or of previously output documents which contain prevalidated data elements and keys.
(6) Verification—second-pass inspection by punched card operators, or key to disk terminals, to enhance quality control.

(7) Format disciplines—provided by form design, data capture devices or screen displays to aid user accuracy.

(8) Administrative disciplines—procedures, organisational constraints and user manuals to enforce data standards.

(9) Internal controls—separation of duties, authorisation procedures and audit trails to ensure data security.

Some of these devices also can be applied to output controls, especially administrative disciplines and internal controls. Further output procedures include:

(1) Output distribution—data control offices to monitor and record receipt of outputs by authorised recipients.

(2) Audit trails—print-outs of data-flows from source to output and from transaction to summary.

(3) Security checks—access restrictions, user codes, terminal locks, confidentiality barriers and password protection to ensure legitimate usage.

The importance of input/output control cannot be over-emphasised. Many operational control systems have failed because the data foundation has been inadequate.

PROCESSING CONTROLS

These controls are concerned with ensuring not only that system, especially computer, processing is reliable, but also that, if the system fails, full recovery is possible. Principal controls include the following:

(1) Processing controls—checkpoint, restart and recovery procedures, operations logs and monitors, hardware and software checks, and standby facilities.

(2) Security controls—physical safeguards, access controls, terminal controls, privacy and confidentiality protection, and hardware and software controls.

(3) Database controls—security protection, back-up files, reconciliation checks, error wash-out facilities, and database administration procedures.

Total system reliability will never be achieved, whilst application of both processing and data controls can be expensive and difficult to enforce. So the value of controls must be set against their cost and practicality. In making these judgements, it can be beneficial to assess the probability of system breakdown and its likely impact.

STANDARDS

In order to encourage, direct, train and assist designers, operators and users in development of reliable systems, standards and disciplines are essential. Indeed the routine and immediate nature of operational control demands working standards. These fall into three groups.

(1) Development standards—design standards, specification and report standards, documentation standards, testing standards, and user authorisation procedures.
(2) Operational standards—operating instructions, data preparation instructions, data control procedures, security standards, and recovery procedures.
(3) User standards—procedures manuals, data control standards and internal control procedures.

Finally it is advisable to consult both internal and external auditors early in the design process, to seek specialist advice on both audit requirements and system controls.

CHAPTER 5—PROJECTS

1. You are the financial controller of the Universal Credit Company, a savings, insurance and credit business which is growing rapidly. The company uses agents to collect premiums from housewives. The premiums are credited to the housewife's account and then this credit can be spent by the housewife on insurance or on goods and services from major chain stores and supermarkets using the Universal credit card. You believe the data supporting this operation is unsound, examples being: (a) inadequate record-keeping by housewives; (b) possible fraud by both customers and agents; (c) poor management decision-making using inaccurate information; (d) an increase in credit defaults. You believe a computer-based system would increase data accuracy with consequent economic gain to the company, but you cannot be sure. How would you evaluate the feasibility of computerisation?

2. A computer salesman is trying to sell you an application package for inventory control. How would you decide whether or not to buy the package system, and how would you implement it?

3. A computer-based purchasing and goods receiving system is to be installed. A similar exercise failed some years ago because of user resistance. How would you ensure success this time?

4. A computer-based payables and receivables accounting system for a golf club is being designed. Members can pay for lessons, buy goods, pay green fees, and purchase food and drink on credit. Visitors from other approved clubs in the vicinity are to have the same privileges. Other visitors must pay in cash. All profits belong to the club, except those made on goods and lessons which belong to the professional. Food and drink stocks are bought and controlled by the steward.

Design the controls, disciplines and procedures which you believe are required for this system.

5. Blumenthal devised a framework of operational control modules for a typical manufacturing company. Devise such a framework for one of the following activities:

(1) A retail bank.
(2) A chain store.
(3) A hospital group.
(4) A local government authority.
(5) Any other organisation with which you are familiar.

NOTES

1. Forrester, J. W., *Industrial Dynamics*. Cambridge, Mass.: MIT Press, 1961.
2. For example, see Tocher, K. D., *The Art of Simulation*. Princeton, N.J.: Van Nostrand, 1963.
3. For example, see Hartman, W., Matthews, H., and Proeme, A., *Management Information Systems Handbook*. New York: McGraw-Hill, 1969.
4. Langefors, B., *Theoretical Analysis of Information Systems*, Vols. 1 and 2. Lund, Sweden: Studentlitteratur, 1970.
5. For example, see Ackoff, R. L., and Sasieni, M. M., *Fundamentals of Operations Research*, London: Wiley, 1968; or Hillier, F. S., and Lieberman, G. J., *Introduction to Operations Research*, San Francisco: Holden-Day, 1967.
6. Galbraith, J., *Designing Complex Organisations*. New York: Addison-Wesley, 1973.
7. Mumford, E., 'Implementing Systems', *The Computer Bulletin*, January 1969.

BIBLIOGRAPHY

Beer, S., *Decision and Control*. London: Wiley, 1966.

Blumenthal, S. C., *Management Information Systems: A Framework for Planning and Development.* Englewood Cliffs, N.J.: Prentice-Hall, 1969.

Boutell, W. S., *Computer-oriented Business Systems.* Englewood Cliffs, N.J.: Prentice-Hall, 1973.

Brandon, D. H., *Management Standards For Data Processing.* Philadelphia, Pa.: Brandon, 1969.

Hartman, W., Matthes, H., and Proeme, A., *Management Information Systems Handbook.* New York: McGraw-Hill, 1968.

Mair, W. C., Wood, D. R., and Davis, K. W., *Computer Control and Audit.* Altamonte Springs, Florida: Institute of Internal Auditors, 1976.

Martin, J., *Design of Real-Time Computer Systems,* Englewood Cliffs, N.J.: Prentice-Hall, 1967.

6 Database Management

'Database' is now common terminology. However, it means different things to different people. The lay-user is prone to ascribe the term to all data in the organisation, whilst the information systems specialist sees database in a technical light. This chapter develops such a technical view. Yet the lay view has conceptual value, conceiving the database as the structural foundation of management information systems, emphasising data as the bedrock and raw material of information, recognising the importance of data availability and reliability.

To the specialist a database is a group of logically related files, independently updated, but available to different applications. Database thus refers to computer files in computer-based management information systems. In this chapter the definition is somewhat relaxed to include all computer file design and management, although the true database concept is also studied at some length. Our exposition thus blends the lay and technical views of database into a concept of decision-oriented files upon which management information systems depend, a concept which in practice requires considerable investment and commitment.

In Chapter 3 the so-called database approach to MIS development was rejected in favour of a decision-oriented design framework. That rejection still holds, for, as conceived at the time it was practised, the approach produced data-oriented systems built round static and rigid computer files and integrated data-flows in pursuit of data processing efficiency. The database concept to be developed in this chapter is one of information-oriented file management and design, in which data is managed as a resource.

File design and management is a complex and specialised task. Data storage and retrieval vitally affect the economics of an MIS, and can influence the capability, flexibility and service expected by the user. Data storage and retrieval can make or break the effectiveness of MIS operation. Despite falling costs of file storage and continuing development of file management software, database design is increasingly difficult. There are many different ways of structuring data with their own advantages and disadvantages, and the needs are so diverse that there is no one optimum method. Indeed database design becomes a delicate course of compromise involving trade-offs between conflicting attributes, such as storage versus speed of access, or flexibility of use against system efficiency. The design process requires managerial judgement as much as technical expertise. Indeed management involvement may avoid expensive solutions where simple approaches may suffice; in other words, managers should know what is possible in database design, and need to understand how alternative designs affect both processing efficiency and effectiveness of use.

Management responsibility goes further. Database design also raises crucial managerial and organisational issues, and demands of management involvement and support in both the design process and subsequent operation. It is for this reason that the chapter is entitled database *management*; management issues as much as technical principles will be discussed. First, however, it is necessary to define terminology more clearly.

DATA DEFINITIONS

Much of the inadequacy of the database design and much of the confusion in database management arises from loose terminology. Data must be organised in order for processing to be feasible and efficient, and organisation is based on a hierarchy of data levels. Data can be defined in three realms:[1]

(1) The real world in which there are entities and in which the entities have certain properties.
(2) The ideas and information which exist in the minds of men and programmers, namely the attributes of entities which we represent symbolically in English or programming language and to which we assign values.
(3) The data in which strings of characters or bits are used to encode entities and their attributes.

The third realm, namely the characters which represent the value of an attribute in the second realm, are stored in a *data-item*. A data-item is the piece of raw data the system stores, retrieves and processes. For example, if the object, or entity, of data processing is an employee, a data-item may describe the attribute 'name' or 'age' or 'grade'. A data-item is sometimes also called a field, data-element or elementary item, but the CODASYL Data-Base Task Group, who are concerned with standards in database design, prefer the term data-item.

A collection of such data-items is called a *record*. A record represents an

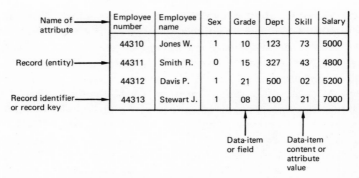

FIGURE 6.1. Data definitions: a personnel file

entity such as an employee (see Figure 6.1) and comprises data-items such as employee number, name, sex, grade, department, skill and salary. A collection of related records is called a file. Each record or entity in the file is identified by a record identifier or record key, in this example the employee number. Records are normally all the same length (fixed length) but can differ (variable length) if storage is at a premium. Some records may comprise a master portion, or header, followed by detail or trailer records. For example, a debtors ledger or accounts receivable system might have an invoice file with header records containing more permanent data-items such as customer name, code and credit rating, followed by trailer records containing data-items describing each live invoice (Figure 6.2).

Customer number	Customer name	Customer code	Credit rating

Invoice number	Invoice data	Invoice amount	Account code

FIGURE 6.2. Header and trailer records: sales invoice file

A *file* is a collection of related records, sometimes called a data-set, such as the personnel or sales invoice files already described. Files are generally held on magnetic tape, disk or drum, and as described in Chapter 3 their creation, updating and extraction form the nub of most computer systems. In processing terms three main types may be identified.

(1) Master files contain relatively permanent records and exist throughout the life of the system(s). They are generally updated in tune with the pulse rate of the function they serve—say, daily for the sale invoice file, weekly for the personnel file and, in the case of a production work-in-progress file, perhaps as each transaction occurs, that is real-time.
(2) Intermediate files are temporary in that they exist only between programs, jobs or runs of the system. They may store transactions ready to update the master file, or be extract or report files derived from master files in order to prepare a report, or carry data from one subsystem to another.
(3) A working file is even more ephemeral and contains records for subsequent sorting, or similar manipulation, after which it is normally erased.

Descriptions of data and of the relationships between data are either *logical* or physical. Physical data descriptions refer to the manner in which data are recorded physically on the hardware medium. Logical descriptions refer to the way the user or programmer sees the data, such as the representation of the personnel file in Figure 6.1. This distinction becomes important, as will be explained later, within the true database concept. A *database* is a group of logically related files or data-sets, or more precisely[2] 'a collection of the occurrences of multiple record types, containing the relationships between records, data aggregates and data-items'. There can be several databases in one system, and more than likely across several systems. Where several such separate and disjoint databases exist, the term database system is used.

Alternatively *data-bank* sometimes refers to a collection of databases, and the terms are often used interchangeably. Data-bank tends to conjure up in the mind, and sometimes in practice, a vast store of data serving known and assumed needs, with the consequent emotional reaction. For this reason and because it is imprecisely defined, the term will not be adopted in this chapter.

Having clarified database terminology, file design can now be pursued in more detail. Then the database concept is discussed and database management and design principles examined.

FILE DESIGN

DESIGN OBJECTIVES

Files are designed to satisfy one or more key variables. Different file organisation methods are available to meet different needs and their structure can be complex and their selection demanding. It is because aspects of effectiveness, may have to be traded off against efficiency, that both users and specialists need to understand file design. A file organisation is sought which facilitates processing, and retrieval of records but without excessive file creation or maintenance problems and at reasonable cost. The solution is derived by weighing up the information requirements to be met and the computing resources available. Typical trade-offs consider storage utilisation versus time utilisation, response time against complexity of data structure, and information potential against data processing efficiency. The more carefully the alternatives are considered, the more likely will be a good file design. And many poor MIS have resulted from poor file design.

The major variables which influence file design include:

(1) Storage cost—the need for economic storage reduces degrees of freedom on other variables.
(2) Dominant processing mode—file organisations which suit periodic batch processing may hinder on-line updating or irregular retrieval.
(3) Processing cost—the more flexible file organisations are likely to be costly in terms of processing time.
(4) Response time—the need for quick response time reduces file organisation flexibility.
(5) Information predictability—complex file structures to meet flexible and changing information requirements affect storage and processing efficiency.
(6) Reliability—complex structures may require more maintenance, and pose recovery problems.

In addition several subsidiary issues may affect file design, for example expandability, data volatility, security and privacy, file size or data-item size. That database design becomes an exercise of compromise must be apparent. Four principal file organisation methods are available: (1) sequential; (2) random; (3) indexed sequential; (4) list and its derivatives.

SEQUENTIAL FILES

The best-known file organisation is the sequential method, wherein records are stored in position relative to other records according to a specified sequence. To order the records in a sequence, one common attribute of the records is chosen. When a data-item within the record is selected for sequencing, that data-item is called a key. In Figure 6.1 the personnel file is sequential, with employee number being the key. The invoice file in Figure 6.2 could also be sequential, in customer number order within which invoice records can trail behind each customer master record. An alternative sequential form is to store records in order of arrival, without keys, and is commonly called a serial file. In all sequential files the logical order of records in the file coincides with the physical order on the recording medium. Sequential organisation can thus make efficient use of the least expensive storage medium, namely magnetic tape.

One particular record on the file is located merely by starting at the beginning of the file and comparing the key of each record with the key sought until a match occurs. Efficient processing therefore demands that input records are first sorted to file sequence. Sequential files accordingly suit batch processing where transactions can be accumulated, sorted and then processed efficiently against the master file. Conversely if a file is referred to infrequently, as in random enquiries or on-line updates, sequential organisation is inappropriate: the whole file has to be searched until the relevant record is found.

RANDOM FILES

Random file organisation allows any record to be retrieved by a single access. Other records do not have to be examined as in sequential files. Random files are usually based on direct access storage (disk or drum), which favour rapid access to individual records. Such devices become inefficient if used for serial or sequential files, however. In random data organisation, records are stored and retrieved on the basis of a predictable relationship between the key of the record and the direct address of the location where the record is stored. The address is used when the record is stored and again when retrieved. Three principal methods of random organisation exist.

(1) In direct addressing the address and the key are identical, whereby the number of physical addresses allocated to the file roughly equates with the number of records likely to be stored. Thus record key 1023 is stored in

address 1023. Obviously such correspondence tends to be difficult to achieve; record keys for example may not be sequential because they occur in groups and ranges, say where department number forms part of an employee number.

(2) An alternative therefore is to derive the physical address from the record key via an index or dictionary in which each record has a unique address. Such searching may be time consuming, and file creation carries index construction overheads, but that may be the price of random retrieval facilities.

(3) The third approach is by calculation. Such 'randomising' or 'hashing' techniques transform the record key into a storage address. There are several methods most of which involve (a) converting the keys, if non-numeric to numeric form, (b) applying an algorithm to the numeric forms to convert them into a spread of numbers of the order of magnitude of the address numbers required, and distributed as evenly as possible over the range of addresses, or (c) applying a constant to compress the resultant numbers to the precise range of addresses. A major difficulty is that some addresses may never be generated, whilst on the other hand duplicates may result. Then overflow handling techniques have to be built in to accommodate duplicate addresses.

Therefore random file organisation aids random record retrieval, but can be inefficient for volume processing through the overheads of processing time for address calculation and of storage for handling overflow and indexes. It may also necessitate complex programming.

INDEXED SEQUENTIAL FILES

Indexed sequential files represent a compromise between sequential organisation and random organisation. Often called ISAM files, records are stored sequentially by record key so that sequential processing may be performed, but indexes are also maintained to allow direct retrieval based on a key value.

To access one particular record directly, the index is searched and the key located which then provides the record address for access (see Figure 6.3). Equally the file may be updated with transactions in random sequence, in batch or real-time mode, using the same procedure. If sequential updating is required then the index need not be used. Since ISAM files are held on direct access devices, updating is in place, that is each record to be updated is read, amended and written back in the same location. Records for

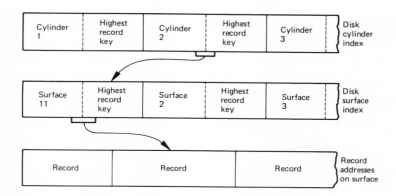

FIGURE 6.3. Indexed sequential organisation

insertion are placed in overflow areas to which a pointer refers, whilst records which are deleted create gaps. Consequently ISAM files are regularly reorganised.

Indexed sequential organisation, especially the indices, may be modified to exploit the characteristics of the particular direct access storage device being used. Unlike most random files, ISAM files are created, organised and accessed using manufacturers' software. They are thus simple to use and are widely employed since they combine the best features of sequential and direct access organisation. The price paid for such advantages includes extra storage space required for indexes and overflow areas, and extra processing time for searching and for the regular reorganisations.

LIST ORGANISATIONS

Where the MIS is oriented towards information retrieval, especially where relationships between records and between data-items in a file need to be exploited, sequential, indexed-sequential and random organisations are limited. The alternative is the list or chain organisation and its derivatives. Three main types may be distinguished: (1) simple list structures; (2) inverted list structures; (3) ring structures.

The basic concept of a list is that relations among records are established by pointers so that the logical organisation is divorced from the physical organisation. In a sequential organisation the next logical record is also the next physical record, whereas in a list organisation, by including a *pointer* to the next logical record, the logical and physical arrangements can be completely different. The pointer can be anything which allows the accessing mechanism to locate a record. In direct access devices it is the direct address of the record.

In a *simple list* structure the first record points to the second logical record and so on in logical sequence through the chain. The last record in the logical sequence contains an end of chain symbol. Figure 6.4 demonstrates a simple list structure of a sales analysis file where all customers' records can be read by chasing the chain established by pointers. Thus record insertion and deletion involves revision of pointers as well as processing of the record itself, and, to aid this revision, backward as well as forward pointers are usually used. This allows the list to be searched in either direction.

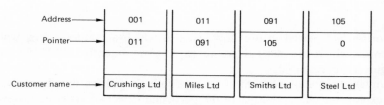

FIGURE 6.4. Simple list structure

Since any data-item in a record may be treated as a key, many lists can pass through a single record, as in Figure 6.5. Here each record is a member of two lists, an area list and a customer list, both logically related in alphabetic order. By allowing a record to be on multiple lists, duplication is avoided and updating it in one list automatically updates it in the other.

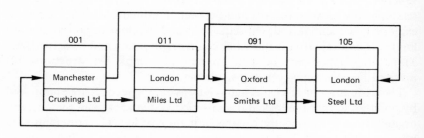

FIGURE 6.5. Multiple list structure

Multiple lists can become extremely long so that search time is excessive. One remedy is to create sublists with their own origin, thus reducing search time but increasing file maintenance. Using the same example, a *partially inverted* list can be constructed with an area index. Each entry in the index has a starting point to the list of records having the same value as the key in the index, in this case area. In Figure 6.6 the area data-item is now removed from each record in the list at the expense of adding a pointer, which will occupy less space.

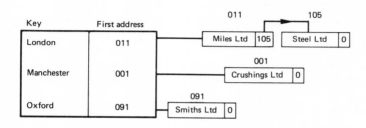

FIGURE 6.6. Partially inverted list

Inversion may be taken further so that each list comprises one record, and each key appears in the index. The index then points directly to the record sought and no pointers are needed. Such an *inverted list* is shown in Figure 6.7 where, if all customers in London of credit rating 99 are sought, then by scanning the index it is established that only record at address 105 is relevant, and it is then retrieved. Thus a request is processed via the index rather than through the file. Every data-item becomes available as a key

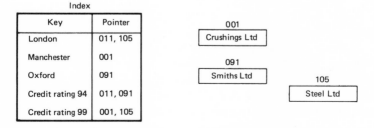

FIGURE 6.7. Inverted list

and thus inverted lists are ideal for information retrieval applications, especially where requirements are unpredictable.

The trade-off for such flexibility is the size of the index, or dictionary, which can become larger than the data itself, and its updating complexity. Consequently an inverted list is sometimes combined with either a sequential or random organisation where only the most popular keys are inverted. The index then is reduced, but all records can still be accessed.

A *ring structure* is a list whose pointers go both forward and backward. The first record is an index record which specifies the nature of the ring, and the last record points back to the first. This allows retrieval to proceed from any record, either backward, or forward, or back to the starter record. Ring structures are very powerful as they provide a means of retrieving and processing all records in any one ring, while branching off at any or each of the records to retrieve and process other records which are logically related. Thus one ring can nest with another so that hierarchical organisations are possible.

Following the earlier example, if a record is retrieved in the inverted list by the key London, no other data from the record than the customer name can be obtained since, for example, credit rating is stored in the index and the record has no pointer back to the index containing this other data. With hierarchical rings, the London area ring could be searched and when one particular record is found, we might wish to know which other customers have the same credit rating. The credit rating ring is then chased and we retrieve all records in this ring until we return to the originating record (see Figure 6.8). Thus this hierarchical ring structure permits us to start with any record in the file and move up or down the hierarchy. It is ideally suited therefore to hierarchical entities such as bills of material.

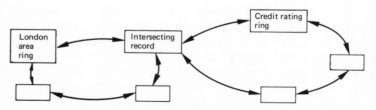

FIGURE 6.8. Hierarchical ring structure

Hybrid variations on list structures to meet special applications include *multi-list files*, where by a sequential index contains key values by which records are indexed. Each key value has a pointer to the list of records having that key value, which are stored in fixed size blocks called cells or pages. They are addressed by page number and record number. This organisation reduces access time where groups of records have to be retrieved, at the expense of index size. Such cellular approaches can be applied to different list structures to reduce the indexes, especially if lists are limited to one page. In general, lists suffer the disadvantage of the storage overhead required to contain pointers. In return a powerful retrieval facility is provided and data-item redundancy is avoided.

Where several hierarchical levels are to be accommodated in logical and physical organisations, *tree structures* may be used. The tree comprises a hierarchy of elements or nodes. The uppermost level of the hierarchy has only one node, called the root. Every node, except the root, has one node related to it at a higher level called the parent. No element can have more than one parent, but each can have one or more elements, or children, at the next level down. In the sales analysis example a tree structure could look like that shown in Figure 6.9.

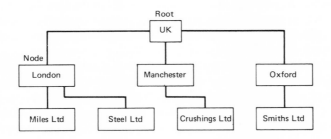

FIGURE 6.9. Tree structure

If a child in a data relationship has more than one parent, the tree structure is clearly inappropriate. Instead it is described as a *network or plex structure*. Here any item can be linked to any other, but still the relationships can be represented in parent and child form as in Figure 6.10. Both tree and plex structures can become complicated in representation and in reality. Their significance is that in database management systems, described later, they are used in logical and/or physical definition of the database.

SYNTHESIS

File design and management involve more than file organisation. There are

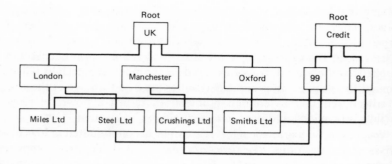

FIGURE 6.10. Plex structure

also techniques of data-item representation, of record addressing and scanning, and of file control which the specialist should know. This is not the place for such issues; this section has aimed to demonstrate what can and cannot be done by file organisation. In particular for the user to participate in systems development, appreciation of file organisation should help ensure the technician does not win arguments invalidly, and that information potential is built into MIS designs.

Other file management issues are important to specialists and managers alike. File security, file recovery, data administration, file maintenance and data standards are examples. Since these are especially crucial to the database concept, they are examined in the next two sections. As a conclusion on file design, Table 6.1 attempts to summarise the attributes of the file organisation methods discussed above. The summary is not rigorous; it cannot be, for as emphasised already, the ultimate choice is a compromise.

DATABASE

DATABASE CONCEPT

A database was defined early in the chapter as a group of logically related files, independently updated, but available to different applications, or 'a collection of the occurrences of multiple record types, containing the relationships between records, data-aggregates and data-items'. Such clinical definitions reveal nothing of the real benefits or mechanics of the database *concept*. To appreciate this, the evolution of computer systems

TABLE 6.1. File organisation overview

Design variable	Sequential	Indexed-sequential	Random	List
Volume processing efficiency	high	medium	low	low
Random access efficiency	low	high	individual records high groups of records low	medium
Information retrieval flexibility	low	low	low	high
Storage requirement	low	medium	medium	indexes, pointers or records can be high
File device cost	low	medium	medium	medium/high
Dominant applications	operational control	operational control management control	operational control	operational control, management control and strategic planning
Programming complexity	low	low	medium	medium if buying software; otherwise high

must be examined. To understand the concept is to understand perhaps the most promising technological contribution to date towards the goal of designing decision-oriented MIS serving user needs.

In the early days of data processing, the horizon of most systems planning and design rarely extended beyond the application currently being developed. If another application could be based on the same data, a new file was invariably created and designed, because file management software could not accommodate the simplest of file restructuring. Soon the goal of integrated systems and eventually 'the total system' became fashionable. Some systems design teams however realised that integration was only a worthy goal where applications were naturally related and were based on common master files, thereby ensuring base data was identical at all times.

In practice this proved difficult wherever independent applications operated on such common files. Discrepancies arose through error, through updating at different times and through failure to add or delete items. Functions which used the common files were not only naturally prone to maintain data for their own uses only, but would exacerbate this tendency by adopting, duplicating or subverting data as the situation went out of control. An example might be that of an engineering company where the production control, engineers, production management, contracts and accounts functions all used common product specification data, but adapted it for their own needs.

Standards, disciplines and technical constraints could sometimes re-establish some control. However, another problem was typical. As new applications were planned and requested, the common files could not cope. The data organisation could not be restructured without rewriting many programs with consequent upheaval. Leaving spare fields in record formats was not enough, and in response to user's new needs, the systems designers replied, 'It isn't possible', or 'We must rewrite the system', to the frustration of all concerned. Furthermore, files were designed for certain sets of applications and modes of processing. Even seemingly simple, yet vital, information requests could not be met, because the necessary data relationships were not built in. A function's data became locked into its own applications and the organisation's own data became a frozen asset— a highly constrained resource increasingly unresponsive to ad hoc information requirements[3] and managers' real information needs.

Nevertheless the concept of a set of common files independently updated but available to different authorised applications, was attractive. It became practicable when developments in both equipment and know-how led to the creation of database management systems. This software, supplied by manufacturers and specialist software houses, created file organisations at the data-item level so that a data-item need only be held once for all applications. Complex data structures—based on trees and networks— provided data-item linkages of considerable flexibility. The programmer was protected from the complexity involved and could construct logical data organisations without regard to the physical organisation implied.This facility is called *data independence*.

The database concept is thus both powerful and simple. Its mechanics, however, are technically complex, but fortunately are hidden from the user and systems analyst. The database thus avoids data redundancy, thereby providing benefits of data and information consistency, together with storage and processing efficiency. (Trade-offs against access time or file recovery may force occasional redundancy, but as an exception.) The database also brings data independence so that data can be restructured, for example introducing new record types or data-items, without program or systems rewrites. In other words the database can grow and change. Data becomes an independent resource, separate from program and programmer. The database is concerned with, and built on, relationships between data-items and records, as well as how and where data is stored. Flexibility is thus provided so that new and unanticipated information needs can be met. In addition, database management systems often provide query languages so that the organisation's data can be searched and interrogated.

Yet the concept can be oversold or misunderstood. It is not the creation of a data-bank with all its emotional overtones. Indeed not all of an organisation's data is kept in the database; there is no black box containing the entire records of a business. There will be several databases reflecting the logical groupings of files. Nor is database the panacea for MIS, constructing a reservoir of all possible data 'in which a diversity of users can go fishing'.[4] Users cannot escape from consciously specifying their principal information requirements, any more than the technicians can escape from careful and rigorous analysis in database design. Indeed computer specialists have fostered much of the misunderstanding of database by applying the term to existing files without building in the non-redundancy, data independence and interconnectedness implicit in the concept. They have often failed also to persuade management of the significance of database and convince them, as will be discussed later, that the concept extends beyond the technical implications.

The technical criteria for judging a database are thus minimal redundancy, data independence and interconnectedness, with perhaps a search and query capability. In reality a complex database is constructed stage by stage and is a considerable investment and commitment for the whole organisation. It will actually comprise several databases, each providing anticipated information for several logically related management information systems, where data can be modified and retrieved with reasonable flexibility. Each database may serve several functions and departments and thus cross organisational boundaries. The reality also is that most organisations do not yet possess the corporate-wide database often imagined; the data is still not collected and will develop over time. The database concept, however, pursues an objective of a reliable and accessible corporate data resource; database software makes it feasible.

Database may now be redefined, borrowing from Martin,[5]

A data-base may be defined as a collection of interrelated data stored together, without harmful or unnecessary redundancy, to serve one or more applications in an optimal fashion; the data are stored so that they are independent of programs which use the data; a common and controlled approach is used in adding new data and in modifying and retrieving existing data within the data-base. One system is said to contain a collection of data-bases if they are entirely separate in structure.

Figure 6.11 represents the database concept and is developed further in later sections.

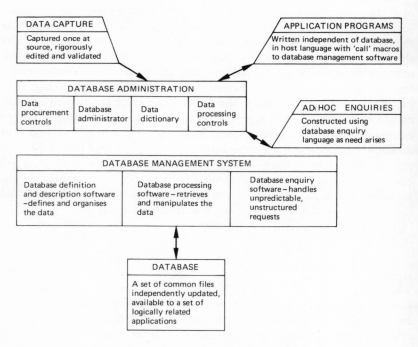

FIGURE 6.11. Database concept

USER IMPLICATIONS

How then does the database concept manifest itself to the user? What are the advantages and what problems arise? Since database implies a high initial investment and brings repercussions throughout the organisation, the user implications warrant further examination. Firstly, the advantages include:

1. *Increased flexibility.* Both the ability to react to changing demands which data independence brings, and the interconnectedness of data-items implicit in database structures, mean that unanticipated needs can be met without the upheaval or cost experienced hitherto. It is the data interrelationships which really bring flexibility, for new or unforeseen information needs now tend to be dependent on programming rather than on data. Furthermore if a database enquiry language is used, then programming becomes less of a constraint. A batch system may readily adapt to on-line enquiries, an operational control system answer management control 'what-if' questions, and an established MIS react to personal information needs and personal views of how data fits together.

2. *Increased data integrity.* Data reliability, accuracy and consistency are encouraged by having one common 'file', with the more permanent data updated by one subsystem only. Emphasis is put on data security and control, with corporate-wide standards and disciplines enforced. These standards are oriented towards the organisation's needs as a whole rather than any one function's parochial quirks or wants. The organisation behaviour stimulated by functional files is modified into a sense of corporate responsibility for the data resource.

3. *Increased efficiency.* The data redundancy and duplication removed by database yields data processing efficiency. File storage is saved since duplicate files no longer exist. In turn, processing economies arise as less data is accessed and fewer files updated. Furthermore sundry manual files, which are developed officially and unofficially in response to unreliable files, are no longer required. Of course some data redundancy may have to be incorporated as a trade-off for faster access times or improved security. Thus the realistic aim is controlled redundancy.

4. *Cost savings.* Initial database development costs tend to be high. Both data collection and database design are expensive. Thereafter considerable savings can result, in particular from the efficiencies described above. Furthermore data-independence, non-redundancy and data-interconnectedness simplify data and system maintenance. Since some surveys suggest up to 50 per cent of EDP budgets are devoted to maintenance, potential savings are high. An established database should also result in lower incremental development and running costs for new applications founded on that data. Finally, the decision to implement the

database concept should be evaluated on a cost–benefit basis; there are considerable commitments and hidden costs, described later, and it is as well to appreciate them from the outset.

5. *Change and evolution.* Data-independence allows data to be added or restructured both quickly and simply. New or evolving needs can more often be accommodated without redesigning and rewriting systems and programs. Data becomes an independent resource, so that the new record types, new data-items and new structures, which evolving decision-making needs require, cause less upheaval.

6. *Integration.* Organising common data into a logically related database, with connections between data-items rather than files, encourages integration of information. This is not pursuit of systems integration for its own sake, but facilitation of integrative perspectives where they are justified. For example, management control decisions often require information which is cross-functional and inter-level in character. The rate of change and uncertainty in the management environment today is apparently calling for new perspectives and linkages in the information which decisions require. The database concept may be one way of responding to such demands.

7. *Easier programming.* The programmers and system designers have less responsibility for file design. Having one structure—in a logically related area—the database itself, they are freed from the constraints of separate and different file structures. The database management system looks after the physical organisation, so that programmers and systems analysts can concentrate on the logical view. Equally problems of security and recovery are increasingly handled by software, whilst the managerial issues of data organisation are delegated to a database administrator (discussed later).

8. *Data a resource.* Information was earlier described as a resource, and data its raw material. The database concept encourages us to manage data as a resource. It asks us to eliminate waste, to focus on how the data will be used, to commit ourselves to disciplined data custody. Those organisations which have successfully implemented the database concept apparently see and manage data on a different scale than previously.

These eight advantages bring an equal number of problems, and maybe more. However, they are not equal and opposite disadvantages, leaving no ultimate benefit from the database concept. They are issues which management has to face, recognise and overcome to implement database successfully.

1. *Data not information.* The reservoir notion of database storing all the organisation's data can lead to development of management *misinformation* systems. The data-orientation rather than the decision-making focus can emerge, whereby too much of the wrong data is stored. The system design principles of Chapter 3 apply equally to database development, whereby a decision framework is required with full user participation, both of managers who will use the information and of those who will supply and maintain the data. A set of databases should be developed, each serving a limited and logically related set of applications. More than likely, development should be gradual.

2. *Omniscience.* Users can readily be persuaded that the database will serve all their needs. The idea of a reservoir of all foreseeable data requirements in which a diversity of users can go fishing has already been debunked. Again the flexibility that database brings has to be constructed from sound design principles.

3. *Overcredence.* Just as there are computer-cynics, there are some who are computer-gullible. For them, database seems to add a further hallowed air to computer output. Whilst increased data reliability is expected, nevertheless users should question the assumptions built into the database. For example, data collected and structured for operational control may perhaps not contain all the nuances relevant to management control. Consequently managers may need assumption-testing, exploratory facilities as much as rapid response enquiry routines.

4. *Centralisation.* Common data can imply centralised database storage which may conflict with the organisational ethos. Certainly some degree of centralised data is normal, but like many issues of centralisation versus decentralisation, there are many variants available. Firstly, database access can be distributed to local points of usage at satellite computers or remote terminals or through hybrid mini-computers. Secondly, the database itself can be distributed so that all data required by all segments of the enterprise is centrally held, with subordinate databases created to meet local demands. It is, however, not a simple question. Data communication costs are high, subsidiary databases may be prone to data inconsistencies and of course managerial sovereignty can be an emotional issue. It is thus likely that the optimal degree of centralisation will vary with each organisation.

5. *Organisational problems.* It is implicit in the database concept that data-relationships do not respect functional or departmental boundaries. Thus management policies and administrative controls are required to protect the data resources from factional abuse and sub-optimisation.

6. *Security and privacy*. The pooling of data, the diversity of use, the flexibility of structure, and on-line access inherent in database, bring problems of security and privacy. Database management systems increasingly incorporate security and privacy controls whilst administrative procedures are required to supplement them.

7. *Recovery*. Despite increased attention to reliability and security, computer systems will fail—through hardware, software, program, user or operator error. Under database, the ability to recover quickly and without loss is more crucial than ever, since that data is held only once and usage is so widespread. Consequently database management systems are constantly improving in terms of recovery capability.

8. *Responsibility*. The database concept broadens the responsibility for the data resource. It is not only the DP function's or controller's responsibility, it is also a corporate asset with widespread commitments. Just as this must be made clear to all concerned, clear lines of responsibility are also required.

TECHNICAL IMPLICATIONS

The benefits claimed for the database concept are impressive. However, they demand that database organisation fulfils several technical objectives. Based on Martin's[6] interpretation of various industry guidelines and standards, these technical implications are summarised in Table 6.2.

A key attribute of a database is clearly data independence. The database can be seen at different levels of organisation. Firstly the application programmer views the database in terms of the file structure or organisation which the program demands. Secondly, however, the physical storage organisation is different and is concerned with indexes, pointers, chains and other means of physically locating records. Data independence is the ability to change either the data or the application program without changing the other, thereby making the database so adaptable. The database software maps the application programmer's file structure into the physical data structure that is actually stored, and vice versa. This process is called 'binding'. The third level of organisation is the overall view of the database, to which all the logically related application programs have access. This global logical structure becomes complex as the database evolves, and it becomes important that it should be able to change without affecting the many application programs using it. The overall logical structure is constantly evolving and thus two levels of data-independence are in fact required, namely: (1) logical data independence, which means

TABLE 6.2. Technical implications of database

Objective	Implication for Database organisation
Relationship versatility	Should represent many data-item relationships and easily accommodate change
Performance	Should provide acceptable response times and appropriate throughput levels
Minimum cost	Should minimise storage cost and simplify programming
Minimal redundancy	Should store data-items once only if possible but maintain relationships
Search capability	Should handle unanticipated requests and provide rapid response
Data integrity	Should recover completely and quickly from failures and should incorporate controls on data values
Privacy and security	Should protect from failure or 'attack' and should incorporate authorisation procedures
Compatibility	Should be able to interface with existing programs, procedures and data so as to prevent major redesign
Change	Should accommodate change and evolution by data independence
Tunability	Should be able to react to new trade-offs as demands change, through monitoring and physical data independence
Data migration	Should be able to adjust storage to suit frequency of usage of data
Simplicity	The user and programmer should have a simple and neat view of the database and the interface with it

that the overall logical structure of the data may be changed without changing the application programs; (2) physical data independence, which means that the physical layout and organisation of the data may be changed without changing either the overall logical structure of the data or the application programs.

When changes are made to the data at any of these three levels of organisation, all programs using that data must be converted. This binding can be achieved through re-compiling or re-linking the program—static independence—or automatically at the time the program reads the data—dynamic independence. Static independence is usually adopted for reasons of cost and performance of throughput and response. Dynamic independence is a luxury and only justified where data change is very frequent, for example where terminal users are experimenting on data formats, or where applications are under constant conversion.

So that the user can view the data in whatever form is most convenient for him, and so that the database software can translate this view into the physical organisation, a formal means of describing data organisation is required. This description is achieved through the *schema* and *subschema*. The schema is the logical description of the database. It is a chart and dictionary of the types of data that are used, giving the names of the entities and attributes, and specifying the relationships between them. It is a framework into which the values of the data-items can be fitted—see Figure 6.12. The subschema is the application programmer's description of the data he uses. Thus many different subschemas can be derived from the schema, which the application programmer need not necessarily see. It is the database management software which assembles the data described in the subschema from the data described in the schema, and gives it to the application program.

The different data organisation levels, their relationships to the schema and subschema, the roles of data independence and the function of database management software are represented in Figure 6.13.

DATABASE MANAGEMENT SOFTWARE

It is evident that the database management software or system (DBMS) is a powerful and crucial element in implementing the database concept. In practice the database organisation is so complex and technical, that the software is usually bought from specialist suppliers. Unlike conventional file management software, DBMS manage the whole database rather than individual files. Consequently they work at the data-item level, since one application's logical file may be quite different from another, yet the data is of course common.

The creation and evolution of the database is thus handled by the DBMS. It creates and updates files, it selects, retrieves, manipulates and returns data, and it may generate reports. The DBMS interfaces with the host language of application programs, COBOL, PL/1, FORTRAN or whatever. In short it is the vehicle which converts the application programmer's view of data into the overall logical view which in turn is mapped into the physical representation. It achieves this for the application program by using the schema and subschema. The process by which the DBMS interacts with, and serves, an application program requiring a record from the database is summarised in Figure 6.14.

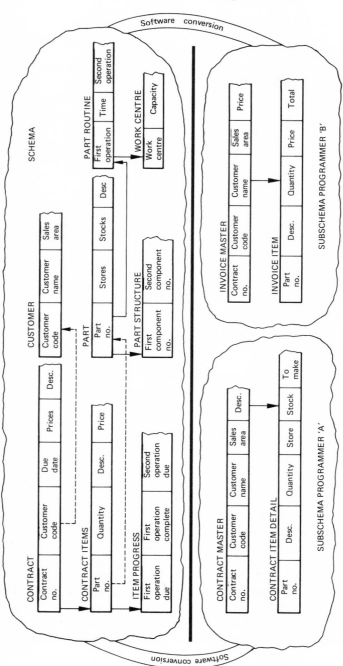

FIGURE 6.12. Schema and subschema of a production database.
N.B. Solid lines represent relationships, the dashed lines are cross reference.

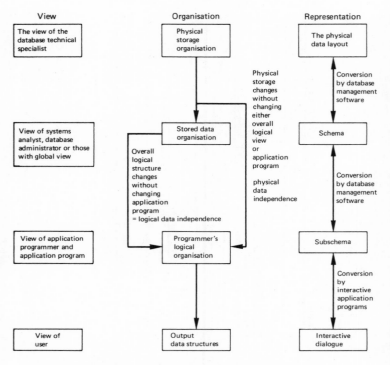

FIGURE 6.13. The different views of database organisation

From Figure 6.14 it is apparent that the DBMS has several components, which may be seen as languages. Firstly there is the host language of the application program which interacts with the DBMS through a data manipulation language (DML). The DML comprises a set of macros which instruct the DBMS to operate on the database, for example reading or writing records, and which also interpret status messages from the DBMS. These macros are thus incorporated in, and need to be compatible with, the host language. Secondly the database is described and defined by a data description language (DDL). The subschema is generally described through the data division or declare statements of the host language in which the application program is written. This function might, however, be handled by the DBMS itself. The schema is described by a schema description language used by the systems analyst or database administrator, or whomever has responsibility for the global logical view. The

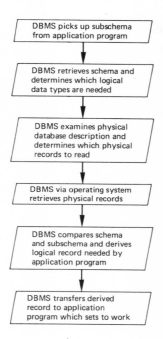

DBMS picks up subschema
from application program

DBMS retrieves schema and
determines which logical
data types are needed

DBMS examines physical
database description and
determines which physical
records to read

DBMS via operating system
retrieves physical records

DBMS compares schema
and subschema and derives
logical record needed by
application program

DBMS transfers derived
record to application
program which sets to work

FIGURE 6.14. How database management system interacts with application
program

schema description language describes the data and defines its relationships
and characteristics. Finally the physical data description language assigns
the data to its physical media and devices, and handles the physical
organisation. Typically the DBMS data description language, for example
IBM DL/1, comprises both the schema data description language and the
physical data description language. It is desirable that all three DDLs
should be independent so that changes at one level do not affect the others.
Also since the schema is a long-term investment, the schema data
description language should be compatible with all major languages and
DMLs.

Most computer manufacturers supply database management software.
IBM's IMS is probably the best known. However, the technology is
developing rapidly and specialist software houses have produced respected
systems such as CINCOM's TOTAL which is widely used. Experience is
already emphasising the value of inbuilt support facilities in database

software, especially security and privacy features, database activity monitors, data validation procedures, space management routines and recovery ability. In addition, data transmission facilities are becoming available in so-called database data communication systems (DBDC), a necessity where remote or distributed processing on a centralised database is required. General-purpose enquiry languages are also being added, or made compatible, so that enquiry and dialogue can exploit the potential of the database concept—without being dependent upon scarce programmer skills.

Users of DBMS have apparently found that the simpler the software, the easier the implementation of the database concept.[7] Also support facilities, especially those which enhance reliability, are proving to be significant criteria in selection of database software.

DATABASE DESIGN

DESIGN PROCESS

Whilst the database concept will probably prove to be a significant stage in the evolution of MIS theory, it is certainly not true that a MIS consists of a database, or even that the database is the most important component. In particular, pursuing a goal of collecting, storing and organising all the data available in an enterprise is likely to be expensive and misguided. The focus in database design, as in MIS design in general, is on providing information in support of decisions. Consequently the database design process is preceded by information requirements analysis. Only then can a *relevant* database be designed. Furthermore in practice, the database concept is only manageable when developed in stages. Thus the design process described below assumes development of a database for one group of logically related applications, not construction of the corporate data reservoir.

After information requirements analysis, the data analysis stage begins—see Figure 6.15. Here the data elements and their relationships are examined in detail to ensure the design team fully understand what is required. A vital input to this process is the corporate long-range MIS plan which provides a framework within which all possible relevant data relationships and database interfaces can be considered. The ideal end-product is a definition of data that is precise and non-redundant and yet incorporates all required relationships. Any constraints of physical organisation or of database software are ignored at this stage. A number of

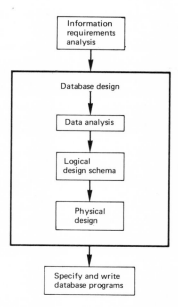

FIGURE 6.15. Database design process (adapted from Tebbs, D., and Kelly, B., 'Major New Techniques in Data-base Project Management', *Computing*, 3 March 1977)

tools exist to aid data analysis, usually based on charts or set theory, such as Third Normal Form.[8] More pragmatic techniques exist, but all aim to help the designer to consider all possible data relationships and to describe them clearly. The resultant data requirements are converted into a logical data structure at the logical design stage. In other words the schema is devised and the data dictionary (see below) specified. The database technicians then map the logical design onto a physical design, subject to constraints of the DBMS and to trade-offs against processing efficiency, recovery ability or local standards.

Once the database is designed, the programs forming the database update and maintenance suite can be written. Experience suggest that database development should be phased, and the maintenance suite is an obvious first stage for several reasons:

(1) It is a logical necessity.
(2) It allows the designers to learn the database technology, and to adapt the design before applications access the database.

(3) It can proceed in step with data collection and rationalisation in user departments.

(4) It raises many of the data administration problems for solution at an early stage.

(5) It allows a 'running-in' period before applications use the database.

(6) It provides an opportunity to evaluate the database management system selected.

In short, this approach is consistent with the prototype methodology advanced in Chapter 3.

DATABASE ADMINISTRATION

The database concept involves far more than competence in technical design. Because it is concerned with logical data relationships which cross functional and departmental boundaries, key administrative issues are raised. Data becomes a corporate-wide resource whose owner and user is the total organisation, so that corporate objectives have to outweigh factional claims. Management support is essential, to set the direction of database development, define responsibilities, and through understanding of the concept and its implications, resolve at an early stage the problems and conflicts which arise. Four elements of database administration have proved to be essential: (1) creation of database administrator; (2) construction of a data dictionary; (3) development of formal data procurement controls; (4) provision of data processing controls.

The concept of a database independently updated but available on an authorised basis to widespread applications demands control. A new role—*the database administrator*—is required to plan and regulate database development and operations. The database administrator is custodian of the corporate data resource, but not the owner. He protects the global logical view of the database but is not concerned with the values of its contents. His prime responsibilities are:

(1) Database definition, namely approval of all additions or changes to data-items. He is concerned with the necessity, redundancy, cost-effectiveness and definition of any data-item.

(2) Data procurement, namely approval of data collection methods and subsequent control to ensure integrity of data before it enters the database.

(3) Database planning, namely advice and ultimate approval of database developments for the future.

(4) Database security and privacy, namely concern that the database can

withstand deliberate or accidental 'attack' and that unauthorised access is prevented.

(5) Database standards, namely development, documentation and monitoring of operations standards.

(6) Database documentation, namely creation and custody of database definitions and descriptions, especially the data dictionary.

Frequently the database administrator is a group or team, rather than one person, for it is an important and demanding task providing an interface between the different views of the database, and ensuring overall database integrity. Conversely these issues no longer concern the application programmer.

The definition and documentation of the database is often achieved through the *data dictionary*. This contains the corporate definition of all data-items at the schema level, in terms of fieldname, description, length and representation (see Figure 6.16). The objective is to ensure that no data-item can exist in more than one form. All users of that data-item agree and understand precisely what it means and thereafter it cannot be amended without the database administrator's approval. Agreement on a data dictionary can be a long and arduous task, of perhaps up to two years duration. In time the definitions become standard terminology. The dictionary is centralised for corporate control, even if the database may be distributed. It is often itself automated, being a file which is referred to by the Data Description Language, thereby also ensuring that programmers conform to the discipline.

So important is data integrity, once the database concept is implemented, that *data procurement controls* are crucial. Unreliable input can

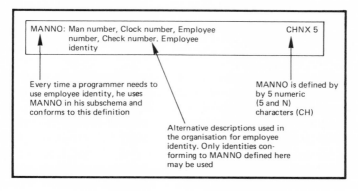

FIGURE 6.16. Data dictionary

undermine the soundest and most sophisticated database structure. Inevitably initial creation of the database is accompanied by rigorous data cleansing activity. No longer can duplicate sets of data be maintained, idiosyncratic identifiers (part numbers, cost codes, or order numbers for example) be suffered, or departmental exceptions be granted. Often the collection and preparation of permanent data has to be 'centralised' in sympathy with the database. Equally, input validation standards must be high. Otherwise errors have multiplying effect where several applications use common data. Consequently editing procedures as close to source as possible are preferred, with logical validation and reasonableness tests applied by program. Overall disciplines have to be established and enforced often supported by concerted training programmes.

Data processing controls are preventive, diagnostic and corrective, all serving to protect database reliability. Preventive controls include privacy and security checks against unauthorised access. Passwords, protected fields and security classifications are common techniques, built into the DBMS operating system or application program. In-process controls are also required to prevent concurrent updates which can produce database inconsistencies. Diagnostic tools include file-scanning programs which seek 'unclean' data, such as data-item values exceeding set limits, or conditions which are illogical and invalid, and monitor programs which observe changes in file activity and could stimulate file reorganisation or reassessment of data organisation trade-offs. Corrective facilities include automatic logging and recovery procedures and file reorganisation and space management programs.

In short a database can represent considerable investment. Unless supporting administrative commitment exists, the database concept is liable to fail. Often the administrative costs can be as high as the computing costs.

DECISION DATABASES

Do strategic planning, management control and operational control decisions require different databases? Examination of the respective decision and information attributes in Chapter 3 would suggest they do, and yet some authorities would not agree; after all, they say, the principle of database is that the inherently flexible data structure can serve many different applications. On both analytical grounds and from the limited experience to date, the need for separate databases seems more likely.

The operational control database(s) is transaction-based, disaggregated and current, serving largely predictable and repetitive information needs.

Management control decisions, however, whilst often based on operational control data in summary and exception form, also require data from wider sources; indeed much operational level data would be irrelevant. Thus perhaps a separate management control database is required, holding summary operational data together with data from other sources. After all the operational control database is liable to be structured for processing efficiency and rapid response times, whilst management control needs might demand a compromise database structure serving both routine data processing and less predictable and unstructured information searches. Or perhaps manager's information thresholds and preferences, not to mention decision-making models, vary so greatly that ad hoc databases should be constructed as necessary?

Probably a compromise is sought, whereby data can be extracted from the operational control database to update summary management control files for routine reporting. Aggregate data does not then impair the operational control database, and the data structure changes endemic in management control, such as alterations to organisational charts, are less disruptive. The less predictable management control information needs may be met by search and interrogation of the operational control database, especially where new needs demand that disaggragated or re-shaped data has to be accessed. Alternatively they may be met by creating special one-off files.

And what of strategic planning decisions? Here the historical, disag-gregated operational control database can be relevant, especially for asking ad hoc questions via DBMS enquiry languages. However, there are no predictable boundaries on strategic information, so formal databases are of limited application. Indeed the managerial problem may be one of ability to perceive the strategic information content in messages already in existence.[9] Likewise, routine and highly aggregated information is prob-ably of little assistance. Strategic planners will probably use operational control databases for occasional searches, specially constructed one-off or semi-permanent files for computer modelling, and extensive non-computer-based information for many major strategic decisions. Figure 6.17 summarises the likely trend for decision database development.

SUMMARY

Database means different things to different people. It is concerned with file design, a complex and specialised task which influences both the efficiency and effectiveness of computer-based information systems. Its ultimate

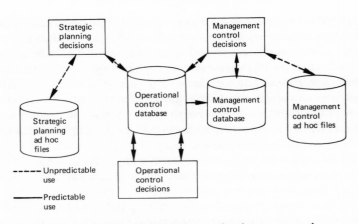

FIGURE 6.17. Decision databases: development trend

expression is the database concept, managing data as a resource, requiring considerable technical and administrative expertise and support.

Much inadequacy of management information systems stems from poor file design. Much inferior file design stems from inattention to the different alternatives and trade-offs which have to be considered and from confusion of terminology and concepts. There are many file design methods available for different purposes. Both specialists and managers should know what is available, to ensure development of effective, efficient and reliable management information systems.

The database concept grew out of systems integration, new information demands and the need to 'unfreeze' the data resource from insular constraints. It was made possible by the development of database management software providing non-redundancy, interconnectedness and data-independence. Three views or levels exist in the database concept, the physical storage view, the application program view or subschema, and the global logical view or schema. Since each changes over time, data independence is required between each level.

In reality there will be several databases, each organised to serve a set of logically related applications. The encyclopaedic corporate reservoir of data, meeting all known and unknown needs, is an illusory and dangerous notion. Yet the database, concept has many attractions to the user, as long as the problems it raises are recognised and overcome at an early stage. This imposes on management a high responsibility to set the direction of database development, to avoid or settle organisational conflicts, to participate in the design process and to ensure adequate database administration.

Design should be founded on decision and information requirements analysis. A number of techniques exist for data analysis. Once implemented the database demands administrative support, in particular aided by a database administration function, creation of a data dictionary and introduction of data procurement and processing controls. Database management software increasingly provides such controls, for example security, recovery and monitoring.

It would seem that one database can rarely serve strategic planning, management control and operational control needs. The dependence of database design on information requirements analysis is thus evident. Equally, management support and participation is essential.

CHAPTER 6—PROJECTS

1. File Design involves assessment of trade-offs. What are the common variables which these trade-offs consider?

2. What are the advantages of: (a) sequential files; (b) random files; (c) indexed sequential files; (d) list files. Describe an application for which each is ideally suited.

3. What are the principal elements of the database concept and the consequent implications?

4. You are commissioned to develop a computer system on student information for a university. Design a database for this MIS. What particular administrative controls would you stress?

5. If you were asked to specify the ideal database management system, what facilities would it provide?

6. How would a database differ in design and operation for:

(a) a production control information system in an engineering company;
(b) a financial control information system in a bank;
(c) a strategic planning information system in a government authority.

7. Your company is characterised by internal and external change. The corporate verdict is that the database concept would be too large a commitment under such instability. What would be your opinion?

8. What are, or would be, the principal responsibilities of a database administrator in your own organisation?

9. 'The more data the computers have access to, the greater is their potential power. In all walks of life and in all areas of industry, data banks will change the realms of what it is possible for man to do' (J. Martin). Discuss.

10. Databases raise crucial questions of security and privacy. If you were designing a personnel information database for the Civil Service, what special security and privacy features would be built in? How would the design process be influenced?

NOTES

1. Martin, J., *Computer Data-Base Organisation*. Englewood Cliffs, N.J.: Prentice-Hall, 1975.
2. *Ibid.*
3. Nolan, R. L., 'Computer Databases: The Future is Now', *Harvard Business Review*, September–October 1973.
4. Martin, J., *op. cit.*
5. *Ibid.*
6. *Ibid.*
7. 'EDP In-Depth Reports', *Current Developments in Data-Base Management*, 2, No. 5 (1973).
8. Normalisation techniques have been strongly advocated and developed by E. F. Lodd. An overview is provided by Martin, J., *op. cit.*
9. Tricker, R. I., *Management Information and Control Systems*. New York: Wiley, 1976.

BIBLIOGRAPHY

Blumenthal, S. C., *Management Information System: A Framework for Planning and Development*. Englewood Cliffs, N.J.: Prentice-Hall, 1969.
Dodd, G. G., 'Elements of Data Management Systems', *Computing Surveys*, 1, No. 2, (1969).
Flores, I., *Data Structure and Management*. Englewood Cliffs, N.J.: Prentice-Hall, 1970.

Martin, J., *Computer Data-Base Organisation*. Englewood Cliffs, N.J.: Prentice-Hall, 1975.

Nolan, R. L., 'Computer Databases: The Future is Now', *Harvard Business Review*, September–October 1973.

'The Cautious Path to a Data-Base', *EDP Analyzer*, 11, No. 6, 1973.

'Organising the Corporate Data-Base', *EDP Analyzer*, 8, No. 3, 1970.

'Processing the Corporate Data-Base', *EDP Analyzer*, 8, No. 4, 1970.

7 Behavioural Aspects of Operational Control

Operation controls relate to tasks or transactions. The primary focus of operational control is usually on economic efficiency. In Chapter 4 we discussed the characteristics of operational control. These characteristics are mainly associated with the tasks and their nature. In this chapter we are concerned with the performance of the tasks. The effectiveness and efficiency of controls in the final analysis depend on their being enacted by people.

The management information system designer's objectives should be to create a system which is both technically perfect and behaviourally acceptable. Many operating systems designers have been found to ignore the behavioural aspects of the system. They give too much attention to the technical aspects, and little or no attention to human aspects. These types of controls are potentially bad for human motivation and job satisfaction, or they may be circumvented, partially or entirely, to make them acceptable to those controlled.

Operating control is by and large mechanistic. Predetermined rules and procedures and rational models guide the actions of human operators. Judgement and intuition are seldom needed. The data for operational controls relate to the immediate past; they are real and accurate. Pressure to produce results is high and immediate. Controls operate at the level of supervisors and operatives. Operational control information, its collection, presentation and use, all have implications for the employee's morale and motivation, his satisfaction, frustration and fatigue.

In this chapter our main focus will be on the behavioural problems associated with the approaches to operating control design.

SOCIO-BEHAVIOURAL ASPECTS OF OPERATING CONTROL

Recognition of the behavioural aspects of operating control and control information is not a new phenomenon. Early authors on management and organisation recognised at least the social aspects of behaviour.[1] The consideration of the psychological aspects did not draw much attention at that time.

The first important behavioural experiment was the Hawthorne[2] experiment, which established once and for all the interrelatedness of social and psychological factors with productivity. The Taylor model, of scientifically measured and designed work, was shown to be incomplete. The careful management of the social environment is also critical to success. As Golembiewski observed, 'in the Taylorian system, when reality did not fit the mechanisms of stop-watch, scale and tape, the attempt was made to change the reality rather than to accommodate the mechanisms to it'.[3] If this approach is followed rigidly by the system designer, he may face frustrating results. His tools should fit the reality and not the other way round.

Operating controls even today, long after the Taylorian era and the pioneering 'Hawthorne' contribution tend to focus to far too great an extent more on non-human and non-social issues.

Division of work into small tasks and jobs is essential before one can institute operating controls. An effective system is associated with increased specialisation and with the application of fairly rigid rules and procedures. However, these measures do not ensure the realisation of the objectives of higher productivity and effectiveness as the following example from a sales office shows.

In this sales office a complete order processing used to be done by each processing clerk. One clerk used to take up the order, prepare further document record, distribute to files, follow-up and close the file. The volume of orders processed was stable. The management wanted to improve productivity. The order processing work was broken down into a number of sub-operations, such as order receiving, recording, checking and sorting, filing and distribution, follow-up and coordination. Each of these operations was assigned to one clerk. The emphasis was upon the physical characteristics of the work only. No attempt was made to analyse its effects on the individuals and the group.

The changes in the work system did not produce the expected results. Output decreased. Dissatisfaction grew. The reasons for the drop in output were analysed from several viewpoints.

The reorganisation failed to get social support from the clerks. Individually, their identity was lost. The feeling of pride they had derived from initiating a job and completing it was no longer there. Moreover, with the previous task organisation there was an established social interaction pattern. The present change obviously disturbed that pattern. There were group norms for productivity. The new system needed reformation of group norms. Also, the new system was designed and introduced at the initiative of the top management. The actual operators were not involved in this process.

Operating system design clearly can upset the social and behavioural patterns in the organisation. This may cause a drop in productivity. Furthermore, the system designer requires support from the people for whom the revised system is developed. One way of ensuring the acceptance is through encouraging their participation in the design process.

In most operating control situations, the rational aspects of the task tend to override the social and psychological man. Operating control models too often seem to perpetuate a machine model of man. This failure to incorporate the social and psychological factors in control designs is caused by the implicit use of inappropriate theoretical assumptions associated with the design of controls, such as:

(1) High productivity depends upon the existence of authority as a formal one-way relation. In our example of the sales office, the order-processing procedure was changed unilaterally without reference to the individual's social and psychological aspects.
(2) Authority can be most effectively exercised through close supervision. The actual evidence is 'that too close supervision can breed discontent and suspicion. Again, authority cannot be exercised for long unless it is accepted by the subordinates.
(3) Working man is physiological; his social ties and psychological peculiarities are not relevant for work situation.
(4) Specialisation and routinisation are the keys to increased efficiency.

These assumptions ignore man as a social and psychological being, and his skills, intelligence, and planning capability. We very often forget the amazing capacity of man to learn. His loyalty, capacity to work without supervision, and trustworthiness are virtually universal attributes, which are often ignored or, even worse, suppressed. Golembiewski[4] observed that, in a patent office, the O & M team emphasised a 'physiological caricature of the copy puller . . . They emphasised 'rhythm', walking distance, time, and 'even flow', all of which reflect an underlying model of man which more than anything resembles a machine'. He concluded that 'in the patent office, authority was not a one-way formal relation', and that 'operators had characteristics other than physiological ones which were job relevant and management at several levels was closer to the work unit'. A blending of mechanistic control theory with social and psychological processes within a work environment is desirable. There is always a temptation to design a control system which supposedly assures high productivity. This leads to adopting engineered-job design. This in turn, leads to alienation of men from work. Standardisation, mechanisation, subdivisions and routinisation are the facets of engineered-job design. These job designs have a high social cost. Engineering design is associated with the distressing effects of (1) anonymity of the individual worker, (2) no control of work pace by worker (3) little or no need for skill, and (4) methods and tools completely specified.

Employees react negatively to increased rationality in their lives. They are afraid of reduced freedom. They think that their performance and career will be evaluated by a mechanism over which they have no control.[5]

Operating people can think as well as any other social human being. The information system should recognise this clearly. The system should include mechanisms to break monotony and fatigue. For example, one man may be entrusted to handle more than one kind of job, thus increasing the variety in terms of information handling and processing. It should be noted that controls are not for the tasks alone but also for the performer. His goals and values, his hopes and aspirations, all are affected by the system.

THE SOCIAL AND PSYCHOLOGICAL OPERATORS

It is recognised now that task characteristics and motivational characteristics of the task performance should fit each other. Empirical research studies support the view that job contents interact with psychological variables and cause variations in users' job satisfaction and performance. Daniel Robey[6] provided evidence that the employee's work value system is responsible for different job satisfactions on the same job. Challenging jobs are satisfying to workers with an intrinsic work value system. Routine and simple tasks provide greatest satisfaction to those with an extrinsic work value system. It was observed that repetitive task performance provides little intrinsic reward and satisfaction. Automated operative tasks fail to stimulate workers with a high intrinsic work value system to the highest performance. On the other hand, larger jobs will not always ensure higher motivation, reduced turnover, decreased boredom and dissatisfaction. Individual differences are more important. Only a certain class of workforce responds favourably to large jobs. Some white-collar and supervisory workers and non-alienated blue-collar workers are in this group. Hulin proved (see Table 7.1) that the degree of alienation from middle-class norms interacts with the task characteristics to produce job

TABLE 7.1. Job satisfaction

Degree of alienation	Task characteristics	
from middle-class norms	Specialised	Enlarged
Alienated from	High job satisfaction	Low job satisfaction
Integrated with	Low job satisfaction	High job satisfaction

Hulin, C. L., and Blood, M. R., 'Job Enlargement, Individual Difference and Workers' Response', *Psychological Bulletin*, 69, No. 1 (1968), 41–55.

satisfaction. Many factors contribute to on-the-job satisfactions of individual workers. Apart from their work value system, it was observed that in a structured operating control situation, workers' satisfaction can be increased (1) by providing opportunity to set goals, (2) by showing their attained success in the task performance, and (3) by giving appropriate feedback of progress in their task performance.[7]

The management information system designer in this context faces a difficult challenge. For example, if the task is already defined and the users are given, he can only try to accommodate the various diversities into one system—obviously, a very difficult task. He may propose to modify the task definition with the help of the client and propose a system appropriate for the people involved. He may also suggest the kind of people who can be effective for a given system characteristic.

One cannot ignore the emotional involvement of the supervisors and operators in control. It should be recognised that emotional involvement is a barrier to communication. The information system designer should recognise this human barrier between his system and the operating task, and his efforts should be directed towards breaking this communication barrier. There is a natural tendency to evaluate others in the light of our own experience and attitudes. Control fails when it ignores or injures the feelings of others. Moreover, when the supervisor has an attitude unrelated to the social environment of the work situation effective control cannot be achieved. Effective control is ensured only through adaptive systems and supervision.

A SOCIAL FRAME OF REFERENCE FOR OPERATING CONTROLS INFORMATION SYSTEM

In a work system, an intimate relationship exists between the physical

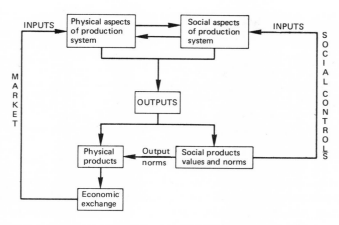

FIGURE 7.1

system and the social products which develop in it. The social products, such as norms, developed in a work situation are likely to persist even when the physical system is changed. Figure 7.1 explains the concept of social products. It clearly signifies that an effective control system at the operating levels needs to deal with the social products. Concerns for physical products only create a partial system. Any production system, involving groups of people working in contiguity creates both physical products and social products. The designers face these as given constraints. Over a period of time the contents and characters of these 'products' change. Should not the controls change also, to fit their frame of reference?

THREAT, MONOTONY AND FATIGUE CONDITIONS IN OPERATING CONTROLS

Operating controls which are perceived as threatening may result in various adverse physical and psychological conditions. A control system which is perceived as threat-arousing and which is intended to increase productivity has the possible effects shown in Figure 7.2.

Arousing a threatening condition is also present in leadership situations. At the supervisory level a widespread attitude towards workers is one of threat. It is assumed that workers require threats to force them to work. Argyris quoted one supervisor, 'I'll tell you my honest opinion, first 5 per

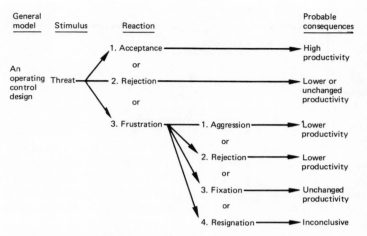

FIGURE 7.2. Possible effect of a threat-arousing control (adapted from Golembiewski, R. T., *Behaviour and Organisation*, Chicago: Rand McNally, 1962, p. 137)

cent of the people work, 10 per cent of the people think they work, and the other 85 per cent would rather die than work'.

The fact that threat is not leadership is illustrated by the following example. Two senior consultants supervised the work of two groups of consulting assistants engaged on the same project. The work was mechanical. The assistants were to collect data through a precoded questionnaire and tabulate the data in the specified form. They were working under the pressure of a limited time schedule. One senior consultant supervised the job in a highly structured way. He used verbal and procedural threats, recorded the daily progress and awarded pecuniary punishment in the form of withholding payments of salary or recommending deductions. The other senior consultant did not have a formal procedure for monitoring the progress except the weekly meetings with the assistants. He reviewed the progress informally and occasionally reminded them of the deadline. There was an atmosphere of trust. The results achieved by these two groups are strikingly different. The work done under the threatening condition had the following characteristics: (1) the total work could not be completed in time, (2) on many questionnaire items, incomplete or unreliable data were collected, (3) the number of mistakes was high, and (4) intentional 'cheatings' were found. On the other hand, the work done under liberal supervisory condition was very satisfactory. It was possible to complete the work in time and mistakes were very few.

What one should guard against in these situations is over-emphasis of any of the following conditions in the operational control design which are legacies of the old, traditional organisation theory:

(1) High specialisation—which prevents completion of a task by an individual.
(2) Limited span of control—which induces a sense of failure and low ability and interferes with individual's expressions and assertions.
(3) Close direction in supervision—from which employees conclude that the leaders cannot really lead.

These are basically Taylorian concepts. Taylorian concepts are useful for analysing many operational controls. Nevertheless, for systems design their limitations should be thoroughly examined. It must be remembered that controls designed to Taylorian methods have high potential for frustration.

Operating controls are said to produce monotony, fatigue, and high turnover. Opinions on these differ. The general impression is that repetitive work is uncreative and causes boredom and monotony. It has been shown in the literature that workers who do not suffer from monotony when doing repetitive work are inferior, placid, extroverted, happy, unable to day-dream and unintelligent.[8] Monotony or boredom in work is a state of mind of the individual.

Repetition is one of the characteristics of task as perceived by the workers and one of the aspects of monotony. Repetition is not the only valid cause for monotony. Workers who report satisfaction with repetitive work are not insensitive or stupid as has been asserted in a section of the literature. Smith, among others, proved that the feeling of monotony is not merely a function of the task performed, but is related to more general factors in the individual worker.[9] Assumptions about the operators' characteristics should not be restricted to a stereotype.

Operating controls designed on the basis of traditional organisation theory involving principles of specialisation, repetitiveness, reduction of skill content, minimum impact of the operators on the control process, fulfil only lower order needs, i.e. physiological needs. Higher needs such as needs for recognition, autonomy, affiliation, achievement and fair evaluation largely remain unsatisfied. Ross and Zander showed that employee turnover is related with the degree of need satisfaction. The study showed that employees who resigned from the job reported these higher order needs as unsatisfied.[10]

Fraser showed that operating controls resulting in repetitive task design may create fatigue conditions.[11] An information system making provision for various forms of feedback reduces employee fatigue. Feedback is also important for employee motivation.

INFLUENCE OF SMALL GROUP IN OPERATIONAL CONTROL

Small groups regulate the individual's behaviour. In operating controls, small groups can play both positive and negative roles. Small groups are behavioural groups. Their effects on successful operational control are very significant. A small group can make a formal organisation effective, or it can emasculate the most elegant technical system.

The most common example of a small group's negative role is restriction of output. The positive effect can include such things as high output norms and group morale. In the case of physical and psychological stress, small groups play the role of shock-absorber by providing emotional support. A large number of research studies have been carried out with small groups at operating levels. The conditions of small groups exist at operating levels much more than anywhere else in the organisation.

The properties of small groups can be grouped as: (1) structural, characterising the group organisation; (2) behavioural, characterising the behaviour pattern; and (3) individual, characterising the individual's psychological aspects. In Table 7.2 a list of such properties is produced. These properties have effects on performance at operational levels.[12] In a situation of high group cohesiveness, productivity tends to be high. Such groups maintain high output norms. All these properties have to be considered to get a complete view of the system domain. To develop a socio-technical operating system, these properties may provide crucial inputs. Small groups are inevitable in organisations. The system designers should utilise their virtues and avoid their ill effects.

In a situation of high group cohesiveness, workers report a lower level of

TABLE 7.2. Small group properties

Structural	Behavioural	Individual
Functional roles	Atmosphere	Intelligence
Status	Role style	Authoritarianism
Leadership	Task	Response repertoires
Status congruency	Norms	Compatibility
Cohesiveness	Style integration	
Structural integration	Threat	

tension at work.[13] Job specialisation, routinisation, narrow span, repetitiveness and mechanisation all imply high threat, and consequently produce high anxiety. Consideration of small group variables and individual variables in operating control design may help ameliorate many of these resultant effects of the inherent control characteristics.

ROLE OF LEADERSHIP IN OPERATING CONTROLS

Leadership plays a significant role at all levels of controls. Much leadership research provides evidence of effective and ineffective leadership at the operating control and the management control levels. It has been shown that a supportive supervisory atmosphere will achieve high productivity.[14] Pressure-oriented, threatening, and punitive management yields lower productivity, high cost, increased absence, and less employee satisfaction than supportive and employee-centred management. Supportive and employee-centred managers use the group method of supervision and encourage participation. Pressure-oriented and threatening supervision can obtain impressive results in the short-run, which are usually associated with the long-run cost to the organisation. Table 7.3 shows the comparative position of leadership characteristics and their effects on productivity and employee morale.

TABLE 7.3. Leadership characteristics, productivity and morale

	Participative *(supportive)*	*Hierarchically* *controlled* *(authoritative)*
Production	Lower increase (short run)	Higher increase by direct order (short run)
Feeling of responsibility and loyalty etc.	Higher	Low
Attitude towards high production	Favourable	Unfavourable
Satisfaction with supervision	High	Low

Source: adapted from Likert, R., 'Measuring Organisational Performance', *Harvard Business Review*, 36 (1958).

Operating control if designed carefully may permit supportive leadership to function effectively. We will observe in a later chapter that the leadership characteristics vary according to individuals and the situations. While the individual traits are more or less stable, the situational characteristics can be varied by the design of the control system and the control information.

Figure 7.3 summarises some influences of the control characteristics on the feelings and sentiments of the individual workers and the resulting behaviour. It illustrates how the basic behavioural responses which are of interest to operating control designers are formed. A large number of variables are candidates for consideration. A limited number of them can be effectively controlled and manipulated. The success in the design hinges on the choice.

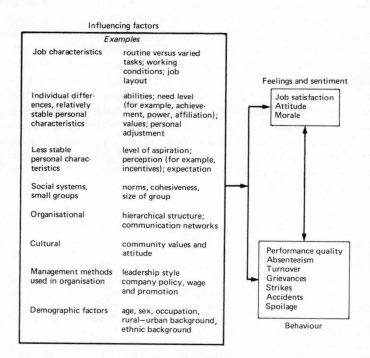

FIGURE 7.3. Interacting influences affecting feeling and behaviour on the job

Source: Costello, T. W., and Zalkind, S. S., *Psychology in Administration: A Research Orientation* (Englewood Cliffs, N. J.: Prentice-Hall, 1963), p. 121.

USES OF OPERATIONAL CONTROL DATA

We have discussed previously the influences of leadership characteristics on the operating people in a repetitive task situation. We observed that in operating situations pressure for production is high. In practice, operational control data may have (1) a production-oriented use or (2) an employee-oriented use.

The production-oriented use is associated with the pressure-oriented supervisory pattern of leadership. The employee-oriented use is supportive to employee morale. Employee-oriented use assures long-term effectiveness of the organisation. These uses of operating control data are made for (1) controlling the operation and, (2) evaluating the operatives. Table 7.4 shows the nature of use of operating control data. The rigid use of operating control data is associated with the production-oriented leadership style. The flexible use, and non-use, of operating control data are associated with the employee-oriented leadership style.

TABLE 7.4. Nature of use of operating control data

	Rigid use	*Flexible use*	*Non-use*
Controlling the operation	Follow the instructions	Follow the instructions but ready to apply judgement	Does not arise
Evaluating the subordinates	ditto	ditto	Does not rely on operating data alone

If the operating control data are used for subordinate evaluation, this can have many unwanted consequences, Operatives do not always accept evaluation with a favourable attitude. Falsification of performance figures is not uncommon at the operating levels.[15] For example, in a system of incentive wages, the operatives were found to manipulate the output record to increase wage levels.

Employees report tensions, anxiety and dissatisfaction when faced with production-oriented use of operating control data. A more detailed discussion of the effects of use of control data for evaluating subordinates is made in Chapter 10.

CONCLUSION

The objective of operational control is to ensure effective and efficient performance of a task or transaction. However, both effectiveness and efficiency of the control in the final analysis depend on the human operators. In Chapter 4, we observed that an operational control by and large is a mechanistic control. The actions of the human operators are not based on judgement and intuition but on the predetermined rules and procedures and rational models.

The data for operational controls are concerned with the immediate past, they are accurate and real. The pressure to produce results is high and immediate.

The control operates at the level of the supervisors and operatives with a limited focus on the tasks and transactions. The operational control information, its collection, presentation and use all have implications for the morale and motivation of the individual control operators and task operators. In this chapter the specific behavioural issues that merit consideration in designing operational control information system have been discussed. The behavioural implications of operating controls may be summarised as below:

(1) Human responses to operational control are mainly of mechanistic-reflex type.

(2) Pressure for results creates behavioural problems.

(3) Higher order motivational needs are not activated and self-actualisation need is threatened.

(4) Autonomy and freedom on the job is minimal, which affects self-esteem.

(5) Restrictions on interaction opportunity.

(6) Little or no mental activity on the part of the individual operators.

(7) Repetitive nature of control creates monotony in human operators resulting in fatigue, physical exhaustion and frustration.

(8) Supervisor's choice of use of control information affects productivity and morale of the operatives.

(9) Falsification of control information by the operatives.

(10) Invalid information to cover poor performance, errors and fraud.

(11) Deliberate use of dummy data by the supervisors because of the time pressure.

(12) Attempts are made by the operatives to sabotage operational control, e.g. restriction of output by the group to fail the work procedure.

(13) Deliberate misuse of control, e.g. postpone repairs to prolong the breakdown.

(14) Use of own independent control information by the supervisors.

The use of operating information and the supervisory behaviour influence the effectiveness and efficiency of the controls. Operating control information systems recognise physical and economic aspects of the task. In spite of the best efforts to design a control system which is elaborate and comprehensive, the best control is seldom achieved. Operating control information systems provide links between tasks, transactions, controls, groups and individuals.

Some considerations for operational control information systems (OCIS) design are given below:

(1) The three aspects of OCIS should be well understood and accepted by the operators: (a) OC information characteristics, (b) processing characteristics, and (c) output (reporting) characteristics.

(2) OCIS must match the cognitive ability of the users and operatives.

(3) System objectives and operation should be well understood by the users and operatives.

(4) Users should have adequate technical competence to work as the system says and to perceive the data correctly.

(5) Create the information system in such a way as to encourage the individual's involvement in control by encouraging participation and building a flexible system, and by creating a balance between mechanical control and human control.

(6) A supervisor's information need (his own information system) may be recognised profitably.

(7) Operating control information has an upward transmission tendency—creating a downward transmission will help increase the understanding and trust.

(8) Operational control is only partially informational. Supervisory influence in operational control can never be eliminated by an information subsystem.

CHAPTER 7—PROJECT

RECEIVING AND STORAGE PROCEDURE OF ALPHA CORPORATION

Purchase and stores are two separate sections under the factory administration department. Stores section has seven assistants and a stores supervisor, while purchase section has eleven assistants and a supervisor. Stores department is responsible for receiving and storing the materials purchased. On receiving the supplies the stores supervisors take necessary steps to check the quality against the standards. Usually people from the concerned indenting department verify the quality of the supplies. The stores clerks count, weigh and measure the materials. When the checking and inspection is complete the stores clerk prepares a quality certificate which is signed and certified by the indenting department supervisor. After preparing the quality certificate the stores clerk prepares the Material Receiving Report (MRR) in four copies and signs them. Store clerk sends them to (1) accounts, (2) purchase section, (3) indenting department and keeps the fourth copy. Generally, no separate control reports are prepared for inspection, counting, weighing and measuring.

Usually all materials flow through the stores department. Sometimes the production departments receive supplies directly from the suppliers in emergency situations. In such a case, the indenting department receives the materials. Sometimes, items of small volume are directly purchased and received by the production departments.

1. Give your comments on the receiving and storage procedure.

2. Does the procedure satisfy operating control characteristics.

3. What behavioural problems will you be likely to face, if you recommend any change in the procedure. What positions are likely to be affected by the change?

NOTES

1. Alfred, L. P., *Henry Lawrence Gantt*. New York: Harper, 1934.
2. Roethlisberger, F. E., and Dickson, W., *Management and the Worker*. Cambridge, Mass.: Harvard University Press, 1946.
3. Golembiewski, R. T., *Behaviour and Organisation*. Chicago: Rand McNally, 1962, p. 13.
4. See Golembiewski, R. T., *Behaviour and Organisation*. Chicago: Rand McNally, 1962.
5. Argyris, C., '*Management Information System*, The Threat of Rationality', *The McKinsey Quarterly*, 2, No. 2 (1970), 25–41.
6. Daniel Robey, 'Impact of Alternative Decision Techniques on Users' Behaviour', *Decision Sciences*, 7, No. 1 (1976).
7. Salvate, J. M., 'The Effect of Introduction of CPM on Middle Management in the Construction Industry', unpublished Ph.D. dissertation, Columbia University, 1970.
8. See Flishman, E. A., *Studies in Personnel and Industrial Psychology for References*. Homewood, Illinois: The Dorsey Press, 1967, pp. 548–9.
9. Smith, P. C., 'The Prediction of Individual Differences in Susceptibility to Industrial Monotony', *Journal of Applied Psychology*, 39, No. 5 (1955), 322–9.
10. Ross, I. C., and Zander, A. F., 'Need Satisfaction and Employee Turnover', *Personnel Psychology*, 10 (1957), 327–38. Daniel Robey, 'Impact of Alternative Decision Techniques on User Behaviour', *Decision Sciences*, 7, No. 1 (1976).

11. Fraser, D. C., 'Recent Experimental Work in the Study of Fatigue', *Occupational Psychology,* 32, No. 4 (1958).
12. Golembiewski, *op. cit.*
13. Seasore, S. E., *Group Cohesiveness in Industrial Workgroup.* Ann Arbor: Survey Research Center, University of Michigan, 1954.
14. Likert, Rensis, 'Measuring Organisational Performance', *Harvard Business Review*, 36 (1958), 41–50.
15. Hopwood, A. G., *An Accounting System and Managerial Behaviour.* Farnborough, England: Saxon House, 1974.

BIBLIOGRAPHY

Hinton, B. L., and Reitz, H. J., *Groups and Organizations.* Belmont, California: Wadsworth, 1969.

Katz, D., and Kahn, R. L., *The Social Psychology of Organization.* New York: Wiley, 1966.

March, J. C., and Simon, H. A., *Organizations.* New York: Wiley, 1958.

McGregor, D., *Human Side of the Enterprise.* New York.: McGraw-Hill, 1960.

Porter, L. W., and Steers, R. M., 'Organisational, Work and Personal Factors in Employee Turnover and Absenteeism', *Psychological Bulletin*, 80 (1970), 151–76.

Stedry, A. C., *Budget Control and Cost Behaviour.* New York: Markham Publishing Company, 1967.

Tannenbaum, A. S., *Control in Organization.* New York: McGraw-Hill, 1968.

Part III Management Control Systems

8 The Nature of Management Control Systems

A management control system is a set of administrative procedures through which one group of people in an organisation intentionally influence or affect the behaviour of another group. If it is effective, it will ensure that the top management policy decisions are put into practice at the level of operations. The design of such a system is a complicated affair— much more so than the systems of operational control which we have already examined. This is because a management control system seeks to control the behaviour of people, and these people are in turn attempting to control the behaviour of others. The word 'control' should not be taken to imply a negative kind of control, an oppressive kind. In many cases, the goal of the control system is to help a manager do his own planning and thinking more effectively, so that he becomes able to do things he could not previously do at all, which is not only useful to the organisation but a source of great satisfaction to the man or woman involved.

A successful management control system will induce (*not* coerce) people to behave, and will cause them to induce (*not* coerce) others to behave, in a fashion congruent with the organisational goals established during the strategic planning process.

For example, a common method of management control is expressed in return on investment terms. The top levels of management require a certain rate of accounting or cash flow return on the investment entrusted to the manager of a division. This desire is expressed in the form of a management control system. The control may be in the form of a profit and investment budget as illustrated in Figure 8.1. The middle level of management is conscious of the measurement procedure in use and attempts to operate the section of the business entrusted to him so that these desired targets will be attained. An evaluation is then made as to whether the middle manager has fulfilled the requirements of the top management group. A comparison is made between the actual results achieved and the original return on

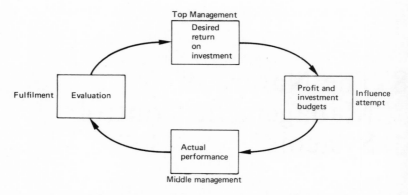

FIGURE 8.1. The management control process, conventional cycle

investment target. The result may be a revision in the procedures employed by the middle manager. Or it may be a change in the return investment target. Or it may involve extensive action in the case of material divergence. In any event, the management control system has set a simplified target and then seeks to measure attainment against that target.

The management control system, however, is usually intended to measure and to influence behaviour which is multi-dimensional. A manager's job cannot really be described only in terms of return on investment. There are personal variables, there are organisational variables, there are psychological variables, there are long-term and short-term variables, all of which must be balanced and monitored if the manager is to carry out his job properly. It may be perfectly feasible for a manager to achieve return on investment in the short term by building up troubles for the future. But few top management groups would really wish to induce that kind of behaviour in their middle-ranked executives.

Management control is a process. It changes over time. It involves setting control procedures and standards and it involves the process of measurement and evaluation. It must change if management control is to be effective and alive. For example, in financial management control, concerns for accounting profitability and return on investment measures are replaced in times of acute liquidity problems by systems which give priority to measurements of cash flow.

THE BOUNDARIES OF MANAGEMENT CONTROL

The management control process merges into operational control procedures below it and into strategic planning procedures above it, in an almost imperceptible fashion. Nonetheless, for discussion purposes it is useful to identify some of the activities of management which are clearly included under the heading of management control. The systems and information systems can provide help to managers engaging in these control activities and thus be identified and discussed. Some of the activities are:

(1) Budget activities—budget formulation, monitoring and evaluation; it includes all types of operating budgets and financial budgets.

(2) Working capital management—working capital planning is a part of the financial management control; it is a vital issue for managers at the enterprise level. Maintaining adequate cash flow and moving the products profitably are among the major concerns of managers.

(3) Capital expenditure decisions—managers are required to take decisions on routine capital expenditure for replacements and improving the operating efficiency of the enterprise.

(4) Personal decisions—developing human resources and planning staff levels, have both short- and long-term implications. Personnel decisions include recruitment, training, development, compensation and retention of personnel.

(5) Product decisions—to remain profitable, the manager must become involved in product introduction, improvement, modification and withdrawal.

(6) Advertising programmes—as a part of a manager's marketing efforts, selection of advertising programmes comes within management control; it also includes other promotional activities.

(7) Research projects—selection of research projects that are necessary to maintain current profitability is a management control activity. Such research projects which are of interest to managers are related to improvement of products and processes.

(8) Operating rules and procedures—developing and reviewing the operating rules and procedures are included in management control; these are important management control functions. Operating procedures ensure success of operating controls and reflect the resourcefulness of management.

(9) Performance evaluation—measuring, appraising and improving management performance. Profit plans, budgetary controls, cost–price

relations etc., are some of the widely-used performance evaluation tools.

It may be summarised from the above that management controls are related to managerial decisions relevant to operations of different functional area controls such as: (1) financial management control, (2) production management control, (3) marketing management control, and (4) personnel management control. Control decisions are primarily oriented towards present performance and future objectives.

MANAGEMENT CONTROL INFORMATION

Information required for management control functions can be analysed on different dimensions, e.g. decision-makers; source; complexity; aggregation and frequency.

(1) Decision-makers—middle-level management personnel. They include people above supervisory level up to the top management. It should be observed that here more than one level of management is involved. The nature and process of controls and information used vary with the hierarchical levels of management.

(2) Source—the data source for management control is both internal and external. Management control uses extensive internal data. It also needs external environmental data, mainly for comparison and for market appraisal, to produce effective decisions.

(3) Complexity—management control information is moderately complex. It is built on relatively simple operating data and is linked with the complex strategic input.

(4) Aggregation—management control data are of two types: (a) aggregated and (b) detailed. The aggregated data are inputs from operating controls. The detailed data are those that are generated by the management control system. Aggregated management control data are employee turnover summary, inventory control reports, etc., while the detailed data are generated on budget performance and employee evaluation.

(5) Frequency—the frequency of monitoring and reporting management control data depends on the levels in the hierarchy for which data are produced. As management control decisions usually involve revision, alteration, deletion or addition of products, processes or procedures, the control system needs data for an appropriate length of time. Time should not be so long as to make the data operationally sterile nor so short as to capture useless details. Table 8.1 puts these characteristics of management control at the intermediate position.

TABLE 8.1

Information dimensions	Operating control	Management control	Strategic control
Decision points	Subordinate and operating supervisors	⟶	Top management and board of directors
Data source	Largely internal data generated at the level of operation	⟶	Largely external data
Complexity	Simple to manipulate and use	⟶	Complex to manipulate and use
Aggregation	Detailed	⟶	Aggregated
Frequency	Very frequent	⟶	Not frequent

Source: adapted from Lucus, H. C., 'An Empirical Study of a Framework for Information System', *Decision Science*, 5 (1974) 102–3.

An alternative viewpoint for classification of management control information is its main purpose: control or decision-making.

(1) *Control information inputs are*:

(a) Internal information, e.g. current production reports, current employee turnover.

(b) Historical summaries—sales trend for a number of years, production volume and efficiency achieved during the past few years.

(c) Goal-performance summaries—budget reports analysed with actuals and targets.

(d) Monetary reports—statements of income, expenses, cost, profitability etc.

(e) Rhythmic reports—regular periodic reports of performance compared with standards.

(2) *Decision-making inputs include*:

(a) Past and future trends—past historical data on sales, production price and demand, and forecasts of future trends.

(b) Monetary and non-monetary reports (e.g. reports to make decisions to make or to buy)—include monetary and non-monetary data analysed on different basis such as opportunity costs, relevant costs, incremental revenue etc.

(c) Special studies—feasibility study, market survey reports etc.

(d) Rhythmic report—regular report to focus attention on exceptions needing decision to change some management variable.

(e) Product and market data—product and market data supplied by regular sales reports and sales analysis. Special analysis and reports also produce product and market data.

(f) Market share, customer and product profile—these data come from special analysis and are reviewed at periodic intervals.

(g) Production efficiency—supplied by regular production reports, quality control reports and production budget performance reports.

A management control information system includes both formal and informal elements. The formal part, which includes the management accounting system and the budget, is often not as important as the informal. The typical manager makes considerable use of informal meetings, discussions, and observations in approaching his decisions, especially in the field of subordinate evaluation. Employee attitudes towards work and towards colleagues are not often formally measured, for example.

MEASUREMENT IN MANAGEMENT CONTROL

The task of measurement in a control system is always hard. But it is particularly hard in the management control systems area. A manager must decide whether profits are satisfactory, whether morale is high enough, whether productivity is high enough, and whether the information system is being used properly, amongst other things. If he is to get help from the management control information system in answering them, it must contain qualitative as well as quantitative information. It must be multi-dimensional information, if it is to represent, reasonably fairly, the complexities of managerial behaviour.

If it is to be measured an activity must have at least two attributes, a unit of measure and a period of time for measurement. Sometimes the time period is rather arbitrarily chosen, at other times is dictated by the natural time-cycle of the enterprise being measured (for instance, a voyage of a freight ship). This problem can usually be overcome. But the choice of a unit of measurement can be quite difficult. Such a unit must fulfil several conditions:

(1) Validity.

(2) Sufficiency—does the measure adequately reflect all aspects of the control situation relevant for the purpose. A profit measure may be insufficient to evaluate a manager's performance if it does not reflect the

controllable responsibility of the manager. On the other hand, data on only cost-effectiveness are not sufficient measure for managerial efficiency.

(3) Stability—it is clearly important that a measure should record the same 'reading' each time it is applied if the underlying variable is stationary. Also each value of the underlying variable should have, as an unambiguous equivalent, a value of the measure. For example, the year-on-year percentage growth rate in a company's income is a most unstable measure. At a very low level, a modest increase will show a very high percentage, while the achievement of a second year of record-breaking results would show a nil growth measure.

THE MEASUREMENT OF CONTROL FACTORS OTHER THAN PROFIT

For many years executives have been concerned about the lack of congruence between the financially oriented control systems and the behaviour which they actually want to induce in their middle-level managers. While a profit content is important, especially in the long term, if the entity is to survive and prosper, it is by no means obvious that managers at middle level should emphasise profit to the exclusion of other factors. In 1952 the General Electric Company of the United States attempted to deal with this issue specifically and many other firms have, since that time, attempted to deal with the problem. GE identified eight key result areas. In each case the problem was one of attempting to measure variables which were both important and not easily measurable. Because the GE project was the first of its kind, it is worth reproducing some of their ideas and some of the methods they used to evaluate progress on the less quantifiable dimensions.

One of the measures which GE applied was of productivity. It was felt that a manager who sustained profitability of his enterprise but did not do things to improve productivity at the same time was less effective than a manager who did both. To assess this they chose a ratio of value added to non-material costs. By this means the company hoped to obtain a measure of productivity which was independent of the contributions made to productivity by suppliers of materials whether partially processed or completely raw. The value-added measure covered the sales value less the costs of goods and services acquired from outside the company. The denominator of the productivity ratio was the sum of expenses other than material purchases. Labour costs and depreciation charges were both included. A manager was expected to maintain and to improve the value of the ratio over time. The use of this ratio permitted the manager to obtain a favourable result by either economising on the controllable inputs (labour and capital equipment and working capital) or by increasing the throughput with existing resources, or both.

$$\text{productivity ratio} = \frac{\text{sales} - \text{purchased goods and services}}{\text{labour} + \text{depreciation}}$$

A second dimension of measurement was personnel development. Personnel development was concerned with the systematic training of managers to fill present and future manpower needs so as to allow for both growth of individuals and growth of the enterprise. Programmes of training and development were expected to produce a continuous flow of potentially promotable employees.

The basic soundness of the programmes which were sponsored by a department for the development of its staff was appraised by informal means. Questions were asked about the selection of candidates for development, about the nature of programmes available, about the periodic review of performance of the people, and about the placement of those once trained in suitable jobs.

A second step involved taking stock of the trained manpower of the department, to see how well off the department was in terms of its ability to fill its own promotional needs. This step was taken by means of a manning table in which the preparation of each manager was listed, and an annual comparison made of the proportions trained internally versus externally.

The third factor in the personnel development area which the management sought to review was in the area of programme effectiveness. A measure was devised of the ratio of the number of people promoted to the number of people who were designated as promotable in each department. A high score on this statistic indicated that the people being trained in that department were perceived as highly usable throughout the enterprise and this was taken as prima facie evidence of effective personnel development procedure. A secondary measure of this kind of progress was the proportions of managers in each department who were seen in the performance review procedure to be improving, unchanged, and deteriorating. A relatively high proportion in the first category was considered to be a good point in personnel development terms for the department in question.

The other variables which the GE project sought to measure were profitability, market position, product leadership, employee attitudes, public responsibility and the balance between short- and long-term goals.

The entire operation was reported in full in Lewis[1] and more briefly in Jerome.[2]

In other companies, a variety of further measures have been devised to assess the performance of a section on quantifiable but non-financial bases. A major hotel chain has established time standards longer than which no guest is expected to have to wait. These time delays are roughly inversely proportional to the prices charged in the hotels in the chain. Major chemical companies are measuring the pollution which may be caused by their factories in advance of legislative demands for such measures to be made. In one such case the top management group has ordered a decline in the tonnage of each chemical pollutant leaked at a rate of so many tons a year. As the firm was growing in volume, the requirement to reduce the absolute weight of pollutant meant that the rate of pollution per ton of product had to fall at a dramatic pace.

The point about control systems design at the management level is that it must be sufficiently diverse, and involve a sufficient number of different variables, so that the task which the manager is being asked to fulfil can reasonably be represented by the measures taken. In the GE case, a satisfactory performance would be attributed to a manager only if a reasonable or better score was obtained on *all* eight dimensions measured. A high score on profitability would not compensate for a series of low scores on the other dimensions at hand. If a manager is asked to perform effectively along a number of dimensions at the same time, then the control system must have at least as many variables in it as the independent dimensions upon which performance is sought. The argument that it will all eventually transform itself into profitability is specious. The time within which a poor personnel development policy will show itself in the profit figures is so different from the time within which poor product leadership will impinge upon profit, that it is just not reasonable to assert that they are merely two aspects of the same phenomenon. A typical manager could expect to be promoted from his post before the results of a defective personnel policy could be detectable. Unless that dimension is formally measured therefore, the manager might be tempted to omit it entirely.

SOME SPECIAL ISSUES IN MANAGEMENT CONTROL

The general problem of measuring performance on a multitude of dimensions is the essence of the management control process. Within that broad framework, however, there are a number of specific issues which have come to the fore in recent years concerning the application of the principles discussed above to the practical corporate situation. There is insufficient space in this book to discuss any one of these exhaustively. However, three have been chosen for an introductory discussion in the rest of this chapter. They concern controls over divisional operations in a decentralised enterprise, management by objectives, and budgetary controls.

1. DIVISIONAL CONTROLS

Control of decentralised operations is a difficult but critical part of management control systems. Decentralised operations are termed profit centres. The usual way of evaluating a decentralised operation is through a profit budgeting system.

The profit budgets are prepared at the beginning of each year. The usual profit budget procedure is that a profit budget proposal is prepared for the coming year and a profit plan for the next few years. The budget preparation activities start at least three to four months before the commencement of the year. The budget is prepared and evaluated by special committee and budget staff to assure that (1) the budgets represent reasonable goals for the coming years, and (2) the plan is consistent with the corporate objectives. Figure 8.2 shows the profit plan process of a dynamic organisation.

Profit plans help managers to exercise control in several ways. The top managers' attention can be focused on divisions which are having trouble meeting their objectives by variances of actual performance from the budget. The manager of a unit can have his attention drawn to corporate targets by the discussions which take place during the drawing up of a budget. Also, a budget can be developed which reflects the potential of each unit separately, in a fashion which simple inter-divisional comparisons can seldom do with equity. The development of a budget is a most effective management control tool.

As is true of any tool, it can be misused of course. The multi-dimensional character of the managerial task has already been discussed. If simple performance against budget is used to evaluate managers, without taking the other factors discussed in the previous section into account, the manager may be motivated incorrectly. Dearden[3] suggested that profit evaluations of managers should not be used, because of the multi-dimensional point made earlier, and because budgets tend to be done on an annual basis. Dearden pointed out that a year is far too short a time over which a manager's performance could reasonably be assessed. He also noted that the budget was inevitably subject to error, as it had to be

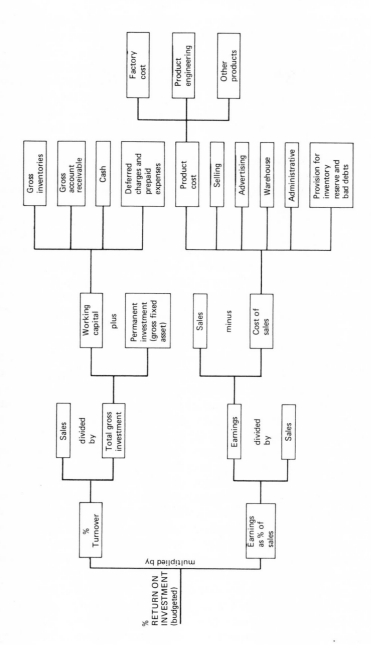

FIGURE 8.2. Budgeted return on investment and profit plan

prepared many months in advance. In changed circumstances, the manager might be absolutely correct to seek to diverge from an obsolescent budget.

The use of budgeting to implement the principles of management control is not rendered inappropriate by Dearden's comments. But his observations, derived from many years of observation, illustrate the dangers of applying the budget as though it were a 'blunt instrument' to the delicate mechanism which is the management system of an organisation.

2. MANAGEMENT BY OBJECTIVES

Of late, management by objectives is being subsumed into the management control systems. Management by objectives requires a clear identification of objectives and the desired results, the establishment of programmes for the realisation of the objectives and finally an evaluation of performance in terms of the results. Many organisations have taken steps to link the organisational reward system with performance measurement and improvement. Management by objectives emphasises increasing productivity and improving employee satisfaction. It, in fact, tends to accumulate into a systematic framework all management knowledge that has been developed so far.[4]

The distinctive features of management by objectives are: (1) clear definition of responsibilities, (2) accomplishment of targets expressed in terms of results, (3) participative goal setting, (4) recognition of achievement, (5) development of measurement for qualitative and quantitative data, (6) ability to analyse qualitative and quantitative data, (7) satisfactory performance in the present assignment leads to advancement in the organisation.

Management by objectives has been extended to a three-stage system. The primary stage of the system is performance evaluation. However, performance evaluation alone cannot assure the realisation of organisational goals. It needs integration of objectives of all employees to produce desired results. Thus the intermediate step is integration. Furthermore, if the efforts are not linked with long-range planning, MBO will initiate only short-run current operating efforts and thinking. Therefore, the final stage is long-range planning. The steps are illustrated well by Howell, from whose work Table 8.2 has been adapted.

3. BUDGETARY CONTROLS

Budgets are widely used management control tools. There is hardly any

TABLE 8.2

	Procedure	Purpose	Contribution	Weakness
Stage I: Performance evaluation	Discussions and agreements on target results	Increased participative motivation, performance evaluation	Managers are able to set realistic and measurable objectives	Does not integrate with objectives of other employees
Stage II: Integration	Discussions with different levels and departments horizontally and vertically	Horizontal and vertical integration of goals and objectives	Managers are capable of assessing the capabilities to measure shared responsibility	Does not involve long-range orientation
Stage III: Long-range planning	Link with budget and long-range planning	Long-range focus is given to the activities of the organisation	Managers are capable of evaluating the results of their actions in long-range terms	Strategic planning horizon not tempered

Source: adapted from Howell, R. A., 'Management by objectives: a three-stage system' *Business Horizons*, February 1970. Also see Brown, N. R., 'Improving, measuring and rewarding performance', *Management by Objectives*, 4, No. 4

organisation where budgets do not assume a pivotal position in the management control system.

Budgets are plans, mainly financial in nature, for a specified future period. Budgets can be current operating budgets and long-term budgets. Current operating budgets are concerned with planning the operations for the current year, and usually start with sales budgeting. Sales budgets then are translated into production budgets and other expense budgets. The operating budgets are hierarchical. For example, a total sales budget is broken down into territories, districts, zones, and salesmen. These are also analysed by products and channels of distribution. The total production budget for a company is subdivided by factories, departments and sections. Other budgets are also simultaneously broken down the hierarchical chain. A list of operating budgets is produced below:

(1) Sales budget.
(2) Production budget.
(3) Materials budget.
(4) Purchase budget.
(5) Labour budget.
(6) Manufacturing expense budget.
(7) Cost of goods sold budget.
(8) Administrative and general expense budget.
(9) Selling expense budget.
(10) Advertising budget.
(11) Research and development budget.
(12) Other income and expense budget.
(13) Cash budget.

Budgetary control works by monitoring the operation through measurement, comparison and feedback. At operating levels these steps are more frequent than at the management levels. At management level, budget comparisons are usually done monthly.

Below are examples of typical budgeting processes of two large companies.

Example A
The budgeting process starts with the preparation of sales budget by the group sales managers and the production budgets by the production managers. These two forecasts are reconciled at the group level. In the preparation of budgets, the unit managers and the sales managers use (1) planning assumptions provided by the head office, (2) previous year's results of the unit, and (3) the data on the present operating conditions. For all expense estimates, managers use local knowledge. However, managers

do not have a completely free hand in deciding budgets. The instructions which they receive from the group office and the head office control them in this respect, and may ignore the local conditions. These instructions sometimes create dissatisfactions among the managers when they find that the instructions are not in conformity with their expectations based on experience and knowledge of local conditions. Figure 8.3 shows the organisational authority and responsibility for budgets and also the budgeting process in the company. The budget responsibility and authority is spread over the three levels of the management. At all levels the managers and the accountants work very closely to compile the budgets and after the approval, to monitor and control the budget expenditures.

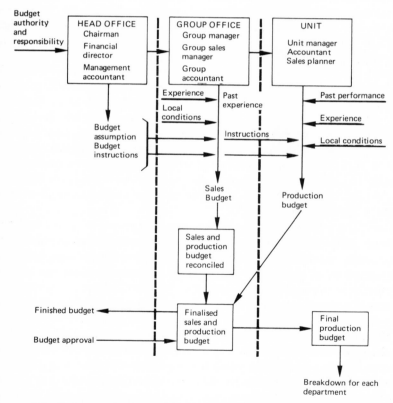

FIGURE 8.3. Budget authority and budget process of company A (adapted from Rahman, M., PhD thesis, Manchester University, England, 1976)

At the unit level, the budgeted production and expenses are broken down to departments and sections. However, elaborate accounting controls did not develop at these lower levels in the units. Managers who tried to institute accounting control at these levels were not successful. The reasons for this may be sought in the following comments of a manager:

> the changes in the supervisory area were not as great as in the management structure, where managers have become more qualified, if you like, more commercially and financially oriented, the shop-floor supervisor is still very much the man who came up from the tough job, and it's a very slow job educating these men.

At the unit levels not all the expense items are controllable by the managers in the same way. There are around 60 items of expenditure which a unit manager is supposed to control. However, the single most important item in terms of the controllability and the amount, is labour cost. Labour and raw material accounts for 80 per cent of the total cost of production.

It may be worth noting that the planning assumptions and the costing formula used for preparing budgets and monitoring expenditures are based on straight-line cost and volume relation. However, this is an inaccurate basis for estimates. The labour is the biggest single item which a manager can influence. However, the managers cannot reduce the labour at the same rate with which the reduction in production may happen. Thus per unit labour cost rises with the fall in production. Pressure from trade unions, fear of losing skilled operatives and government regulations are among the reasons. Again, a greater portion of the fixed costs are beyond the influence of the unit managers. The most important and common example of such costs is depreciation.

Over and above these, in some cases allocations of items and the averaging of the expenses create further problems. In the case of some units accounting results are the allocated and the averaged sums of the performances of more than one unit. In such instances the accounting results belie managers' knowledge of their own performance. As one manager stated:

> allocation could be done any way the accountants wanted to. My allowable expenditure was £1,200 for the following year. I ended up spending only £1,000 according to the accountants. The very next mill, with an allowable expenditure of, say £3,000, ended up spending £2,900 on paper. Both figures look very nice. They would not have caused a second look from anybody high up. The truth of the matter in this instance is that I probably spent half of my budget due to certain factors, and the other mill spent double its budget due to other factors.

The units are subject to detailed evaluation in counts, quality, price and costing. Each month is an accounting period, a monthly trading account for each unit shows its profitability.

The budget performance is reviewed at the head office every half year. This half-yearly budget review explains the wages, prices and expenses. However, the ultimate measurement is profit.

The budget is production-oriented. Sales expenses form a small part of the total expenses. Thus, an elaborate accounting control is not used for sales expenses.

The managers are very much aware of the elements which enter into price quotation which includes their input costs and profit.

Example B

As in any large company, budgeting is the mainspring of accounting control for the company. The budgeting process starts from a long-term projection of sales and profitability. An outline forecast is made for ten years from which the detailed forecast is built for five years. The company, in the outline forecast, projects a total sales demand for ten years and gross estimates of profits. These estimates also include price index forecast to adjust for inflation.

The budgeting process begins in August/September each year and the final approved budgets become available by the end of December. The two components which are the outputs of the budget process are capital budgets and revenue budgets. The process of evaluating capital budget is rather stringent. The flow of budget responsibility and authority is presented in Figure 8.4. The operating budgets are broken down to cost centres and territories. The marketing function is broken down to territories, and the production and research functions are broken down to cost and expense centres.

The sales budget is made for 12 months and is revised every quarter to the next 12 months. The forecast is synthesised into a production budget.

The sales forecast is matched with production capacity which is coordinated by the operations department. Thus, the start of the planning activity in the production is the setting up of a quota which is based on the expected level of outputs of the various products that will be needed for the next budgeting period, on the basis of the sales forecast and planned inventory level. The setting up of the quota is the basis for the preparation of a production budget. The cost elements in the budget are derived from the expected yield for each batch. The product standard cost is based on a batch costing system.

Figure 8.5 shows the production budgeting process which ends up in a

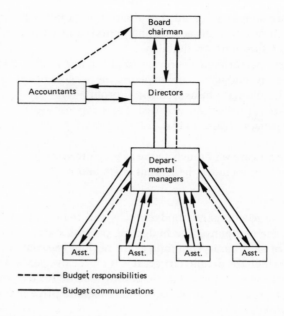

FIGURE 8.4. Budget responsibility and authority of company B and budgetary process

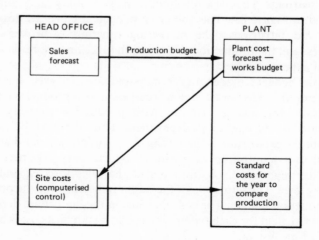

FIGURE 8.5. Production budget process

works budget and site costs—which is the standard cost for the year to compare production with. The budgeting system is a flexible one. However, where changes occur during the year which are not permanent in nature, the budget standards are not altered.

Budgeting as a system of planning and control has its inherent weaknesses, the fundamental of which is the behavioural aspect. This will be discussed in the next chapter. Many new techniques and concepts are now used to overcome many of the shortcomings of budgeting as a planning and controls system. Some of these are (1) flexible budgeting, (2) responsibility budgeting, and (3) bracket budgeting.

(1) Flexible budgeting—budget forecasts are adjusted to the actual level of operations for performance evaluation.

(2) Responsibility budgeting—budgets are segmented as to the nature of responsibility of the manager: (a) accountable budget, (b) partly account- able budget, and (c) allocated budget.

(3) Bracket budgeting—bracket budgeting is a comparatively new tech- nique. It reflects sensitivity of financial results to variation in the major elements in the profit equation. It is an extension of risk analysis.[5]

CHAPTER 8—PROJECTS

1. Beta Pharmaceutical Company evaluates the branch managers' perfor- mance on the basis of return on investment criterion. At the beginning of the year the target return is fixed on the basis of past performance. Managers take their operating decisions freely. For investment decisions they need approval from the head office. Head office has a system of investment proposal evaluation which evaluates the opportunities, risks and future profitability and cash flow. Managers are not always happy with the system.

Questions:

(1) Is return on investment a proper basis for evaluating the managers of the company?
(2) Should head office apply rigid control on investment proposals?
(3) What are the problems that the company is likely to face owing to the present management control system?

2. Performance appraisal for Companies A and B. The two companies have formal systems of performance appraisal for their employees which they do once a year. However, there are some variations between the two systems. Company A has recently set up the system, which is primarily an appraisal interview. This formal interview happens once a year. A subordinate is interviewed by his superior. The basis of interview is the past performance of the subordinate. A wide range of criteria are considered in this interview which include the quantitative and the qualitative criteria such as the attitude of the person, his character, integrity, budget performance etc. The managers are expected to make their recommendations on the basis of these interviews. However, in actual practice the subordinate appraisal is a continuous process. As one manager observed: 'You are actually appraising the people on a day-to-day performance. In your mind you build up the picture of a particular person, what his good points and bad points are'.

Similar to Company A, Company B has a standard appraisal system. It begins with the setting up of the objectives for the people for 12 months. The objectives are agreed between the managers and the subordinates. This is done on a pyramid basis from the bottom to the top of the organisation. The nature and contents of these objectives vary from department to department. For example, a research manager outlined the content of the objectives as:

We have a list of criteria which is more meaningful to working scientists than anyone else. It is concerned with his technical skill in the laboratory, how much direction he needs, how capable he is in the establishment of new techniques, handling new equipment, ability to design experiments, ability to design strategic objectives, how he plans his work in moving towards those objects, the ability to write reports, the ability to communicate, the number of contacts within and external—an overall picture of the person's effectiveness as a scientist.

Again, the list of criteria the marketing managers follow is a different one. A marketing manager included in his list of criteria the following: profit against forecast, sales against forecast, market penetration, and quality of programme and quality of advertisement.

A production manager focuses on a different kind of criterion. He is interested in his subordinates' performance in: establishing new processes for some existing products or a new product, cost reduction, material variance control, etc.

At the end of the year, the performance is discussed at the appraisal meeting with reference to these objectives. The subordinate may agree or disagree with the manager. In the case of disagreement the subordinate is allowed to ask for reassessment. It may be noted that in spite of the simplicity and 'some objectivity' of the system it has some weaknesses. As one manager observed: 'we think the system works well for new managers who are still on the progressing part of their career path. It tends to be a bit hollow for the people who are on the job for 5–10 years'. The fact that the performance appraisal of subordinates involves both qualitative and quantitative aspects is recognised by the managers. However, it is deeper and more complex than it is usually viewed. As one manager observed:

I think our quantitative procedures are very good. The most important ones at this department are qualitative ones. The whole industry is moving away to a new form of industrial relations and the traditional form of management giving way to the participative management, a changing attitude of staff—the whole area is new to us all. Therefore, we have to go very carefully, very slowly, make sure that we are not creating precedents with which we can't live, on the other hand, we are suppressing natural motivations and instincts which we should not be suppressing which are creating resentment among the workforce. I think it is the subjective areas where we would like to have better ability to monitor them, and indeed guidelines are very difficult to find. I think our quantitative procedures are very well worked out. The fact that they are numerical perhaps presses too much attention on it and perhaps too little attention on the very subjective parameters.

Questions:

(1) What measurement problems are the companies likely to face?
(2) Evaluate the similarities and differences in the performance appraisal systems of both the companies.
(3) How do performance evaluation criteria vary from department to department? List possible criteria for performance evaluation of production, marketing, research and accounting personnel and suggest methods of measurement for the criteria listed.

NOTES

1. Lewis, Robert W., 'Measuring Reporting and Appraising Results of Operations with reference to Goals, Plans and Budgets', *Planning Managing and Measuring the Business* (A case study of management planning and control of General Electric Company), New York Controllership Foundation, 1955.

2. Jerome, W. J., *Executive Control—The Catalyst*. New York: Wiley, 1961.
3. Dearden, J., 'Appraising Profit Center Managers', *Harvard Business Review*, May–June 1968.
4. Carvalho, Gerard, *Some Critical Problems Encountered in Installing Management by Objectives: A New Perspective on Organisational Change*. Salt Lake City, Utah: Utah Management Institute,1975.
5. See Curran, H. W., 'How Bracket Budgeting helps Managers Cope with Uncertainty', *Management Review*, April 1975 and May 1975.

BIBLIOGRAPHY

Anthony, R. W., *Planning and Control Systems: A Framework for Analysis*. Division of Research, Graduate School of Business Administration, Harvard University, Boston, 1965.

Barnard, C., *Functions of Executives*. Cambridge, Mass.: Harvard University Press, 1936.

Beer, S., *Decision and Control*. London: Wiley, 1966.

Bonini, C., Jaedicke, R., and Wagner, H., *Management Control: New Direction in Basic Research*. New York: McGraw-Hill, 1964.

Clayden, Roger, 'A New Way to Measure and Control Divisional Performance', *Management Services*, September–October 1970.

Edwards, J. D., and Irvine, V. B., 'MOR and an Objective Accounting System', *Managerial Planning*, January/February 1974.

French, W. L., and Holiman, R. W., 'Management by Objectives: The Team Approach', *California Management Review*, XVII, No. 3 (1975).

Horngren, C. T., *Accounting for Management Control*. Englewood Cliffs, N.J.: Prentice-Hall, 1970.

Humble, J. W., *Management by Objectives in Action*. New York: McGraw-Hill, 1963.

Johnson, R. W., *Financial Management*. Boston: Allyn and Bacon, 1971.

Morrisey, G. L., *Management by Objectives and Result*. Reading, Mass.: Addison-Wesley, 1970.

9 Design of Management Control Information Systems

The management control system is the means by which management control is achieved. Its function is to motivate and guide managers in making decisions in the best interests of the organisation. This relies on a mix of organisational structure and information systems. It is the design of the latter, which cannot for long be divorced from the former, which this chapter addresses.

The scope of management control, its decision types and information characteristics were described in Chapter 3. It became apparent in Chapter 8 that management control faces complexity and uncertainty, relies on judgement and interpersonal interaction, focuses on line management, and seeks goal congruence, however ambiguous organisational goals may be. Management control information is thus both internal and external, broad in scope, sometimes detailed and sometimes aggregated, and equally variable in currency, accuracy and frequency of use. This information serves the twin functions of decision and control.

The complexity of management control comprises complexity of goals, interrelationships and environment. The uncertainty comprises the turbulence of the environment and the unpredictability of responses to control actions. Consequently few management control problems are structured. Many are semi-structured with all three of Simon's phases of intelligence, design and choice being a mix of programmable and non-programmable elements. Therefore many management control information systems tend to be *decision support systems* where man's judgement, insight and evaluative strength are combined with the analytical and processing power of the computer. Indeed the man–machine continuum (Figure 3.6) again provides a useful framework. Management control information systems are rarely machine-dominant, but tend to the left of the continuum because creativity and judgement are as necessary as compliance, and because both formal and informal information flows are essential. Thus the man–

machine interface is commonly with the database. Alternatively where man and machine combine to draw inferences and evaluate alternatives, a predictive model is feasible.

Our prime concern is with design of formal MIS. However, they are only part of the information fabric of management control. In order to provide adaptive responses to instability and change, to ensure flexibility in the face of complexity and uncertainty, and to meet needs of social and self-control, complementary informal MIS are required. Indeed such systems perhaps better suit managers' behaviour, especially their style and use of time.[1]

The principles of MIS design developed in Chapter 3 and the procedures of the systems development life cycle described in Chapter 5 are relevant to management control applications. However, there is as yet not the same confidence about designing MIS for management control, as for operational control. The opening paragraphs of this chapter explain why. In particular, there is no one best design, for the environments are so diverse and the interacting variables so many. A contingency approach seems most appropriate, designing the MIS to fit the circumstances. Certainly models rarely can be borrowed from other organisations, or lifted off the shelf. The task is one of model explication, not application, and of defining information requirements afresh each time.

Thus an understanding of the management control *process* is vital, not only because controls, measurement and information are interdependent, but also because they all function within the context of the organisation's behaviour and in a rapidly changing environment. A decision-oriented framework for management control is therefore developed in the next section, from which design generalisations can be drawn. Essential design principles are then developed, followed by an examination of some crucial issues for the future.

FRAMEWORK FOR DESIGN

Figure 9.1 represents a decision-oriented view of the management control process. Strategic planning, by setting objectives and specifying resources, gives direction to management control. Long-range planning (LRP), by environmental monitoring and formal planning procedures, constructs major programmes to achieve strategic aims and initiates responses to major changes in the external environment. LRP thus defines the key control variables and sets the guidelines, for example target rates of return or market share. Short-term planning (STP) then develops refined operational plans to be achieved over a shorter time-frame, commonly one

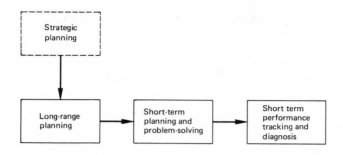

FIGURE 9.1. The management control process

year. It comprises the classical budgeting process, based on hierarchical bilateral commitments, together with irregular problem-solving activities, such as pricing or capital investment appraisal. Thus planning, both long-term and short-term, is inseparably linked with control, setting the sub-goals to be achieved and taking decisions to be monitored. Performance tracking and diagnosis (PTD) then takes over by measurement and reporting—or tracking and diagnosis—of subsequent performance.

These three activities thus make up the management control process, each having its own information requirements, each in turn refining the control variables.

LONG-RANGE PLANNING

LRP is a formal planning process of scanning, forecasting and decision-making which sets the global, and primarily externally-derived, premises for subsequent shorter-term control. It also includes continual monitoring of those external variables which the organisation cannot influence but whose impact may be significant, such as competitor innovation or government legislation.

Scanning in LRP is confined to the substantial environment, namely that part of the environment which affects, or is affected by, the organisation, (Figure 9.2) in the shorter time-span of management control. Information inputs therefore include: market statistics and trends, competitor information, customer information, supplier information, general economic indicators, technological change, product innovations, cost trends, government and political action, and industry practice. The sources are varied, mainly being publications and meetings plus informal contacts and

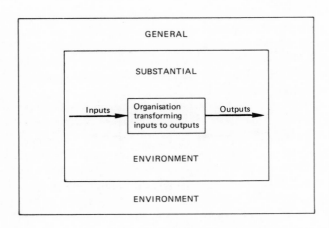

FIGURE 9.2. The substantial environment of long-range planning[2]

hearsay.[3] This informal intelligence is generally part of a structured process which includes subsequent analysis, interpretation and presentation.

Forecasting depends on more formal information systems. Three classes of forecast are used: (1) global economic forecasts; (2) industry or market forecasts; and (3) local forecasts. Generally the macro-level forecasts will be bought, often by subscription, or by access to commercially available database enquiry systems. Local forecasts, for example sales forecasts, will be constructed in-house commonly using one of the following four methods:[4]

(1) Time series analyses giving trends, highlighting cycles and fluctuations, and indicating leads and lags.
(2) Regression analyses to determine interrelationships between the forecast variable and other independent variables (with correlation coefficients and standard errors).
(3) Adaptive forecasting, or exponential smoothing, giving simple, cheap and routine forecasts with flexible weighting to recent events.
(4) Informal forecasting, such as sales predictions, from internal data and judgement.

Decision-making is concerned with analysing these information inputs, strategic directives and occasional internal feedbacks, and evaluating alternative plans. Increasingly corporate planning models are used, varying the assumptions about key factors and asking 'what-if' questions. Use of both deterministic and probablistic models[5] allows the uncertainties of the external and internal environments to be assessed and aids the search for, and testing of, alternatives. Without such computer models, LRP decision-making has often proved too slow, inconsistent, error-prone and simplistic. In this task, the models are serving as much as a communications device as a decision support system.

LRP is thus mainly dependent upon informal information or intelligence, derived from the strategic planning process or culled from the business environment. This intelligence may then be stored and processed in formal database, enquiry and reporting systems. The subsequent planning process may well employ formal forecasting and decision support systems which will be very much man–machine systems relying on managerial experience and judgement, and operating in tandem with informal, less structured decision-making.

SHORT-TERM PLANNING

Budgeting and problem-solving demand forecasts from LRP, recent trends from the management control and operational control database, and judgements and predictions from managers. The process is thus data-processing intensive, often in iterative, interactive and enquiry mode, requiring considerable coordination, and frequent revision. So formal MIS, such as cost accounting systems, are a necessary support.

Since short-term plans become the sub-goals or standards of control, it is vital that they are as valid and robust as possible. Computer simulation models therefore are increasingly relevant, enabling management to assess risk, react to change, test interrelationships, consider more variables and apply their own judgement. Such models are equally appropriate for problem-solving, improving decision rules, and evaluating alternatives. Examples are pricing models for examination of the interrelationships between price, volume, competitor reaction, promotion and other marketing variables, capital investment appraisal models for assessment of risk and uncertainty in cost, revenue and other functions, and budgeting models for exploration of alternative volumes, market share, cost behaviour, inflation rates and the like.

Such is the complexity and uncertainty inherent in these tasks, and so dependent are they on managerial judgement, that optimisation models are of limited value. However, such models may assist in formulation of policies and decision rules, for example indicating optimal policies for production planning or distribution. Linear programming models are the commonest.

PERFORMANCE TRACKING AND DIAGNOSIS

Tracking is the measurement of *actual* performance, whilst diagnosis is the analysis of any deviation from plan, determining how much deviation is controllable, who might be responsible and what is the cause. Much tracking and diagnosis is shaped by hierarchical organisation structure in the form of responsibility accounting—departmental cost reporting, standard costing, divisional performance measurement and the like—but can also focus on lateral, global, matrix and other alternative decision and control structures.

MIS do much of the tracking and aid the diagnosis, thereby providing the feedbacks of control. The conventional feedback loop initiates corrective action if deviation occurs; the adaptive feedback loop triggers amendment of short-term plans or standards where corrective action is an inadequate response to the variance; the third feedback loop is a less frequent, but sometimes necessary, response to severe or uncontrollable deviations, and triggers modification of long-range plans. These three feedback loops may derive from the same controls; it is the transmission of the information messages and their absorption into the three decision processes which the MIS has to ensure.

Measurement, diagnosis and feedback are the stuff of controls. Thus design of information systems and design of controls are inextricably linked. Chapter 8 emphasised that measurement must satisfy criteria of validity, stability, sufficiency, objectivity, appropriateness, congruence and controllability. Information designed without attention to these criteria can be quite dysfunctional to control. Indeed *potential* tracking data is often over-abundant and must be carefully selected, for focusing on a new variable may give it undue emphasis, assumptions (especially of the immeasurable) may not be explicit, qualitative measurement may be dominated by the quantifiable, or obvious indicators may be crude and do great harm. Often 20 per cent of available information will cover 80 per cent of key areas.[6] Conversely, sometimes critical feedback is hidden in less obvious functions. Above all, the ready availability of internal information may lead to vital external information being ignored. The boundaries of control do not follow those of the organisation, but extend into the substantial environment. External variables, especially those which interact with internal variables, are perhaps the most influential on ultimate performance.

Diagnosis is just as problematic. The aim is to identify and convey causality, controllability and responsibility. Building causality into PTD is confounded by the multiplicity of interacting variables at work. Thus 'effective causality' often must suffice, measuring surrogates and symptoms, expressed in financial terms, and relying on managers' own diagnoses, sometimes aided by analytical tools. Where its use can be guaranteed, elaborate and informative variance coding can be built into data collection, especially if mechanised.

Report information is often too superficial to indicate controllability. For instance a purchasing manager once claimed that all his import raw material price variances were uncontrollable because of constant currency escalation. What the MIS failed to do was monitor his forecasting ability properly, calculate the opportunity cost of his forecasting error, and evaluate his decision-making model. The purchasing manager in fact could have changed his raw material source to a country of weaker currency, but the inadequacies of the MIS reinforced the 'uncontrollable' syndrome and never encouraged the search. For this reason Demski and others have proposed use of optimisation models in diagnosis.[7] Using ex-post values of inputs, in other words hindsight, the model is run to produce the optimal solution. The actual performance is then compared with the model's solution and control decisions analysed, and adaptive responses initiated to formerly 'uncontrollable' conditions. Certainly simulation models can be used as diagnostic tools to discover and evaluate remedies to deviations in performance.

Responsibility reporting and accounting is largely a matter of providing PTD information to fit the organisational design. However, programme responsibility, typical of matrix organisations for example, may not match hierarchical responsibility structure. Thus two sets of information flows may be required. Equally the information required for decision-making can cut across that required for control, so that yet another flow is necessary. Add the growing conviction that information for budgetary planning may conflict with that embodying motivational factors for budgetary control, and still another dimension is introduced. Fortunately computers have made multi-purpose and multi-flow information systems feasible.

Indeed computer systems hold great promise in PTD. They can provide the hierarchy of control and decision reporting described in Chapter 8. As uncertainty and rate of change accelerate, real-time computing can enable information frequency to keep in step. Likewise enquiry systems provide the information flexibility which increased complexity demands, whilst the needs of coordination and integration may be met by the information interrelationships which database technology affords. Furthermore computers may make the concept of requisite variety feasible.[8] Tracking recorders can become more extensive and continuous in coverage, whilst filtration can become more sensitive by event and time-triggered exception reporting, together with improved tests of significance.

Yet more controls and information do not guarantee motivation and action. Maybe half of management control information is unused.[9] Therefore we need to study the use as well as the provision of information. Behavioural factors explain why action-oriented budget reports often are more effective when manually produced, why tracking and diagnosis is often informal and why much control information is abused or unused.

SYNTHESIS

Figure 9.1 can now be updated with the information flows and processing that this decision-oriented view of management control has uncovered (Figure 9.3). MIS provide information and feedback which, when combined with organisational structure, form a management control system. Both formal and informal MIS are required to match the structured and unstructured problems which the uncertainty and complexity of management control present.

Four types of formal MIS can be distinguished:

(1) Database systems comprising detailed internal data from operational control and the aggregate and external data specific to management control. Examples are cost accounting systems or marketing information systems.

(2) Enquiry systems allowing pre-planned and ad hoc interrogation of database systems. Examples include enquiry of commercially available forecasting databases, or inter-active enquiry of costing systems.

(3) Monitoring and reporting systems which track and report on the organisation's activities and environment. Examples include standard costing or budgetary control systems.

(4) Computer-based models allowing exploration of alternatives and consequences under probabilistic conditions. Examples include budgeting or capital investment appraisal models.

As Chapter 3 suggested 'computability' is limited in management control. However, computer assistance is becoming more essential in order to raise the information thresholds that management control today demands. Evidence for this claim includes:

(1) Growth in use of models.
(2) Need for multi-dimensional information flows.
(3) Need for multi-purpose databases.

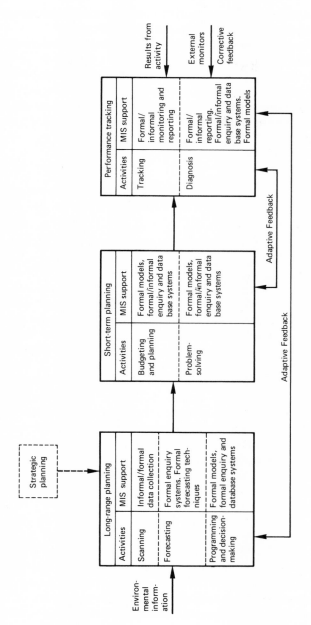

FIGURE 9.3. The management control process—MIS support

(4) Growth of more complex variance reporting and analysis.

(5) Need for greater variety in tracking recorders.

(6) Need for information filtering, especially by exception reporting and significance testing.

(7) Need for greater information frequency in the face of change and uncertainty.

(8) Need for more frequent revision of plans.

(9) Aid in design of control systems.

(10) Need for more flexible enquiry systems.

(11) Growth of new analytical techniques.

(12) Development of, and need for, new report/output media and mechanisms.

(13) Need for improved data validity and accuracy.

Whatever technological advances are made, however, the MIS design process will remain crucial. The overriding aims of management control, namely to pursue goal congruence, to motivate managerial action and to ensure a viable organisation, demand great sensitivity in MIS design. We must be concerned with information use, as well as with its provision, and with organisational development as well as information design. This synthesis provides the backcloth against which the next two sections on models and the design process can be examined.

MODELS

Use of models in both decision and control is growing rapidly. Intuition, experience and rules of thumb are no longer a match for today's complexity and uncertainty; analysis, exploration and understanding are also required. Models are bridging this gap.

DEFINITIONS

A model is a simplified abstraction of reality, for example the geographer's map or the architect's scale model. Business models are mathematical approximations, sets of related expressions that represent the key operations of the organisation. Often they are little more than accounting statements linked in a straightforward way, yet they can be very effective. They are computer-based, employing the processing power of the computer and thereby enhancing the manager's analytical ability with time and cost savings and flexible input/output mechanisms. They allow the manager to recreate part of his environment at low cost, nil risk, in a simplified way and in a problem-solving manner. Examples of both long-range planning and short-term planning models were briefly described in the previous section.[10]

Computer-based models may be classified into:

(1) Optimisation models which derive the best solution for a given set of assumptions in terms of a precise objective function. Linear programming, integer-programming and dynamic programming models are examples.
(2) Simulation models which imitate the behaviour of key operations (analogous to wind-tunnel experiments) to explore the outcome of different conditions and relationships.

Simulation models may be divided into:

(1) Deterministic models which assume certainty, by only allowing single-point estimates for each important variable, for example one sales forecast in a budgeting model.
(2) Probabilistic models which incorporate uncertainty by allowing multiple-point estimates and including probability frequencies for the important variables, as shown in the example of a capital investment simulation in Figure 9.4.

It is possible with most types of model to assess risk by sensitivity analysis. In optimisation models, the coefficients of variables can be 'wobbled'. In deterministic models, several runs with different values can be arranged to ask 'what-if' questions. In probabilistic models, risk and uncertainty can be incorporated in the model's structure.

Many computer-based models are run in batch mode with no conversational man–machine interaction. Increasingly, however, where time-shared computing is available, interactive decision support systems are used. The flexible and rapid dialogue which these provide allow the manager and the model to 'learn' together, redefining objectives, reshaping the problem and creating new alternatives. However, many of the other benefits attributed to interaction, for example using managers' own data, estimates and assumptions as the circumstances demand, apply to all models. A computer-based model generally comprises all the components of Figure 9.5, although with the availability of dedicated mini- and micro-computers, the terminal, communication link and computer become one.

The advantages of computer models in management decision and control include:

(1) Ability to explore complex interrelationships.
(2) Ability to assess risk and uncertainty.

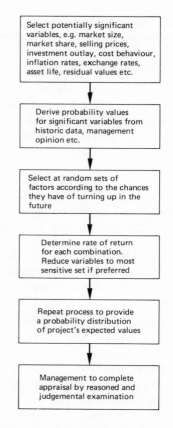

FIGURE 9.4. Simulation in capital investment appraisal

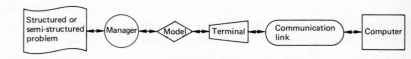

FIGURE 9.5. A computer-based modelling system

(3) Flexibility in the face of change.
(4) Speed, cost and accuracy from mechanisation.
(5) Ability to handle optimising or less structured problems.

(6) Ability to distil key aspects.
(7) Opportunity for understanding, learning and insight.
(8) An aid to communication between decision-makers.
(9) Release of managerial time for strategic and analytical thinking.
(10) Ability to consider longer futures.
(11) A method of checking decision-making consistency.
(12) Ability to handle complex calculations.

The limitations include:

(1) Risk of emphasising the quantifiable at the expense of the qualitative.
(2) Limited to what they are designed for.
(3) Sensitive to quality of data and estimates.
(4) Can become passive rather than creative.
(5) May overlook the politics of decision-making.
(6) May be abused in the politics of decision-making.
(7) Dependence on data availability.
(8) May demand special hardware and software.

These limitations are not generally sufficient to deter model development, for essentially computer models are simple devices—or should be—despite their powerful impact. The benefits are not guaranteed, however; the design process, examined in detail later, is crucial.

MODEL DEVELOPMENT

Computer-based models either can be purchased or built in-house, using one of the following four approaches:

(1) Packaged models can be bought from computer manufacturers, software houses or bureaux. Optimisation models are freely available, simulation models less so. Packages are likely to be either so general that they tackle simple problems, or so specialised that they meet few users' requirements. However, they provide an easy and available induction to modelling, from which users can progress. Most packaged simulation models are financially oriented.

(2) Modelling systems are commercially available high-level programming systems. Increasingly popular, they comprise sub-routines, utilities, and macros which users customise to their own requirements through parameter selection, interactive dialogue and occasional user coding. Examples are STRATPLAN, ORACLE and PROSPER which are typical of the financial and corporate planning orientation that modelling systems

generally adopt. They do not depend on specialist programming skills and can now be developed and operated by managers. However, they may be locked-in to commercial bureaux.

(3) In-house model development by simulation language is more dependent on specialist programming skills. In return more complex, tailor-made models can be built. SIMSCRIPT, GPSS and DYNAMO are well-known examples which are easier to use than conventional programming languages, as they give guidance on model construction, incorporate input/output and statistical routines, and provide diagnostic facilities.

(4) In-house model development by conventional programming is the most specialist-dependent route. Languages such as FORTRAN, PL/1, or APL are used. Their advantage is compatibility with local standards, interface capability with other systems, and lack of design constraints.

These four routes to model development are compared against several criteria in Table 9.1. Discernible trends[11, 12] in model development are:

(1) Development of custom-built rather than packaged models.
(2) Use of modelling systems rather than general-purpose languages.
(3) Use of simulation rather than optimisation models.
(4) Use of deterministic rather than probabilistic models.
(5) Use of planning and problem-solving rather than control models (that is LRP and STP rather than PTD support).
(6) Use of both batch and conversational mode with movement towards the latter.
(7) Emphasis on financial rather than physical models.
(8) Emphasis on meta-models rather than disaggregated models, but extension into the latter.
(9) More user development and operation as well as specialist-dependence.
(10) Use of specialists in advisory/training roles.

The route to model development and the selection of model type should be a managerial decision. Models are manager-dependent; they should be simple, robust, understood, available and meet the circumstances. Above all they should be *used*; thus model selection cannot be solely a specialists' decision.

The preference for simulation models reflects the mismatch between optimisation models and management control. A precise objective function is rarely apparent, interrelationships are too complex, the variables are too probabilistic, the data is too approximate, and reactions of managerial

TABLE 9.1. Routes to model development

Criterion	General-purpose language model	Simulation language model	Modelling system	Package model
Operating mode	Batch or conversational	Batch or conversational	Batch or conversational	Batch or conversational
Computer used	Own or bureau	Own or bureau	Own or bureau; often bureau	Own or bureau
Size and complexity	Few constraints	Few constraints	More constraints	Many constraints
Programming skills required	High	Medium to high	Medium to low	Low
Speed of development	Slow	Medium	Fast	Very fast
Cost of development	High	Medium to low	Medium to low	Variable
Cost of operation	Low	Medium	High	Medium to high
Fit with local needs	High	High	Medium	Low
System interfaces	High	High	Medium to Low	Low
Ease of use	Variable	Variable	High to medium	High
Supporting facilities, e.g. forecasting	Extra development	Extra development	Often available	Available but separate
Ease of updating	Medium to low	Medium to low	Medium to high	Low

experience are required. Managers seem to prefer simulation models because:

(1) They are more intelligible.
(2) They express complexity more easily.
(3) Competing objectives and constraints can be flexibly weighted by the manager not the model.
(4) Thus objectives are implicit in the alternatives chosen.
(5) Ranges of solutions are available.
(6) Risk and uncertainty is better handled.
(7) The simulation process is one of learning and insight.

Despite management control's uncertainties, however, managers seem to prefer deterministic to probabilistic simulations. Reasons include:

(1) Model cost—since many more instructions and iterations are involved in probabilistic models.
(2) Difficulty in understanding and interpreting probabilistic models.
(3) Difficulty or reluctance in supplying probabilistic estimates and ranges.
(4) Difficulty in empirically establishing probability distributions.
(5) Closer coincidence between deterministic models and conventional logic.
(6) Ability to do backwards iteration, or normative planning, for example determining what levels of sales etc. are required to achieve certain profit targets.
(7) Ability to perform sensitivity analysis by multiple runs of deterministic models with different inputs.

Where sums at risk are large, then probabilistic simulations are preferable. However, in many cases, simple deterministic models provide sufficient insight, and the users feel more comfortable. Such models have been built in two to three days or less by using modelling systems. A corporate planning model can be developed for as little as £1000, and few models cost more than £10,000.

MODELLING TRENDS

Who designs, develops and operates the model? Design decisions are the user's responsibility, although specialist advice may be necessary. Specialists will normally develop the models, though the user may be involved if modelling systems are used. Modelling systems have fused together design and development, since they guide the design within established architecture. The modelling process is examined in depth in the next section.

Evidence is less clear on who operates the model. The input, alternatives and iterations should be user-controlled. However, direct interaction between the manager and the model is rare in practice. Assistants usually operate the model, advising and consulting the user on each step.[13] Even under conversational modelling, managers often prefer straightforward alternative testing to interactive dialogue.[14] Such processes are consistent with traditional managerial decision-making practice, where advice is taken from staff. As long as the manager takes the final decision with full insight, the model has served its purpose. The intermediary becomes another component of the decision support system.

Models are commonly regarded as purpose-built systems. However, continued usage brings demands for flexibility in:

(1) Structure, so that interfaces can be built between the model and other models, systems and routines such as forecasting and statistical packages.
(2) Logic, so that changes can be easily accommodated or the model enjoy wider usage.
(3) Input, so that data can be input in different forms, units, trends, rates, changes, ranges, etc.—and by different media.
(4) Output, so that report formats can be changed, reports selected and alternative media, such as graphical devices, used.

Such refinements must be rigorously justified, because a major attraction of models is their simple construction and ready availability.

One interesting aspect of flexibility, however, is usage of models for purposes not originally envisaged. Examples include a production manager's optimisation model being used to persuade a marketing manager to seek orders which would use the plant more effectively, a company's capital budgeting model being used to persuade banks to provide finance, and a corporate planning model being used by a managing director to evaluate his managers' performance.

Alter[15] has classed such uses of models as 'offensive' or 'defensive'. His use of these terms is interesting, as it suggests that models may be used as weapons in attaining manager's goals, as well as serving as tools for devising them. Perhaps this indicates a change in the status of models, from being innovations towards being routine. It is probably a sign of maturity in model usage.

Another trend is to seek integration between models. Disaggregation of corporate financial models into divisional or to forecasting models and databases is another. Certainly access to more relevant input data, 'devolution' towards the workface and the ability to reconcile top-down and bottom-up decision-making are attractive ideas which are likely to gain increasing acceptance. However, in uncertain environments and with such approximate data, models perhaps should not be too tightly coupled; nor should they become too complex. Often simple manual interfaces suffice and are more flexible.

Finally, concern about security of models is growing. Output reports such as draft company plans can be highly sensitive. Thus limited access, through password protection and the like is preferred, and if external computer bureaux are used data files can be deleted after each run.

A MODEL-BASE

Computer-based models have become part of the kit of management control, combining man and machine to grapple with an unstable and complex problem-space. Yet they represent a process rather than a technique, for the manager directs, controls and manipulates the model as a learning and educative system. The model's output is never sacrosanct. Indeed preference for deterministic models emphasises that they are tools for the manager, not mechanistic automated problem-solvers. Models serve managers by helping the decision process, not by providing more and more information.

The concept of the *model-base* is therefore attractive. This is a decision support inventory of models, modelling systems and languages, analytical and forecasting routines, and enquiry links into the database. To prevent the concept being taken over by technical specialists, four rules are apparent and will be developed in the next section:

(1) Models should be sponsored, supported and controlled by managers.
(2) Models should be simple and available, serving specific and significant decision-making needs.
(3) Models should be firmly embedded in the decision and control process; otherwise they will be cosmetic.
(4) Models should be seen as learning enablers, not problem-solvers.

THE DESIGN PROCESS

Whilst the arena of management control is generally less structured than in operational control and the supporting information systems more diverse, system development is nevertheless amenable to, and benefits from, a systematic approach. The systems development life cycle outlined in Chapter 5 is applicable; only certain emphases and skills differ. For example, faced with less structured decisions, model explication becomes a key task of system analysis. Since management's own control systems are being designed, manager participation is essential. Because of the many interrelationships of management control, a holistic approach—'systems thinking'—is required. As system success is dependent upon the managerial behaviour it stimulates, sensitive implementation becomes crucial. Finally pragmatism is necessary, for design is concerned with effectiveness as much as with efficiency. Thus systems thinking, modelling and participation are examined below. Firstly, certain other nuances of the management control system development life cycle are considered.

SYSTEMS DEVELOPMENT LIFE CYCLE

The feasibility study must involve managers. Often the MIS is directed and designed at too low a level where perspectives are limited and cost–benefit analysis is unrealistic. Benefit streams tend to be uncertain in timing and gradual or unpredictable in nature. Thus continuous monitoring is essential.

Whilst systems analysis is a critical phase, system design is often undervalued. The flexibility that management control requires places considerable demands on database design, enquiry facilities and system modularity. Output design, which should aim to stimulate management action or enquiry, can be a skilled task. Likewise efficient processing is essential in any interactive MIS, such as models or enquiry facilities.

System implementation, because of its organisational consequences, is a critical phase. Besides effects on individual jobs and the problem of introducing change, power balances may be disturbed, authority structures altered—especially between superior and subordinate—and organisational boundaries crossed. Very often it is beneficial to retain some familiar procedures, confining change to where it really matters. Local, unofficial and private routines, procedures and systems present a challenge. On the one hand, some may need to be expunged so as not to harm the momentum of the new MIS. In other cases they should be retained as more effective, sensitive or economical systems—and also to encourage adaptation in the future.

Organisations often expect too much, too quickly, of management control information systems. Such are the complexities of the control process, that a two- to three-year implementation period may not be excessive. There are many instances of 'failed' systems which were killed off or discredited too soon; the PPBS experience of United States federal agencies is perhaps an example.[16] It should be explicitly recognised by all that management control information systems generally succeed where development and implementation are gradual and evolutionary; in short it is a learning process. Nevertheless, MIS should be monitored to ensure the potential is being realised and that both the organisation and the system do learn from experience. Furthermore as the environment, and thus the key control variables, change, the MIS must keep in step. It is ironic that management control systems which centre on feedback principles frequently provide no feedback on themselves.

SYSTEMS THINKING

Optimisation is not possible in management control. The complexity of interdependence and interrelationships in organisational decision-making prohibit it, the conflicting organisational loyalties, values and thus goals prevent it, and the need to decompose organisations into manageable parts hinders it. Thus suboptimisation is inevitable. The aim in management control systems design is thus to *minimise* sub-optimisation. Systems thinking provides a valuable conceptual and practical framework in this task.

Systems thinking forces us to consider the likely interactions of our design. Control variables *within* a system interact so that introduction of a new control may reduce the impact of another. Control variables *between* systems interact so that, for instance, rigid pursuit of production targets may result in industrial relations inflexibility. Control variables *outside* our systems interact so that an external event, say competitor innovation, may render our internal controls useless.

Three further attributes of systems are relevant. The *boundary* must be defined with care, not only to ensure all significant variables are included, but because, inevitably, the system we define is a construct meeting the purpose in hand. The boundaries therefore should be continuously reviewed and of course interaction across them be explored. Then the system's *function* must be defined. Despite conflicting goals, an explicit understanding of the system's objectives and constraints is required in order to direct design and monitor performance. Finally the system *level* is important. Many 'control in the small' systems, such as functionally oriented, responsibility-oriented or programme-oriented MIS, are themselves subsystems of a 'control in the large' system. The interaction should be examined, and in designing the large or meta-system, conflict resolution and sub-optimisation-minimising devices should be incorporated.

The *industrial dynamics*[17] approach can be used to make these concepts happen. One such project at MIT found that in many organisations systems design was in fact causing disequilibrium and creating new control problems. Industrial dynamics modelling can be used to describe, hypothesise and test interactions between programmed decision rules and non-programmed actions, between subsystem and subsystem, between control in the small and control in the large. It seeks by experimentation, rather than hit-and-miss design, to identify the important variables and relationships.

The technique has been used in designing performance and tracking systems. Industrial dynamics assumes PTD behaviour[18] as in Figure 9.6,

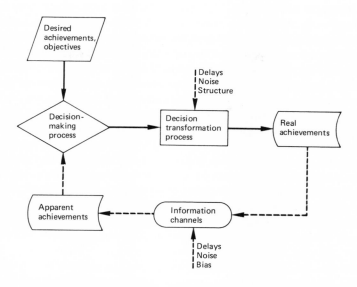

FIGURE 9.6. Control system structure—industrial dynamics view

and then by constructing a descriptive simulation model, experiments with typical data and typical managerial responses. Bonini[19] examined control in the large by this method, observing how different information flows and decision rules affected organisational performance. In the firm he studied, overall performance was found to improve not when the environment was stable, but when conditions were variable. Another unexpected discovery was that whilst tight production standards reduced costs, sales also decreased. However, when production standards were loose and costs were high, sales rose in compensation. Such surprising behavioural discoveries are typical and have stimulated further experimentation on the interaction between controls and behaviour, for example evaluating different approaches to transfer pricing.

Industrial dynamics is one example of how the process of building such a simulation model is in essence no different from that of building decision support systems; in this case the alternatives being evaluated are different system designs.

MODELLING

Little[20] suggested some reasons why models are not used more widely: (1)

good models are hard to find, particularly models which contain the manager's control variables, have direct implications for action and attack significant problems; (2) good parameterisation is even harder, particularly measurements and data; (3) managers do not understand the models, in particular they reject complexity they cannot grasp. What is clear from such diagnosis is the importance of *modelling* rather than of models. Establish a sound modelling process and models will improve.

Modelling, like MIS design in general, is a creative process but requires a disciplined approach. The support managers require is not technical; it is aid in eliciting their views—their implicit models—of their organisation and its environment. A proven approach is represented in Figure 9.7. This process is iterative. Construction of successful models usually requires at least two complete iterations. Since objectives may not be at all precise at the outset, it is not unusual to begin by deriving a descriptive model and specifying objectives subsequently.

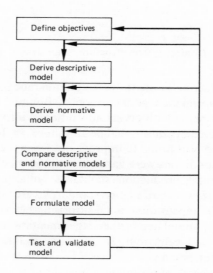

FIGURE 9.7. Modelling process

The descriptive model is built by the manager describing the system as he currently understands it. He is generally helped by a specialist who will flowchart the description, narrate it or translate it into formulae. The specialist's task is to question and probe the manager's assumptions, intuition and rules of thumb, to sketch and amend the picture, to apply common-sense and experience, to clarify and then improve the manager's view. At first only the essentials are captured, any assumptions and simplifications being made explicit. When the manager begins to recognise things previously unrealised, the explication is working.

Once the manager and specialist agree upon the descriptive state, a normative model is constructed. This represents the way things ought to be, drawing from theory, practices in other organisations, consultants recommendations, special analyses and other available sources. A normative solution may be impossible but it is pursued via normative goals, until a desirable solution is achieved. Once derived, this ideal is compared with the descriptive model and gaps analysed and explored, defining the key elements, relationships and functions the eventual model will incorporate.

The design or formulation of the model should aim to make the model an extension of the manager, by incorporating his special requirements, being easy to use, control and adapt, and yet being robust in operation. Some elements may not be fully understood by the manager—especially mathematical equations, probability distributions and the like—but he should appreciate their function.

Finally, testing and validation should be as rigorous as possible. Approaches include:[21] empirical testing with live data; using historical data to compare the models results with historical outputs; other research and experiments; using prototypes; field testing. It is likely that if the results do not meet initial expectations, the model will be ridiculed. The manager then should be asked to test the model—his model, his assumptions and his data—further. Of course, since managers prefer simple models at first, the initial results may be poor. Confronted by questionable output, the iteration and evolution towards a more realistic model begins. The decision on when to stop developing the model further also becomes iterative. If a tractable model is constructed, then enrich it; if it is intractable simplify it. Finally if results still amaze the user, it may be salutary to remember that surprise content is one indicator of valuable information.

Clearly modelling is a joint process. The model's source is the manager. The specialist provides the modelling equipment and strives for explication. He helps the manager to identify key variables, to factor the problem, to build it up again, to provide the parameters and to understand the end result—in other words he enables the manager to overcome the problems which Little reported. Modelling is a process of analysis, education and decision.

Rules for success therefore are:

(1) Keep the model simple—within the managers' experience and grasp, avoiding quantum jumps.

(2) Tackle significant problems—tackling complexity in incremental stages.

(3) Ensure managers design the model—assisted by specialist enablers.

(4) Rigorously test and adjust the model—using it whenever opportunity allows, and maintaining it as factors change.

(5) Document the model—managers move on and successors may wish to use it.

Finally it must be emphasised that a model which is simple, meets the manager's needs, and is used is to be preferred to one which is sophisticated, complex, not understood and therefore ignored. This does not mean model efficiency is unimportant; once 'converted' to models, managers expect rapid response times, easy formatting and reliability.

JOINT DESIGN

Arguments for joint manager–specialist systems design were advanced in Chapter 3. Participative design of management control information systems is essential. By themselves, MIS cannot control; their role is to help managers in the management control process, providing information, improving decision-making and stimulating action. So, unless these MIS serve managers' real needs and are actively used by managers, they are worthless.

Only managers themselves can be sure of their own needs; and managers are no different from others—if they are involved in design, they are more likely to use the system and use it properly. Indeed, information is so vital to the management control process, it cannot be left to specialists in particular techniques and technology to design it. Furthermore as the control task grows more complex, the experience and views of managers are an invaluable and necessary source of relevant ideas. Indeed, managers' own unofficial and private systems designed in their own interest are often more impressive than the official systems supposedly controlling the business. Furthermore managers in the classroom have been found to specify highly effective and often complex controls and control systems.

Examples outside the classroom also exist. In a hospital a management control system designed by systems experts stressed financial control. The MIS was effective in that costs were controlled. However, medical service deteriorated and innovation was curtailed. When medical staff were involved in design, medical and nursing variables, as well as financial controls, were made visible by the MIS. Consequently both financial and medical performance improved.

In many practical situations, the manager himself is the main source of data. He has the problem, and the responsibility to solve it. So he must have a dominant role in devising the model which is to help generate the solution. This will not only ensure the validity of the model, but will also increase the manager's confidence in it.

In many cases, especially in the design of performance tracking and diagnosis systems, multi-level management participation is required. Performance measurement, however, raises many issues of superior-subordinate relationships and of crossed boundaries. Disagreement on what are key variables, what is relevant information and what are the measurement implications are just as likely between managers themselves, as between manager and specialists.[22]

Possible devices and processes for joint design were explored in Chapter 3.

DESIGN FOR TOMORROW

In conclusion, six current issues are addressed, resolution of which will guide future design of management control information systems. This is by no means speculative: both research and experience are rapidly indicating directions for future design.

FORMAL AND INFORMAL

Management control is dependent upon both formal and informal information systems. Designers must recognise this and develop judgement on where to draw the boundary between the two. Because informal systems are spontaneous, they provide flexibility and adaptation. They often collect, store and transmit information which is more current, concise, significant and outward looking than that provided by formal systems. Because of their social milieu, they can convey nuances which the formal system cannot handle, but they also suffer from consequent noise, bias and amplification.

Managers often are information manipulators who work in a stimulus–response environment favouring live action, being receptive to gossip and preferring verbal channels.[23] Managers thus find informal systems comfortable. Formal systems, especially if computer-based, cannot handle such characteristics, nor can designers easily gain access to such managerial preferences, or predict their occurrence. What is more, systematic procedures often are inappropriate for the ambiguity of management control and offer weak protection against unpredictability. For example, in long-range planning, formal and systematic procedures may be so constraining—or even overlook the obvious by slavish addiction to extrapolative forecasts—that they can be dysfunctional. Grinyer and Norburn[24] found no correlation between formal planning procedures and financial performance across 21 companies; instead informality and diversity of information seemed the critical variable. Formal systems can all-too-readily incorporate static assumptions, or designers' assumptions, about the external and internal environments.

Furthermore, social control and self-control is perhaps better served by informal information. The functions being controlled may themselves comprise largely informal behaviour—for example, workplace industrial relations. One significant trend may be the development of formal information systems under informal (that is self- or social-) control, such as the workshop control information systems controlled by work groups at the Volvo car-plant at Kalmar in Sweden. So it is likely that informal information systems will often capture the essential characteristics of management control better than formal systems. The information super-structure is provided by formal systems; informal information systems are complementary and compensatory, filling in the interstices which formal systems cannot handle and providing adaptation over time. Informal systems should be reviewed periodically to ensure that the boundaries are optimal—see Chapter 11.

Finally, intermediate systems between the formal and informal have been proposed. Typically they would comprise specialist intelligence officers scanning the internal and external environment and presenting messages in the managerial idiom. This is not a helpful idea; this intermediate system would be part formal and part informal—just as are many information systems. What is more, by creating an extra interface, another set of assumptions intrudes. The challenge is not to devise another type of system, but to recognise when an information system should be formal or informal.

LINKAGES AND COUPLINGS

Management control is dependent upon linkages and couplings—linkages to planning, to operations and to the external environment, and couplings between subsystems and between functions. How tight should these associations be?

Long-range planning represents a positive attitude to both the future and to an unstable environment. By setting the control variables, defining expectations to be achieved and monitoring the environment, it becomes firmly embedded in the management control process. This linkage tightens as it demands feedback and forward-looking attitudes from short-term planning and control. To be manageable in practice, this tight linkage demands organisational devolution such as responsibility accounting,[25] and perhaps integrative devices such as matrix structures.[26] Thus the linkage between planning, control and action is dependent upon a strong fabric of both information and organisation structure.

Performance tracking and diagnosis implies linkage between management control and operations. This linkage is beset by difficulties of establishing causality in variances and of ensuring sufficiently rapid responses. Accordingly, tighter coupling between operational control and management control systems may be required, despite the differing nature of their activities. On the other hand loose coupling may be more flexible and allow the intervention of managerial judgement which management control requires. The more stable and predictable the environment of the firm, the greater is the chance of a successful system of tight coupling.

Early concepts of management control systems suggested the need for an integrated MIS ensuring goal congruence. The reality is that such tight coupling is impossible and that task specialisation and decentralisation, with some consequent sub-optimisation, is inevitable. Therefore a loosely coupled set of management control subsystems is a more tenable concept, but it should be designed with due attention to system interactions, and supported by organisational mechanisms for conflict resolution.

ACCOUNTING AND CONTROL

It is not unusual to encounter organisations that see management control and accounting as synonymous. Certainly accounting has contributed much to control, whilst financial control systems will continue to be important. However, accounting information has limitations and over-reliance on it is liable to be dysfunctional. Reasons include the following:

(1) Accounting inadequately reflects the multi-dimensional nature of control problems.
(2) Accounting is generally internally oriented; furthermore accounting devices linking into the environment are rarely used e.g. sales variances.
(3) Accounting practice often ignores its social context.

(4) Accounting controls, because of their financial bias, may become the end rather than the means.

(5) Accounting can only provide some of the stimuli in the intelligence, design and choice phases of decision-making.

(6) Accounting is generally historical; today 'what if' and 'what might be' are more important than 'what was'.

(7) Accounting controls, because they imperfectly represent reality, are often ignored by line managers.

(8) Accounting fails to provide requisite variety.

(9) Accounting tends to emphasise performance measurement rather than improvement and change.

(10) Accounting, despite advances in cost accounting (marginal costs, relevant costs, etc.), tends to be influenced by control rather than decision needs.

It is the last reason that is perhaps most pernicious. An organisation's approach to management control can often be judged by the extent of accounting influence. Table 9.2 suggests where the emphasis might lie in management control, depending upon the relative influence of accounting and non-accounting and of decision and control. Accounting dominated organisations frequently emphasise responsibility accounting, with the result that problem-solving information is deficient (box a). Pressures for change, improvement and analysis lead to construction of decision-oriented costing systems (box b). Inflation has accelerated this movement. Only when non-accountants, especially line managers, exert influence do broader-based, enquiring systems develop (box c) and integrative, wider-perspective control systems (box d) evolve. Increasing complexity and uncertainty are accelerating this trend.

TABLE 9.2. Emphases and influence of management control

	Accounting	*Non-Accounting*
Decision	(b) Decision costing systems	(c) Modelling systems
Control	(a) Responsibility accounting systems	(d) Multi-measure or lateral systems

The attack on accounting may seem excessively harsh. It probably is; but breakthroughs in management control may well depend on wider perspectives than accounting has offered hitherto.

ADAPTATION AND LEARNING

In the face of an unstable environment, the need for open adaptive management control information systems is clear. Adaptive feedbacks, external controls, new measurement bases and methods of assessing risk and uncertainty are meeting this need. However, it seems that as complexity and uncertainty increase, information systems must incorporate *self-adaptive* elements, which increased formalisation may prevent.

For example, it has been suggested[27] that self-designing organisations are required to provide this adaptation, where rigid structures of 'palaces' have to be replaced by looser, flexible arrangements or 'tents'. Since the nature of management control places limits on structure and formalisation, and since adaptation is essential, perhaps supporting MIS should also be more flexible, where decision and control 'tents' are provided by modelling, database enquiry facilities and encouragement of unofficial and informal systems.

Thus we are designing and providing a process, not a product. The process is one of learning, from which managers design and select their own management control information. The product view of rigid controls and routinely formal information flows may be too claustrophobic for today's needs. Participative design, model-bases, enquiry facilities, multiple feedbacks and experimentation thus are all vital self-adaptive processes.

INFORMATION AND ORGANISATION

Leavitt[28] has provided a very simple but powerful model of organisation (Figure 9.8) comprising four basic interacting variables. Accepting this model, it is evident that the MIS technology must fit the other three variables of task, structure and people. MIS design cannot be divorced from organisation design: the interfaces are crucial.

Clearly these variables differ from one organisation to another and over time. Therefore there is no one best design for an MIS or organisation; they must vary with circumstances. The contingent theorists,[29] however, go further. They tend to explain different organisational designs especially in terms of strategy, task uncertainty and environmental instability. Galbraith[30] suggests that in highly uncertain environments the need for information processing increases. Alternative organisational forms there-

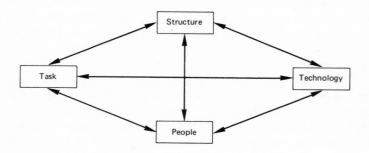

FIGURE 9.8. Leavitt's view of organisation

fore may represent variations in the ability to process varying amounts of information and crucially one must support the other. Management control information system design and organisation design are inextricably linked.

For example, faced with increased uncertainty, Galbraith suggests that four information processing strategies are available. Slack resources can be employed, such as investing in buffer stocks or spare capacity. Alternatively, self-contained tasks can be designed, for example creating specialist functions or decentralising responsibility. Thirdly, investment in vertical MIS is possible, for example devising new tracking devices, filtering information signals, increasing report frequency, enhancing system efficiency or introducing new techniques. Importantly, each of these strategies has MIS implications, each generally requiring information system support or change. Then the fourth strategy, creating lateral relations, often is required as the other three strategies are found not to support the global and interdependent needs of organisational decision-making and control. Laterally integrating structures are then developed, such as project teams, coordinating managers, global databases, and, perhaps ultimately, matrix organisations. Thus organisation and information evolve together.

Both designers and managers therefore need to appreciate how information and organisation are crucially linked in management control. They must also understand the critical forces which influence the relationship.

INFORMATION AND BEHAVIOUR

In management control, the interface with one of Leavitt's organisational variables—people—is especially critical. Management control information systems are influenced by, and in turn influence, human behaviour. Systems designers are not blind to this interaction; often, however, their assumptions about the relationship of information and behaviour are invalid. Frequently the system is amended because of behavioural 'difficulties' without trying to understand the root causes.

We have seen that controls do not guarantee control, that goals and values conflict and that what is information for one manager is of no impact on another. We know the way that information is used—the interpretation, the biases, the fiddles, the over-credence, the disregard—can render any system worthless. We can recognise that unofficial responses also compensate for design inadequacies. And we observe that information is power and that power—its distribution and application—is at the heart of control.

The value of participation, the promise of industrial dynamics modelling and attention to output presentation all have been stressed because of the critical interaction between information and behaviour. If we are to create socio-technical information systems in support of management control, then behavioural aspects deserve more explicit attention. The next chapter is devoted to this topic.

CHAPTER 9—PROJECTS

1. The managing director of a shoe manufacturing company believes that computers have no role to play in management control. 'I have supported computerisation of our basic operational systems', he said recently, 'but management control depends on informal relationships and on people. Computers will get in the way and provide all the excuses'. How would you reply to this statement?

2. Albion Contractors Limited have just appointed a new Financial Director who previously worked for one of the largest contracting firms in the country. He is expected to implement many of the management control systems which his old firm pioneered. What analysis would you expect him to do first and how would you advise him to implement the new systems?

3. Bill Fields is a corporate planner with Universal Holdings, a major retail store group with shops in most large towns and cities. Universal sell clothes, toiletries, hardware and food and have close relationships with their suppliers. The board feel that the current uncertainties of the business environment, the pressures on costs and margins and the growing competition in the marketplace demand more sophisticated planning techniques. Bill Fields has been asked to investigate and implement use of computer-based modelling.

After researching into the possibilities, Fields has found that a business planning model could be developed by the following methods:

(1) Use of a package planning model employed by other retailers.
(2) Hire a consulting group to build a model of the firm.
(3) Ask Universal's DP department to construct a model using FORTRAN.
(4) Develop a model himself using a modelling language.

How would you advise Bill Fields to proceed?

4. How might design of a management control system differ for a non-profit organisation from a profit-seeking enterprise? Would any alteration in the design process be required?

5. Information disclosure, co-determination, participative management and industrial democracy are all current trends and issues. What implications, if any, do they have for the design of management control information systems?

6. 'Financial control systems have proved to be the most effective means of management control.' Do you agree with this claim? Suggest why non-financial information is or is not important in management control.

7. Design a management information system to support a budgetary planning and control system in one of the following situations: (1) a local government authority; (2) a multiple retailer; (3) a steel manufacturer; (4) any other business activity with which you are familiar.

NOTES

1. Mintzberg, H., 'The Myths of MIS', *California Management Review*, Fall 1972.
2. Lowe, E. A., and McInnes, J. M., 'Control in Socio-Economic Organisations: A Rationale for the Design of Management Control Systems', *Journal of Management Studies*, May 1971.
3. Aguilar, F., *Scanning the Business Environment*. New York: Collier-Macmillan, 1967.
4. For further information on forecasting techniques see Wood, D., and Fildes, R., *Forecasting in Business*. London: Longmans, 1976.

5. See next section for definitions and classification of models.
6. Drucker, P. F., 'Controls, Control and Management', in Bonini, C. P., Jaedicke, R. K., and Wagner, H. M. (eds.), *Management Controls: New Directions in Basic Research*. New York: McGraw-Hill, 1964.
7. Demski, J., 'An Accounting System Structured on a Linear Programming Model', *The Accounting Review*, October 1967.
8. See Chapter 5.
9. Dew, R. B., and Gee, K. P., *Management Control and Information*. London: Macmillan, 1973.
10. For detailed descriptions of computer-aided decision models see McCosh, A. M., and Scott-Morton, M. S., *Management Decision Support Systems*. London: Macmillan, 1977. A corporate planning model is described in Gershefski, G. W., 'Building a Corporate Financial Model', *Harvard Business Review*, July–August 1969.
11. Grinyer, P. M., and Wooler, J., *Corporate Models Today*, Institute of Chartered Accounts in England and Wales, 1975.
12. Naylor, T. M., and Schauland, H., 'A Survey of Corporate Planning Models', *Management Science*, May 1976.
13. Boulder, J. B., 'Computerised Corporate Planning', *Long-Range Planning*, June 1971.
14. Keen, P. G. W., 'Interactive Computer Systems for Managers: A Modest Proposal', *Sloan Management Review*, Fall 1976.
15. Alter, S., 'How Effective Managers Use Information Systems', *Harvard Business Review*, November–December 1976.
16. Anthony, R. N., and Herzlinger, R., *Management Control in Non-profit Organisations*. Homewood, Ill.: Irwin, 1975.
17. See Chapter 5 for description of industrial dynamics.
18. Roberts, E. B., 'Industrial Dynamics and the Design of Management Control Systems', in Bonini, C. P., Jaedicke, R. K., and Wagner, H. M. (eds.), *Management Controls: New Directions in Basic Research*. New York: McGraw-Hill, 1964.
19. Bonini, C. P., 'Simulation of Organisational Behaviour', in Bonini, C. P., Jaedicke, R. K., and Wagner, H. M. (eds.), *Management Controls: New Directions in Basic Research*. New York: McGraw-Hill, 1964.
20. Little, J. D., 'Models and Managers: The Concept of a Decision Calculus', *Management Science*, 16, No. 6 (1970).
21. Van Horne, J. C., 'Validation of Simulation Results', *Management Science*, 17, No. 5 (1971).
22. Dew, R. B., and Gee, K. P., *Management Control and Information*. London: Macmillan, 1973.
23. See Mintzberg, H., 'Impediments to the use of Management Information', National Association of Accountants (US), 1974, and 'The Myths of MIS', *California Management Review*, Fall 1972.
24. Grinyer, P. M., and Norburn, D., 'Planning for Existing Markets: Perceptions of Executives and Financial Performance', *Journal of the Royal Statistical Society*, Series A, pp. 70–97, 1975.
25. Gilbert, X. F., 'Does your Control System fit your Firm?', *European Business*, Spring 1973.
26. Vancil, R. F., 'What kind of Management Control do you need?', *Harvard Business Review*, March–April 1973.

27. Hedberg, B., Nystrom, P., and Starbuck, W., 'Camping on Seesaws: Prescriptions for a Self-designing Organisation', *Administrative Science Quarterly*, March 1976.
28. Leavitt, H. J., *Managerial Psychology*. Chicago: University of Chicago Press, 1964.
29. For example, see Lawrence, P. R., and Lorsch, J. W., *Organisation and Environment: Managing Differentiation and Integration*. Division of Research, Harvard Business School, 1967; Burns, T., and Stalker, G. W., *The Management of Innovation*. London: Tavistock, 1961; Woodward, J. (ed.), *Industrial Organisation, Behaviour and Control*. London: Oxford University Press, 1970.
30. Galbraith, J., *Designing Complex Organisations*. Reading, Mass.: Addison-Wesley, 1973.

BIBLIOGRAPHY

Anthony, R. N., and Herzlinger, R., *Management Control in Non-profit Organisations*. Homewood, Ill.: Irwin, 1975.

Bonini, C. P., Jaedicke, R. K., and Wagner, H. N. (eds.), *Management Controls: New Directions in Basic Research*. New York: McGraw-Hill, 1964.

Eilon, S., *Management Control*. London: Macmillan, 1971.

Galbraith, J., *Designing Complex Organisations*. Reading, Mass.: Addison-Wesley, 1973.

Grinyer, P. H., and Wooler, J., *Corporate Models Today*. Institute of Chartered Accountants in England and Wales, 1975.

Hopwood, A. G., *Accounting and Human Behaviour*. London: Accountancy Age Books, 1974.

McCosh, A. M., and Scott-Morton, M. S. S., *Management Decision Support Systems*. London: Macmillan, 1978.

Rappaport, A. (ed.), *Information for Decision-Making: Quantitative and Behavioural Dimensions*. Englewood Cliffs, N. J.: Prentice-Hall, 1970.

10 Behavioural Aspects of Management Control and Control Information

Management control involves individuals and their behaviour within organisations. Controls seek to influence individual behaviour in order to achieve organisational objectives. Control aims at producing goal-congruent behaviour. Management control ensures that organisational behaviour of the individuals effectively contributes towards the realisation of the objectives of the organisation.

Management controls are human controls. Human controls cannot be achieved mechanically. Here the process of control is organic. Management control tools and techniques may be fabricated through elaborate rules and procedures. Yet their successful operation depends on the social and psychological aspects of the people involved in the control. Control originates from individuals and its effective operation rests on the individuals and their psyches.

The basic disciplines for management control are sociology and social-psychology. Management control is a socially defined aspect of management affecting psychologically conscious individuals. So management control information has social and psychological meanings. Management controls designed without the consideration of this social and psychological aspects of the people involved very often fail to produce effective results. Furthermore, it may affect the long-term health of the organisation.

An MIS is to reflect in its information contents and characters the individual and social aspects of the organisation as well as the organisational aims and objectives. For example, if sales budgets are used as control tools for sales managers, the sales target should meet the expectations of the individual managers and also should assure the realisation of corporate profit objectives. The sales manager's success or failure has behind it many social and psychological factors emanating from the environment and the individual, interacting in different ways. Our plan in this chapter is to describe those social and psychological intricacies involved in the management control process and to provide factors for consideration in the design of an effective management control information system.

THE BEHAVIOURAL ENVIRONMENT OF MANAGEMENT CONTROL

A management control system is operative in an environmental milieu which is a resulting force of many interacting forces. For example, the system of subordinate performance evaluation should focus on the needs and expectations of subordinates, the power and influence of the manager, the character and contents of the task and broadly the socio-economic environment of the system itself. This means that management control and information systems should be built on a contingency model which consciously considers the forces in the manager, the forces in the task, the forces in the subordinates, and the forces in the environment.

Figure 10.1 reveals that manager's control behaviour is decided by individual traits and the pressures and purposes of the environment. Forces in the manager result from his individual motivation, needs and expectations, his leadership style and managerial traits. We intend to emphasise here that formal recorded information for management control gives only a partial view of control. For example, the budget variance report, or the employees appraisal reports are the results of social and psychological processes of control. These reports contain nothing about the processes of interaction, bargaining and the persons involved in the production of report data or in their use. Therefore these control reports are partial replications of the actual control situations. In other words, these reflect only the structural variables and not the process variables.

FIGURE 10.1. (Adapted from Shetty, Y. K., and Cerlisle, H. M., 'A Contingency Model of Organisation Design', *California Management Review*, Fall 1972)

BEHAVIOURAL MODELS OF MANAGEMENT CONTROL

The behavioural aspects of management control can be best explained by
the model shown in Figure 10.2. Here the manager's intention to influence
behaviour (actions of subordinates) and subordinates' willingness to
accept his authority produce management control. These again will depend
on the organisational rewards system, organisational objectives and
constraints. A rightly poised information system helps to maintain these
essential links between the parties involved in the control, i.e. the managers,
the subordinates and the objects of the organisation.

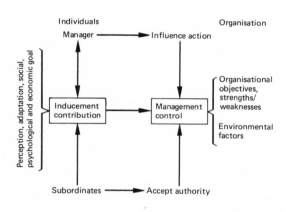

FIGURE 10.2

Beagioni and Lavely, using the Porter and Lawler model (Figure 10.3)
showed how a particular type of management control information enters
into and influences the behaviour of the individuals in the organisation.
The model is based on the expectancy theory. It shows how the effort (3) of
an individual results from the interaction of the value of the reward (1) and
the perceived probability of effort–reward relationships (2). If either is zero
the effort is zero. In the next stage the manager's abilities and traits (4) and
his role perception (5) are positively related to his performance (6). It
indicates that abilities, traits, role, perceptions of efforts–reward relationships contribute to producing the performance efforts of a manager.
Actual rewards (7) received may not have any relationship with the
performance. The manager's satisfaction (9) depends on his perception of
rewards as being equitable. Two feedback loops are provided here. One
influences the perceived probability that higher effort will produce a higher

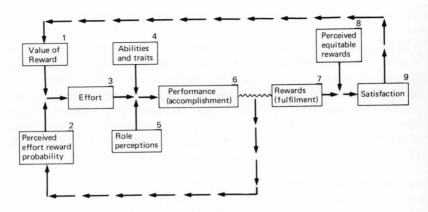

FIGURE 10.3. (From the Porter–Lawler Model; Porter, L. W., and Lawler, E. H., *Management Attitudes and Performance*, Homewood, Ill.: Irwin, 1968, p. 17.)

reward; while the other links the value of the rewards to the manager, with his satisfaction. The higher the satisfaction the higher is the value.

The management control information system enters into the process of control through its influence on the manager's role perception. Information system output is active in communicating the manager's role in the superior–subordinate relationship, and in influencing the manager's role, his behaviour and his perception of his role. This can be illustrated with the most widely used management control tool, the budget.

The budget is considered as the main goal-setting device and goal communication machinery. The organisation prescribes roles (set of tasks assigned) for its managers through budgets. It also provides boundaries to the roles. The budget is considered as a role-sending device also. The budget reports measure and communicate manager's performance. The manager is expected to link his performance, efforts and rewards through the budget performance reports. If he perceives that the rewards are not linked with his performance and if he is not satisfied with his rewards this may influence the intensity of his efforts.

BEHAVIOURAL PROBLEMS OF MEASUREMENT IN MANAGEMENT CONTROL

In Chapter 8, we discussed the concept of measurement in management control. Management control involves the behaviour of people and it focuses more on personal and interpersonal aspects of performance in the organisation than on the impersonal relationships. So the criteria for measurement we set out in Chapter 8 need careful consideration. Management control information systems face the task of capturing data pertinent to the system of control. In the face of the natural absence of appropriate measures for many control aspects, surrogate measures are used. These surrogate measures are mainly financial (accounting) in nature. Apart from its inadequacies in measuring and reporting all relevant organisational aspects, accounting also faces the problem of criteria selection.

Accounting data are inherently partial and incomplete reflections of the transactions they seek to measure. A transaction is a social process of exchange of utilities. It involves the people and the organisational environment. Accounting never attempts to reflect these. It only records and reports the results of the transactions and not the process. Therefore it becomes very difficult to derive social and behavioural meanings from the reported data. In essence, management control using these data fail to produce the desired social and psychological effects.

Let us take a very simple example. In a purchase transaction, the process of purchase decision involves many steps, searching for the vendor, evaluating the price, quality, delivery conditions and so forth. The result of the transaction is the purchase of goods at some specific price. The only things which are primarily of accounting interest are the quantity and price, and the accounting records show the cost and quantity of goods purchased. If a manager wants to control the cost of raw materials he cannot rely on accounting records only. He needs to go beyond them. Conventional accounting records only tell him whether his costs were high or not. It does not tell him why his costs were high or what his future costs will be.

This brings us to another aspect. We observed previously that a management control system is a measurement and feedback system where the purpose is to create congruent conditions between (1) organisational objectives, (2) systems of reward, (3) subordinate managers' goals, and (4) a formal measurement system. In actual practice this is difficult to achieve. Figure 10.4 shows the incompatibility between organisational purposes (A), subordinate manager's goals (B), and the formal measurement system (C). It shows that subordinate managers' goals and organisational purposes do not form identical sets. Furthermore, through our formal measurement system we can capture only a portion of the intersections of subordinates' goals and organisational goals. A large portion of the formal measurement domain is not relevant to organisational and managerial purposes. Therefore, it is quite likely that use of such control tools will give

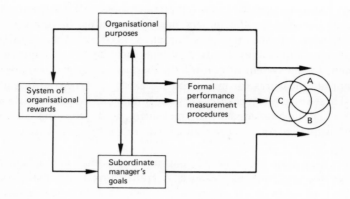

FIGURE 10.4. A—behaviours having organisational significance; B—behaviours having managerial significance; C—formal measurement process. The overlap is, inevitably, partial. (Adapted from Hopwood, A. G., *An Accounting System and Managerial Behaviour*, Farnborough: Saxon House, 1973.)

rise to unwanted and unwarranted behavioural responses. Managers usually overcome the constraints of controls by circumvention or dysfunctional behavioural responses not related to the organisational objectives. Later in this chapter we discuss some of these issues in more detail.

VARIATIONS IN MANAGEMENT CONTROL INFORMATION USES

The ways in which managers use control information vary. The variations can be systematically explicated. The differences in control information use depends on the manager's personal characteristics and his organisational environment.

One of the present authors evaluated the influence of organisational climate and managers' individual characteristics on the use of management control information (specifically, management accounting data).[1] It was observed that managers who attached primary importance to accounting control data for performance evaluation and operating decisions were task-motivated, had a short time-perspective, and perceived the environment as highly structured. These managers were found to have low supervisory ability, relatively low intelligence, low occupational achievement and self-actualisation needs but high decisiveness and moderate self-assurance and initiative.

Contrarily it was observed that the managers who attached minor importance to the accounting control data were of different types. They were relationship-motivated managers, having longer time-perspective for their actions, who perceived the environment as less structured. They had high supervisory ability, medium intelligence, occupational achievement and self-actualisation needs and low initiative, self-assurance and decisiveness. This study in fact suggested that while designing a system, the designer should consider along with the technical aspects of the system the individual characteristics of the managers as far as possible.

Managers' use of control information is influenced by their decision-making behaviour which means that decision-making styles of the user determines the nature of the use of control data. Driver and Mock differentiated the styles of decision-making and the use of information. An awareness of these variations should be a useful input for the system designers. Future system designs will increasingly be influenced by these considerations. Figure 10.5 illustrates a decision-making model. It shows that there are four decision-making styles: (1) decisive, (2) flexible, (3) hierarchic, and (4) integrative. These styles are differentiated on the basis of the degree of focus and the amount of use of data. For example if a decision-maker seeks only one solution, his use of data will be minimal and he will be decisive in style.

Degree of focus in use of data	Multiple solutions	Flexible	Integrative
	One solution	Decisive	Hierarchic
		Minimal (satisficer)	Maximum

Amount of information used

FIGURE 10.5. Decision style model. (Adapted from Driver, M. J., and Mock, T. J., 'Human Information Processing, Decision Style Theory and Accounting Information Systems', *The Accounting Review*, July 1975.)

Table 10.1 (adapted from Driver and Mock) summarises some attributes of each style mentioned. The minimal information processor uses just enough data to make an adequate decision and then moves on. He processes data to break-even on information use only. On the other hand the maximum data user massages all data perceived to be relevant. He aims at producing the maximum benefit. Again there are information users who perceive only one relevant conclusion while there are others who see information as having varied meanings.

Though most of these conclusions are tentative, the fact remains that

TABLE 10.1. Summary decision style chart

	Decisive	Flexible	Hierarchic	Integrative
Values	Efficiency Speed Consistency	Adaptability Speed Variety	Quality Rigorous method System	Information Creativity
Planning	Low database Short-range Tight control for results	Low database Intuitive	High database Long-range Right control of methods and results	High database Long-range Adaptive
Goals	Few; organis- ation-focus	Many; self- focus	Few; self-focus	Many; self- and organisation-focus
Organisation	Short span of control Rules Classic organisation	Control by confusion Loose	Wide span of control Elaborate pro- cedures Automation	Team process Matrix organisation
Communication	Short summary format Results focus one solution	Short summary format Variety, several solutions	Long, elaborate reports Problem, methods, data, give 'best conclusion'	Long, elaborate Problem analysis from many views Multiple solution
Amount of information used	Minimal			Maximum

Source: adapted from Driver, M. J., and Mock, T. J., 'Human Information Processing, Decision Style Theory and Accounting Information Systems', *The Accounting Review*, July 1975.

managers use control information differently. We definitely believe that the production of control reports having the same contents and formats is not ideal. Garbutt proposed a flexible ideal format for information (FIFI)[2] which merits attention from the system men. Under this system, the content of reports can be varied to meet the requirement of the users. The assumptions for producing control information should be based on a marketing orientation; the information user is assumed to be right. This is illustrated in Figure 10.6. This also focuses on the requirement to modify the control reports to suit the individual's need.

FIGURE 10.6. (Adapted from Garbutt, D., *Accounting*, October 1973.)

THE EFFECTS OF THE USE OF CONTROL INFORMATION

The use of control information in different ways has significantly different behavioural effects on subordinates. Hopwood showed that the use of control information for subordinate evaluation had behavioural and psychological implications. Subordinates who were evaluated by rigid use of control information reported high financial and job related tensions, disturbed supervisor–subordinate relations and dysfunctional behaviour. The rigid use of control information had been characterised by the short-term concerns of managers. Contrarily, where the subordinate evaluation was made on a broader basis and with a long-term perspective, unfavourable behavioural and psychological indications were not observed. The control data in such a case was used on a flexible basis.

SOME BEHAVIOURAL PROBLEMS

The behavioural responses which are associated with the use of information for management control have been classified by different authors from different points of view. We discuss some of these below.

1. Dysfunctional behaviour
One of the most common and widely used examples of the failures of

management control is the dysfunctional behavioural response to controls by the managers. It means management control may wrongly motivate managers to produce apparently good results at the cost of long-term corporate health or growth. In the budgetary control literature these types of behaviour are extensively illustrated. Managers sometimes prefer to postpone the repair needed for the future if it exceeds the current operating budget. Such examples are commonly observed.

Again, managers may postpone investment in fixed assets to show improved return on investment.[3] For example, a manager found it convenient to justify claims for a higher budget allocation for machinery repairs by showing a loss of volume of production. His attitude towards loss of volume is favourable if he can use it to justify claims for a higher allocation.

> I suppose for machinery repair this year there is £50,000. I want to spend sixty. I put it back to the group manager, he has come back to me and said, 'no, you can spend fifty'. I put it to him why I want to spend sixty. But still the decision is fifty. I would be thinking in terms of loss of volume rather than anything else to justify my claim.

2. *Superstitious behaviour*

Superstitious behaviour arises where the control is taken to be the end, and not as the means of achieving corporate objectives. On the use of accounting control, Becker[4] observed that 'Superstitious behaviour occurs when accounting systems are stimuli to responses which are totally unrelated to the problems of the organisation. The means–ends substitution occurs when accounting stimuli acquire reinforcing properties, when they are associated with rewards and finally become an end in themselves'.

This question of superstitious behaviour was investigated by one of the present authors with respect to budgetary controls. A classification of managers was developed on the basis of their uses of budgets (1) as the means (the means type) and (2) as the end (the end type).[5] The means type managers maintained an attitude of using the budget as a guideline. They considered the budget as a facilitating link which helped them to aim at a preselected target. Budgets did not appear as a constraint to them. As one manager said:

> It is not an aim—you might be able to do better than a budget . . . I have in my mind a distant budget and this is an interim budget . . . a budget is supposed to be an agreement . . . The budget is intended to show what

you may spend, if you won't spend it you may cause some damage. I think without spending I would show more profit this year—but this would cause problems next year.

Whereas the end type manager's aim is limited within the budget targets. The achievement of budget becomes a matter of immediate concern to them. One end type manager observed that:

at the end of the day I have got to go before the board. My accounts are straight. I want to say that I spent exactly what I said I would do. I think really, to mean anything, it should be a programme of action. I see little point in drawing up a budget if it is not going to mean anything. It's a wastage of time. Therefore, I would see the budget as an actual target in itself.

3. *Circumvention*

When managers face a system of control which is rigid and which does not fulfil their expectations they tend to bend the control towards their objectives. The constraints of control are overcome by various ways. To illustrate this aspect we have quoted below a research manager describing the budgetary control in his department.

To an extent I feel the budget is a constraint. The budgets do not allow me enough flexibility. I am evaluating the safety of a drug. Suppose a drug given by inhalation. To find out the right way, I can give an estimate of what I may require. Until you actually get working with the problem you just don't know all the problems, and if the project is important enough I think I should be allowed to spend enough money to get a satisfactory system. If I work to a sum, I think it could be harmful . . . We built a fair amount of contingency figures into our annual budgets—which enables us to make purchases within reasonable limits of unforeseen items . . . Furthermore, we share allocations between departments behind the doors to purchase new equipment.

4. *Creation of Informal Information System*

If a management control information system cannot produce the information which fulfils the needs of managers in content, character and quality, managers create their own information systems. Numerous growth of such 'information systems' may create confusion, produce unreliable data, duplication of effort, make coordination difficult and finally may alienate the managers from the corporate control system. One very successful shopfloor production manager was found to keep a separate information system of his own because (1) the formal information report came late to him, (2) it did not tell him the things which he used in his control decisions, (3) it was difficult to understand, and (4) it carried a large mass of data.

5. *Falsification*

Much management control data is initially recorded at the supervisory level. If the supervisors want to they can manipulate the control reports so as to look good. They may record the data in a way that makes their short-term accounting profit look more favourable. When the pressure from the control is excessive then supervisors are found to resort to manipulation or falsification of records, as in quoting another department's number on their requisition slips or making 'midnight requisitions', i.e. stealing from other departments. However, falsification is possible at the point of recording the data. Hopwood[6] reported various forms of manipulation and falsification. For example a few managers were found to report pseudo-production by creating recorded production which had not taken place at all.

CONCLUSIONS

We conclude this chapter by making some unoriginal recommendations to produce an effective and adaptive management control and information system.

(1) Participation—to improve the performance, encourage participation by the people in setting control objectives and in designing the control information system.[7]

(2) Improve supervisor—subordinate manager contact for creating a social environment for control: (a) use departmental meetings; (b) use results in the performance measurement; (c) provide frequent person-to-person contacts about results; (d) avoid creating pressure situations.

(3) Consider cognitive complexity of people—control systems which are highly complex fail to attract the attention of people with low conceptual ability. Many complicated management accounting reports are ignored by production people as rituals only because the managers understand neither their meaning nor their mechanics.

Again, research studies indicate that low conceptual level subjects need to process more information than their high conceptual level counter-parts.[8] Miller and Gordon[9] observed with respect to the accounting information system that 'the accounting information system (true for other MIS also) can affect the individual's decision-making behaviour through its effects on his conceptual level in two ways: (1) by influencing the immediate environmental complexity; and (2) by affecting the long-term training conditions which may shift an individual from one dispositional conceptual level to another'. Thus, the design of the accounting system may be very influential in determining how decision-makers respond to given situations.

A properly designed system can have effects which are beneficial in both the short run and the long run. The introduction of computer-oriented MIS also affects the cognitive styles of managers.[10]

(4) Prepare flex-data based system—it increases the system capability to match varied output requirements depending on the persons and the situations. It should enlarge the scope of the information system and increase the system capability of data manipulation according to the requirements of the users.

(5) Humanise management information systems—Mintzberg's[11] conclusions on this aspect are very appropriate. His humanising formulae are:

(a) Managers need broad-based formal information systems, in large part independent of computers.

(b) In an ideal MIS the rate of information bombarding the managers would be carefully controlled.

(c) Concentration on intelligent filtering of information is a key responsibility of the MIS.

(d) Careful determination of channels is necessary in MIS design.

(e) The formal information system should encourage the use of alternative and in-depth sources of information.

(f) Stored information must be conveniently available to the manager.

(g) The information specialist must be sensitive to the manager's personal and organisational needs.

(6) Tailoring concept—the tailoring concept[12] in information system design recognises the differences in persons, organisations and time.

(a) Recognise the innate differences in the abilities of individuals who must operate the system to perceive, assimilate, and decide.

(b) Recognise the information available to and required at each decision point.

(c) Match these factors to achieve best possible decisions at each point. Determine the 'floor' and 'ceiling' of the information possibilities within the firm. The system 'floor' is the minimum amount of information needed at each decision and control point. The system 'ceiling' is the maximum theoretically possible. The attainable information goal lies between the two, and is the amount of information the organisation is capable of comprehending and using effectively.

Finally, our conclusions are that the management control system is a behavioural system. The management control information system designed to support the management control system should consider the wide range of behavioural variables in the persons, tasks and environment. The system should be modified and revised with the passage of time.

CHAPTER 10—PROJECT

Mr Altaf Gahur, a behavioural consultant had recently visited a medium-sized production plant of a nationalised corporation. He was interviewing the people in the different departments of the organisation. Below we quote results of his interview with the production supervisor.

The production supervisor had a different story to tell than the general manager. He had 40 workers to supervise. There were eight processes and four machines. Products were standardised and produced through a partly automated system. He got his monthly production plans from the general manager. His concerns were the control of production as to targets, maintaining the quality and minimising the wastages.

Even then I do not have much to do. Everything is fixed for me. The plan says what to produce. There are standards for output quality and quantity. Moreover, I do not hire or fire the workers. Of course, I can recommend sanctions or rewards for the workers. However, due to the absence of specially defined authority my power is limited. My recommendations are not always accepted. The general manager evaluates me. I never know what it was. I sometime think my efforts are not rewarded appropriately. I have been in this position for more than 15 years. I have not seen any change in the management policies. Now I have stopped expecting rewards for my good work. Financially, I do not say that I am not well paid. Still I feel the need for some changes. Well, you may call it I am bored! I do not blame anybody for that. I even do not know what I want. I have had very little opportunity to know what actually is happening outside the boundary of the factory. I feel that I do not have time to do anything else. Furthermore, 15 years is quite a long time to learn the tricks of the trade.

I do not say that this general manager is not good. He is excellent. He is a graduate manager. He is young, he needs more time to master the aspects of the trade. I sometimes fail to understand him. I never did so much paperwork before. Doing so many reports for him every day. Sincerely, I hate it. But I love him. He has never bothered me.

I tell you what. There was one shop floor general manager, I still remember. He did not do his degrees, but had long experience. During his time our mill was number one in the production in the whole industry. I was then shift supervisor. He used to come to the factory several times during the day. On many occasions before we were in the mills he was there. We knew what he was thinking about us. We could tell from his attitude about the forthcoming raise or bonus. Now it's impossible. You cannot tell by reading papers what is coming for you.

We do not argue with the present system. We have accepted it. We feel that managers today are more and more administrators. They are armed with modern tools which are not our cup of tea. In the future more and more will happen in impersonal ways than it used to be.

QUESTIONS

1. Analyse the interview from the following angles and make useful comments as to its effects on employee motivations: (a) variety in the job; (b) autonomy in the job; (c) feedback in the job.

2. What transformation is occurring in the management control system? How does it affect the motivation of individuals?

3. Describe the information systems used for management control.

NOTES

1. Rahman, M., and McCosh, A. M., 'The Influence of Organisational and Personal Factors on the Use of Accounting Data: An Empirical Study', *Accounting, Organisations and Society*, 1, No. 4 (1976).
2. Garbutt, D., 'Flexibility as the Ideal', *Accountancy*, October 1973, p. 38.
3. Return on investment (ROI) = Net profit divided by Total assets (fixed assets plus other assets). Managers, instead of investing in fixed asset, may acquire the asset on a rental basis so as to show a higher ROI at the cost of the long-term health of the organisation.
4. Becker, S. W., 'A Critique', in Burns, T. J. (ed.), *The Behavioural Aspects of Accounting Data for Performance Evaluation*. Ohio State University, 1968, pp. 263–6.
5. In Rahman, M., and McCosh, A. M., *op. cit.*

 6. Hopwood, A. G., 'An Empirical Study of the Role of Accounting Data in Performance Evaluation', Supplement to vol. X, *Journal of Accounting Research*, 1972.
 7. See Milani, K., 'Relationship of Participation in Budget Setting to Industrial Supervisors Performance and Attitude', *Accounting Review*, L, 1975.
 8. Schroder, H., Driver, M., and Strenfert, S., *Human Information Processing*. New York: Holt, Rinehart and Winston, 1967.
 9. Miller, D., and Gordon, L. A., 'Conceptual Levels and the Design of Accounting Information Systems', *Decision Sciences*, April 1975, pp. 259–69.
10. Kriebel, C. H., Van Horne, R. L., and, Heames, J. T., 'Management Information Systems: Progress and Perspective', *Graduate School of Industrial Administration*. Carnegie Mellon University, 1971.
11. Mintzberg, H., 'Making Management Information System Useful', *Management Review*, May 1975.
12. Nichols, G. E., 'Four Systems Analysis Tools', *Journal of Systems Management*, April 1976.

BIBLIOGRAPHY

Anthony, R. N., Dearden, J., and Vancil, R. F. (eds.), *Management Control Systems: Cases and Readings*. Homewood, Ill.: Irwin, 1965.

Argyris, C., *The Impact of Budgets on People*. New York: Controllership Foundation, 1952.

Argyris, C., *Personality and Organization*. New York: Harper & Row, 1957.

Argyris, C., *Integrating the Individual and the Organization*. New York: Wiley, 1964.

Atkinson, J.W., and Feather, N.T., *A Theory of Achievement Motivation*. New York: Wiley, 1966.

Burns, T., and Stalker, G.U., *The Management of Innovation*. London: Tavistock Publications, 1961.

Caplan, E.H., *Management Accounting and Behavioural Science*. Reading, Mass., Addison-Wesley, 1971.

Fiedler, F. E., 'The Contingency Model—New Directions for Leadership Utilization. Current Perspectives in Leadership', *Journal of Contemporary Business*, Autumn 1974.

Hopwood, A. G., *Accounting and Human Behaviour*. London: Accountancy Age Books, 1974.

Likert, R., *Human Organization: Its Management and Value*. New York: McGraw-Hill, 1967.

Miner, J.B., *Personnel Psychology*. London: Macmillan, 1969.

Porter, L.W., and Lawler, E.E., *Managerial Attitude and Performance*. Homewood, Ill.: Irwin, 1968.

Ridgeway, V. F., 'Dysfunctional Consequences of Performance Measurements', *Administrative Science Quarterly*, 1 (September 1956) 240–7.

Vroom, V. H., 'Decision Making and Leadership Process Current Perspective in Leadership', *Journal of Contemporary Business*, Autumn 1974.

Vroom, V. H., and Yetton, P. W., *Leadership and Decision Making*, Pittsburgh, Pa.: University of Pittsburgh Press, 1973.

11 Measuring System Performance

It is ironic that whilst many MIS exist to provide intelligence and feedback for planning and control, monitoring and measurement of the MIS themselves is frequently inadequate. System performance should be measured for three reasons: (1) to ascertain whether the MIS has met its stated objectives; (2) to ensure that the ongoing MIS operates reliably and efficiently; and (3) to ensure that the MIS adapts to change. Just as in the performance, tracking and diagnosis activities of the management control system model described in Chapter 9, three feedback loops are involved: (1) system corrections and modifications to meet stated objectives; (2) modification and extension of system objectives themselves to meet changed needs; and (3) the decision to replace or kill the system when it no longer can meet current needs, or no longer is required.

The aim, as with all feedbacks, is learning—either correction or adaptation. Since it is primarily *use*, rather than design, of the MIS which is being measured, the process is dependent upon user involvement. In particular, if user participation was lacking in design, the performance measurement process permits some compensation.

Our focus is on the individual MIS. The wider issue of management control of the entire information systems function is equally important, but is well covered elsewhere.[1] Whilst we have separated evaluation of a MIS from its design, the two processes are of course interdependent, evaluation being a crucial iterative step in the design life cycle.

Systems performance measurement faces many problems, for example:

(1) What criteria should be used?
(2) How are these criteria assessed?
(3) Who is involved with performance measurement?
(4) What records are required?
(5) How is information use evaluated?
(6) What action is taken after measurement?
(7) How is this action agreed?

(8) Do different systems need different measurement methods?
(9) How are informal systems assessed?

These are some of the issues addressed in this chapter. The performance measurement task divides into three processes:

(1) System monitoring—continuous tracking and diagnosis of system performance, focusing particularly on system efficiency.
(2) Post-implementation review—investigation after the system is installed to establish whether stated objectives have been met and to learn from the project experience.
(3) Periodic review—occasional investigations to assess system effectiveness and establish changed needs.

Finally two related problems are discussed: the increasing concern over system security and the contribution of auditors.

SYSTEM MONITORING

OPERATIONS MONITORING

The operation of the management information system can be a major activity in an organisation's daily life. For example, running a production control system or a product costing database becomes a production function in itself. Processing has to be scheduled, data assembled and routed, quality control tests applied, departments coordinated, and resources accounted for. In addition capacity has to be planned and standards formulated. All this demands its own operational control information—a system of monitors, logs and records. This monitoring information is of value to performance measurement in: (1) triggering day-to-day operational corrections; (2) providing records of use in post-implementation and periodic reviews; and (3) directing attention to perhaps more significant problems. Mostly the focus is therefore on technical aspects of operational performance, although operational symptoms when diagnosed may reveal design disorders.

Typical monitoring devices include the following:

(1) Hardware logs—generally sensors, they are useful in recording scheduling, activity, failure recovery and operator performance. Technical efficiency is often important, so hardware logs provide critical planning and control indicators.
(2) Software logs—generally resident or 'snoopy' programs, they focus on

program and operating systems performance. Again they may provide valuable guidelines for efficiency improvements or stimulate 'tuning' exercises, from which efficiency gains of up to 25 per cent have been reported.

(3) Operation logs—generally worksheets, checklists and job reports, they record operational events and failures. Essential in task control, they also aid disaster diagnosis and special reviews, indicating quality of timeliness, frequency, reliability, turnround and the like.

(4) System monitors—recorders can be built into manual or mechanised formal systems to monitor activity levels, data volumes, facilities usage and so on. They aid capacity planning, particularly of files and hardware, and may indicate design needs. For example, unused facilities can be withdrawn and heavily used routines perhaps be improved, whilst unexpected usage could suggest unofficial adaptations to changed needs. System monitors thus provide essential inputs to reviews.

(5) System documentation—the documentation which exists at installation is maintained throughout the system life cycle. Amendments are recorded, major errors, and recoveries documented and criticisms or suggestions noted for possible action. Systems documentation thus aids ad hoc queries, but particularly forms a basic input to systems reviews.

(6) Management controls—financial and other controls commonly are applied to the MIS function, especially to EDP. MIS plans provide review reference points, operations budgets provide systems' costs and benefits, whilst MIS charging may stimulate user control. Such management controls can be knotty. For example, charging for data processing can create user awareness, provide evaluative information, and encourage pursuit of efficiency and effectiveness. Equally it can be dysfunctional, emphasising short-run performance, stimulating conflict and restricting innovation.[2] Thus implementing management controls for MIS administration, like all management control, is interrelated with management style, organisational structure and organisation climate (Figure 11.1)—and also perhaps with the evolutionary stage of MIS development that the organisation has reached (Table 11.1). Nevertheless if management controls exist, or are being devised, they may provide useful system monitoring information.

None of these monitors should be underrated. Besides providing valuable planning and review data, they help sustain technical efficiency and reliability. Once management information systems are operational, efficiency and reliability are important. User confidence can soon be dissipated by late batch processing, database breakdowns, real-time 'constipation' or amateur recoveries.

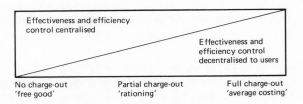

FIGURE 11.1. Relationship between charging procedures and control philosophy (from McFarlan, F. W., Nolan, R. L., and Norton, D. P., *Information Systems Administration*, New York: Holt, Rinehart and Winston, 1973, p. 480.)

DESIGN MONITORING

Information from any of the above operations monitors may, when diagnosed, reveal design inadequacies. However, design monitors *per se* can be deliberately built into information systems—but often are not.

MIS, especially computer-based models, generally incorporate assumptions. Assumptions, such as decision parameters, coefficients, formulae or distributions, become outdated and yet may remain unamended for years. Reminders can be built into the system to trigger reassessment or to flag obsolescence. Input can be monitored and compared with design assumptions, reporting significant deviations; examples might be order size, inflation rate, machine capacities and the like. Physical assumptions—of volume, usage, frequency, data life-span for example—are also incorporated in MIS design and influence input/output configurations, processing modes and database organisations. Physical assumptions can be monitored by periodic housekeeping programs, data control procedures or statistical facilities built into application programs.

Finally, no MIS is devoid of errors, several of which can go unnoticed and build up in the system. Error scanning routines and programs—searching for unclean data, file inconsistencies, redundant or obsolete items and the like—are invaluable and should be complemented by error-correction facilities, such as cleansing programs or reorganisation utilities.

POST-IMPLEMENTATION REVIEW

The purpose of the post-implementation review is two-fold: (1) review of the product, that is to ascertain whether the MIS has achieved its stated objectives, and (2) review of the process, that is to discover from project

TABLE 11.1. Evolution of EDP and management control

Evolutionary phase	(1) Initiation	(2) Contagion	(3) Control	(4) Integration
Phase characteristics	Applications to prove computers	Multi-functional applications	Consolidate applications	Integrate applications
	Operational control applications	Some management control applications	Some strategic planning applications	Control and planning important
	Management pursue cost savings	Management support extension	Management control in crisis	Management direction and acceptance
	User resistance	User enthusiasm	User frustration	User involvment
	DP functionally located	Multiple DP locations	Centralisation of DP	Integration of DP into organisation
Controls and charging	No chargeout	Allocate costs	Full costing	Direct costing
	DP budget	Tax control	Proliferated controls	Balance of and Informal Controls

Source: adapted from Nolan, R. L., *Management Accounting and Control of Data Processing.* National Association of Accountants, 1973.

performance any lessons for future MIS development. Product and process review are clearly quite different. Accordingly they do not occur simultaneously. Process review ideally begins soon after system installation, when all involved in the design are still available and can remember the project experience. Product review takes place somewhat later, since systems take time to settle and benefits are released gradually; in other words the review should occur well into the system's learning curve. We use the term 'review' rather than 'audit' for two reasons. Firstly, audit implies compliance and checking; review also suggests improvement-seeking and adaptation. Secondly, audit can be confused with the activities of the audit profession, whose objectives and emphasis are somewhat different.

PROCESS REVIEW

According to one source,[3] fully three-quarters of failures in the design of computer-based information systems are a direct result of the management of the design process. Indeed, the importance of the design *process* in devising effective management information systems was stressed in Chapter 3. Consequently explicit attempts to learn from experience should be encouraged. This is the rationale of process reviews.

In Chapter 3, it was stressed that project management must be flexible, fitting each set of circumstances. Alloway[4] confirmed this when he discovered that unlike many organisational activities, the MIS design task is temporary and the product unique. The luxury of iterative learning is not available, yet failure is no longer tolerated. The process review must therefore be distinct from the product review, as the latter will incorporate unique criteria which can confuse and distort any conclusions on improving the design process in general. Process review asks the following questions:

(1) Was project performance—costs, time, etc.—according to plan?
(2) What were the reasons for any discrepancies?
(3) Were any other problems encountered?
(4) Are there any outstanding requirements to be completed?
(5) Were any lessons learnt?

The process review thus firstly concentrates on evaluating project performance, also establishing any facilities which are outstanding—it is not unusual for users and designers to differ on when the system is complete. Then any generalisations about future design methodology are sought, but taking into account any uniqueness of the particular system.

Process review should be a joint specialist–user activity, for both will have been involved and both have views. User tasks—data preparation, training, etc.—should not be excluded from review. In particular those design activities dependent upon participation, notably information requirements analysis, can be assessed with the objectivity of hindsight—perhaps with third party contributions to avoid collusion. Apart from opinion and judgement, information is available from the project file, and from project planning and control systems.

A process review report provides useful reference in the future. Senior management, when assessing performance, should not be reluctant to draw specific conclusions about individuals, about project climate and the like. Many of the 'harder', procedural tenets of managing MIS design appear to be myths,[5] so that 'softer' or more subjective judgements may be valuable.

PRODUCT REVIEW

In assessing if the system's stated objectives have been met, two points should be remembered. Firstly, besides economic criteria, operational and technical performance are relevant. Secondly, the stated objectives will by iteration have evolved through the systems development life cycle and can still evolve. So improvements are also sought during product review.

In contrast to the feasibility study, *ex-post* evaluation is *relatively* simple. Criteria exist, fewer conflicts arise and benefits are no longer abstract. Nevertheless, product review is still not generally practised, or is often inadequate. Economic performance tends to be the meta-criterion; it also represents to some extent operational and technical performance. We shall therefore describe product review methodology in terms of economic measurement,[6] and then examine key issues of operational and technical evaluation.

Costs and benefits are now measurable. The intangibles as well as the tangibles can be evaluated. Many of the costs can be collected from the project file, from operations monitors (especially budgets) and from the process review. User costs as well as producer costs are included. Benefits, especially from operational control systems, should be apparent in departmental and programme budgets. However, there are less direct benefits, such as improved decision-making from models, and hidden benefits and costs which must be assessed by in-depth investigation.

The investigation team should be composed of both design specialists and users, with supporting direction and catalysis from senior management. The technicians cannot evaluate the benefits (and would not be believed) but can learn from the process. Users thus must be involved but can be inconsistent, unreliable and biased evaluators. Therefore third party representation helps—or sustained senior management direction—providing balance, asking questions and ensuring all relevant issues are considered. Third party evaluation alone—perhaps internal auditors or consultants—may seem attractive. However, since system improvements are sought, technical and user inputs and dialogue are also required.

Two major problems have to be faced. Firstly, how are realistic and consistent estimates of costs and benefits derived? Secondly, the product review should be presented to senior management for, besides providing feedback to designers and users, it should contribute to overall MIS planning and control by influencing system resource allocation decisions and demonstrating the value of the information resource. However, how can senior management be convinced that the results are reliable? Proven approaches to these two problems include: (1) ensure both users and specialists are involved in the evaluation; (2) only consider quantifiable benefits; (3) estimate benefits conservatively and costs generously; and (4) check out results for accuracy and plausibility.

The evaluation procedure must therefore tap all information sources and involve successive management levels, as shown in Figure 11.2, returning to earlier phases where necessary. Each step involves the following:

(1) System acquaintance—by consulting system documentation and the project file and by widespread discussion, ensure all evaluators understand the scope, purpose and mechanics of the MIS.
(2) Collect established information—collect recorded costs and benefits, and documented problems, plans and suggestions, from management control systems, the project file, operations monitors and the like.
(3) Conduct operational user interviews—by interviewing those primarily involved with system input/output, ascertain user costs and derive views of the MIS impact on local activities. These users are generally knowledgeable and dedicated supporters of the system and will reveal both its benefits and 'warts'. They may prefer to express benefits in operational rather than financial terms. The results of the interviews should be documented and then corroborated by the users.
(4) Conduct user management interviews—by interviewing departmental or programme managers, translate operational user verdicts into financial terms. Doubts, conflicts and problems are discussed and the more difficult issues addressed, such as 'intangibles' or unexpected results. Ultimately only quantifiable costs and benefits are recorded and then agreed by the managers.
(5) Conduct cross-location checks—where possible similar functions and users are examined to provide checks and balances on results. Where

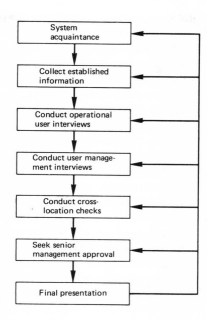

FIGURE 11.2. Product review procedure

significant differences emerge, the relevant parties can be brought together to probe reasons, and perhaps learn from the diagnosis. If the results are unclear, conservatism is preferred.

(6) Seek senior management approval—difficulties and uncertainties are resolved before the results are finally approved and support gained.

(7) Final presentation—for the reasons outlined earlier top management (often the MIS steering committee) should be informed of the product review conclusions.

Throughout this process, six points should be borne in mind:

(1) Economic appraisal is often helped by comparison with an alternative—perhaps what would exist if the MIS had not been developed.

(2) Such an alternative must be conceptual for circumstances will have changed since the new system was installed. Activity levels, organisation structure, legislation and so on may be quite different.

(3) Economic benefits may be due to several causes, not only the MIS. So other variables should also be examined.

(4) Some systems may be very local in application, for example decision support systems. Cross-checking may therefore be limited. Other indicators—such as frequency of usage—may therefore help in evaluation.
(5) Variances from expectation should be investigated. There may be good reasons for discrepancy—changed needs, premature assessment, or perhaps deeper technical or operational issues.
(6) Whilst user opinions and statements should be corroborated by cross-location or senior management surveys, subjective user judgements often provide trenchant and relevant appraisal. They should not be neutralised or theorised away too readily.

Operational performance measurement is susceptible to the same procedure. Historical data is generally available from the operations monitors described earlier. In particular, error and recovery histories provide guidance on recurring problems and design inefficiencies. Information use can only really be measured by interview. This is examined in detail in the next section. It can be particularly fruitful to ask what facilities are *not* used, not only to reveal design inadequacies of timeliness, relevance, aggregation and the like, but also user indifference and resistance. These behavioural issues then need cautious and careful probing—perhaps by behavioural scientists—through further interviews and questionnaires. The original social benefits established by the feasibility study, for example easier work, better conditions or improved job satisfaction, can also be assessed by these means.

Technical performance can also be evaluated from operations monitors. However, interviews of users and specialists are also required, because technical faults or potentials are not always obvious. Users, in reporting breakdowns, delays, poor input/output mechanisms and so on, may be revealing symptoms of deeper or latent technical problems. Specialists may be aware of improved technology of relevance to the particular application. A key question is the reliability, maintainability and recoverability of the system.

In evaluating economic, technical and operational performance, the criteria vary with each MIS and may be constrained or biased by failure to consider all the stakeholders. The concept of stakeholder participation in system design advanced in Chapter 3 is just as relevant to system evaluation. Indeed, the same team may be involved. Each set of stakeholders—Figure 11.3—is represented and agrees, redefines or re-negotiates its own objectives. Collectively they agree the relative weightings. The sectional subgoals are then assessed, using the procedure in Figure 11.2. The results are aggregated and compared against the group's

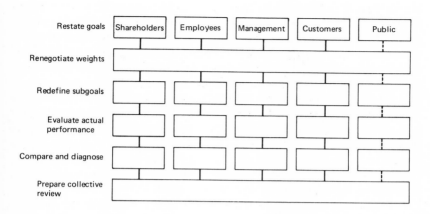

FIGURE 11.3. Stakeholder product review

multi-dimensional expectations. Variances are diagnosed, discussed and negotiated to produce an agenda of improvements, and a collective product review is prepared. It is likely of course that changing values and power balances are reflected and so this procedure fuses into the adaptive process of periodic reviews.

Such multi-dimensional stakeholder evaluation may well appeal to those organisations that wish to foster participation, but do not yet feel able to do so in the design phase. Product review would then commence with *ex-post* definition of sectional goals.

An alternative evaluation methodology which also encompasses a broader view of system effectiveness has been proposed by King and Rodriguez.[7] They recommend four broad varieties of assessment which may be made before, during and after MIS design and development. These are:

(1) Attitudes, i.e. user attitudes on the likely effect of the MIS on job performance, interpersonal relations, organisation structure, managerial goals, top management support and the like.
(2) Value perceptions, i.e. user perceptions of certain values such as the probability that the system will be used and will succeed, that it will be worthwhile and meet the information criteria specified.
(3) Information usage behaviour, i.e. whether the information will be used, how it will be used and whether new uses will be found.
(4) Decision performance, i.e. whether the MIS has an effect on decision-making performance.

Measurement techniques have been devised to evaluate these four dimensions. Comparisons are then made in two ways. Firstly, changes in the four dimensions from the pre-system time period, through design and development to the post-system period are compared and analysed. Secondly the behaviour and benefits of system users are compared with those of non-users. Conventional statistical techniques are then used to explore and test any changes for significance. If significant changes and differences are established, they then provide valuable feedback in product or process review. The design and development process may need revision, the system may need to be 'sold' more strongly, the system objectives may require modification or the system design itself may need amendment. The major value of this approach may be that it is systematic, broad-based and practical—since the measurement techniques exist.

This method, together with the previous approaches, tends to assume a stable environment because major change is unlikely between system installation and review. In the longer term this assumption is invalid. The comparative method could be applied subsequently on a periodic basis, but it does not explicitly seek to capture and record environment change. Hence the need for quite different, formal and structured periodic reviews.

PERIODIC REVIEW

With reinforcement from the post-implementation review, the MIS should meet its initial objectives. In time the system's environment changes and improvements are possible so that adaptation is required. The periodic review is an occasional appraisal providing adaptive feedback. It is one mechanism for prolonging the system life cycle—an aid to producing a dynamic system.

Our contingency approach suggests the effective MIS will fit the circumstances, and the circumstances change over time. The contingent variables which should be appraised are: (1) the external environment; (2) the organisation's strategy; (3) the organisation structure; (4) the available technology; (5) the system's particular task; and (6) the behavioural context (people). These will vary in impact, especially differing between operational control and management control MIS—see Figure 11.4. Methods of appraisal are not common to each variable. In general review methodology is pragmatic; any source of information is tapped and any available means adopted. The six contingent variables provide a framework. Clearly they can only be assessed by a joint user–specialist team.

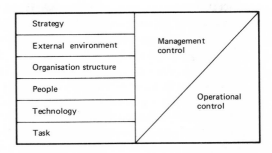

FIGURE 11.4. Relative impact of contingent variables

STRATEGIC CHANGE

Strategic changes have more impact on management control than operational control systems, as the organisation's key control variables are affected. Long-range planning has to adapt and so may the controls of short-term planning and performance tracking and diagnosis. For example introduction of strategic planning demands forward-looking rather than rear-view controls together with action-oriented reporting.[8] How are strategy changes discerned? MIS planning should operate within an umbrella of strategic thinking set by top management—Figure 11.5. The strategic context of each MIS should therefore be known; if not, direction must be sought from top management and detail filled in by senior functional management and corporate planners.

There are of course implications for operational control systems. New market entry may require additional routines in a sales analysis system,

FIGURE 11.5. MIS planning

new production technology may impose substantial modifications to a production control system and so on. The challenge very often is to detect the strategic message for management information systems in such changes.

EXTERNAL CHANGE

Not all changes in the external environment trigger strategic change; they may not be so significant. Yet external factors—markets, competition, legislation, politics, etc.—may have impact on the MIS. For example, if management control systems ignore external factors, dramatic strategic change may eventually be needed for survival. At the operational level, external factors may require detailed adaptation—for example, incorporating credit transfer trends in the payroll, or increasing costing field sizes as inflation increases.

Adaptation to external change relies on continuous scanning by those with MIS awareness. This is not easy. Consequently a periodic review team must interview key users in the MIS application area, seeking views on the major external changes.

ORGANISATION CHANGE

Both strategic management and environmental instability may demand new forms of organisation structure. For example, managerial flexibility, adaptation, fluidity and innovation may be better achieved by organic, rather than mechanistic, organisation forms.[9] New information flows may then be required. Indeed environmental and task uncertainty seem to demand more information processing, strategies for which include use of slack resources, improved channels of communication, development of vertical information systems or better lateral coordination.[10] The MIS and the organisation must adapt therefore in tandem. Likewise management control systems and organisation evolve together, strategic thinking and long-range planning seemingly aided by profit responsibility accounting.[11]

Whatever the causal factors, in any organisational change there are likely to be MIS implications. Minor changes, such as creation of new cost centres, will be accommodated in normal ongoing MIS maintenance. The periodic review should aim to establish how the organisation structure has altered since the last review, or since system installation, and consider whether the MIS is still congruent with it. At the management control level, information flows often become inappropriate over time as structures evolve. At the operational control level, the man–machine interface may have changed and the locus of decisions, and thus their mechanisms, be quite different. This in turn may invalidate the assumptions of the management control system. Industrial dynamics modelling then can be used to assess and predict the consequences of such changes.

Organisations themselves are a mix of our other contingent variables— Leavitt's view of this interdependence is reproduced in Figure 11.6. It is therefore important when assessing the remaining variables to return and reconsider the implications for the different interfaces between the MIS and the organisation.

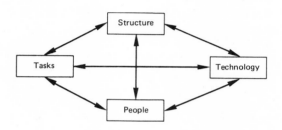

FIGURE 11.6 Leavitt's view of organisations (from Leavitt, H., *Applied Organisation Change in Industry. Structural, Technical and Human Approaches*, New York: Wiley, 1964)

PEOPLE CHANGES

The periodic review is here concerned with how changes in human behaviour may affect the MIS, and vice versa. Information use and its relationship with human behaviour is as important as the technicalities of systems design. The mere availability of information does not ensure its acceptance and appropriate use. However, there is a danger in reviewing use, namely that in response to behavioural 'difficulties', either the MIS is modified or the people are altered, without the true, and probably complex, underlying causes being understood.

Chapter 10 stressed how information is interpreted and used according to the recepient's beliefs and motives, his pressures and expectations, the demands of the organisation environment and individual psychological make-up. Analysis of information use is therefore complex. Key questions can be asked such as:

(1) What information is not used and why?
(2) Is information use too rigid?

(3) Is formal information interpreted with too much credence?
(4) What biases or fiddles are incorporated?
(5) Do managers manage their reports rather than their actions?
(6) Does the MIS encourage short-run behaviour?
(7) What informal or private information is used?

Interpretation of the answers, or even asking the questions, is, however, not simple. In-depth survey and questionnaires are required, carried out with behavioural science awareness and statistical care. For example, use of management control information, by being linked with managerial performance evaluation, can be particularly complex to analyse.[12] Questionnaire approaches to MIS evaluation are examined more fully later in the chapter.

Of course, information use, abuse or non-use may reflect a mismatch between the social and technical system. Technology—or its application—is not always neutral. Periodic surveys can be used to assess MIS impact on job satisfaction and the quality of working life in general. Such mismatches not only will be socially damaging, but also reduce MIS effectiveness. At the operational level, many inadequate interfaces are not wholly apparent until sought out.

In Chapter 9, the delicate boundary between formal and informal systems was discussed. The qualities of informal MIS—their spontaneity, flexibility and social nuances—were seen to provide adaptation and variety in the face of complexity and uncertainty. Thus informal systems complement formal systems. In addition we can recognise unofficial (or perhaps private) MIS which represent managerial responses to in-adequacies of the official MIS, perhaps restoring control to users who have been provided with a technically oriented and inappropriate system. These often suit local needs, private motives and managers' individual styles and may be more responsive to change. Table 11.2 classifies these MIS alternatives, giving examples of each.

Both informal and unofficial systems can be a rich source of design ideas. Periodic reviews should establish therefore what other information besides that provided by the formal, official MIS is used and why. Only if these alternative systems are duplicate or redundant, should they be abolished. Equally they should only be formalised or 'adopted' (made official) if one of the following conditions exists:

(1) The user is overloaded with information, and formalisation or adoption would provide filtration and condensation.
(2) The information is crude and can be improved by formalisation or adoption.

TABLE 11.2. The information system mix

	Formal	*Informal*
Official	Production control system Budgetary control reporting system	Memoranda Task forces
Unofficial	'Black books' Parallel or supplementary records 'Just-in-case files'	'Grape-vine' 'Lunch-table meetings'

(3) Scarce resources are being inefficiently consumed by unofficial or informal systems.

(4) The assumptions and model at the core of the unofficial system are more realistic than those of the official system.

Abolition, formalisation or adoption therefore must be pursued with care. The very effectiveness of alternative MIS may depend on their unofficial status or informal behaviour. They may be crucial to the MIS mix, being complementary, interstitial, flexible or dialectic in purpose. To disturb them may also impair a climate of spontaneity and innovation.

TECHNOLOGICAL CHANGE

MIS need not keep in step with technological change. However, technological enhancement may be relevant if: (1) it would increase MIS efficiency; (2) it would extend the scope of the MIS; (3) it would allow previously non-feasible requirements to be met; (4) it offers social benefits or opportunities; and (5) it offers an opportunity for technical experimentation without undue risk.

Technological change tends to have greater impact on operational control systems as they tend to be more machine-oriented and demand efficiency. Improved data collection, data communication, database and real-time technology have, for example, had considerable impact in recent years.

Technological change is not confined to hardware. It includes:

(1) New techniques, e.g. management science models.

(2) New information sources, e.g. availability of forecasts, or commercial databases.

(3) Potential interfaces, e.g. with other systems.

(4) New hardware, e.g. input/output media.
(5) New software, e.g. new application packages or operating software.

Such opportunities have to be scanned. Organisations frequently appoint someone to monitor technological advance, but this does not guarantee that potential applications are recognised. MIS planning processes will be concerned with exploiting new technologies, but only the user may see the valuable and relevant implications. Thus scanning is only an aid; the periodic review also contributes by tapping all sources and interviewing users and specialists alike.

TASK CHANGES

Task changes in this context include adoption of new working methods, engagement in new activities and operating at changed activity levels. Thus they particularly affect operational control systems; but the management control system may have to respond with newly relevant controls. Equally there may be behavioural repercussions.

Many task-induced MIS modifications will be accommodated through ongoing system maintenance. However, it is not unusual for task changes to be overlooked, their MIS significance to be underestimated or temporary amendments to be made. Task surveys are thus an essential element of periodic review.

EVALUATION BY QUESTIONNAIRE

In both post-implementation and periodic reviews, we have suggested that information use can be evaluated by questionnaire survey. Seward[13] has experimented with this methodology, measuring user satisfaction with an MIS as a surrogate for system effectiveness. User satisfaction may indeed be a valid measure, since dissatisfaction is likely to lead to users disowning or abandoning the MIS. Such questionnaire measurement, however, is a delicate exercise, as Seward admits.

Firstly, users may not know their true attitude to the MIS and thus demonstrate a superficial reaction which in turn may be true or false. This generally can be overcome by ensuring that the real users or decision-makers are identified and surveyed and that the questions they are asked are clear and relevant. Secondly, however, the user may have a perception of what are 'right' and 'wrong' responses and give a reply which he thinks the organisation expects of him. Alternatively if he is threatened by the system or the survey, he may give a protective or defensive reply. Where there are minimal social expectations of 'right' and 'wrong' responses a direct approach should work. Where such social expectations are likely to be strong, where personal threats are involved, an indirect approach is preferred. The indirect approach disguises the true nature of the inquiry. Results from indirect surveys, however, may be difficult to interpret.

In all cases, Seward recommends anonymity in questionnaires, and also stresses the need for top management support to ensure the survey is taken seriously. A non-threatening climate should also be fostered. Seward's procedure then involves eight steps:

(1) Define the MIS to be evaluated by reference to its outputs, rather than by decision analysis.
(2) Determine the user groups, ensuring the real users, plus legitimate secondary users, are surveyed.
(3) Determine the user functions.
(4) Determine the most important information dimensions of the MIS.
(5) Design and test the questionnaire, ensuring that there is a question to cover each combination of user group, user function, MIS component and MIS dimension. Use pilot tests to eliminate any doubts and to refine the questions.
(6) Administer the questionnaire. Use conventional questionnaire techniques to ensure an adequate response. The evaluation may have to be 'sold' first.
(7) Perform statistical analysis. Questionnaires should be designed with both ease and rigour of analysis in mind. Computer assistance is invaluable.
(8) Report the analysis results to appropriate staff and line personnel.

Questionnaire analysis generally should form only part of the evaluation process. Follow-up interviews may well add value to the results. Furthermore the evaluators may need to add their own normative comparisons, since user standards of satisfaction may be influenced by previous experience of MIS, or by inadequate appreciation of what is possible. Also subjective statements and less constrained opinion may well add valuable texture to the questionnaire results.

REVIEW PERIODICITY

Timing of periodic reviews must vary with circumstances. However, it is likely that most MIS require an in-depth review at least within three years of installation; otherwise system decay will be premature. It is quite feasible, and sometimes more manageable, to break down periodic reviews into discrete studies of each variable. However, the interdependence of these factors, and the desirability of combining system amendments together, make integrated reviews preferable.

MIS SECURITY

Information is a key resource. A management information system is an asset. Organisations become dependent upon information systems. So MIS must be secure and, should any breaks occur, recovery must be possible.

As systems grow in complexity, errors, security breaks and crime become both more costly and more difficult to detect. Internal controls are of course vital, as stressed in Chapter 5, but computerisation has made controls more diffuse, while data and know-how have become more concentrated and vulnerable. Real-time systems, data communication, mini- and micro-computers, database technology, distributed computing and integrated systems have all posed new security problems.

Because information systems are so central to managerial activity and because their design and operation involves the entire organisation, security is a management responsibility. Unfortunately, managers frequently lack security awareness because they fail to see the implications, because their computer or MIS education is inadequate and because security rarely appears as a priority issue. Yet consider some recent events:

(1) A fifteen-year-old London schoolboy gained access to secret computer files of company accounts and payrolls and was not detected until later.
(2) A disgruntled employee erased all debtor records on the sales ledger files six months after he left his firm. The company never recovered and went bankrupt.
(3) Computers were central in the insurance fraud of $2 thousand million at Equity Funding Corporation.
(4) A computer operator suddenly went ill while on duty and crashed all the disk-drives before anyone could stop him.
(5) At Cape Kennedy a space launching failed because, during a computer program amendment, a symbol was inadvertently omitted. This resulted in the rocket going so far off course that it had to be destroyed.
(6) A programmer in a bank managed to steal large amounts of money simply by programming the computer to by-pass his account number when reporting on overdrafts. He was then free to overdraw his account by any amount he pleased.
(7) A computer room was sited on the first floor of a building, in the belief

it was safe from fire, flood and explosion. When the ground floor caught fire, the first floor collapsed and the computer room with it.

Of course these are dramatic examples and it is often such cases, especially computer-dependent ones, which reach the headlines. However, it is the simplest frauds which work, the innocent errors which cause chaos and the unwitting mistakes which are most frequent. Because historically security has often been underemphasised, managements are now initiating security reviews.

SECURITY DEFINITIONS

Security can be defined as the ability to withstand attack whether deliberate or accidental.[14] Therefore a secure management information should satisfy three criteria:

(1) Availability—the system should be operational when required.
(2) Integrity—the system should be accurate and meet its designed intent.
(3) Confidentiality—access to the system and its information should be controlled where necessary.

System security is a problem of risk management and two concepts of risk are of value:[15] (1) vulnerability is the cost that an organisation would incur if the security break occurred, and (2) exposure is the vulnerability to that security break multiplied by the probability of its occurrence within a given time.

Complete security is impossible and too expensive. The possible risk has to be balanced against the cost of prevention; hence the concept of exposure involving probabilities. By estimating a financial amount at risk and the probability of attack, security priorities can be assessed. Martin[16] offers the following formula if these two factors can be quantified:

$$E = \frac{10^{(P+D-3)}}{4} \, \pounds \, \text{p.a.}$$

where E = exposure, P = probability of attack, and D = vulnerability.

SECURITY DESIGN

Designing secure management information systems requires three sets of counter-measures: (1) to minimise the probability of security breaks, (2) to minimise the danger if they happen, and (3) to provide a method of recovery.

It helps in devising these measures to be aware of potential threats. These can be classified as: acts of God, hardware/software failure, human carelessness, malicious damage, crime, and privacy invasion. The traditional approaches to internal control go a long way to ensuring acceptable security levels. In particular the notion of multiplicative probabilities is valuable—setting more than one control or safeguard, so that if one fails, it is unlikely that the next will. This is the rationale behind keeping three or more generations of master files. It also leads to the concept of security layers—Figure 11.7—where different sets of controls provide an envelope of security around the system.

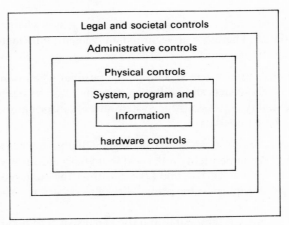

FIGURE 11.7. The security envelope

The techniques, controls and procedures available within these layers are numerous and can be consulted in many reference books.[17] It should be remembered that as formal systems grow more complex and sophisticated, there are as many opportunities for designing counter-measures as there are new security threats.

MIS PRIVACY

MIS privacy is a subset of the security problem, and many of the counter-measures required are similar. However, privacy problems hitherto have been rare. For instance, in the UK it seems that neither private nor public sector computing have posed major threats hitherto.[18] Nevertheless, several governments are legislating to provide machinery to safeguard privacy of information.

The growing formalisation and computerisation of information systems does increase exposure through: (1) the extent of record systems and data retention, (2) the ease, speed and distribution of information access, (3) the rapid transfer of data, (4) the possible combination of data not otherwise practicable, (5) the coding and thus language of data, and (6) the advances in applications. So the dangers which these trends present can be classified as: (1) inaccuracy, incompleteness and irrelevance of data, (2) access by unauthorised parties, and (3) use of information in a context, or for a purpose, not originally envisaged.

Clearly while these dangers may be remote, should they arise the consequences could be disturbing. It is for this reason that legislation is growing. The objectives set out in the recent UK white paper[19] for safeguarding privacy of information are indicative of worldwide trends. They provide a sound set of criteria to adopt in a privacy or security review:

(1) Those responsible for holding all personal information in computers must be under an obligation to take all reasonable protective measures to ensure that information cannot fall into the wrong hands whether by design, inadvertance or deliberate penetration.

(2) Those who hold personal information in computers should not conceal the scope of their operations—particularly from those to whom the information relates.

(3) The existence and purpose of such information should be publicly known, as well as the categories of data handled, what is done with the data and which interests have access to data.

(4) People asked to provide information should know who will access it, and for what purpose.

(5) The information provided should not be used for purposes other than that originally intended, unless the subject gives consent.

(6) Only personal information necessary for declared purposes should be collected.

(7) The operator of the system should be responsible for the accuracy and relevance of personal information, while the subject should be able to satisfy himself about this, for example by visual check and, if necessary, by correction.

(8) The subject should be able to find out what the information has been used for and by whom.

(9) The information should only be kept for as long as it is needed.

(10) Analytical statistics based on personal information should not reveal individual identities or details.

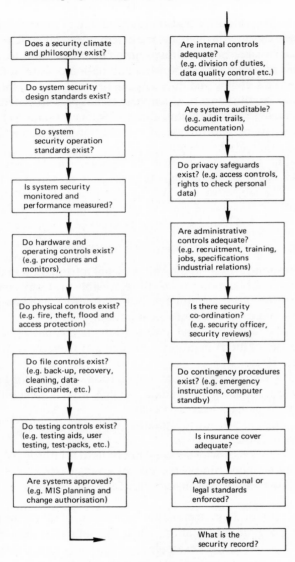

FIGURE 11.8. Security checklist

SECURITY REVIEW

The aim of the security review is to appraise MIS security and possibly create a security climate. Clearly the major task is to verify that effective security controls exist. The flowchart in Figure 11.8 provides a valuable checklist. It also often helps to consider how the system might be attacked. However, three further tasks are important: (1) to define security objectives if none exist, (2) to define security levels and responsibilities if none exist, and (3) to create security awareness.

Security can be perceived as desirable but all-too-vague without clear objectives. Martin[20] offers the following objectives which one company adopted:

(1) Ensure integrity and accuracy for planning and control.
(2) Ensure privacy of data.
(3) Protect employees from temptation.
(4) Protect employees from suspicion.
(5) Protect assets from hazard.
(6) Ensure survival and recovery.
(7) Protect management from charges of imprudence.

Defining responsibilities and levels of security must vary with each organisation. It helps however to consider the three major processes of MIS administration and identify who should be responsible at what point, and what levels of security are desired. The three processes are:

(1) MIS planning—requires top management direction on security, establishment of criteria for selecting security projects, and security awareness in project approval.
(2) MIS design—requires security awareness in systems analysis phases and security standards for system implementation phases.
(3) MIS operation—requires security awareness in user areas and standard security disciplines and controls in operation.

Creation of security awareness can only be achieved by ardent review and sustained training. Security performance measurement can help and security reviews might assess the following:

(1) How appropriate are existing security measures to the particular organisation and its interests?
(2) To what extent are security techniques applied?
(3) What is the level of security awareness and motivation?
(4) How much advice and cooperation on security has been sought?
(5) Is there any overall security coordination?
(6) What is the history of security breaks?
(7) How effective were the recoveries?

Above all, however, top management direction helps create awareness, for it should be stressed that security is not just a technical matter. Technicians have an important responsibility, but all managers and users are involved. It is the users who depend on management information systems. They often have most immediate knowledge of the application and have most to lose.

MIS AUDITING

A specialised form of MIS performance measurement is that practised by auditors. External auditing may be classified into substantive and compliance auditing. Substantive auditing is the verification of financial results, normally by external auditors. If these results are derived in part from formal information systems, then their derivation must be checked. Compliance auditing is the examination of the technical process by which the results are produced. If formal systems are involved, in order to predict their reliability, the auditor must examine the processing, procedures and controls. He is concerned with the accuracy and reliability of data, the validity of its processing and the relevance and objectivity of the information produced.

Compliance auditing is also the concern of internal auditors. Their brief, however, is not confined to financially-oriented systems, so that any formal MIS can be examined. Increasingly internal, and occasionally external, auditors are being asked as a third party to do performance audits. These are special studies such as efficiency audits or security reviews.

AUDITING TECHNIQUES

Only compliance and performance audits are relevant to systems performance measurement. Several techniques are now used and are summarised in Table 11.3. Many of these can also be employed in post-implementation and periodic reviews.[21] Auditing techniques can be classified into auditing around or auditing through the computer. If the formal MIS is not computer-based, then the former class of techniques is of course appropriate. Auditing around the computer treats the computer as a black box and concentrates on verification of inputs and outputs and on examination of supporting and manual controls and procedures. Auditing through the computer examines the black box by checking files, reviewing programs and using the computer itself as an audit tool through use of special audit programs. Selection of appropriate techniques depends on the problem in hand, the cost involved and the expertise available. In many circumstances a mix of methods is applied.

TABLE 11.3. Auditing techniques

Class	Technique	Advantages	Disadvantages
Auditing around	Audit trail review	(1) Little training required (2) Results-oriented	(1) Not necessarily comprehensive (2) May need supporting techniques
	Internal control questionnaire	(1) Sound for security review (2) Provides a total view	(1) Does not test actual processing or results, so needs supporting methods
Auditing through	Parallel simulation	(1) Provides a realistic test (2) Under auditor control (3) Thorough method	(1) Needs expertise (2) Costly to run (3) Needs maintenance
	Test-decks	(1) Tests significant areas (2) Under auditor control (3) Thorough method	(1) Relies on sound documentation (2) May miss errors
	Snapshot	(1) Designed to test and collect specific data (2) Can help DP staff	(1) Is only a partial approach
	Special audit enquiry programs	(1) Can test specific issues (2) Multiple facilities	(1) Needs expertise (2) Costly
	General-purpose audit programs	(1) Easier than special programs (2) Tests results and processing	(1) Needs expertise
	Program review	(1) Tackles detailed problems (2) Probes suspicions (3) Anti-fraud measure	(1) Needs programming expertise (2) Can be costly
	Integrated test facility	(1) Little training required (2) Low cost (3) Tests actual operation (4) Understood by everyone	(1) Needs rigorous control (2) May miss conditions
	Flowchart review	(1) Can be easier than program review in same circumstances (2) Aided by flowchart generation software	(1) Needs expertise (2) Can be costly (3) May be operational constraints
	Audit review files	(1) Can be ongoing (2) Can be run down (3) Can collect data	(1) May be resisted (2) Costly investment (3) Needs maintenance

Systems designers have three responsibilities to auditors: (1) to consult them during system design, seeking advice and establishing audit requirements, (2) to provide an auditable system, and (3) to help auditors during execution of the audit task.

As legal, professional and social codes grow tighter, the audit profession will be called on to examine management information systems in greater depth. As management's awareness of system security increases and as its concern for efficient, as well as effective, systems operation grows, then internal audit may well expand. Both designers and users will then have to improve their understanding of the purpose and practice of MIS auditing.

CONCLUSION

Measuring system performance can readily become an end in itself, rather than a means to an end. It should be seen as a phase of the systems development life cycle which leads to MIS correction and adaptation. Unfortunately this depends on organisational learning—which cannot be guaranteed. There are many inhibitors and obstacles to learning. Goals conflict, politics confuse and preconceptions obstruct. Argyris[22] suggests that learning and correction will only happen if the original MIS objectives, or the loyalty and competence of those involved, do not need to be questioned. Otherwise the inhibitors are activated, such as cover-ups, accusations, coalitions, inertia and the like. So a climate of organisational learning must be fostered. Many of the design principles advanced in earlier chapters—participation, prototype systems, simple but relevant models—may be conducive, although Argyris has questioned this.[23] In all probability learning climates depend on balance, a balance of congruence and conflict, of consensus and antithesis. Hedberg and others,[24] when they prescribed self-designing organisations founded on adaptation and learning, suggested that an ideal set of 'minimal balances' might be pursued. These are reproduced below and seem to fit the context of MIS design and review equally well. The interpretations are mainly ours.

(1) Minimal consensus, i.e. too much agreement may be stifling.
(2) Minimal contentment, i.e. alarms and questioning are necessary.
(3) Minimal affluence, i.e. to prevent stagnation.
(4) Minimal faith, i.e. over-reliance on plans and original objectives and design may be too inflexible.
(5) Minimal consistency, i.e. avoid drastic revolutions and consider some incrementalism.

(6) Minimal rationality, i.e. some imperfection and unconformity may aid creativity and insure against invalid assumptions.

Measuring systems performance is therefore not a mechanistic procedure. It is a delicate process, heavily dependent upon a learning climate.

CHAPTER 11—PROJECTS

1. What are the strengths and limitations of the user satisfaction questionnaire method of evaluating system performance?

2. If in the course of a periodic review of a marketing information system, you discovered that a local unofficial MIS was being used in preference to the official system, what questions would you wish to ask of whom and why?

3. You are employed as an internal auditor and have been asked to assist in ensuring that your organisation's new computer-based purchasing and purchase accounting system is secure. What controls and procedures would you recommend?

4. As director responsible for information systems, you believe it would be beneficial to evaluate the performance of your firm's stock control system. The computer department have been reluctant to cooperate and the users believe no good will come of it. How would you proceed?

5. 'We know so little about the value of information and do not yet understand the complex process of information use, that measuring MIS performance is a lost cause.' Discuss this assertion.

NOTES

1. Nolan, R. L., *Management Accounting and Control of Data Processing*. New York: National Association of Accountants, 1977.
2. For example, see McFarlan, F. W., 'Management Audit of the EDP Department', *Harvard Business Review*, May–June 1973; or Dearden, J., and Nolan, R. L., 'How to Control The Computer Resource', *Harvard Business Review*, November–December 1973.
3. Alloway, R. M., 'Temporary Management Systems: Application of a Contingency Model to the Creation of Computer-based Information Systems', Executive Summary, Stockholm School of Economics, November 1976.

4. *Ibid.*
5. Dickson, G. W., and Powers, R. F., 'MIS Project Management: Myths Opinion and Reality', Working paper 71–01. The Management Information Systems Research Centre, University of Minnesota, Minneapolis, 1971.
6. Many of the following economic performance measurement procedures have been drawn from: Hall, P. G., and Lincoln, T. J., 'A Cost Effectiveness Study of Production and Engineering Systems within a Tightly Integrated Manufacturing Environment', *Management Datamatics*, 5, No. 6 (1977).
7. King, W. R., and Rodriguez, J. I., 'Evaluating Management Information Systems', Working Paper 251, Graduate School of Business, University of Pittsburgh.
8. Gilbert, X. F., 'Does your Control System fit your Firm?', *European Business*, Spring 1973.
9. Burns, T., and Stalker, G., *Management of Innovation*. London: Tavistock, 1968.
10. Galbraith, J., *Designing Complex Organisations*. Reading, Mass.: Addison-Wesley, 1973.
11. Vancil, R. F., 'What Kind of Management Control do you need?', *Harvard Business Review*, March–April 1973; Gilbert, X. F., 'Does your Control System fit your Firm?', *European Business*, Spring 1973.
12. See, for example, Hopwood, A. G., *An Accounting System and Managerial Behaviour*. Lexington, Mass.: Saxon House, 1973.
13. Seward, H. H., 'Evaluating Information Systems', in McFartlan, F. W., and Nolan, R. L. (eds.), *The Information Systems Handbook*. Homewood, Ill.: Dow Jones–Irwin, 1975.
14. Martin, J., *Security, Accuracy and Privacy in Computer Systems*. Englewood Cliffs, N.J.: Prentice-Hall, 1973.
15. National Computing Centre, *Where next for Computer Security?*, NCC, 1974.
16. Martin, J., *op. cit.*
17. See, for example, Martin, J., *op. cit.*, or Mair, W. C., Wood, D. R., and Davis, K. W., *Computer Control and Audit*. Institute of Internal Auditors, 1976.
18. HMSO, *Computers and Privacy*, Cmnd 6353, December 1975.
19. HMSO, *Computers: Safeguards for Privacy*, Cmnd. 6354, December 1975.
20. Martin, J., *op. cit.*
21. For more detailed information on these techniques see, for example, Mair, W. C., Wood, D. R., and Davis, K. W., *op. cit.*
22. Argyris, C., 'Organisational Learning and Management Information Systems', *Accounting, Organisations and Society*, 2, No. 2 (1977).
23. *Ibid.*
24. Hedberg, B., Nystrom, P., and Starbuck, W., 'Camping on Seesaws: A Prescription for Self-Designing Organisations', *Administrative Science Quarterly*, 21 (1976).

BIBLIOGRAPHY

Hopwood, A. G., *An Accounting System and Managerial Behaviour*. Lexington, Mass.: Saxon House, 1973.

Mair, W. C., Wood, D. R., and Davis, K. W., *Computer Control and Audit.* Institute of Internal Auditors, 1976.

Martin, J., *Security, Accuracy and Privacy in Computer Systems.* Englewood Cliffs, N.J.: Prentice-Hall, 1973.

McFarlan, F. W., and Nolan, R. L., *The Information Systems Handbook.* Homewood, Ill.: Dow Jones–Irwin, 1975.

NCC, *Where next for Computer Security?* The National Computing Centre Limited, Manchester, England, 1974.

Part IV Strategic Planning

12 The Nature of Strategy

There is a great deal of confusion of terminology on the subject of strategy. It does not matter too much if one person uses the word policy where another uses strategy and yet another uses the term procedure, as long as each knows what the other means. But this knowledge is often absent, so it seems sensible at the start of this part of the book to define some of the terms we will be using.

The first and most important is the term 'goal'. This is sometimes used synonymously as the 'objective' or 'mission'. It is the condition in which the person (or company or other organisation) intends to ensure that he (or it) will be at some specified future date. Normally, one goal is insufficient. Life is too complicated for that. So many firms specify a series of goals, each covering a single dimension of the firm's operations. One might specify the target return on investment. Another, the target growth rate. Another, the penetration of the firm's principal market. In most instances, these subgoals will be subordinated to a general target, which may well be published in the firm's annual report. Some examples of the umbrella objective statements are given below, taken from published sources.

The Dowty Group Limited organisation has taken shape from its main purpose, which is to develop original [engineering] products for a variety of markets where the product tends to sell itself. The main emphasis is always on the technical side.[1]

The objective is that the group should remain an oil-based industrial enterprise with a still substantial stake in the North Sea, a share in profitable LNG ventures, and in due course a profitable reduced tanker operation based principally on the Bahamas terminal.[2]

. . . our determination to be a prime mover in the UK leisure industry. 'Ladbroke's Leisure' is the sign recognised and accepted by the public as that of a hard-working and imaginative company dedicated to the concept of quality and reliability.[3]

The principal activities of the Company and its subsidiaries in the UK and the Republic of Ireland comprise the purchase, transportation and refining of crude petroleum and the marketing of the resultant fuels and other petroleum products and derivatives.[4]

Once a goal has been set for a company, one must consider how the goal will be approached. The method of approach is here called a strategy. As the range of possible goals is close to infinite, so the list of possible strategies for attaining them must also be vast. There is even an extensive list of bases upon which strategies can be classified. So any approach to strategic studies that seeks to identify and evaluate strategies by taxonomic means must be suspect. The dimensions of variability are, at least at present, too numerous for the approach to be productive.

This assertion can be supported by a simple review of the taxonomic studies already in the literature, and by noting that no two of them have used the same basis for classification except in cases where a study was a deliberate replication of an earlier one.[5]

If, however, we are going to reject the taxonomic approach to the study of strategy formulation, we must decide upon an alternative. In view of the great diversity of circumstances affecting companies and the wide differences between their respective resources and their attitudes, any attempt at a general-purpose model will fail. For any rule that can be devised at the strategy level, there will be more exceptions to it than examples of conformity.

The approach to strategy analysis which occupies the bulk of this chapter would never have been possible without the field data supplied by the taxonomists already mentioned. But it attempts to deal with that data in a rather different way.

In statistical investigations, it is customary to establish a 'null hypothesis' at the outset. This, generally, is a statement that two or more groups of interest are exactly the same as each other with respect to some variable of interest. Thus, for example 'there is no difference on the average between the height of British adult males and adult females'. This null hypothesis is now in a form which can be addressed; the required measurements can be made. The results can be summarised, and the null hypothesis can be accepted or rejected. In addition, in most instances, one can make statements about the degree of confidence with which the hypothesis is accepted or rejected.

In the study of strategy formulation, the ideal of the null hypothesis can very usefully be borrowed, to aid in formulating the decisions to be addressed. The 'null strategy', as we shall here call it, is a statement that the company is completely satisfied with the existing state of affairs. It has normally been found useful to subdivide the null strategy into elements, as we shall demonstrate below. Unfortunately, it has not usually been possible to carry out the statistical analysis normally associated with the null hypothesis idea; firms must accept or reject the null strategy concept by direct observation and the use of informed judgement. But the null strategy method does help the executive group pin down the segments of the firm needing attention. Also, the method helps the manager identify segments of the evolving environment which may be becoming opportunities or threats.[6]

The objective of the exercise is to ensure that a number of specific aspects of the enterprise are carefully and regularly considered by the management. The firm cannot afford to assume that all aspects of its world are in good condition except for those few in which there is a 'brushfire' at the moment. Of course, no executive would ever admit to making such an assumption, but there is often a tendency to carry on the business of the enterprise as though it were true.

THE AGENDA FOR STRATEGY FORMULATION

The subjects which are addressed in the following agenda for strategy formulation are, the geographic region served, the product line at present, the customer groups, material resources, people resources, and organisation. The goal in each case is to ask a series of questions which will help the managers find out what strategic options exist, and which will ensure that they cover the entire spectrum of the firm's operations in doing so. Each section of the agenda has a reference code, and this coding will be used to demonstrate the use of the agenda in an example at the end of the chapter. The coding is summarised in Figure 12.1.

(A) GEOGRAPHIC AREA

'The existing geographic region serviced by the firm is perfectly satisfactory.' This is the statement of null strategy with respect to geography.

(A1)   The characteristics of each of the *Neighbouring regions* not now serviced must be measured with respect to:

(A1A)   *Accessibility*. Includes transport costs for the existing product line, and tariffs if applicable. An estimate of the 'capital' cost of

(A)   Geographic area

    (A1) Characteristics of neighbouring regions
        (A1A)   Accessibility
        (A1B)   Surfeit
        (A1C)   Sophistication
    (A2) Chatracteristics of present region (subdivided)
        (A2A)   Accessibility
        (A2B)   Surfeit
        (A2C)   Sophistication
        (A2D)   Market growth
        (A2E)   Current sales growth, our firm
        (A2F)   Gross margin trends

(B)   Product line

    (B1) Adjacent products
        (B1A)   Supportiveness of existing lines
        (B1B)   Surfeit of means to fulfil end user need
        (B1C)   Channel convenience
        (B1D)   Breakeven volume required
    (B2) Existing products
        (B2A)   Growth history, sales and profit
        (B2B)   Surfeit
        (B2C)   Immediate future prospects, from budget
        (B2D)   Availability of special-purpose manufacturing capacity

(C)   Customer groups

    (C1) Existing customer groups
        (C1A)   Volume, growth, channel, site
        (C1B)   What do our present customers do with the product?
        (C1C)   Discretion of customers in product selection
        (C1D)   Description of the customer groups
    (C2) New possible customer groups
        (C2A)   What industry do our high-growth-rate customers service?
        (C2B)   For which of our products do the customers of our customers have low discretion?
        (C2C)   In which industries are the customers concentrated who have high discretion with respect to our product groups?

(D)   Materials source

    (D1) Existing sources
        (D1A)   Financial history of relations with each major source of supply, covering volume, growth, dependability
        (D1B)   How important is our firm to each of the major supply sources?
        (D1C)   Duration of existing contracts
        (D1D)   List the sources that are less than satisfactory on the above criteria, and derive a list of the commodities for which new suppliers may usefully be sought
    (D2) Alternative sources
        (D2A)   Location, accessibility, and transportation costs associated with each major alternative supplier
        (D2B)   Nature and feasibility of substitution of the commodity causing trouble. Supply sources for the alternative to be obtained in similar fashion

(D2C)   Feasibility of internal sourcing. Both R&D and acquisition approaches to be considered

(E)   Labour supply

(E1) Existing suppliers of skills
    (E1A)   History of relationships
    (E1B)   Importance of our firm to each of the major groups of suppliers of skills
    (E1C)   Existing contract form
    (E1D)   List of difficult skills, with reasons
(E2) Alternative sources of supply of skills
    (E2A)   Similar supply in different locations
    (E2B)   Substitution of skills
    (E2C)   Training and development of skills in short supply
(E3) Opportunities for suppliers of skills to share in success of enterprise, and vehicles for such sharing
    (E3A)   Information about success
    (E3B)   Financial sharing

(F)   Organisation

(F1) Who decides what? Survey of a reasonable batch of recent successful decisions.
(F2) On what issue does the firm have a decision-making procedure?
    (F2A)   How does the firm keep itself informed about innovations in capital equipment?
    (F2B)   How does the firm decide to obtain a new capital asset?
    (F2C)   How does the firm decide to create a new job?
    (F2D)   Who has the right to initiate a strategic review such as the one now being conducted?
    (F2E)   Who is responsible for monitoring the actions of competitive firms?
    (F2F)   Who is responsible for monitoring the rest of the firms environment, notably government?

FIGURE 12.1. The topic headings for an agenda for strategy formulation

obtaining access, as well as the ongoing costs should be made if possible.

(A1B)   *Surfeit.* Number of firms making existing product line in the new region. Preliminary guess at the size of these firms from published sources if possible.

(A1C)   *Sophistication* of the new region as a market. Is it ready for the existing product line? Or already ahead?

(A1D)   There are obviously numerous additional items that can be important with respect to any single region. But at the early stage of a strategy analysis, it is not appropriate to go into them. It is essential to hit the top items, so do not add more than one other element to section (A1) unless you are sure they are vital.

(A2)   The characteristics of the *present region* served must also be
         reviewed as there may be bits of it which you do not really want to
         continue to service. If the region divides into convenient segments
         the analysis should obviously be subdivided similarly.

(A2A)   Accessibility

(A2B)   Surfeit.

(A2C)   Sophistication.

(A2D)   Growth in market in aggregate.

(A2E)   Growth in current activity by our firm.

(A2F)   It is tempting to put in profit by region in this segment. But it is
         probably misleading except at the gross margin level. Net profit of
         a region is an accounting artefact of no real meaning for most
         firms, because the differences in circumstances swamp the other
         elements entering the net profit calculation—but the net account-
         ing process produces apparently precise comparisons which are
         very likely to be wrong. Stick to gross margin reporting.

(A2G)   Do not add anything else to this list. It is long enough already, and
         we want strategic guidance, not a book. If you must insert an
         (A2H), delete one of the earlier items or you will just get confused,
         and so will the answers.

(A3)   There is a temptation to carry out a region analysis for places
         neither presently served nor neighbouring. Don't. Going into a
         distant region, with long lines of supply, and with customs you are
         not used to, is a good recipe for disaster. Napoleon found that in
         the Moscow campaign. So do not even bother to analyse it. It
         might look very tempting if you did, and then you might find
         yourself sucked into a quagmire.

(B) PRODUCT LINE

The null strategy on product lines is described by the statement that there is
no need, nor is it desirable, to add to the range of products offered, nor to
delete from the existing range.

(B1)   The first set of questions on this topic relates to *adjacent products.*
         These are products which fulfil an end user need which is the same
         as, or closely related to, the need fulfilled by one of the existing
         range of products. For instance, if the firm is currently distributing
         conventional golf tees, adjacent products would be golf tee
         holders, and silver golf tees.

(B1A)   The adjacent products must be reviewed with respect to *sup-*

portiveness of the current range or a part of that range. The addition of a further product may, and if it is an adjacent product probably will, affect the success of the existing product to which it is adjacent. The measure of the impact is the covariance. This is a statistical term which means the degree to which quantities move together or in opposite directions. As we are looking to the future, these can only be estimates. If a covariance is believed negative, so that sales of the new product will reduce sales of the old, then the new product should not be analysed further unless the existing product is in decline.

(B1B) Each adjacent product must be reviewed for its *surfeit*, the extent to which the end user need it could fulfil is already met from other sources.

(B1C) The adjacent product must be reviewed for its *channel convenience*, the extent to which the main channels of distribution now used for existing products can be employed to distribute the new one. If they cannot, the firm is in for a big investment in getting the additional channels activated. For instance, you sell most golf tees through professional shops, but silver ones are sold through the 'luxury executive toy' units of big department stores.

(B1D) It is not worth it unless a proposed adjacent product has come out well on all three of the above dimensions, but if it has succeeded on all three you might want to estimate the *breakeven volume*. Do not try to estimate the sales volume directly at this stage unless you are very sure of a major contract or have some other reason for abnormal certainty. But costs to make, fixed and variable, can be estimated roughly and the market price of the current method of fulfilling the end user need can be found. Division gives the breakeven volume.

(B1E) Now stop. You have spent enough time on this product for a strategy study. Go back and analyse another adjacent product idea. Only if you are sure there is nothing worthwhile left should you move to (B2).

(B2) Existing product line items can be studied more closely than adjacent or distant products, as the internal accounting information system is full of data about them. It is therefore vital to ensure that you spend *less* time on reviewing the existing line than you spend on the others. The temptation to analyse the data you have instead of studying the problems which actually exist, can be very great and must be resisted at all costs.

(B2A) The first thing one needs to know about a product or group is the growth history with respect to both sales and profits.

(B2B)   *Surfeit*, as (B1B).

(B2C)   *Growth prospects* for the product in the existing geographical regions served. The estimates used in the preparation of the annual budget will do. If these do not go forward far enough, ask the sales head. If you promise not to quote him, and have a history of keeping promises, you will probably get a better estimate than if he has to sign his name.

(B2D)   There may be a constraint or an opportunity because of productive capacity of a kind which can only be used for a single product or product group. This will be unimportant in the case of general-purpose production machinery. An estimate of the increase in specialised capacity which would arise from buying one additional machine or other constrained resource, together with the costs of such an addition, may be added here if available.

(B2E)   Stop. You have lots of extra data on every product in the factory, but if you put any more into the strategy review you will swamp the vital external data.

(c) CUSTOMER GROUPS

The null strategy on this issue is given by the statement that the groups of customers with whom business is done directly at present should not be changed in kind at all and should only be augmented in size at a rate adequate to allow for the inevitable drop-outs.

The current facts are vital in all the areas of strategic concern, but they are nowhere more vital than in the study of customer groups.

(C1)   The study of the existing customer group must precede the review of possible further groups, as this study defines the people who can be classed as adjacent groups to the present customer population.

(C1A)   The routine *classification of present customers* by volume, growth, location, and channel of distribution is useful here as it helps concentrate attention on the customer groups which matter. Also the information is readily to hand in most companies. But it is much less important than the other data sought below.

(C1B)   What do our present *customers do with the product* they buy from us? In the case of the retailing of consumer products the answer may be very simple and obvious, though even here a few surprises may be discovered. But in other sectors, the product is reprocessed or resold or used in production. It may be handled by several organisations before it reaches its final destination. If the firm wishes to trace the product through to its final destination, the technique of input–output analysis[7] can be used. But for most firms, especially smaller ones, it may be a sufficient approximation to use one of the government-produced input–output tables for the industry and to assume that the firm's product mix is sufficiently like the industry's in aggregate to allow the comparison. This is much cheaper than carrying out a full-scale analysis and should certainly be tried first. But in the short term, the small-to-medium company will not wish to go so far. A description of uses made by direct customers, not ultimate customers, is required at the start. The classification will normally be sufficiently precise if it is by sector or industry. Thus the output of the analysis will be a list of industries serviced by customers of the firm, with percentages. For some simple and specialised firms this task will be trivially simple. For others, such as manufacturers of general-purpose components, it will be a major undertaking. It is very important, however.

(C1C) The next matter of concern with respect to our existing groups of customers is their *discretion*. Does the customer have a large choice of firms from which he could meet the need he presently meets by using our product? Is there a range of substitute products or materials which could be used to fulfil the need, whoever may supply them? A negative answer to both questions indicates low discretion. It is better, in carrying out a strategy formulation step, to make an estimate of discretion on a relative basis among either our products or our customers, without trying to measure this discretion on any absolute scale. Such scales do not exist.

(C1D) Now we must stop looking at our existing customers and begin to consider adjacent groups of customers. But before we can do that we must define what we mean by adjacent in this setting. Evidently we must include customers of the exact same kind as our own who have just not picked us, so far, for no particular reason that can be discerned. By all means let us try to convert such customers by promotion, advertising, and other efforts, if the present level of direct growth in volume is less than satisfactory. But the strategic issue, with regard to customer groups, is to select by deliberate planning and analysis the group of customers you will go for next from the almost infinite list of customer groups you do not serve at the moment. We need descriptions, of the following general format, of each customer group. 'The buyers of this product group use it as a high-quality sub-component in the assembly of an intricate machine for use in the heavy engineering industry, which machine is vastly more costly than our component. The buyers have no substitute material they could use instead, but there are several firms which could make the sub-component quite well; its patent has now run out. At present these buyers account for all our sales of product X and 40 per cent of product Y, which are between them 10 per cent of total sales.' Once a series of these statements has been drawn up, so that we can characterise our existing customer groups effectively, we can study the strategic options. The details of the exact questions to be answered in such study cannot be written down in general terms—there are just too many variables to be taken into consideration. So all we can do is to write down a list and invite the reader, with a particular firm in mind, to expand it into a full set of questions.

(C2)   Descriptions of possible *new customer groups.*

(C2A) The high-growth-rate customers are the ones who use our products to service the requirements of the P industry and to a lesser extent the Q industry. We have several other products also serving these industries, namely products A, B, and C.

(C2B) The customers of our customers have low discretion with respect to our product types C and D. We may be able to serve these indirect customers directly,

(C2C) The customer groups with high discretion with respect to our product groups seem to be concentrated in the Q industry and the R industry. Our volume to these industries has been X per cent and Y per cent of our estimate of the market size.

(D) MATERIALS SOURCES

The null strategy here is given by the statement that we cannot expect to improve our quality or price or service received with respect to any important raw material, neither by moving to new sources of supply nor by renegotiating contracts with existing sources of supply, nor by substituting an alternative raw material.

(D1)   *Existing sources.*

(D1A) Financial *history of relations* with each major source of supply, covering volume, growth, dependability.

(D1B) Review importance of our custom to each of the main suppliers. *Are we important* to them, relative to their own customers?

(D1C)   Duration of existing contracts. In general, a long contract is better if we are becoming less important to the supplier and vice versa.

(D1D)   Produce now a list of those sources of supply which are less than satisfactory, either in terms of reliability, or in terms of contract terms, or in terms of our importance to them (low importance will normally imply an unsatisfactory source though there are exceptions). Re-define the list of *materials*, the supply of which seems to need attention.

(D2)   *Alternative sources*
This area of study should be confined to the unsatisfactory sources identified in (D1D). A full study of all sources may be appropriate at times, but most of the important strategic changes are likely to be found in the 'unsatisfactory' list. With respect to each group of products, goods, and materials appearing in the (D1D) list, prepare an intuitive analysis of the following issues.

(D2A)   The location of *alternative suppliers* and the accessibility of each, including estimates of the further transportation costs, is an obvious first step. If a capital cost arises, such as a cancellation fee to a current supplier or a start-up stock from the new one, this ought to be estimated roughly and included.

(D2B)   More importantly, the firm must study the possibility of substituting a new material for the unsatisfactory one. For each such new material, the information required in (D2A) must be obtained.

(D2C)   The firm must consider the feasibility of supplying the materials of concern from *internal sources* instead of by purchasing them. In addition to considering the use of research and development talents to find a substitute, the firm may consider acquiring the unsatisfactory supplier, or another (probably smaller) firm with similar capabilities with a view to improving the acquiree's competence in creating the main firm's required product. Do not make an acquisition in haste, make sure you know all the gory details first; also, always double your first estimate of the management time you are going to have to supply from the main firm in order to get the acquired firm sorted out. And remember to cost out that management time at three times salary in working out the effective price of the acquisition. Once for his pay, once for his overhead, and once for the loss of his efforts in doing something else.

(E) LABOUR SUPPLY

The firm makes use of a number of different skills, some of which are largely controlled, either by a union or otherwise, and some of which are 'free' in the sense of being individual. There is really no difference between the supply of labour and the supply of other materials products and services: all are essential to the workings of the firm, and all are the subject of contracts, implicit or explicit. The process of acquiring labour inputs looks different, and is subject to different laws, but it is economically identical. So we must ask exactly the same questions as we asked of suppliers of materials.

(E1A)   History of relationships.
(E1B)   Our importance to the labour force.
(E1C)   Existing contract form.
(E1D)   List of difficult skills.
(E2A)   Alternative sources, including similar sources in new locations.
(E2B)   Substitution of skills.
(E2C)   Training and development of skills in short supply.
(E3)   The only point that really matters in dealing with suppliers of skills is to ensure that they share in the success of the enterprise. If they see it succeeding and can share in its success there should be relatively few entries in the list in (E1D). If they do not share in the success, or if they are not informed about that success, there will be trouble. The task of reporting results to suppliers of skills has been addressed in Part I of this book, and more specific recommendations are also obtainable.[8] If the enterprise is not succeeding, a clear statement of the facts may appear to be damaging. But it is likely to be far less damaging than the rumours that build up quickly in a firm having difficulties.

(F) ORGANISATION

The null strategy with respect to organisation is given by the statement that decision-taking powers are vested at present in the right offices and that the reporting relationships within the firm should be left undisturbed. A 'stock-taking' must obviously form the first part of this phase of the analysis.

(F1)   *Who decides what.* It is not practicable to try to study 'decisions' in the abstract. The majority of firms arrive at decisions by implicit procedures which can only be isolated and described by a 'protocol' procedure, in which a number of examples of decisions taken in the very recent past are traced back to their origins. In doing this work, the best results will be obtained by selecting a batch of decisions of which a quarter were notable successes and the rest were at least reasonable. Trying to trace the origins of disasters leads inevitably to attaching blame for them, and will lead to complete lack of cooperation on the part of all staff involved. So pick some good ones. The least benefit that can accrue from the protocol study is an appreciation of who does what, which can inform both recent and more senior staff valuably. The most benefit can be obtained by a careful study of the protocols to seek opportunities for delegation of powers and responsibilities away from the central group. This not only gives practice and training to the group of middle-rank managers from which at least some of the next top group will be drawn, but also enables some of the existing top group to be freed for strategic review and thinking.

(F2) On '*what issues* does the firm have a decision-taking procedure?', one can often discover, in the course of the analysis under (F1), that there are a number of significant areas with which the firm has no means of coping at all. This is perfectly all right if the decision to take no action is a deliberate decision to take a risk. But it quite often is not. It is worth going through the list to ensure that the omissions are deliberate.

(F2A) How does the firm keep itself informed, on a worldwide basis if required, about developments in and costings of *capital equipment* required for normal production procedures?

(F2B) How does the firm decide upon the *acquisition* of capital assets. Is there a formal appraisal procedure, and does it have any real effect on such acquisitions?

(F2C) How does the firm decide to *create a new job*. In view of the recent legislative procedures[9] in the United Kingdom, which make it very hard indeed to abolish a job, the creation of a new one becomes a much more serious matter than was the case formerly. The casual process of allowing a senior executive to create a new position to deal with a temporary problem may well be insufficient in the new legislative climate.

(F2D) Who has the right to initiate a *strategic review* of the kind this present agenda represents. Is there a mechanism for ensuring that it takes place at some prescribed interval. Is there a clear-cut means of making the review and its results available within the enterprise, and is there someone who has that task?

(F2E)   Who has responsibility *for monitoring the behaviour of competitive firms?* If this monitoring is left to the salesforce, who will react to the arrival of a new product only when rumours of it reach the market, then the firm cannot really expect to meet that competitive advance without a lengthy delay, except by good fortune. Alternatives obviously include the careful sifting of public statements by such companies, the hiring of important members of competitors' staff at strategically chosen moments and the review of scientific papers published by the competitors' research staff. Outright bribery has the same effect, of course, but has the disadvantage of being a violation of the recipient's employment contract and also of laws in certain countries.

(F2F)   Who has responsibility for monitoring the rest of the firm's environment? The firm must somehow or other keep a sharp lookout for changes in government policy, changes in tax law, changes in the investment climate and interest rates, changes in the labour markets, changes in the raw material markets, and so on. Obviously the specific list of things to look out for will vary from one firm to another, but there is bound to be a list of some sort. Who is responsible for drawing up the list of things to be monitored? And who is responsible for carrying it out?

(F2G)   Please add no more than two extra items of your choice to the above list of things to be checked. These should be chosen with the firm's characteristics in mind, rather than those of the industry.

AN EXAMPLE OF THE AGENDA IN USE

In the following section we show what results can be found in a very simple business when the agenda for analysis is followed as discussed above. The firm chosen is a chain of six retail establishments in the pharmaceutical and related products field operating in the UK outside the Greater London region.

A   GEOGRAPHY
A1   *Neighbouring regions* not now serviced [only one of five regions studied is shown here].
A1A   Accessibility. Fairly easy, firm's own transport could feed the area and the main product suppliers could also oblige. Capital costs of access can be limited pending promising initial results.
A1B   Surfeit. Not too bad. The five big national chains seem to be

under-represented in the region, compared to most. Not known why this is so.

A1C Sophistication. The market has previously obtained pharmaceutical services from small specialist shops which have not been diversified nor have they operated as self-service. A certain resistance to self-service for related products can be expected, though as long as the actual drugs are served this should not be serious.

A1D This is a high-unemployment area; the bad debt experience has been awful. Strict cash if we go in.

A2 *Present region.* Not divisible.

A2A Access; no problem at all.

A2B Surfeit. Getting serious. Major encroachments by major national chains. Hurting our volume but not our margins.

A2C Sophistication, no problem.

A2D Market is rated moderately prosperous on national scale, slightly above the national average. Rate of growth also (just) over national average, but that is a pretty poor average. Real growth probably 2 per cent over next two years at best.

A2E Firm has not grown at all in the last three years. The sixth shop was added four years ago, and the first two years after that were spent on consolidating the gains made. Nothing much has happened since. Profit has recently declined with volume.

A2F Gross margins holding.

B PRODUCT LINE

B1 *Adjacent product.* [The firm has for many years provided a service in photo developing and printing, and has sold film. One adjacent line is shown here to illustrate, though twenty were considered in the real situation].

B1A Adjacent product-retail sales of cameras at low end of the price spectrum. Supportiveness: good. Regular requests for camera sales in early days, though this has been less noticeable recently. Covariance with all existing products positive or zero.

B1B Surfeit. Specialist store in vicinity of our two largest units sells general optical goods; tends to emphasise the high-priced goods, and is not doing too well in the present economic climate of the region as a consequence. But he may react violently if we go into cameras. NB: nephew serves on local council.

B1C Channel convenience. Fine; just need an extra display cabinet, or two in the larger outlets. Space is available.

B1D Breakeven volume. To be credible, would need to invest about

£20,000 in displays and in stocks; interest cost about £3000. Mark-up 35 per cent, thereafter breakeven at wages increment of £6000 would be £26,000 approximately. A requirement of pre-tax return on investment of 25 per cent would increase the breakeven to £40,000. Corresponds to 25 cameras a week approximately.

B2   *Existing product line.* [the firm had decided to break down the existing product lines into forty groups. Only one is shown.]

B2A   Film sales and processing. Growth history has been uninspiring but steady. $3\frac{1}{2}$ per cent average annual cash volume for four years. Profits growth: 4 per cent.

B2B   Surfeit. Not applicable.

B2C   Growth prospects for the product. Existing volume can only increase if more people in this area buy cameras and take pictures. They show no signs of doing so at present, though this firm has done little to stimulate them. Growth prospects as per growth history at the moment.

B2D   Processing capability very adequate. Could double the volume with no trouble and only a very small amount of overtime work.

C   CUSTOMER GROUPS. [Only one shown, though basically the same grouping was used for all the product lines separately.]

C1A   Film sales and processing customers:

	Volume	Prior year
Local professional photographer	11	10
Shoppers buying other items	25	24
Regular enthusiastic amateurs	30	20
Other	34	46
	100 %	100 %

C1B   Use of the product by customers:
       (a) film sales—self-evident

(b) film processing— One more print each negative	45 %
Two or more	6 %
Multiprint from negative previously singled	19 %
Enlargements (portrait)	11 %
Enlargements (other)	19 %

C1C   Discretion of our customers. There are thirty other shops within reasonable reach of those customers who use our service which provide film processing. However, only eight of these offer 'next-day' service through on-site working. The discretion is high.

C1D   The bulk of our film custom is from regular shoppers who may buy other goods in the shop but who only want one print of each picture they take. An important subgroup of these bring back at least one picture for either enlargement or for multiple reproduction, as, for instance, in use as a personal greeting card.

C2   *New customer groups.*

C2A   The high growth rate customers are the enthusiastic amateurs who use our services for private entertainment and to a lesser extent for gifts. At the present time we do not have any products intended as gifts, except for a few cosmetic items which are sold primarily during the holiday season.

C2B   There are no products over which our customers have low discretion, except for pharmaceutical products in the case of those customers who have little private mobility. Our customers do not really have customers of their own, except for the occasional professional photographer with whom we have no expertise to compete.

C2C   Not applicable.

D   MATERIALS SOURCES

D1   *Existing sources.*

D1A   Financial history of relations with major film supplier. Excellent in every way. Good service, adequate credit, complaints only very minor indeed. Very dependable deliveries, relative to other product suppliers.

D1B   We are not in the least important to the film supplier. Each outlet of which we have six represents about 1/100th of 1 per cent of total volume. They say, of course, that we are all-important.

D1C   We have no contract at all with the film suppliers. As we do our own processing, there is no need for a contract in this area.

D1D   There are no unsatisfactory suppliers in relation to the part of our business that relates to the film sales and processing industries.

D2   As there are no unsatisfactory sources, this section is inapplicable.

E   LABOUR SUPPLY

E1A   We have always had good relationships with our labour force. This has been true both at the assistant and at the professional levels.

E1B   We are of some importance to the assistant group, as unemployment is high in the area of such people. We are not very important to the professionals, such as the pharmacists, as there is a permanent shortage of these skills.

E1C   There are no labour contracts in force.

E1D   We could certainly make use of more pharmacists. But they are

	very scarce indeed, and the big chains can afford to pay them more than we can.
E2A	Not applicable.
E2B	Substitution is illegal.
E2C	We could send some of our brighter assistants off for training as pharmacists, but there is no guarantee that they would come back.
F	ORGANISATION
F1	The most important decision relating to the photographic section relates to the decision to stock a particular range. The quantities are determined by the supplier once the initial decision is taken to take the range, and we have found the right, which they always provide, to override their allocation of product, to be pointless. This decision is taken by the senior assistant at the main unit. None of the senior photographic assistants at the other units can alter that decision.
F2A	The owner takes all capital investment decisions personally.
F2B	The owner intends to continue taking such decisions.
F2C	The store managers may hire any new assistants they want. Only the owner can hire a professional, either a photographic or a pharmaceutical.
F2D	Nobody has the formal right to initiate a strategic review, but the owner's son initiated this one. So he and the owner are effectively the only people who could initiate a review.
F2E	Nobody has formal responsibility to monitor competitors' behaviour.
F2F	Nobody has responsibility to monitor the other changes that may take place in the firm's environment.

IMPLICATIONS OF THE STUDY

Clearly, the study shown above is incomplete, as only one general product range has been discussed out of a much larger number. But the analysis of the photographic section gives ample food for thought. The firm is in a moderately prosperous area, though one in which unemployment is high. Nonetheless the neighbouring area is in worse shape as far as unemployment goes. The competition in camera sales seems fairly weak, though the possibility exists that the competitor may take frantic action if we move into that field. It is a question of whether we want to ride out the storm. We have an incentive to take some action, as the big chains are moving in on our territory. The required volume for breakeven is shown, and there would be costs attached to breaking into the market, not least in training the sales personnel to deal with customer inquiries. There is little prospect of building up film processing and sales directly, as the customers have a great deal of discretion. Consider acquiring the specialist optical firm. Consider driving him out, and recruiting his specialist staff. We can do little at the input end, as the supplier is far too big. If we do decide to move into the low end of the camera market only, we could hardly hope to retain the interest of the highly trained personnel of the optical firm. It would be necessary to consider a full move into the optical business, which would be a major innovation, and in which no present expertise exists in the firm above the level of senior assistant.

In the case being studied, the owner was afraid of a geographic diversification, as the big chains which were starting to hurt volume already could easily move into such neighbouring areas and they could do so with more power than the owner could muster.

For this reason, he was enthusiastic about the product line diversification idea. The move into opticals was made, eventually, by investigating and eventually acquiring the specialist optical shop. A major addition was made to that shop's product range, to include lower-priced cameras and equipment. This down-market move was profitable.

Evidently, there are an infinite number of possible applications of the agenda. Some pieces of it are not applicable to any given firm. But there are certain features of it which are important to any business. In the first place, it puts heavy emphasis on the external environment and on the competition which the firm must meet. Secondly, it does not pay very much attention to the internal resources of the firm, nor to its cost accounting and management control procedures. These are, of course, vital to its success, but they bear only slightly upon the strategic questions with which the top management must, at least sometimes, be concerned.

We suggest that the cautious but thorough application of the strategic analysis agenda will be of considerable help to a large number of firms, especially smaller and medium-sized firms, which have tended heretofore to react to events in their environment instead of attempting to manage that environment to their own organisational benefit.

CHAPTER 12—PROJECT

Apply the strategy agenda to a small-to-medium-sized firm in your area You will be better advised to do the work in teams, and to carry out a preliminary revision of the agenda to take account of obvious characteristics of the firm you are going to look at. When you have completed the agenda, discuss it with the proprietor(s) or their delegates.

Once an opinion has been expressed on the issues raised by the agenda study, draw up a financial forecast to facilitate the implementation phase. Feed this back into the agenda, and then use the results to amend the strategy decided upon. Report back to the management group upon completion of this revision, or after several repetitions of the cycle of revision if need be.

NOTES

1. Edwards, R., and Townsend, H., *Studies in Business Organisation*. London: Macmillan, 1961, p. 33.
2. Burmah Oil Company Limited, 1975.
3. Ladbroke Group Limited, 1975 Annual Report.
4. Esso (UK) Limited, 1974.
5. Studies of this kind have been made by Chandler, Channon, Steiner, and Bower, amongst others. The full references are in the bibliography of this chapter. The value of these analyses is great, as the observational data they collectively contain is extensive. But it has proved very difficult to apply their generalisations without the original population of study.
6. Ansoff, in his book on corporate strategy (see Bibliography), was the first to use the opportunities and threats idea as a basis for analysis. He also measured the strengths and weaknesses of the firm, to try to bring out imbalances between these elements. The null strategy method here discussed is offered as a more practical method of attaining the same goal, as it is rather less prone to opinion.
7. Gols, A. G., 'The Use of Input–Output in Industrial Planning', *Business Economics*, May 1975, gives a detailed view of how to benefit from this method.
8. The Hundred Group, *Financial Information for Employees*. London District Society of Chartered Accountants, 1978.
9. *The Employment Protection Act*, 1975, HMSO.

BIBLIOGRAPHY

Allison, G. T., *The Essence of Decision*: *Explaining the Cuban Missile Crises*, Boston, Mass.: Little, Brown, 1971.
Ansoff, I., *Corporate Strategy*. New York: McGraw-Hill, 1965.
Argenti, J., *Corporate Planning—A Practical Guide*. London: Allen & Unwin, 1968.
Bower, M., *The Will to Manage*. New York, McGraw-Hill, 1966.
Chandler, A. D., *Strategy and Structure*. New York, Anchor, 1966.
Channon, D. F., *Strategy and Structure of British Enterprise*. London: Macmillan, 1973.
Gutman, P., 'Strategies for Growth'. *California Management Review*, 6 (1964).

Henderson, B. D., 'Strategy Planning', *Business Horizons*, Winter 1964.
Steiner, G., *Top Management Planning*. New York: Macmillan, 1969.
Stotland, J. A., 'Planning Acquisitions and Mergers', *Long-Range Planning*, February 1976.

13 Methods of Formulating Strategies

We have seen in the last chapter what a strategy is. In the chapters to follow we shall consider strategic forecasting and the management of strategic databases. In this one we are concerned with devising a procedure for formulating strategy. The modern corporation, especially the larger ones, cannot normally adopt the free-ranging opportunistic style. There is inevitably a degree of inertia which comes with size and with success. It would be very easy for a firm to adopt the null strategy which we discussed in Chapter 12. Nonetheless, almost every top manager would agree that his company would not pursue the null strategy. He would say that its adoption would lead in the medium-to-long term to a moribund company, to which he would have no desire to remain affiliated. But how does a company set about a job of formulating new strategies? What machinery must it set up?

Mintzberg,[1] has analysed this problem and has identified three different ways of going about solving it. The entrepreneurial approach, characterised by bold strokes and a young, strong, pro-active, flexible leadership, is very difficult to sustain in the larger firm. The choice really is between the two methods he described as the 'adaptive' and the 'planning' approach. Under the adaptive approach, the company establishes its strategic posture in a reactive fashion. It operates in a complex and changing environment, and attempts to deal with its short-term strategic needs by small incremental steps which are devised to meet the needs of the moment. The tidy mind of the planner tends to view this approach with disdain. But there is no evidence that the other method is better.

The planning approach, typically used only in the largest firms, is at its most effective in companies facing a predictable and stable environment. The top executive group formulate global strategies, and then attempt to ensure that the desired results come about. The time horizon over which decisions may be viewed under such an approach can be quite long, although even in these situations plans stretching more than twenty years ahead tend to be rather hazy.

The choice between these two methods, to judge by the management literature on the subject, was an open-and-shut case until 1974. The planning style, which was adopted successfully by some of the largest firms, appealed to a lot of writers on the subject and seemed logical and complete. The resulting plans were tidy, well thought out, carefully balanced and integrated one with another. However, they were no more correct than the less expensive approaches taken by the adaptive school in dealing with the major discontinuity which arose, notably in energy-related industries, as a result of the 1973 Middle Eastern War. Since then the benefits of the adaptive approach have been promoted more vigorously. The untidiness could be seen to be creative. The involvement of line managers and the absence of professionalisation of the planning process began to be seen as a material benefit rather than an untidy drawback. The jury is still out.

Firms adopting the planning approach tend to favour more organised and fully developed systems and procedures for strategy formulation. Obviously that is not really the objective. The objective is to assist the executive who has the decision to take to do a better job of taking those decisions. No-one would argue with this. As Taylor,[2] has put it: 'the planner should focus on the end (decisions and actions) rather than on a particular means (e.g. programme budgeting or some other package)'. It is not reasonable for the planner to adopt an extremely formal and structured system for planning and strategy formulations, if the management of the company has always favoured a more adaptive and less organised approach. Obviously, the best planners have always taken account of the political environment within which they are operating. The problem has been to spend just enough time and effort on scanning the business environment and on the development of new strategies to ensure corporate survival and growth without spending so much time and effort that there is no-one in the company who has any time left to put the new strategic proposals into practice.

THE PLANNING GAP

An obvious first step in deciding how many resources to devote to strategic matters is to find out how far short of target one is initially. Many consultancy firms have produced variations on the techniques of gap analysis for this purpose. This attempts to quantify the difference between the financial growth objectives of the firm and the financial consequences of the null strategy. The results of gap analysis are often presented in a diagram of the general form shown in Figure 13.1. The financial growth objective is shown in the dashed line, expressed in this particular case as earnings per share. The forecast outcome on the continuation of existing policies and practices is shown as a series of circles. The problem is obvious. The target calls for an earnings per share of 14·5p in 1985, as indicated by the point A, whereas the projection of existing activities suggest an attainment of 8p (B). A difference of this scale would signal urgently for the development of a coherent new strategy.

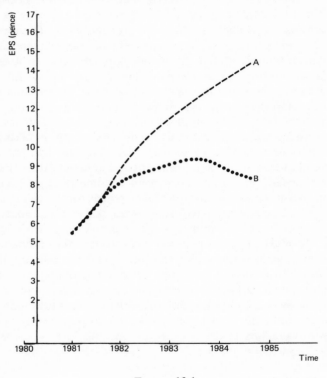

FIGURE 13.1

Weir,[3] has extended this idea by plotting the five-year plan of a series of companies as derived at each of a series of years after the fashion shown in Figure 13.2. The chart indicates the manner in which the planning of the company evolves through time. A stable, predictable company will show patterns of only slight movement. But companies confronting significant uncertainty may well show patterns as dispersed as the one in Figure 13.2.

On the basis of the figures in Figure 13.2 the company may have felt, in

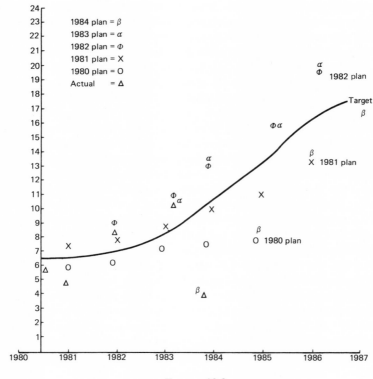

FIGURE 13.2

1983, that it was doing rather well. The actual result (denoted by the triangle) is substantially above the planned figures estimated for 1983 in 1980 and in 1981 and is exactly on target according to the plan devised in 1982. Also, the actual results are above the target growth rate. The planned figures for 1983 indicate that the earnings per share should reach 24p in 1987.

The appalling results obtained in 1984, in which earnings per share were 5p instead of the planned 13p, could be expected to cause the management to initiate an urgent reappraisal. The plan for 1984 (denoted by the beta symbol) is a very typical reaction to the sudden and severe drop. The plan derived in 1984 attempts to reinstate the previous profit growth trend at a very rapid rate. Generally speaking, this growth rate will only be obtainable if the sudden decline in 1984 was traceable to a single non-repeatable mishap.

Gap analysis is a useful strategy point from which to begin a strategic planning process. It can help you estimate the size of the problem. But that is really all the technique can do. It is not designed to help fill the gap, merely to identify it. We must now consider how to fill it.

INFORMAL SYSTEMS FOR STRATEGY FORMULATION

The top management of any company are the people who formulate strategy. Therefore, the system for strategy formulation has to be of a kind that the top managers will use. It need not be tidy and organised, unless top management want it that way. It need not comprehend the entire firm, unless they want it to. It may involve a trained staff of professional planners, or it may involve only the top two or three executives without any staff support at all. Many studies have been conducted of the process,[4] and they all come up with the unsurprising conclusion that planning systems are as different as the firms in which they operate.

The principal advantage of having a system for strategy formulation is that it provides a gap in the daily routine, during which the top management can give their full attention to the longer-term and more fundamental issues affecting the firm. These issues tend to be crowded out otherwise. The top management group's time is a very scarce resource, so the system should be designed to help that group use it effectively. In particular, it should provide current data on the status of the firm and on the status of the industry and the market in a suitably summarised form so that the strategic decisions taken are thoroughly informed. But the system should only go beyond this if the top group explicitly require it to do so. There is no inherent merit in having an integrated planning system, designed in accordance with advanced concepts.

The task is one of helping the strategist make up his mind,[5] and the information requirement of that task depends on his or their character and style. One of the present authors,[6] has already established the importance of this factor in terms of accounting information, and there is no reason to believe that style would matter less at the strategic level.

Aguilar[7] has shown, in studying two small firms' scanning methods, that the size of the top management group can affect the methods of scanning used in small firms, and he also placed considerable weight on the informal contacts among the management and upon their individual characteristics in his analysis of their various methods of scanning.

Given the above emphasis on the personalities of the managers involved, and given the diversity of companies among and within industries, it is clear that any attempts to generalise on strategic planning and thinking systems for small and medium firms must be doomed from the start. So we will not try to.

In the previous chapter we have shown how the null strategy method may be used to analyse the current state of a small firm and the environment within which it operates. We continue to hold that this approach is the most promising; this is especially true in view of the emphasis there placed upon the study of 'adjacent' products and markets to those currently served.

However, a few general comments can be made concerning the goals which strategic systems must seek to fulfil and the characteristics such systems must display.

INFORMAL METHODS—THE SMALL BUSINESS

The function of strategy formulation must be informed by a data system based upon the same relevance principles as any other function requires. The data system must meet the decision options, exactly as we say in earlier chapters. The difference is that the decision options are broader than in other functions. This implies that the strategic data system must be designed to make a series of simple but accurate statements about a broad range of issues. The human mind may have a great capacity for data, but most of us have limited patience. If we are attempting to think strategically, the last thing we need is a planning or control report in infinite detail; but too often that is exactly what we get, because the strategic data system is an aggregation of the management or operational data systems, or both. Instead, the strategic data system must be designed to offer simple guidance on the questions asked in Chapter 14, many of which are not, and can never be, answered by means of a lower-level system, however the aggregation is done.

For instance, one of the null strategy assertions made in the last chapter was, 'The customer groups now being served include all those who can be expected to be interested in our offerings'. You cannot test that one by looking at present activities, by definition. The present group are interested in the firm's offerings, obviously, but many other groups may be or may become interested. The strategic data system must address first the identity of the null strategy event or assertion and then must assist in taking the next step.

In the case of the above assertion, the strategic data system must first measure the characteristics of the current customer group. Having done this, it must then facilitate a search for a new group by showing the effects of relaxing the descriptive constraints. For instance, the strategic data system for a small tobacco shop may assert that the present customer group consisted of 'middle-aged male pipe-smokers living or working or shopping within 800 metres of the corner of Main Street and Central Avenue'. This part can be assessed by aggregation and analysis of existing operations. But the next step, of relaxing the description, one feature at a time, must be done by using external data. But the very act of identification at once raises the questions that must be asked. Are there a significant number of *young* pipe-smokers in the area? Can we attract a proportion of them, and how? What about cigar-smokers or cigarette-smokers? Can we draw people in from an area larger than the immediate neighbourhood? The questions flow at once from the specification of the current null strategy answer to the customer group question.

The answers to these questions must be produced by the top management group. If they so choose, but only if they so choose, the strategic data system may be designed to help in formulating an answer. In making that choice, the top managers are selecting, from among the questions listed above, those which they feel should be addressed most carefully. In the small and simple business mentioned, the choice may be made to look more closely into the younger group of potential customers. The 'system' in this case may merely involve a count of the male passers-by. Or it may require the shopkeeper to make the count, sub-analysed into non-smokers, and cigarette-smokers. Or it may require an interaction with his strategic review of product line, in that the observed group of younger potential customers may seem to be more interested in products not presently carried in the shop.

The strategic data system cannot be rigidly defined because of the very nature of strategic decisions. But the system must help us to organise our thoughts around the crucial factors. By focusing on these, by helping us to aim at the relevant target, the system must eventually lead us to the critical questions that will allow us to accept or to reject the null strategy. The system must help the manager to broaden his thinking.

Take, for example, the case of a small manufacturer of a specialised do-it-yourself product. This firm, in answering the 'customer' strategy assertion, may find that they presently serve 'all the important chains of hardware, ironmongery, and DIY shops in the northwest of England'. The questions to be addressed by the strategist flow at once from this statement. Would we be well advised to consider serving the less-important chains? How about individual stores? What market penetration would we achieve by adding non-specialist chains? Is the northeast worth looking into?

Once the entrepreneur has reviewed the questions thus generated, and has thrown a proportion of them out as unworthy of further consideration, the design of the strategic data system can be commenced, with the surprising questions firmly in mind. In the present instance, the firm wanted to review the possibility of selling through individual shops within the northwest region, in addition to the chains presently served. At once, the specifications of the relevant portion of the strategic data system became apparent. Where were these individual shops, and what share of the market did they have? How many of them were there, how did they at present service customers interested in products like the company's, and how did these shops seek information and place their orders? The firm decided upon a very simple strategic data system for dealing with these matters. The 'system' consisted of a recently retired salesman and his car, both hired for a month, a telephone directory, a business directory, and a carefully devised list of questions. The reader is invited to draft a list of the questions which one would need to be asked in order to meet the needs of the strategy formulator without at the same time irritating the proprietors of the shops being examined.

The decision to 'throw out' some of the questions generated by the null strategy approach is clearly an important one. The proprietor may make this choice on a very personal basis. In the larger firm, it may be a statement of corporate policy. For example, one well-known retail chain refuses to handle goods that sell for more than twice the price of the cheapest item in the same product area—they want to be known as the place for price-conscious shoppers. The important thing is that the decision not to consider a question further must be taken consciously and deliberately in the light of a formulated policy statement. The decision should not be taken by default.

SOURCES FOR THE SMALL FIRM

Apart from such direct methods of strategy formulation, the smaller firm may also gain useful help from published sources. Hiring consultants to prepare special strategic studies is beyond the means of most smaller firms, and is not really necessary in any case. Intelligent use of the null strategy method will lead to a reasonable answer, and has the added advantage of requiring the active involvement of the entrepreneur, who must make the chosen strategy work. But published sources are reasonably cheap and can be effective sources of answers to some of the questions thrown up by the null strategy approach.

The selection of published sources for strategic development of the smaller business is a topic worthy of a whole book on its own. Unfortunately it would be a very difficult book to write, because the sources applicable in one area or to one industry are of little use in another. The only general comment that can be made on this issue is to recommend intelligent search and a time budget. If the proprietor of the smaller firm takes the strategic development of his business seriously, he must expect to allocate a regular time to reading. One such entrepreneur has a regime which requires him to read trade material every Sunday evening. He has chosen four monthly periodicals, two on his industry and two general business publications. He reads the weekly of his trade association, and a local weekly in which he and most of his competitors advertise. In addition, he reads three or four business books a year, of which, two are usually read during the Sunday evening sessions and the others while on holiday. Obviously, this particular regime would not suit everyone, but it is an example of the structured management of time which a busy manager of a small firm must undertake if he is to keep up with new developments and, if possible, keep slightly ahead.

Another source of strategic data for the smaller firm is the education industry. There are courses available on almost any subject and of almost any duration. They vary considerably in quality, but reputations, both of institutions and of people, are readily accessible and usually reliable. In general, a short course on a specific topic is likely to have the most to offer the smaller firm, not only because its goals are clear-cut and it can therefore be chosen with confidence, but also because others attending it are likely to have very similar problems and experiences from which much can be learned.

For a medium-sized firm, with a dozen or more managers, the possibility of a specially designed course should be considered carefully. Once the entrepreneur has set forth the statements of current position, and has gone through the questions thus generated to pick the issues he feels need most attention, a seminar on these matters, using the firm's own experiences, can be a valuable way of concentrating the minds of all those in the management team. The services of a suitably qualified team from a neighbouring institution may be a useful way of broadening the discussion and bringing to bear experiences from other sources.

Nonetheless, our most important recommendation for use by the small-to-medium-sized firm is contained in the null strategy method described in detail in the last chapter, and illustrated in part by reference to the photographic section of the small pharmaceutical chain. This approach, augmented by carefully budgeted reading, and by training programmes of appropriate design, will throw up the issues very clearly. The technique is simple. It helps the manager identify the really strategic gaps in his defences in a systematic and yet reasonably straightforward style. It does not produce a strategy that will answer the need it identifies; but the range of possible strategies which may fit the needs will be fairly narrow, in most instances. The choice among the strategies that do fit the need is still to be made, and this can never be made by an information system. This choice is the basic entrepreneurial decision, now reduced to its irreducible form.

In the case of the larger firm, however, the possibility of spending more time and effort and being more systematic in answering the questions of strategy exists. It can afford to. Its mistakes are both larger and more conspicuous. It has governments and politicians perpetually under its corporate feet, confusing the environment in a fashion that most smaller firms can ignore. So it has to be systematic in its strategic planning, even if only because of the number of people that tend to become involved in the strategic thinking process.

THE LARGER BUSINESS AND STRATEGIC THINKING

An important innovation in practical strategic planning systems development was effected by Shell Chemicals[8] in 1975. The 'directional policy matrix' technique was devised to help the firm make choices among the numerous investment possibilities open to them. It was publicised in the hope that its general adoption by competitors would help save the industry from the chronic condition of over-supply which had been so costly for so long. Shell reasoned that if everyone used a sensible strategic investment system, then firms which had no hope of success in a market would not invest, leaving the way clear for others to invest profitably in the capacity really needed. The decision to stay out of an active market is not an easy one, especially for the big firms making up most of the chemical industry; but it may be correct, at least for some of them.

The concepts underlying the directional policy matrix are closely related to the Delphi method of opinion-gathering and the Boston Consulting Group method of analysis.

The basic matrix, Figure 13.3 displays the desirability of an investment prospect. A project in the bottom right-hand corner is in a business sector of high potential in which the company has a powerful position. A project in the top left-hand corner is in an unattractive sector which the company does not know much about or in which it has poor present capabilities. Clearly, we want the ones in the bottom right-hand corner.

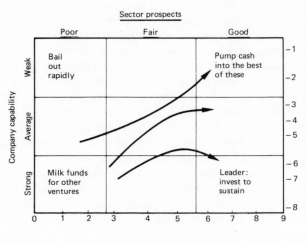

FIGURE 13.3

The job of saying where a given project should be put on the matrix is obviously crucial. The two dimensions can be judged separately, and each of these is in turn multi-faceted. The facets used in petrochemicals would obviously not fit the analysis required in another industry. The peculiarities of each industry must be analysed to decide what its facets should be. The example used has been borrowed from the Shell paper cited, with permission.

In assessing sector prospects, Shell decided to use four factors. Market growth, market quality and environmental considerations would clearly apply to almost any industry. The fourth element, the industry feedstock situation, was, equally clearly, unique to petrochemicals.

An eight-point scale was used for each of the four factors, and the four were weighted equally. A panel of specialists discussed the topic with a group of non-specialists who could bring a more detached viewpoint to bear, and a consensus score was reached. The Delphi technique, which is discussed in Chapter 16, and in which the consensus is reached by letters rather than discussion, may be a way of getting results that are thought out more fully, and which are subject to fewer political influences. However, the objective is the same in each case. To arrive at a measure of the four factors influencing sector prospects.

On market growth, the industry expected growth rate was assigned a score of four points; a zero growth rate got zero points, and any rate above double the average was given eight. The feedstock rating was set by the same consensus approach: a high score if the raw material is scarce or hard to make, a low one if it is plentiful or cheap and easy.

Market quality was a more difficult factor to assess. The consensus on this could only be approached through a series of sub-factors:

(1) Have sector profits been low?
(2) Have sector profits been unstable?
(3) Do prices collapse when demand goes below capacity?
(4) Is the product a commodity, so that its price is unpredictable?
(5) Can the technology be freely reproduced?
(6) Are there a lot of suppliers in the market?
(7) Are there only a few big customers?
(8) Does the customer have only a low margin on resale?
(9) Is the market likely to become very large so that other producers will come?
(10) Can the product be processed without special machinery?
(11) Are there natural or synthetic substitutes?

A series of negative answers to these questions led to a high market quality score, and vice versa.

In the vertical dimension of company capabilities, the Shell factors were market position, production capability and product R&D. The process of assessment was identical to that used for sector analysis. It seems likely that most non-petrochemical firms would need to devise a very different group of factors for this variable.

Once the analytical process is complete, the project can be plotted on Figure 13.3. Then one must decide whether it is worthwhile to attempt to plot the locations of competitive firms on the same chart. If there are relatively few of them, it probably will be worthwhile. A strategic choice can then be made, whether to pump money into the project or to suck cash out. In general, one wishes to suck cash from the projects in the left column (weak industry prospects) and put it into the right column. Also, within the high-prospects right-hand column, one would generally wish to invest so as to strengthen one's corporate position, thus moving downwards in the column. The reason for this is to strengthen market command as far as possible. When the sector matures at a later stage, and the market growth rate slows down, the project will tend to drift to the left. With a strong position, the firm will still find the project generating a steady cash flow. With a weak position one would have little choice but to abandon the product entirely.

In addition to the analytical application mentioned, on which projects are evaluated for investment, Shell suggest that the technique can be used to assist firms in reviewing the strength of their competitors, and that it may also be helpful to institutional investors in analysing the long-term strategic prospects of a firm. A company would be attractive as a long-term investment if it showed a heavy concentration of activity in the lower right section, and would still be reasonable if its activities included projects evenly spread over the matrix. The latter profile would suggest an even balance of new and old activities, and general stability. A less attractive matrix would be one in which the company's projects were concentrated in the left-hand column. Such a firm may be creating a lot of cash, but has little hope for the future unless it is revived which will involve new funds, new projects, new industries, and probably new management.

A continuing process of re-investment in the direction of the arrow in Figure 13.3 is required, if a firm is to sustain itself and grow in the long term.

AN EXTENSION OF SHELL CHEMICALS SYSTEM TO CAPITAL INVESTMENT APPRAISAL

One apparent difficulty, which arises when implementation of the directional policy matrix is considered, is that of relating it to the financial control system. The Shell Chemical paper does not address the problem of institutionalising the process. One possibility would be to relate the discounting rate applied when projects are being evaluated for investment to the location of the project in the matrix. Another would be to set a capital charging rate at varying levels for business segments located at different matrix points. This would suck funds out of divisions at varying rates—rapidly from the mature divisions, slowly from the high-prospect new ones. A combination of variable discount rates and capital levies would be devised, of course, but would run the risk of creating confusion because of its apparent complexity. The following illustration uses a fixed capital charge and variable discounting rates to implement the financial controls required. The capital charge is levied on all the divisions at a fixed pre-tax level of 20 per cent. Corporate headquarters require the transference of funds at regular (monthly) intervals from the divisions, based on the gross book value of the assets in use in the division at the last accounting date, which may be the end of the prior month. In this respect the divisions are treated identically, no matter where their primary business lies on the directional policy matrix.

With regard to capital investment appraisals, however, the rate of discount to be used will be a function of the location of the division on the matrix. If a division is in the unattractive top left corner, a discount rate of, say, 50 per cent pre-tax would apply to its investment projects. In other words, only freakishly profitable new projects would be engaged in, and the normal extraction of funds through the capital charge would ensure the steady dissolution of the division.

In the relatively highly favoured lower right-hand corner, where the firm is a market leader in a highly attractive field, the investment hurdle would be set much lower. A pre-tax discount rate of 15 per cent would, for example, ensure that the bulk of the reasonable projects went through without group interference. The specific numbers in this analysis are less important than the concept of institutionalisation of the sound planning concepts embodied in the directional policy matrix idea. No system, not even a strategic one, can last long if it is necessary to analyse every proposal from scratch. There must be rules of operation so that the system can progress decisions without requiring a complete review of operations each time.

The rates of discount shown in Figure 13.4 are offered as an illustration of how the system might be applied. The various divisions are required to

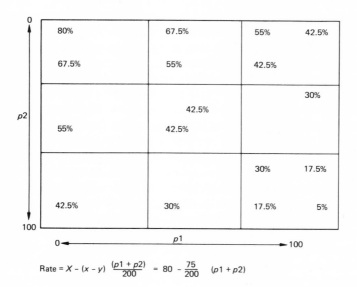

$$\text{Rate} = X - (x - y)\ \frac{(p1 + p2)}{200}\ =\ 80 - \frac{75}{200}\ (p1 + p2)$$

FIGURE 13.4. The target rate of return required of an investment depends on the location of a division on the matrix. The rate ranges from 5 per cent to 80 per cent according to the formula

show that a project they want to invest in will show a return in excess of the figure corresponding to the division's site within the directional policy matrix. Full discretion is given to the divisions to make investments which promise a return above their respective targets. Obviously, any division which is unfortunate enough to find itself in the top left-hand corner would find relatively few opportunities to exercise that discretion.

The use of a 20 per cent capital charge rate would ensure that the flow of funds in the direction of the arrow in Figure 13.3 could be effected. The reader may note that the requirement of a project in the centre of the matrix is much more than 20 per cent, in fact, it is 42·5 per cent. This difference allows for the inevitable optimism with which managers of divisions view their own projects. It also seeks to ensure that a reasonable amount of discretionary funds will find their way to the corporate headquarters, so that re-investment in the 'right-hand column' can be to that extent more assured.

There are many alternative systems in use which purport to do for their respective companies what the Shell Chemicals system we have been talking about (and which we have extended a little) does for that firm. The essential characteristics of the system are simple enough. Within a broad industrial environment, the opportunities for development are tested against a range of criteria to ensure that the firm will truly benefit, in a strategic sense of the word.

Another approach to strategic thinking is to compare the activities of companies, one with another. We have chosen one formal system of comparison for study, as an example of the genre.

PROFIT IMPACT OF MARKET STRATEGY

In 1974, a new procedure for the analysis of strategies, of particular import to the larger business, was introduced to the United Kingdom and to Europe. This was the PIMS programme,[9] which was based upon an earlier programme devised in the United States. At the outset, the programme involved the use of a data bank which included firms of several nationalities, of which the American group was by far the largest. Over time, however, the databases from each of the other nations in the programme have expanded so that a more national view can be taken.

The purpose of the programme is to allow participating firms to supply data in a pre-defined format about each of the businesses in which they are engaged. These data are fed into the database, and the management may then analyse the data bank results to seek guidance on a number of planning and strategy matters. How much is the 'normal' profit of a business in a particular industry, with a particular market position and structure? What future will it have in financial terms if it makes no change in its style of operation? What changes in strategy are likely to improve the results? What effects will such changes be likely to have on financial results?

The PIMS programme is based upon the business as distinct from the company. The two may be synonymous, of course, but the typical company, especially a large one, is likely to be operating in a group of businesses at the same time. Each of these must be separately dealt with if the PIMS system is to operate successfully. The idea originated at the General Electric Company of USA, which decided to re-organise itself into a series of 'strategic business units' in the mid-1960s. Each such unit could be looked upon as carrying on a separate venture from the other parts of the entity, with its own market, its own sources of supply, its own unique labour situation, and its own technological peculiarities. These strategic business units were only by coincidence the same as the divisions of the General Electric entity. In general, several strategic business units were to be found in any division, and in a few instances several divisions were found to comprise a single strategic business unit.

The outcomes from the PIMS system are numerous and can, to a certain extent, be set by the user. However, there are a number of standard reports generated by the computer model on the basis of each submitted set of data. The first such report is an average report, in which the results obtained by all the businesses in the data bank are examined and the ones confronting similar environments (market, competitive position, etc.) are selected and averaged. This gives a PAR figure against which the firm may choose to compare the results obtained by its own business. The second report is a strategy change regression study. This one examines a given strategic change (such as, for instance, a major step towards vertical integration) and isolates those businesses in the data bank which have started from a situation similar to that of the submitting firm, and have carried out that strategic change some time before. The results of the average of such businesses since the change are then reported. The problem attaching to such a report must, evidently, lie in the size of the database of firms with the required characteristics. Nonetheless, in those instances where there is a reasonable number of business reports in the data bank, the results will be of considerable interest to the reporting firm. Obviously, there can be no assurance that the same results would be achieved by it if it were to adopt the same strategy.

The third report is one which purports to identify the optimum strategy, which is that combination of several strategic options which 'promises the

TABLE 3
EFFECT OF FACTORS IN THE PAR ROI EQUATION
ON "PAR" RETURN ON INVESTMENT

Factors	Base period values for:			Impact of Factor on Par	
	All PIMS Businesses	This Business	This Class of Business	on ROI	Par (%)
Environmental factors					−2.70
Industry (SIC) growth, long-term	8.050	12.872	8.180		0.2
Market growth, short-term	5.870	5.008	5.940		−0.1
Industry exports (% Total SHPTS)	7.629	10.000	9.604		0.4
Type business-consumer	0.000	0.000	0.000		0.0
Type business-serv or distrib	0.000	0.000	0.000		0.0
Sales direct to end user (%)	51.010	100.000	64.460		−2.2
Buyer fragmentation index	13.600	10.000	13.750		−1.0
Competitive position					11.58
Your market position	22.460	32.000	24.220		1.2
Share of 4 largest firms (SIC)	51.640	55.000	52.070		−0.1
Instability of your MKT. share	2.888	3.333	3.270		−0.3
Price relative to competition	2.685	1.000	2.652		5.9
Relative pay scale	6.442	5.000	6.400		2.5
Product quality	23.150	48.333	24.680		1.8
New product sales (% Tot sales)	12.130	20.000	12.060		0.6
Structure: Capital					−4.48
Investment intensity	63.780	51.944	71.320		−5.0
Fixed capital intensity	57.470	35.182	61.200		0.3
Receivables/Sales	14.410	13.056	14.900		0.2
Structure: Produc process					5.45
Vertical integration	58.770	71.456	60.110		9.6
Manufacturing costs/sales	30.690	37.353	33.570		0.3
Capacity utilization	75.740	62.667	75.860		−2.8
Raw & in proc. invent./purchase	33.180	66.757	39.250		1.5
Sales/employees	47730.	26627	42860.		−3.1
Structure: Budget alloc'n					−0.11
MKTG Less sales forc. exp/sales	4.114	7.071	3.027		−2.3
R&D expenses/sales	2.900	5.134	3.376		2.2

* Missing data replaced with mean for this class of business
Column 3 is not used in the calculation of column 4. It is for reference only.

FIGURE 13.5

best results for the business', either on an earnings basis, return on investment, or discounted cash flow. This report may well be a useful stimulant to strategic thought on the part of the top management group. It is most unlikely that any board would ever choose the 'optimum strategy' produced by the model directly, of course. But the outcome of the analysis

TABLE 3 (*Continued*)
EFFECT OF FACTORS IN THE PAR ROI EQUATION
ON "PAR" RETURN ON INVESTMENT

Factors	Base period values for:			Impact of Factor	
	All PIMS Businesses	This Business	This Class of Business	on ROI	Par (%)
Company Factors					−0.53
Corporate payout ratio	0.620	******	0.632		−0.1
Degree of corp. diversification	2.132	******	2.251		−0.4
Corporate size	1588.	******	1431.		−0.0
Growth rate of corporate sales	0.101	******	0.103		−0.0
Change/action factors					6.58
Change in your market share	2.258	12.500	3.064		2.6
Change product quality (%)	3.202	10.000	3.328		0.1
Change in price index	2.867	7.382	2.323		0.2
Competitive market activity	0.110	0.130*	0.130		−0.0
Change in capital intensity	−3.303	−6.520	−4.301		1.2
Change in vertical integr (%)	0.500	1.485	0.296		0.2
Point change Adv & Prom/Sales	−0.146	−0.510	−0.113		0.3
Change in sales forc Exp/Sales	−0.268	7.249	−0.335		0.7
Point change return on sales	1.086	2.677	1.312		1.2

NOTES ON TABLE 3

1. Components of "your market position":

Your market share	22.460	32.000	24.220
Your market share/share Big 3	54.320	53.933	58.750

2. Components of "investment intensity":

Investment/sales	63.780	51.944	71.320
Investment/(value added−. 5NI)	120.000	78.036	125.300

3. Focus on the Net effect of "investment intensity", "vertical integration", and "sales per employee" by adding their separate impacts
    −5.00 +9.60 + −3.10 = 1.49 (net effect)

4. Interpretation of relative scales:
    "Price relative to competition"
    If "2" your price is higher
    "4"   lower
    "Relative pay scale"
    If "4" your pay scale is lower
    "8"   higher

may play a useful role in strategic thinking analogous to the null strategy we have already discussed in this book.

The table shown in Figure 3.5 is reproduced with permission from a PIMS study. This report is a part of the PAR report, and indicates the factors which were apparently influential in causing the business under study to be materially different from the aggregate of all the PIMS businesses. The definitions of the variables are clearly important, and they cannot be reproduced in this chapter. However, it is worthwhile noting the three items that are described as having the greatest impact on the return on investment. The derivation of these impact figures is a correlation and regression calculation, based upon the entire database in the system. The root cause of a factor having an impact, however, is the difference between the base period values for all businesses in the database and the value for the business under study.

In the case of the firm in the tables, the three most noticeable impacts are said to be 'price relative to competition' which is fairly self-explanatory, 'investment intensity' and 'vertical integration' which have powerful negative and positive effects respectively. The investment intensity is the inverse of the turnover ratio, and is computed by dividing the book value of long-term capital employed by the annual sales. The degree of vertical integration is assessed by dividing the amount of value added by the firm by its sales for the year. A great deal of discussion could undoubtedly take place on the precise meaning of the terms in use. But the implication of this report seems to be that the firm in question is highly integrated, sells at very competitive prices indeed, and would be in an extremely strong position but for a certain tendency to invest funds in the business above the level competitors have found essential. It is clearly something for the top management group to think about—and thoroughly.

SUMMARY

The strategic information systems design process is a very much more complex matter than the design processes that govern the development of management and operational control systems. The boundaries of the latter can be broad, but they are usually fairly clear. This is not normally true at the strategic level. The attainment of a strategic goal can usually be attempted in a large number of different ways. The system must somehow help to identify these, or at least a fair proportion of them. In order to do this, the system must help the top management group to analyse, in as systematic a fashion as possible, the current activities of the firm and the important aspects of the environment in which it is operating and of the environments adjacent to its current field of operations.

In addition to the null strategy approach discussed in the previous chapter we have discussed three techniques which can be of help in strategic thinking. The first and simplest is often called gap analysis, in which the target growth rate is plotted, the actual growth rate on the basis of present activities is also plotted, and steps are then taken to fill the spaces. The null strategy methods may, of course, be applied to the gap-filling task. The second approach is exemplified by the Shell Chemicals system, in which the strengths of the firm and the prospects of a market segment are independently studied, leading to a view being taken on the overall desirability of a given proposed innovation.This approach is more suitable for the larger and more stable entity.

The last topic considered was the PIMS model, in which the strategic options available to a firm are analysed by comparison with a large group of other business enterprises. Some strategic options can also be analysed in this fashion, as certain of the firms in the data bank will undoubtedly have attempted at least a proportion of the conceivable strategic changes open to the firm. Obviously, there is no guarantee that the strategic changes which worked for one firm will work for another. But then there are no guarantees that other methods of analysis will work either.

The basic issue in strategic information systems is one of achieving breadth and simplicity without becoming trivial and obvious. But it is better to err on the side of obviousness than to make the system so ornate and complicated that the top management group do not trust the results. After all, many of the most important strategic changes ever made have been very obvious indeed—afterwards.

CHAPTER 13—PROJECTS

1. Apply the directional policy matrix technique to a company on the basis of published information. You will no doubt find it useful to refer to sources in your library for the prospects of the various industries within which the firm is operating. Some industrial reports give market share information, but in most instances you will have to go through the rather laborious task of looking up the sales in the annual reports of each of the largest firms in the industry of concern. As far as the company itself is concerned, the various requirements of the law and of the stock exchange can often be helpful in finding out where its strengths lie. Extel cards normally provide very useful analyses of sales and profits by both geographic area and industrial speciality.

2. One of the clichés of modern management is that 'we must learn to expect the unexpected'. Mintzberg identified the adaptive approach to strategic planning as an important variant of strategic thought. Consider, if possible in the context of a particular company, the implications of this statement for the design of strategic information systems. Do we need to create new systems to deal with each new major change in the environment? Or can we design the data-gathering system in a disaggregated fashion that will allow us to assemble a reasonably useful strategic report fairly quickly, once a major discontinuity has been identified?

NOTES

1. Mintzberg, H., 'Strategy Making in Three Modes', *California Management Review*, Winter 1973.
2. Taylor, B., 'Strategies for Planning', *Long-Range Planning*, August 1975.
3. Weir, G. A., 'Developing Strategies. A Practical Approach', *Long-Range Planning*, October 1974.
4. Litschert, R., and Nicholson, E., 'Corporate Long-Range Planning Groups—Some Different Approaches', *Long-Range Planning*, August 1974.
5. Taylor, B., 'Strategies for Planning', *Long-Range Planning*, August 1975.
6. Rahman, M., Unpublished Ph.D. thesis, Manchester University, 1976. See also Rahman, M., and McCosh, A. M., *Accounting, Organisations and Society*, 1, No. 4 (1976).
7. Aguilar, P. J., *Scanning the Business Environment*. New York: Macmillan, 1967.
8. Shell Chemicals, *The Directional Policy Matrix—A new Aid to Corporate Planning*. London, Shell, November 1975.
9. The European operation of the PIMS programme is controlled and administered by the Strategic Management Centre, Manchester Business School, Booth Street West, Manchester M15 6PB. The Director is Mr Gordon Mandry.

14 Forecasts for Strategy

The null strategy method was advocated in Chapter 12 for analysing the adequacy of the firm's current plans, postures and markets. Some methods of strategy selection were discussed in Chapter 13. But in neither chapter did we attempt to deal with the problem of forecasting. The future was taken, in those chapters, as a given. While that was appropriate enough in view of the subjects of these two chapters, it is patently clear that the future is not given at all. But the probable future state of the world is crucial to success in strategy selection. Strategic forecasting is necessary—even if it is only intuitive. This chapter considers some approaches to this topic, and suggests the circumstances under which each is best.

Before starting, it is best to sound a warning. Strategic forecasting is very difficult indeed. Errors are inevitable, and big errors are common. The extent of the errors does not appear to depend upon the effort put into the forecast. Large, complex, expensive and intricate systems for strategic forecasting are just as likely to mislead as are small and simple ones.

The following broad methods of forecasting will be considered: (1) visionary descriptions of the future, (2) scenario writing, (3) collections of expert opinion, (4) mathematical projections, and (5) large complex models, either simulators or input–output.

VISIONARY DESCRIPTIONS

By far the most numerous, most popular, and most readable strategic forecasts are visionary descriptions of the future. An individual has thought about a future, has decided either that he likes it very much or is appalled by it, and writes a description of that future age, in the hope of either making it come true or of averting it. Forecasts in this class obviously include futuristic novels such as those by H. G. Wells or George Orwell. One or more aspects of an assumed new world order are analysed descriptively for their effects on the lives of those involved. In the 1940s for instance, Orwell discussed the implications of increased drug use, greater involvement of government in the affairs of individuals, growth in sexual permissiveness, and the amalgamation of nations into a few super-powers.

It seems probable that Orwell, in writing *1984*, was hoping to prevent, or at least alleviate, the effects he was describing. No doubt many of his readers felt revulsion towards the new world order he was forecasting, and many still do. But if one were to regard his book as a strategic forecast, and leave the moral issues aside entirely, the results are quite impressive. When several randomly chosen portfolios of firms in the industries which are positively indicated by Orwell were identified, as of his date of publication, a large gain was found to have accrued on these portfolios by the time of writing. No attempt has thus far been made to establish the statistical validity of this for the entire London Stock Exchange list. Records are incomplete in many cases, and the computerised lists do not go back far enough. But the randomly chosen portfolios out-performed the market by a factor of three or more over the thirty years. Clearly the decision to use Orwell, rather than someone else, as one's visionary, remains a major problem.

Visionary forecasts are not, of course, confined to the work of novelists. Political and academic manifestos are plentiful, and one can be found to advocate almost any point of view on almost any subject. The policies advocated can hardly be used as a basis for corporate strategic planning, therefore. But the assumptions upon which these writers base their pronouncements are normally much less diverse, and these underlying assumptions can be used as the underpinning of a corporate strategic forecasting process.

As an illustration, let us take Cottrell[1] and his powerful polemic about the need for an appropriate industrial policy and contrast the underlying thoughts of this with those from a very different source. The other book, by Jenkins and Mortimer[2] was intended to get leaders of unions to push for a more sympathetic legal environment within which to operate. The bulk of Jenkins and Mortimer's recommendations have now been carried out, but we are not really concerned with that in our present chapter.

Cottrell, amongst other points, made a series of assertions: (1) that manufacturing industry was such a huge proportion of British enterprise that no conceivable expansion of the other parts of the economy could ever replace it if it were to be lost; (2) that governments were in large part responsible for the problems of manufacturing industry because they were unwilling to give it the priority required to get it into a healthy condition at the expense of other projects; (3) that unions have become very powerful and so would need to be consulted by any government that wished to implement any industrial policy at all; and (4) the strength of the unions also required them to become involved at the market end of the major firms, there being few fields left to conquer inside them. He also advocated an 'examination', to which any industrial policy ought to be subjected; namely, would the proposed policy help Britain make more goods that the rest of the world would buy.

Jenkins and Mortimer were concerned with a less global problem, and were writing quite a few years earlier. But some of their assertions are interesting in the light of Cottrell's remarks: (1) that there was a world trend towards a more effective law on minimum labour standards, but that the unions had not taken nearly enough action to bring this into being; (2) that governments had an obligation to provide a framework of law within which unions and firms could go about their business, and should not leave that framework in its then patchy condition—especially, the government should not vacillate, but had an obligation to promote and to pioneer a new and clear framework for conditions of work; (3) that there were inexorable forces at work, which could not be gainsaid for long, which would ensure a greater role in the governance of companies for the workforces of those firms or for their representatives.

The similarity of these basic concepts, given the very different points of view of the authors, the difference in timing of the pronouncements, and the difference between the objectives they were trying to promote, seems quite striking. The reader is invited to come to his own conclusions concerning the strategy a firm ought to adopt in their light.

THE SCENARIO APPROACH

The visionary approach to strategic forecasting is also the essence of the scenario method. But instead of taking a political stance on the desirability of the outcome, as the visionaries tend to do, the scenario writer takes a more neutral line. The scenario writer seeks to forecast by observing the forces at work at the time of writing, and assumes these will continue in the future. His basic forecast is the result.

But, in addition, the scenario writer tries to test the validity of his assumptions about the durability of these forces by simulation. By allowing each of the forces to change in strength, the scenario writer seeks to describe the future that would arise if the variation happened in practice.

One of the best known examples of this approach to strategic forecasting is to be found in the publications of the Hudson Institute. Kahn and Wiener[3] made a forecast based upon the continued operation of 13 forces. These were listed in their Table 1 on page 7 of their book and are reproduced as Table 14.1 here. The resulting forecast of the economic

TABLE 14.1. Kahn and Wiener's 13 forces, upon which their scenarios were constructed

There is a basic, long-term multifold trend towards:

1. Increasingly sensate (empirical, this-wordly, secular, humanistic, pragmatic, utilitarian, contractual, epicurean or hedonistic, and the like) cultures.
2. Bourgeois, bureaucratic, 'meritocratic', democratic (and nationalistic?) elites.
3. Accumulation of scientific and technological knowledge.
4. Institutionalisation of change, especially research, development, innovation, and diffusion.
5. Worldwide industrialisation and modernisation.
6. Increasing affluence and (recently) leisure.
7. Population growth.
8. Urbanisation and (soon) the growth of megalopolises.
9. Decreasing importance of primary and (recently) secondary occupations.
10. Literacy and education.
11. Increasing capability for mass destruction.
12. Increasing tempo of change.
13. Increasing universality of the multifold trend.

status of the countries studied was a fairly simple one. But the bulk of their work was devoted to exploring the consequences of variations on the original assumptions.

For the United Kingdom, Kahn and Wiener forecast a population of between 55 and 64 millions in the year 2000. This forecast was made in 1965. They next suggest a productivity improvement range of between 2 per cent and 5 per cent which leads to an estimated gross national product of between $US 200 and $US 527 thousand million[4] in 2000 expressed in 1965 dollars. This may well be an accurate estimate. But the range, a factor of 2.5 from the high to the low, makes it very difficult to obtain any strategic meaning from the estimates. This problem is especially acute since the figures mentioned relate only to what the authors call the 'surprise-free' situation, in which existing trends are extrapolated without material changes.

In defence of Kahn and Wiener and others in the same field, it has to be said that a 35-year forecast is a very long-range one indeed, so that errors are inevitable. Indeed, major errors are highly likely. After all, half of those alive when the forecast was made will be dead before its truth can be observed. And of the surviving half, more than half will have been too young to pay any attention to the forecasts, or to act upon them.

A similar approach, but with a much less ambitious objective, was taken by Palmer and Schmid.[5] They sought to forecast the environment in the

USA for New York banks. The objective was to forecast the share which the major banks would have in the financial market in 1985. Palmer and Schmid tackled a smaller number of variables (39) and a smaller error range was reported. A condensation of their exhibits is shown in Table 14.2.

In the Palmer–Schmid model, there are two sets of numbers which are combined to give the overall 'net expected value' of a scenario. The first set is a measure of the importance of a factor to the market share of the large New York banks which were the clients. These numbers were obtained by numerical and regression analysis of the relationship between each such factor and market share (or an intervening variable) in the past. These numerical studies were supplemented by interviews, from which informed opinion on the importance of each element was gleaned.

The other set of numbers represented the probability of a given opportunity or risk under the assumptions of the scenario being tested. Each factor is linked by a logical chain of causation to one or more external environmental events. For example, one of the variables studied was competition with non-financial institutions, and this was felt to be more intense if inflation was high, GNP grew quickly, data processing became better and cheaper, and so on. The latter group were the external variables which made up the scenario between them.

The scenario that turned out 'best' for bank market share was one in which inflation was high, GNP grew slowly, bank regulation was relaxed, New York had problems, and technological developments proved very difficult, notably in data processing. The 'worst' was characterised by high GNP growth, high inflation, relaxed regulation, fast technological development, problems for New York, and others. It appears to be in the bank's interests to slow down technological improvements.

The scenario approach has been widely adopted, but has also been subject to considerable criticism. Merritt[6] has pointed out that a scenario is very difficult to study after its preparation, as it is normally impossible to carry out sensitivity analysis on a scenario. There are too many variables, and too many of these variables are both qualitative and interlocking. A change in the values of one variable at the beginning obviously changes the final result derived, but the connection between the inputs and the outputs is seriously over-simplified. No assurance can be had that the effect of the change will really be anything like the simplistic simulation. The delicate judgemental balance which a skilled scenario writer has built into the original scenario can be seriously disrupted by the sensitivity test change. At the same time, it must be said that the scenario method is often the only method of strategic forecasting available.

As the scenario writer is forced to present a coherent 'total' view of the

TABLE 14.2. A condensation and simplification of the scenario scores of Palmer and Schmid

	Factor importance measured by historical study and interviews	Best scenario		Worst scenario	
		Probability of occurrence by 1985	Expected value	Probability of occurrence by 1985	Expected value
Opportunities:					
Legal obstacles to interstate banking lowered	0·12	1·0	0·12	1·0	0·12
Fewer bank holding company restrictions	0·18	1·0	0·18	1·0	0·18
Business reliance on banks increased	0·23	1·0	0·23	0	0
Risks:					
More banking units compete	−0·12	0·5	−0·06	1·0	−0·12
New York declines as financial centre	−0·14	0·5	−0·07	1·0	−0·14
Other financial institutions gain access to funds-transfer system	−0·09	1·0	−0·09	1·0	−0·09
33 other factors, some opportunities, some risks	−0·18	various	−0·16	various	−0·28
Net expected value			0·16		−0·33

future he must make an attempt to build all the factors in and to give each its proper weight. Even if he fails, he has subjected the problem to a degree of disciplined analysis which is limited only by his energy, resources, and personal professionalism.

THE COLLECTION OF EXPERT OPINIONS

Another widely used method of strategic forecasting is that of gathering and collating the opinions of a group of relevant experts. Of course, this method can be used in conjunction with several of the other methods. For example, MacNulty[7] made use of a panel of experts in feeding data to her scenario procedure; Palmer and Schmid used interviews to build up their 'importance' measures.

At its simplest, this method simply involves asking the acknowledged expert what he thinks will happen next. At its most complicated, a panel of a dozen skilled people may spend weeks trying to agree on the nature of the variables that need to be considered and the extent to which movements in each of these variables can be expected to bring about changes in each of the others. The latter procedure has the obvious advantage of involving more people (and therefore, presumably, more points of view) in the forecasting process. If this process makes these people feel committed to the attainment of a forecast once made, a substantial motivational gain may have been achieved. There is little evidence at present in the literature that the more complex methods produce more accurate forecasts than the simpler ones, principally because the latter are seldom reported in articles.

We have discussed the null strategy questionnaire approach in an earlier chapter. Under this method, the largest group of experts used has been four at the time of writing. The results seem to have been adequate or better, but there can be no guarantee that improvements would not have been obtained from using a larger group.

The more formal methods of collating larger groups of expert opinion include the Delphi and cross-impact methods. The former seeks consensus by repetitive questioning. The latter, a computer-dependent technique, seeks to domonstrate the mutual interaction of forces so that their resultant effect on a variable of interest can be described from some time into the future. The two methods are quite different in procedure but similar in goals and in limitations. As Delphi has been widely discussed in the literature already[8,9] and has also been firmly criticised, we shall only cover the cross-impact method and our experience with its use in this chapter. It should be said, before we leave the Delphi approach aside, that our correspondents in practice have left us with the impression that the technique is either extremely hard to use or that its results are very dubious. If the method is used properly, so that the results can be given credence, the executive time cost is very great. But if this is not done, the results cannot be trusted.

The cross-impact method of forecasting is an attempt to acknowledge the interconnected nature of the variables normally found in strategic forecasting situations. It is not at all uncommon for each variable to be affected by several of the others, and for each in turn to affect another selection of the remainder. In an early paper on the technique, Gordon and Hayward[10] used a simple weather forecasting illustration of this point. The probability of being able to reduce crop damage would be materially enhanced if we were able to exercise limited short-term weather control. Short-term weather control would become more likely if we could make reliable short-term weather forecasts. And the forecasts would become more reliable if we could make limited short-term weather control possible. Given the connection between all these factors, what is the overall likelihood of being able to reduce crop damage?

In using the technique, a preliminary estimate of the value, within its feasible range, of each of the variables must be made. In addition, a matrix of coefficients must be developed by a group of experts in the field, each coefficient being a measure in size and in direction of the impact expected on the value of one variable owing to the present value of the other. For instance, the experts might assert that a coefficient of $+2$ should be used to denote the improvement in the likelihood of short-term weather control given the availability of reliable short-term forecasts. On the other hand, a stronger relationship, perhaps $+5$, might be supposed for improving the weather forecasts given the actual occurrence of a viable system of weather control.

The mathematical equations which are used in the cross-impact model to connect first estimates to the final estimates were developed by trial and error. In the normal situation, the use of a quadratic relationship has been found adequate. The coefficients mentioned above, after normalisation, are used to calibrate these equations.

The technique of cross-impact analysis has been used to explore how the US Navy can expect to man its ships in the future,[11] to help decide how much water Canada should sell to America,[12] and to study the technological evolution of farm equipment.[13]

Perhaps the most useful output from a cross-impact analysis is the fact that it requires the participating executives to think through the relationship between the variables in the system. The systematic review of the variable relationships, taken in pairs, has been found to reveal relationships which would have been completely ignored under a less formal method of analysis. These unsuspected relationships have, on occasion, been of vital importance.

The following example of using cross-impact analysis arose from a research project on which one of the authors has been engaged for some time, into the financing of research and development.[14,15] A series of companies have been investigated, and the forces at work in the research finance area identified. While the research reported on the current status of these forces, the obvious next question was to ask where they would lead. If, for example, a firm has a history of emphasising current pay-off in its research programme, and if the firm has been in an industry of low competitiveness, then what is the prospect of this firm being able to sustain a scientifically creative research team? The cross-impact method has been applied to the study of this issue.

In the first place, a table was assembled for each company of the impacts of each force on each of the others, as is shown in the example company. Table 14.3. The first row of the table indicates the present strength of the force in its range of possible values. For example, the force 'stability of the research institution' was felt to be very high, and a score of 80 per cent of the possible maximum was assigned.

The rest of the table is made up of estimates of the consequences of these values for the other force values. For instance, in row 3 column 3 the impact of the fact that the firm is in a relatively low competition business (index 0.3) upon the scientific interest of the work done in research has been stated to be powerfully negative, which is consistent with the research finding mentioned earlier. The value assigned, −4, is towards the lower end of the scale of values used in the cross-impact computer program available at the Manchester Business School. Other versions of the programme use different scales and it would be appropriate for the reader to become familiar with his own installation's 'Users' Manual' before starting to use the method. The numbers can be obtained either from the researcher's own opinion, or from the collective opinion of a relevant group obtained by discussion. Direct measurement may also be possible in certain cases, though this is not common.

The second tabulation, shown as Table 14.4, is not required in order to make the system work but may be used if desired. The numbers in this table represent the impact of a *change* in the value of one of the variables.

The top right-hand number in Table 14.4 is a 3. This is a moderate positive quantity in terms of the scale. It means that an upward change in the emphasis placed upon diversification from the present low base of 0.2

TABLE 14.3. The cross-impacts of the *values* of the variables upon each other, and the initial values

The impact of value of Upon the value of		1 The stability of the research institution	2 The need for scientific challenge	3 Competition in the firm's markets	4 Technology transfer rate	5 Top management emphasis on current profit	6 Top management emphasis on growth in present markets	7 Top management emphasis on diversification
Initial value		0·8	0·6	0·3	0·4	0·9	0·5	0·2
	Symbol							
1. Stability	+	3	2	1	0	−3	0	−3
2. Challenge	*	2	3	−4	3	−4	5	−3
3. Competition	@	0	0	−1	0	0	2	3
4. Transfer	ε	−1	−1	−1	0	5	3	−5
5. Current profit	$	3	0	2	0	3	−3	−3
6. Growth	0	0	1	3	−3	−3	3	−3
7. Diversification	×	3	3	−2	−2	−3	−3	4

TABLE 14.4. The cross-impact of *changes* in the variables upon the values of the other variables

The impact of changes in value of / Upon the values of	Stability of the research institution	Scientific challenge	Market competition	Technology transfer	Top management emphasis on current profit	Top management emphasis on growth in current markets	Top management emphasis on diversification
Stability	-10	-2	-2	0	-5	4	3
Challenge	5	0	10	-2	0	6	3
Competition	0	0	0	0	1	2	-3
Techno. Transfer	2	-2	10	0	0	0	0
Current profit	3	6	-1	2	0	-3	-3
Growth	0	0	6	2	-3	3	-3
Diversification	3	0	7	2	-3	-3	4

(see Table 14.3, column 7, row 1) would have a moderately positive impact on the stability of the size of the research entity of the firm. Each of the other numbers in Table 14.4 can be similarly interpreted. The cross-impact model is used to process the sets of values shown in Tables 14.3 and 14.4 to give the output shown in 14.5. The mathematical conversion has been discussed by Kruzic[16] and elsewhere. The computer models which can be used are varied, but most connect adjacent values of each variable over time by raising the earlier to a power, the exponent of which depends on the matrix values fed in. The function is a very simple one compared to most other simulations, though it looks a bit fierce at first sight. The exponent, P, is given by:

$$P_i = \frac{2 + t\sum_j (|\alpha_j x_j + \beta_j y_j| - (\alpha_j x_j + \beta_j y_j))}{2 + t\sum_j (|\alpha_j x_j + \beta_j y_j| + (\alpha_j x_j + \beta_j y_j))}$$

where the α values are taken from the ith row of Table 14.3, the βs from the ith row of Table 14.4, the xs from the top row of Table 14.3 and the ys are computed as the change in the x value during the basic interval of time, which is t. Then apply the P value to the old x and get the new figure, thus:

$$\chi_{t+1} = \chi_t^P$$

While it is clearly not our business to explore the *results* of this particular application of the technique, it may be worth looking briefly at Figure 14.1 to see how these results are conveyed. The values of the variables are plotted, with their values shown at the top, and the time axis down the side. The majority of the variables remain reasonably close to the starting values given in Table 14.3, row 1. But two of them are expected to change very materially over time. The first change is a marked improvement in the rate of transfer of technology denoted by the symbol ϵ. This is largely caused by the very heavy emphasis on current profits by top management. The second change is a very serious decline in the prospects of the firm for growth in its current markets, which is denoted by the variable 0 in Figure 14.1. It is not our purpose here to analyse these figures, but only to note them as an example of the cross-impact method in use.

The important things to note about the cross-impact method are three in number. First of all, the consequences of changing one or two assumptions can be displayed on a visual display unit or other computer terminal very quickly. Secondly, the task of filling up the matrices of input values has been found a valuable way of getting groups of people to form and express opinions on future states of their environment. Thirdly, there is a strong

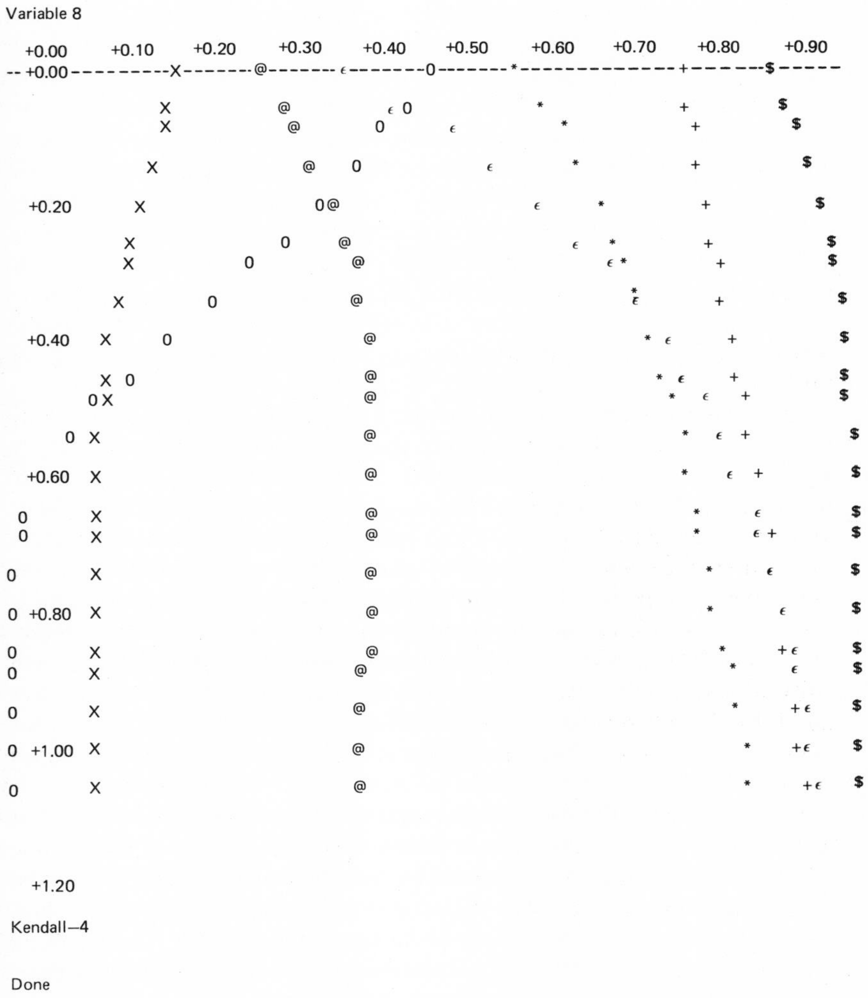

Variable 8

+1.20

Kendall—4

Done

Figure 14.1

temptation to change the input assumptions to make the answers conform to preconceived notions. Obviously, if one succumbs to this temptation the results are valueless. The same might, of course, be said of many other forms of forecasting package.

PROJECTIONS

The commonest and perhaps the most dangerous of all the methods of strategic forecasting is the projection. The methods discussed earlier are projections to some extent, of course. The scenarios of Kahn and Wiener and the cross-impact approach of Kane and others contain projecting calculations as a part of the exercise. But only as a relatively small part. The bulk of the effort is put into assessing the nature and strength of the forces at work and on evaluating the relationship between them. The mathematical projection, in the cross-impact case, is confined to the task of putting these assumptions to work in the manner already discussed.

There have been a number of forecasts prepared, including some highly successful ones, in which the mathematical element has been much more significant in proportion to the total effort. Bean[17] has carried out an historical analysis of the peaks and troughs of the American business cycle, and has observed that the high and low points have occurred at certain times in each decade. He found, by plotting fifty years of data, that the highs were very likely to happen in years ending with a three, a six, or a nine. Lows tend to be found in years ending with zero, four, and seven. Nobody can dispute the factual truth of Mr Bean's observation. But it would seem risky, at best, to expect such a result to hold in future decades. On the other hand, Mr Bean's record as a forecaster in practice requires us to treat his methods with respect, even if the logical basis upon which they are built seems unclear.

For example, in attempting to forecast the level of steel production that was entailed by a full employment policy, Bean simply plotted the volume of steel production against time for the first half of the century. He then erased the points which related to years of less than full employment, and fitted a smooth curve to the rest as shown in Figure 14.2. The resulting forecast was less wrong than many alternative expert opinions of the time.

One tends to be intuitively uncomfortable about such simple methods. One has the feeling that the world is a more complicated place than such simple methods are making it look. But this feeling of discomfort is misleading. We do not improve our understanding of a complex world by using a complex model to describe it, *unless* the complexities of the model

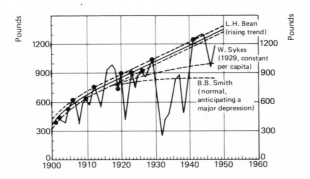

FIGURE 14.2. Three estimates of steel (ingots and castings) production per capita required for full employment, United States

are accurate representations of the world's complexities. If the model's complexities relate to, say, a dozen dimensions of the problem, and the true complexities relate to a different dozen dimensions, then our complex model has at least 24 possible ways of being wrong. And it is awfully hard to tell which of these is operating. With a simple model, at least one can be reasonably sure of the ways in which the model behaves, and one can add on further dimensions, if essential, after the simple edition has been explored to its limits.

LARGER AND MORE COMPLEX MODELS

The use of the large models discussed in this section should only be undertaken after a full exploration of the problem by the much simpler, smaller, and cheaper ones discussed in the last section. But there are times when such simple models just cannot handle the problem at hand. And there are other times when a larger and more powerful model can be justified, simply because earlier simple ones have led to such an improvement in our understanding of the basic issues governing the process being studied that the details and intricacies of that real-world process can now be examined.

There are many kinds of complex model, but two of the most important for strategic forecasting work are input–output analysis and simulation modelling. We shall discuss the former approach briefly.

INPUT–OUTPUT MODELS

The input–output model was devised for the study of economic measurement by Wassily Leontief, one of whose books[18] still offers the clearest description of the mathematics underlying the idea. He made the point that the economic product of any industry forms the input of some other industry, counting consumers, governments, and foreigners as 'industries' for this purpose. If one can measure the destinations of the outputs of each industry, then one is also measuring the inputs at the same time. A table can be developed, with the industries listed down the side and along the top, showing the quantities or values moving from each industry to each other industry in any given time period. This is a massive data-gathering job, and even very large firms have found it difficult to justify the cost. But governments can do it, and have done, and groups of large firms have also been formed which have each found their share of the cost to be well rewarded by the analytical output obtainable.

Of the latter category, an outstanding example is Almon *et al.*[19] This major research programme involved the construction of a complete input–output table relating the industries of the United States to one another. In many cases data had to be gathered from scratch, because they chose to study 130 different product markets, which is more than other input–output model builders have tried. A number of exogenous variables, such as employment levels, household formation, defence expenditure, and population were then forecast, and the resulting states of each of the 130 industries was computed. This gave a view, seen from 1973, of the state of these industries in 1985.

The economy of the USA was seen to become rather sedate in their forecast. A 52 percent fall in the rate of growth in gross national product from 4·6 per cent in 1969 to 2·2 per cent in 1985 was forecast. This represents a compounded decline in the growth rate of $4\frac{1}{2}$ per cent annually. They suggest that the expected decline in the growth of the labour force was only partly to blame, and that the main reason was the movement of labour from sectors with high rates of productivity growth, such as agriculture and railways, into sectors with low productivity growth rates such as medicine and finance.

The assertion has often been made (though not by Almon *et al.*) that many other industrial nations 'enjoy' similar trends to those in the USA, after a lag of between three and seven years.

In the light of the above assertion, it may interest readers in Western Europe to note that a population growth rate over the last 35 years of the century was forecast by Kahn and Wiener. They said that the annual rate for the USA would be 1·5 per cent, while the rate for the four largest EEC countries taken together would be 0·44 per cent. In the UK, the movement of people between industries seems to have been similar to the movements forecast by Almon for the USA. The monthly digest of statistics notes the transfer, between 1967 and 1973, of 7 per cent of the workforce from production to services. The production sector, including agriculture, forestry, fishing, mining, manufacturing and construction, employed 50·85 per cent of the workforce in 1967. The services sector, including transport, distribution, finance, professional, catering, and government, employed the remaining 49·15 per cent. By 1973, the figures were 43·75 per cent and 56·25 per cent respectively. The major growth sectors were finance, professional, catering and government. The 7 per cent of the workforce transferring to the service sector in Britain between 1967 and 1971 may be compared with a transfer in the USA, between 1965 and 1971 of 4 per cent of their workforce. It is at least possible, from these figures, that the sedate growth rate forecast by Almon for the USA may be replicated in Western Europe, and may indeed prove more sedate still. OECD forecasts for the remainder of Western Europe are less quantified, but seem to suggest that the transfer of manpower into the service sector is happening throughout the continent at rates approaching the British.

From a corporate forecasting point of view, one of the most interesting applications of input–output models must be the inter-industrial comparisons. Merritt[20] has suggested that makers of producer goods must be the main beneficiaries of input–output models, as theirs are the firms which depend most on secondary demand functions.

There are two main problems with input–output tables, apart from their high cost which has already been mentioned. First of all, the data tend to be quite old. It seems to take about five years to get a new table out, so the most recent historic actual figures are at least of that age. Secondly, the tables are presented as aggregates, showing the total trade done by one industry with another. For many business decisions, the executive is interested in the marginal effects, the changes in the amount of trade, rather than the total at any particular moment. Nonetheless, the tables provide a view of the interconnections of an economy which no other approach can give, and they ought therefore to be studied with care by all those interested in strategic forecasting. As mentioned earlier, it is not likely that an individual firm can justify the cost of developing a full table, but the intelligent use of a governmentally prepared table can be most valuable.

Almon mentions, for instance, the use by one of his sponsors of his model to choose a merger partner. After sifting out firms that were too big or too expensive in price/earnings terms, they listed the industrial classifications in which each remaining firm worked. They then forecast which industrial mixture was likely to enjoy the greatest progress over the next ten years and picked those firms which offered the 'best' industrial profile. At least two mergers resulted from this process. Ironically, though, the parent firm was itself taken over before it could absorb the two newcomers. Almon does not record whether the ultimate predator used an input–output model!

The most easily obtained input–output tables of the UK economy are those produced by the Department of Industry.[21] Table F of these input–output tables shows the sources from which each of the major industrial groupings draw their supplies—the 'direct requirement' table. Also indicated are those groups of input which are crucial to each of the major industrial groups. A comparison of Table F between years can indicate important changes in demand. For instance, in the 1972 table, it is shown that the building materials industry needed £912 of service from the road transport industry to generate £10,000 worth of final output, and only £65 of other transport services. In contrast, the 1971 table indicates figures of £846 and £71 for road and other transport respectively, which suggests a policy shift by the building materials industry about which road transport executives might well be pleased. An intensity growth of just under 8 % [912–846] has occurred, so if the haulier felt a decline in construction probable, he might still not reduce his fleet in view of the compensation.

SELECTION OF A METHOD FOR STRATEGIC FORECASTING

The range of methods mentioned in this chapter is extensive, and even then is only a sampling from the total list of available approaches to forecasting. How, then, does one go about choosing the 'right' method for use in a particular firm at a particular moment?

For the smaller business, the best approach to strategic forecasting is probably to subscribe to a forecasting service, preferably one which specialises in the relevant industry. By this means, one avoids the expense of having an internal forecasting unit, and can also change over with relative ease if the entity subscribed to proves inadequate. A small firm cannot afford to have input–output models built, and the entrepreneurial leader of a small firm cannot often spare the time to read, analytically, the visionary forecasts discussed at the outset. But he may be able to make use of some fairly straightforward projections, to test whether some forecasts made available to him are within rational bounds. For instance, a small business man was offered a company for sale in 1975. The firm was producing a gross profit of £2·3 million in that year and had grown at 21 per cent from the prior year. The vendor suggested that it would therefore reach a gross profit total of about £15·5 million[22] in ten years time, and wanted to negotiate a price on that basis, suitably discounted for the ten-year delay. The buyer thought this seemed high, and borrowed Kahn and Wiener's simple model. If the population is growing by 2 per cent and the GNP by 4·4 per cent, then the GNP ought to grow in ten years from £66 thousand million to £104 thousand million[23] or so. If the sales of the firm were to hold its proportion of GNP, then the calculation leads to a gross profit in ten years' time of £3·6 millions.[24] This led him to suspect the figures offered, and the price was eventually settled at a much lower figure than the vendor had wanted at first.

There is, of course, no real reason to believe the Kahn–Wiener model to be the perfect answer either. But the use of that simple approach enabled the small businessman to establish that the seller was assuming the firm would attain five times its existing proportion of GNP over the decade. As no particular reason was given for this assumption, his suspicions were aroused, and were acted upon.

A medium-sized firm, in addition to the simplified forecasting projections already discussed, may be able to allocate up to one man-year of effort to strategic forecasting in any given year. In this period, it would be quite reasonable to attempt a cross-impact study, and to make use of existing governmental input–output tables in the preparation of a forecast at the firm level. The analytical reading of a few visionary forecasts may also be attempted, though a medium firm might do well to confine this approach to books written about the geographic region in which it is principally involved.

The very large firm, which can afford almost any technique, is unfortunately not greatly benefited by this fact. The large firm has the problem that the forecasts are usually prepared by people who are organisationally divorced from the executive group who actually run the enterprise. If the forecasters employ a highly sophisticated technique to do their job, then the divorce analogy becomes more appropriate still. The executives, however capable, do not have the time to learn the methods, and there have been many instances in which the output from such advanced methods do not get used because of the mistrust which this lack of understanding generates. If this should occur, the cost-effectiveness of the sophisticated technique is quite undermined. The use of a larger number of simpler methods is therefore to be commended, at least until a thorough rapport between the strategic forecasting unit and the top management group has been established.

CHAPTER 16—PROJECTS

1. Take a forward-looking popular book and read it analytically to extract the essential assumptions about the future environment upon which the argument is built. Better still, take two of them written from completely different viewpoints, and read both analytically. Then compare the resulting lists of essential assumptions. What implications can you detect for the future strategy of a business of your choice in the list of common assumptions?

2. Set up a cross-impact model on your local computer installation. Then, working in groups of no more than four, analyse a business policy case study of recent date. Define the elements that seem likely to impinge upon the welfare of that firm. Then build a cross-impact matrix to describe the relationships between these elements, both as regards the impact of their current values and that of their growth trends. Study the trends in the future, and adjust the model to cater for your changing opinions. Write up a group report, describing the scenario which the firm may be said to confront. Suggest courses of action the firm might follow to capitalise upon its opportunities or to mitigate potential obstacles.

NOTES

1. Cottrell, A., 'Grasping the Nettles in British Industrial Policy', *Journal of General Management*, 4, No. 1 (1976).
2. Jenkins, C., and Mortimer, J. E., *The Kind of Laws the Unions Ought to Want*. London: Pergamon, 1968.
3. Kahn, H., and Wiener, A. J., *The Year 2000: A Framework for Speculation about the Next 33 Years*. New York: Macmillan, 1967.
4. The figure was obtained by multiplying the 1965 GNP by population growth (0·2 per cent per year) and by productivity growth (4·7 per cent). Thus $(1·002)^{35} \times (1·047)^{35} \times 98·5 = 527$.
5. Palmer, M., and Schmid, G., 'Planning with Scenarios—The Banking World of 1985', *Futures*, 8, No. 6 (1976), 472.
6. Merritt, T. P., 'Forecasting the Future Business Environment—The State of the Art', *Long-Range Planning*, June 1974.
7. McNulty, C. A. R., 'Scenario Development for Corporate Planning', *Futures*, April 1977.
8. Helmer, O., 'Analysis of the Future: The Delphi Method', in Bright, J. E. (ed.), *Technological Forecasting for Industry and Government*. Englewood Cliffs, N.J.: Prentice-Hall, 1968.
9. Decker, R. L., 'Future Economic Developments—A Delphi Survey', *Futures*, 6, No. 2 (1974).

10. Gordon, T. J., and Hayward, H., 'Initial Experiments with the Cross Impact Matrix Method of Forecasting', *Futures*, 1, No. 2 (1968).
11. Kruzic, P. G., *Suggested Paradigm for Policy Planning*, Menlo Park, California, Stamford Research Institute, 1973, Ref TN-OED-016.
12. Kane, J., Vertinsky, I., and Thomson, W., 'KSIM, A methodology for Interactive Resource Policy Simulation', *Water Resources Research*, 9, No. 1 (1973).
13. Sahal, D., 'Cross Impact Analysis and Prediction of Technological Developments: A Case Study of Farm Tractors', *IEEE Transactions*, EM22, No. 2 (1975).
14. McCosh, A. M., 'Simulation Study of the Research Accounting Problem'. *R & D Management*, July 1975.
15. McCosh, A. M., and Kesztenbaum, M., 'A Small Sample Survey of the Research Funding Process', *R & D Management*, February 1978.
16. Kruzic, P. G., *op. cit.*
17. Bean, L. H., *The Art of Forecasting*. New York: Random House, 1969.
18. Leontief, W., *Input–Output Economics*. New York: Oxford University Press, 1966, especially Chapter 7.
19. Almon, C., *et al.*, *1985: Interindustry Forecasts of the American Economy*. Lexington, Mass.: D. C. Heath, 1974.
20. Merritt, T. P., *op. cit.*
21. For example, Department of Industry, *Input Output Tables for the UK, 1972*, Business Monitor, HMSO, 1976.
22. $2 \cdot 3 \times (1 + 0 \cdot 21)^{10} = 15 \cdot 47$.
23. $(1 \cdot 002)^{10} \times (1 \cdot 044)^{10} \times 66 = 103 \cdot 6$.
24. Gross in year 10 = gross in year 1 × (GNP).

BIBLIOGRAPHY

Ansoff, H. I., *Managing Surprise and Discontinuity—Strategic Response to Weak Signals*, Brussels, European Institute for Advanced Studies in Management, Working Paper 75/21, April 1975.
Beer, S., *Cybernetics of National Development*, The Zaheer Lecture, Manchester Business School, 1976.
Central Statistical Office, *Monthly Digest of Statistics*, January, 1975, HMSO.
Cole, S., 'Accuracy in the Long Run—Where are We Now?', in Fildes, R. A., and Wood, D., *Forecasting and Planning*. London: Saxon House, 1978.
Lorange, P., *Survey Research in Strategy and Planning: Methodological Considerations*, Working Paper 73/15, European Institute for Advanced Studies in Management, 1973.
Milne, T. E., *Business Forecasting–A Managerial Approach*. London: Longman, 1975.
Raynaud, H., 'Long-Range Forecasting Within Organisations', *Futures*, 8, No. 5 (1976), 420.
Sobek, R. S., 'A Manager's Primer of Forecasting', *Harvard Business Review*, May–June, 1973.

Wood, D., 'Forecasting and Planning National Industrial Strategy', in Fildes, R. A., and Wood, D., *Forecasting and Planning*. London: Saxon House, 1978.

Wood, D., and Fildes, R. A., *Forecasting the Business Environment: The National Economy*. London: Longman, 1976.

15 Design of Strategic Information Systems

It is clear from the previous three chapters that information processing is central to strategic planning. It is equally clear that strategic MIS design presents distinctive challenges. For example most strategic techniques are data-dependent and yet the data are scarce. Thus the emphasis of strategic MIS is as much on *developing* information, or on intelligence, as it is on subsequent processing. Secondly much strategy-making is non-routine and unstructured with information needs being difficult to predict, so that formal MIS may have a limited role. These characteristics also make strategic planning difficult to organise and manage, so that responsibility for strategic information is dispersed and diffused and strategic awareness is not easily cultivated. Thus potential strategic information may be lost and critical strategic messages may not be recognised.

Our understanding of strategic information processing therefore in some ways is still limited; so limited, some say, that extensive development of formal MIS may be harmful. Certainly it seems probable that informal systems, or other alternatives, have an equal and complementary role. Furthermore as strategic planning increasingly has to focus not only on economic questions of product–market strategy, but also on socio-political issues, and as the rate of environmental change possibly exceeds our ability to understand it, or react to it, the MIS designer faces further challenges. Indeed Ansoff[1] suggests that a complete cultural transform-ation of the organisation is required to meet these demands. Certainly strategic MIS and strategy formulation techniques must not be developed in isolation from their organisational context. For this reason, the chapter concludes by emphasising the need for *strategic management*.

STRATEGIC INFORMATION

Both the sources and characteristics of strategic data are diverse. So much was evident from the data collection demands of the null strategy approach described in Chapter 12. Generally, strategic data is:

(1) External rather than internal. The critical and most difficult strategic questions concern the environment, for example economic trends, competitor performances, new technologies, the financial climate, political risk or social pressures.

(2) Future rather than historical. Strategic planning inherently is concerned with futures. Trends, forecasts, intentions and early warnings therefore are invaluable and sensitivity or risk analyses, evaluation procedures and access facilities are important.

(3) Aggregate, yet must be robust. External and future information inevitably tends to be aggregated. Aggregates are sufficient for most strategic decisions, but they must be reasonably accurate. Validation, evaluation and security procedures therefore may be important.

(4) Quantitative and qualitative. Many strategic techniques demand quantitative data, but qualitative data, such as opinions, insights, observation and rumour may be equally relevant. Indeed much social and political data can only be qualitative.

(5) Partial and transient. Strategic decisions often have to be made on imperfect or inadequate information, using judgement, or indeed inspiration, as much as analysis and computation. Equally the non-routine nature of strategic planning means that the permanent or fixed proportion of a strategic database is relatively small.

(6) Formal and informal. Systematic data collection and processing is important in strategic planning, but not at the expense of informal processes which may be more timely, penetrative, efficient or sensitive and may frequently provide the missing link in the chain of strategic thought.

The strategic database, therefore is complex, drawing on at least the sources depicted in Figure 15.1. It is however difficult to specify and design a strategic database, for no one item of data is intrinsically strategic. Aguilar[2] suggests that data only becomes strategic if it relates to a strategic opportunity or problem. Collection, selection, storage and dissemination of strategic data is therefore far from simple, for who determines strategic relevance, how are strategic needs defined, how are potential users identified and how is strategic thinking developed? The answers lie in creation of a strategic culture as the following example demonstrates.

A publishing manager heard of the imminent failure of the coffee crop in Brazil. For him this was strategic information. His company was actively considering expansion in Kenya. He reasoned that with a shortage of Brazilian coffee, demand for Kenya's coffee crop would increase and at

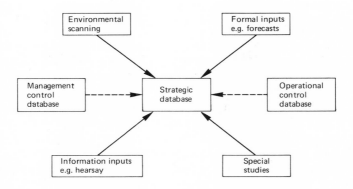

FIGURE 15.1. The strategic database

high prices. With a consequent growth of Kenyan GNP, the nation's education budget might increase providing new market opportunities for the publisher's books. Thus described, the deduction sounds simple, but the conditions which translated this data into strategic information were the product of a strategic culture. First, management awareness of strategic directions had been created in the publishing company and secondly, this particular manager was able to interrelate apparently disconnected facts. In other words, information is as much a process as a commodity, and at the strategic level organisational and human information processing is as important as the more obvious technologies.

STRATEGIC DECISION-MAKING

To provide information relevant to strategic planning, the MIS designer must first understand the process of strategic decision-making. Simon's[3] model of the decision-making process again provides a framework, but it must be modified in the light of recent empirical research. In the strategic context, Simon's *intelligence* phase comprises environmental scanning for decision stimuli, such as business threats or opportunities. The *design* phase is concerned with development and analysis of strategic responses to those stimuli. The *choice* phase comprises the selection of a strategic alternative, followed by its implementation. The nature of strategy-making suggests that these phases are largely non-programmable, since each situation is new, uncertain and complex. The role of the formal MIS therefore will have limits.

However, this view of strategic decision-making may be rather naive. It

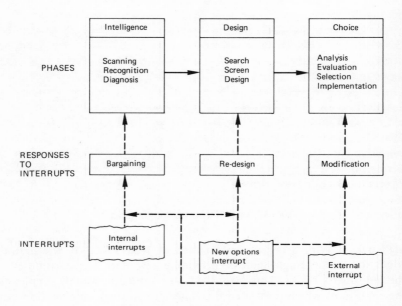

FIGURE 15.2. The strategic process

seems from empirical research[4] that the intelligence, design and choice phases are by no means simple, smooth and sequential. They are broken by significant *interrupts*, so that strategy-making is not the commonly perceived exercise of systematic forward planning, but an evolutionary fragmented and lengthy process (Figure 15.2). This is perhaps not surprising when one considers the complexity of strategy.

The interrupts may be classified[5] as:

(1) Internal political interrupts during the intelligence phase, where there is disagreement on the existence of a decision situation. Resolution is achieved through bargaining, delays and political design.

(2) External interrupts which hinder the choice phase. Examples include resistance from affected parties and lobbying by pressure groups. Resolution is achieved through modification of strategies, development of a new solution, or bargaining.

(3) New option interrupts which occur during the design and choice phases. Here, as conditions change, new alternatives may appear so that either re-design occurs or choice is amended. Clearly these interrupts should not be seen as deviations or exceptions to normative strategic decision-making. They are constituent parts of the strategy-making

process and strategic MIS must therefore help in devising sound responses.

Another view of strategic decision-making may be derived from Thompson and Tuden.[6] They related organisational decision-making to states of uncertainty, distinguishing between uncertainty of objectives and uncertainty of cause and effect (or the means of achieving objectives). The four different decision situations which may arise, and the resultant decision processes, are shown in Figure 15.3. Uncertainty about cause and effect is typical of strategic decisions, and thus judgement and inspiration seem likely to be important requirements. Increasingly in a world where economic, political and social orders are changing rapidly, uncertainty of strategic objectives is also to be expected, with compromise and bargaining a likely means of resolution. The computational philosophy of many MIS developed for other situations therefore has limited utility in strategic planning. The design emphasis has to be on aiding judgement, facilitating bargaining and stimulating inspiration.

Uncertainty about objectives

		Low	High
Uncertainty of cause and effect	Low	Decision by computation	Decision by bargaining
	High	Decision by judgement	Decision by inspiration

FIGURE 15.3. Decision-making under uncertainty

Finally, Toffler[7] has drawn a simpler, but nonetheless valuable, picture of strategy-making. He suggests that strategists consider three different futures (Figure 15.4). The possible future is limited only by artistic

FIGURE 15.4. The strategists' futures

imagination and creativity. It is reduced to a probable future by decision science, such as the use of strategic techniques as in the previous chapter. The preferable future is the feasible region of the probable future and is determined by politics internal and external to the organisation. Whilst the conventional role of strategic MIS is perhaps often seen as helping to define the probable future, a wider perspective is required. Otherwise the possible future may be overly constrained and the preferable future unduly biased.

Toffler has also emphasised how today's rate of change exceeds any previous experience, so that our knowledge system is undergoing upheaval. Today's facts, he suggests, become tomorrow's misinformation. Faced with such a transient environment, old ideas, former models and frameworks, outdated values and assumptions, and poor or wrong procedures have to be discarded before new views and perspective are developed and adaptation occurs. In other words, not only must strategic MIS help us learn and relearn, they must especially assist in unlearning.

STRATEGIC INFORMATION SYSTEMS

From these different perspectives on strategic decision-making, we can begin to define and describe appropriate MIS. Simon's framework is used in Figure 15.5 to predict the different MIS that strategic planning may require. It is clear that rather than developing *a* strategic information system, a mix is required. Different phases of strategic decision-making may need different MIS at different times, in quite disjoint modes. The intelligence phase is typically supported by ongoing scanning systems, by forecasting facilities and by access to strategic databases. The design phase is enhanced by database enquiry systems, by modelling systems which allow analysis and learning, and by 'decision-environments' or 'information centres' which facilitate group decision-making. The choice phase again may be supported by modelling systems to evaluate alternatives, and by feedback systems and decision environments monitoring implementation.

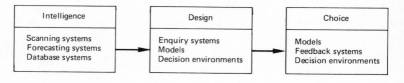

Intelligence	Design	Choice
Scanning systems Forecasting systems Database systems	Enquiry systems Models Decision environments	Models Feedback systems Decision environments

Figure 15.5. The strategic systems mix

Besides this mix of MIS *types*, the other views of strategy-making suggest that a mix of MIS *forms* or philosophies is also required. The complexity, uncertainty and diversity of strategic decisions demand varied forms of information processing. Many MIS may be temporary, serving a particular need at a particular time, whilst the emphasis in the more permanent systems will be on flexibility of use and adaptive design. Most strategic MIS will tend to the left of the man–machine continuum (Figure 3.6) focusing primarily on data collection, database and predictive functions, and having many interfaces with human and organisational information processing.

For example, the interrupts of strategic decision-making may place special, and perhaps unpredictable, demands on MIS design and use. It is likely that during internal political interrupts, formal MIS may not be used as originally intended, or that alternative, *unofficial* systems are employed. Important strategic information can be rejected in such situations through value dissonance, that is a dissonance between the organisation's value environment and its own value system.[8] Adaptation, therefore, may be impaired because we only select strategic alternatives which are compatible with our own values. Unofficial MIS that managers themselves develop, that other stockholders use or that local sub-cultures create, can help counteract the values of technocrats and 'rational men', the rigid premises of officialdom, the narrow perspectives of tradition and the outdated assumptions of the official MIS.

The possibility of external interrupts emphasises the need for environmental scanning, or intelligence in its broadest sense, and for multiple and varied information flows. Where resolution is achieved through bargaining, the need is for multi-dimensional information inputs reflecting the goals and views of the different stakeholders. Certainly corporate financial information alone is likely to be inadequate. For example, a senior manager of a major industrial company reported that when major investment and divestment decisions were being made, the information presented was nearly always financial. Once the decision was made and implementation was discussed, other inputs were made available, such as personnel or engineering information flows. As a result, bargaining only occurred over implementation and not in making the original strategic decision. It may also be possible to influence stakeholders *through* MIS; public-relations exercises, information disclosure and inter-organisational processes are examples of this.

The likelihood of new option interrupts indicates the need for scanning systems which focus on technological, political and social trends as well as on the more obvious economic issues. Resolution through re-design or modification may be assisted by exploratory, experimental or learning systems, especially flexible and dialectic enquiry facilities and pliable modelling aids.

Thompson and Tuden's model is a warning against developing strategic MIS which only seek to optimise or compute answers. Decision by judgement demands learning catalysts, for example decision support systems where the manager's experience is combined with the computer's power as is typical of planning models. Decision by bargaining again emphasises the need for multiple, dialectic, multi-dimensional and perhaps partial and conflicting information flows. It may be impossible and self-defeating to specify the likely information needs of decision by inspiration. Probably simple, bold information flows are required. Indeed *simple* systems may suit many strategic decisions, for over-emphasis on analysis, enquiry, conflict and multiple viewpoints may impair entrepreneurship by inducing risk aversion and stifling creativity. Once decisions are made, however, especially those made by inspiration, the more complex MIS may in fact serve another purpose, namely justification and rationalisation of the decision *ex-post*. Bower[9] in his study of the resource allocation process, showed that such decisions were political rather than rational, and discovered that most capital budgeting procedures were rationalisation devices.

Toffler's model of strategists' futures tends to confirm the picture so far. Too narrow a view of strategic MIS may unnecessarily delimit the futures and bias preferences. The definitions of strategic MIS have to encompass all forms of formalised, human and organisational information processing. Above all, where the possible future depends on creativity, and the preferable future is determined by a political process, *informal* systems will be as important as the formal. Grinyer and Norburn[10] in their study of strategic planning in 21 UK companies found no relationship between formality in planning procedures and successful financial performance. Conversely, the use of both informal channels of communication and informal decision-making processes was found to be associated with success. Informality appeared to fit the politics of strategy-making, and because of its general acceptability, ensured that more and broader information items were used.

An example from a publishing firm suggests another reason why informal systems are required. This company, a publisher of children's books, so formalised its planning procedures that they became mechanistic. The rolling five-year plan was derived by asking the same set of questions and doing the same analyses each year. As a result the management failed to recognise a significant external and obvious event.

The birth-rate was falling and soon the market for children's books would decline.

Strategic thinking can therefore be influenced by the design of strategic techniques and information systems. Toffler's concern with the rate at which information becomes obsolescent is especially relevant here. In stable environments we tend to routinise information processing and standardise operating procedures in order to make best use of managerial skills and allocate available decision resources to problems which are new, different and unstructured. In changing environments this policy may be dysfunctional, for routinisation and standardisation offer weak protection against the discontinuous and unpredictable, and accordingly adaptation may be delayed or prevented. It takes a significant amount of counter-evidence to challenge old behaviours and further efforts and time are needed to unfreeze these behaviours and replace them with new ones. Hedberg and Jönsson[11] recommend the design of *semi-confusing* information systems to overcome this inertia. Instead of seeking absolute certainty, stability and rationality, such systems inject some ambiguity, warnings and discomfort into our thinking in order to trigger both learning and unlearning; hence the concept of semi-confusion. Such systems are feasible, for they are routine formal MIS which deliberately embody some of the following features:

(1) Obsolescence factors such as decay signals to warn that decision parameters, formulae, models or assumptions are out of date.
(2) Crude filtering of data to ensure that inconsistencies are identified and examined.
(3) Short-circuits in communication channels such as irregular distribution lists or authorisation procedures to break down inertia.
(4) Dialectic and enquiry facilities to aid challenge and interrogation.
(5) Alternative modes of presentation and format to stress ambiguity and choice.
(6) Local databases and sub-culture-creating systems to bring different views and perspectives.
(7) Predetermined review and revision points.

Clearly such features alone cannot be relied on to keep in tune with a transient environment. Accordingly *disposable* systems are also required. These serve a particular purpose and then die; they too are transient. They may be deliberately experimental, created to assess new opportunities, ask different questions and scan new areas of potential. Examples include many modelling systems, ad hoc or special exercises, one-off enquiry and analysis routines, or temporary task forces. Periodic systems may be developed to ensure environmental changes are examined and alternative views and opinions are cultivated. One form of periodic system is an annual workshop or conference of senior managers who are encouraged to report and share their potentially strategic findings, anxieties or knowledge with their peers and board-level superiors. It is important to recognise the need for disposable systems, otherwise resources are rarely available to develop them when required.

STRATEGIC SYSTEMS

It is now clear from the descriptive views of strategy-making that a mix of both MIS types and forms is required, for strategic MIS influence strategic thinking and too narrow a view may be detrimental. This diversity required of strategic MIS and the relative disappointment with strategic planning techniques up to now have led to pleas for more spontaneity and less direction and design. However, to hope that the necessary breadth and variety of information, the requisite enquiry and analysis facilities, the dissemination and communication of strategic messages and indeed the very important subjective and personally derived information needs can all be met without some systematisation would be folly. Consequently, this section describes each of the strategic MIS types summarised in Figure 15.5—unless like forecasting systems they have been examined earlier.

SCANNING SYSTEMS

Strategy-making is dependent upon understanding the environment and the future, and understanding is dependent upon intelligence. Scanning systems provide this intelligence by both purposeful search and undirected viewing.[12] Scanning is costly and difficult, but is justified by the greater cost of strategic mistakes. Two problems are paramount. Firstly, the wider the environment that is scanned, the more complex, tenuous and expensive the task becomes. Secondly, the effectiveness of scanning is limited by the information processing ability of the organisation and its members. Consequently scanning systems are always likely to be incomplete and imperfect, and the approach will generally adapt to meet changing needs and priorities. King and Cleland[13] suggest that to systematise business intelligence the following questions must be answered and the answers made operational.

(1) What needs to be known?
(2) Where can the data be obtained?

(3) Who will gather the data?

(4) How will the data be gathered?

(5) How will extracted information be stored most efficiently for equally efficient retrieval?

(6) How can extracted intelligence be disseminated to the proper parties at the right time for consideration?

(7) How will the system be protected from leakage or sabotage?

Some of these questions are examined in this section, and the remainder subsequently.

The scanning sources upon which organisations rely have been surveyed both in the UK [14] and in the USA. [15] Both agreed that personal sources were used more than impersonal sources and that internal contacts, through meetings, and happenstance, were more important than external antennae. Clearly, therefore, informal or non-routine scanning systems are significant. Conversely, market research and the like were found to be least important. Table 15.1 summarises the findings of the two studies.

TABLE 15.1. Scanning sources

	External	*Internal*
Personal	Customer + competitor contacts	Unscheduled meetings with colleagues
	Supplier contacts	Unscheduled meetings with sub-ordinates
	Bankers' contacts	Formal scheduled meetings
	Conferences, etc	
Impersonal	Scanning publications	Written communications
	Market research	Special reports
	Special surveys	

Aguilar[16] classified four modes of scanning:

(1) Undirected viewing—where the manager has no specific purpose in mind save possibly exploration or the feeling that something significant has changed.

(2) Conditioned viewing—where the manager has been directed by cues and experience to recognise certain events or data, but as they are encountered rather than by active search.

(3) Informal search—where the manager actively seeks specific information, or information for a specific purpose, but in a relatively limited and unstructured fashion.

(4) Formal search—where deliberate efforts are made through especially designed procedures or systems to secure specific information, or seek information relating to a specific issue.

Which mode is adopted depends on the scope, magnitude and urgency of the issue, on how well-defined is the objective, on the cost of scanning and on the resources and capacity which exist. For each mode to be effective, awareness of strategic issues must be fostered and cognitive abilities developed, both being functions of strategic management.

Central amongst the data that are scanned are economic facts. Chapter 12 suggested specifications of key data and Chapter 14 examined forecasting systems. Competitive intelligence systems are also fundamental. Sceptics exist who doubt both the utility and feasibility of such systems, and question if they are legal and ethical. Cleland and King[17] answer these doubts by pointing out that product–market data is generally inadequate unless competitive behaviour has been studied. They also point out that the data sources are so wide that hit-and-miss collection is insufficient, and possession of any competitive information is so valuable that haphazard dissemination is profligate. The basic elements of competitive analysis are:

(1) Marketing information, on prices, volume, products, market share, sales methods, distribution channels, customer relations, advertising programmes, etc.
(2) Production and product information—on quality, performance, lines, technology, costs, capacities, new developments, production facilities, packaging, delivery, R&D capability, etc.
(3) Organisational and financial information—on identification of key decision-makers, financial condition, change in philosophies, expansion and acquisition programmes, major problems and opportunities, new investments, organisational changes, etc.

This information is collected both by continuous scanning and special studies. Much of it is available from public sources. A military analogy is revealing: the US Navy obtained 95 per cent of its intelligence in the Second World War from public sources, 4 per cent from semi-public sources and only 1 per cent from secret sources.[18] Potential sources of competitive data include the following:

(1) The field sales force—who are 'in contact' but whose reports often need verifying.
(2) Purchasing department—who learn from suppliers about competitors.

(3) Treasury department—who have comparative data and meet financial experts.
(4) Key executives—who meet industry peers.
(5) Research and development personnel—who attend conferences and read reports.
(6) Business periodicals—which may describe competitors' operations.
(7) Books—which may describe and evaluate competitors.
(8) Business reference services—such as financial guides, supplier directories, etc.
(9) Catalogues and indexes—which may lead to articles on competitors.
(10) Government sources—such as reports, statistics and committees.
(11) Professional associations—where peers exchange problems.
(12) Customers—who like to compare vendors.
(13) Suppliers—who keep customer information.
(14) Trade and commerce associations—where immediate problems and future intentions are discussed.
(15) National, local and trade press—for reports on competitors.
(16) Stockbroker and investment reports—for financial analyses and future prospects.
(17) Annual reports—for financial results, major events and future plans.
(18) Conferences and courses—where competitor examples and problems may be used.

Increasingly, however, organisations need to be sensitive to the accelerating rate of change in the political and social environment. They need to keep updated on, and ask questions about, the meaning and possible consequences of, political and social trends. For example, what are the strategic implications of industrial democracy, indigenisation, international cartels, increasing government involvement in business, consumerism, environmental protection, or the emergence of 'newly poor' nations of the west? The MIS which scans and interprets such issues is clearly remote from systematic procedures and computers. It is more likely to be the directors' dining room, the occasional conference, dips into the 'futures' literature, specialist studies and periodic employment or entertainment of experts, journalists, academics, politicians, policy-researchers and others who may have the insights of 'marginal men'.[19] In particular, strategic thinkers may need to join or 'plug into' inter-organisational networks to explore current issues and share common concerns and experiences. Examples include top management seminars, government–industry committees or business 'think-tanks'.
    It is by now evident that much scanning is informal, not only because top

managers and those who interact with the environment naturally build their own information networks, but because informal systems tend to capture nuances, transmit bad news, convey meaning, stimulate insights and creativity, and cope with qualitative considerations better and quicker than formal procedures. However, this poses validation problems, for how are these information flows tested for reliability and credibility? It is often said that businessmen judge intelligence on its source rather than on its content. An explicit validation procedure which classifies separately the reliability of source and content, much as in military intelligence operations, can be valuable. This validation can be done by functional heads, a cross-functional team or even a strategic information group. They also can be given the responsibility for analysing and interpreting intelligence gained from scanning activities.

Finally, whilst scanning focuses primarily on the external environment, internal trends are important, especially in highlighting corporate strengths and weaknesses. Most of this data is collected by feedback systems which are described later.

DATABASE SYSTEMS

Having collected strategic data by scanning and augmented it with forecasting data and feedback information, how is it stored, made available for retrieval, disseminated and rendered secure? This is the challenge of strategic database design. The encyclopaedic database in which strategists fish as required for hitherto unforeseen information needs is particularly appealing. It is also impracticable and expensive.

Strategic database design is a matter of compromise, based on rational information requirements analysis but also admitting of some speculation. The concept of a formal integrated database is attractive, but the practical reality is more likely to be a loose arrangement of a core data supported by temporary or disposable data within a framework of strategic profiles or key strategic statements (Figure 15.6). Developed in this form, strategic databases are manageable and therefore can be used directly in supporting the strategic planning process. More ambitious systems are likely to be extravagant and lie unused.

(1) Core data is that strategic data which the organisation collects and stores continuously, for example economic statistics, market trends, etc. It may be held in summary files produced by operational control or management control systems, or in especially designed and maintained files.

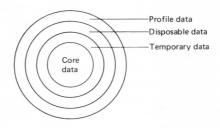

FIGURE 15.6. A strategic database system

(2) Temporary data is that data which is collected and stored for particular strategic planning exercises. An example would be mergers and acquisition data built up during a growth by acquisition phase. Typically it is stored in report of manual file form.

(3) Disposable data are stored speculatively as potentially relevant to an imminent strategic need. An example would be a salesman's report of competitor plans which could impinge on new product or market strategy. Typically it would be held in memo form.

(4) Profile data[20] comprises concise statements of strategic direction, strategic methodology and user interests. It is the envelope around the database which provides guidance on what data is strategically relevant. These strategic statements are documented, displayed and disseminated to explicitly guide strategic data collection, storage and communication.

The development process by which profile data is derived is crucial, for profile data is *evaluated* data and affects the organisation's strategic choices. Typically a staff group will help top management specify the most important strategic factors about the organisation, the environment and strategic choices. Clearly these managers must have the expertise, breadth and authority to make strategic choices, whilst the number of statements should be limited to ensure relevance and to force critical analysis, judgement and negotiation. Statements will be made about the key success criteria in the industry, the competition, the environmental threats and opportunities, corporate strengths and weaknesses, management values and viewpoints and the current strategy. Then the staff group will determine the methodological procedures for administering the strategic database. Finally user interest profiles are constructed and stored alongside the database. Then when any new data is added to the files, it is matched up with the user interest profiles to trigger intelligence reports, vital messages and the like. Of course, profile database development is not a one-off exercise; in today's turbulent environment, assumptions and premises guiding strategic choice must be monitored and profile data updated as they change.

Profile database development is thus an intrinsic part of the strategic planning process, and can help in developing strategic managers (as discussed later.) Indeed, given the obstacles which impede strategic information processing—fractionalised organisations, day-to-day pressures, lack of awareness of others' strategic interests, and diverse cognitive barriers—investment in design processes, such as profile database development, may well yield greater benefits than collecting more and more bodies of information.

Selection of database storage mechanisms will depend on criteria of capacity, life cycle, urgency, cost, security, access, retrieval and data-type. It is likely that core files will be computer-based to aid efficient storage and retrieval. The disposable database, being ephemeral and speculative, probably only warrants manual storage. Temporary databases will be designed to meet their particular purpose, whilst profile databases may well be represented by one guiding document or manual. Thus strategic database systems may incorporate any of the following: computer-based files, manual files, information indexes, memo and correspondence files, publications, reports and surveys, manuals and procedures, managers private systems, and 'black books'. As organisations extend their scanning activities and improve their database systems, and as strategic planning develops beyond the individual organisation into sector, national and international horizons, public database systems are becoming available. Computer bureaux now offer terminal access to such systems, one well known collection of files containing: economic trends and forecasts, business conditions, treasury forecasts, banks' financial data, IMF international financial data, demographic data, price indices, agricultural statistics, energy statistics, securities data, exchange rate data, and government statistics. One way of ensuring that a strategic database is used is to provide enquiry facilities which actually relate to strategic issues.[21] This permits database enquiries to be made in terms of the use to which data are to be put, rather than in terms of the data themselves. Such a facility, for example, would allow a manager to ask about the capability of competitor X to introduce a new product Y next year. He then is presented with system responses which successively identify sub-classes of data in which he may be interested, say the competitor's financial capability, production capability, marketing capability and technological capability, all being elements of the overall issue. The manager could then ask for further data sub-sets, perhaps breaking down the competitor's marketing capability into distribution, sales, service and advertising profiles. Clearly such a system is limited to strategic issues and questions which have been pre-programmed. It is therefore somewhat speculative, but can be kept relevant by involving the same team that specifies the profile database, together with other key users. Such a system is obviously computer-based.

Finally a strategic database which is manageable, and therefore used, is a precious asset. It must, therefore, be secure, for it could be the target of competitors' intelligence activities. Safeguards on input, access and dissemination are required, but within limits, for otherwise strategic awareness may be impaired and important strategic messages may be lost. Security safeguards include assigning total responsibility to a database administrator, validation procedures for input, identification codes for users, password protection on computer files, locks on manual files, classification schemes to distinguish 'open' information from 'closed' information, periodic audits and administrative controls on dissemination.

MODELS

Computer-based models have a role in both the design and choice phases of strategy-making. This role has been enhanced by the availability of timesharing facilities, of databases and of modelling software. An example of modelling in mergers and acquisitions analysis demonstrates the potential. Databases of company financial data can be scanned and analysed by simple deterministic models to produce a list of potential companies for acquisition. Then selection can be aided by use of financial projection models. Finally, once a 'victim' is selected, a model built on standard financial algebra can be used to generate the offer package.[22]

The benefits of strategic modelling are now apparent. The quality of search and analysis is improved. Furthermore if conditions change, say the share price of a candidate company in a merger situation, the model can quickly adapt and react. Then by further what-if questioning, contingency plans can be devised, for example in generating acquisition terms. Finally mechanisation frees managerial time for consideration of important qualitative factors and for due application of the judgement, intuition, creativity and experience which such decision-making requires. However, there are pitfalls. It is tempting to use planning models developed in other activities and by other specialists. The distinctive nature of strategic data and decision-making makes such 'bottom-up' approaches inappropriate. Equally, the 'top-down' approaches of corporate, modular or comprehensive models are likely to fail, as each strategic decision is different, because decision-makers have different styles and since the model becomes too complex either for operational reliability or user comprehension. Modelling therefore must be firmly embedded *within* the planning process, responding to genuine, specific needs, and being applied with temperance and intelligence. From such a 'modelling within' approach follow certain guidelines:

(1) Generalised strategic models will fail.
(2) Each strategic decision, decision-maker or situation may require a specific model.
(3) A strategic decision may require several supporting models, not least to cope with the interrupts of the decision process.
(4) Managers must control strategic modelling and not yield responsibility to technicians with different goals, such as the building of bigger and more complex models.
(5) Participative model design and development is essential.
(6) A model-base of modelling software, core model components and modelling data is likely to be beneficial.
(7) The role of strategic models is to aid learning and judgement as much as to improve analysis *per se.*

This last guideline is perhaps fundamental. Unthinking, computationally oriented modelling can transmit technocratic values, impart rationality and suggest answers where judgement, bargaining, compromise, politics or inspiration are more appropriate. Yet, as strategic planning moves away from financial extrapolations, single point estimates and narrowly-defined futures towards qualitative assessments, alternative scenario testing, range forward estimates, sensitivity and risk analysis and incorporation of political and social variables, models are being used as learning enablers. The technology of MIS can be harnessed in developing managers with more environmental sensitivity and understanding. Models can be used in sensitivity analysis to discover the most important parameters making or breaking a current or potential strategy, for discovering value premises, to expose inconsistencies, in offensive or defensive persuasion, in continuous review of strategies and perhaps in after-the-fact justification of strategic choices. As in other application areas, models should be seen as learning systems.

DECISION ENVIRONMENTS

Interest is growing in constructing 'decision environments' or what often are called chart-rooms, decision-making centres, war-rooms or information centres. Whether decision environments are a form of MIS is perhaps arguable, although they are certainly formally designed to input, process and output data. Also they are often MIS-dependent in operation. Decision environments aim to engender creative thinking and to facilitate control of complex operations. Typically, they comprise a loosely integrated set of charts, graphs, tables, models and screens for effective presentation of information. They need not be computer-based, although supporting modelling facilities are sometimes incorporated and random-access remote controlled display systems may be computer-driven. Most surveys suggest that the prime rationale of the decision environment is effective presentation and communication of information. So computer support is only necessary if it improves storage, access, retrieval, display or analysis. The advantages claimed include:

(1) Improved comprehension because we tend to absorb more of what we see and hear.

(2) Improved group problem-solving because all decision-makers have access to the same data.

(3) Exploration of issues because ad hoc staff and computer help are available.

(4) A better mix of formal and informal information.

Decision environments grew out of war-rooms[23] and still they may be more relevant to operations planning and control. Several firms and utilities, for example the Pillsbury Company, have used chart-rooms for operational and management control,[24] and at the national level the operations room developed by Stafford Beer[25] in Chile is well-documented. At the strategic level, however, the decision-centre concept has to overcome the problems of defining strategic information and developing a strategic database. In addition cost and management's anxiety to avoid gimmickry, may have constrained development.

Yet decision environments for strategic planning have been built. They are not necessarily constructed around advanced technology. For example, if modelling facilities are included, they may be provided off-line in an adjacent room; the model's output is then displayed after a short delay. So decision environments, like all MIS, should be designed to meet their purpose and no more. On balance, however, it seems unlikely that they offer a breakthrough in strategic planning. They are still data-dependent and only relate to a small part of the strategy-making process. Yet any aids to presentation and communication of information should not be totally dismissed in an area where cognitive barriers are so strong.

FEEDBACK SYSTEMS

The rationale for feedback systems in strategic planning is threefold:

(1) Strategy is not just concerned with decision-making. Strategies have to be implemented and so corrective feedbacks, to ensure actions conform to plan, and adaptive feedbacks, to ensure plans react to change, are both necessary.

(2) Strategy-making is not entirely a creative, inspirational and political process. Strategists can learn from experience and thus strategy audits, or reviews of strategic performance, are valuable.

(3) In addition to scanning systems which seek strategic intelligence, valuable feedbacks can also be captured from other planning and control systems in the organisation. A 'nose' for strategic feedbacks is therefore worth cultivating.

The first class of feedback system is designed to track and diagnose implementation of strategic plans. They monitor results not only to aid those responsible for implementation, but also to inform top management of the operational consequences of their strategic decisions. It is equally important to monitor the assumptions upon which the plans were founded, because an additional strategic change may be required long before implementation is complete. These feedbacks therefore serve corrective, adaptive and learning purposes. Each such feedback system is likely to be a simple, formal information routine focusing on key factors and results.

A strategy audit is a formal term for what is normally a very informal review of strategic performance. An audit team, perhaps made up of top managers, staff specialists and developing managers, will conduct a periodic review of enterprise goals, recent important events, and strategic performance. Such feedbacks are then used to improve strategic information systems, to assess and review the organisation's decision-making structure, and to modify any current strategy which is found to be inadequate.

Many potential strategic feedbacks which exist in organisations may be captured by adapting or re-designing other planning and control systems. To ensure that major exceptions, sudden discontinuities or persistent trends are flagged by these systems, occasional performance reviews may be instituted, infrequent summary statistics produced, or more external tracking incorporated. In other words, linkages between management control and strategic planning can be valuable.

A second strategic feedback difficulty can occur because of the complexity of modern organisation design. Lorange[26] points out that in multinational corporations organisation structure is frequently oriented towards integration and control. For example, constituent companies and divisions may be organised by product, or by geography, to make smaller businesses out of large, and to delegate responsibility. Information flows then follow the organisational structure, being either product-oriented or geographically-oriented but rarely crossing these boundaries. Strategic planning, however, is concerned with adaptation and unless information flows cross the control boundaries, key environmental information may be lost. For example, in a product-oriented structure, if market or political information were aggregated on a geographical basis previously unrecognised, strategic messages might be detected. Thus a re-alignment of MIS, with corporate analysis, can compensate for the strategic inadequacies of MIS designed to meet control objectives.

STRATEGIC MANAGEMENT

Successful strategic planning depends on more than employment of strategy formulation techniques and development of strategic information systems. A broader perspective is required whereby both these activities are integrated into the organisation. Strategic management is required in order to create a facilitative context and framework within which strategy formulation techniques and strategic MIS can be developed and used effectively (Figure 15.7). These three elements of strategic planning are interdependent and must be in balance. Strategic planning is far more than forecasting; it is an active attempt to influence the organisation's future. Strategic management, therefore, is required to ensure that strategy formulation is purposeful and that no strategic stimuli are ignored. A reverse influence exists whereby strategy-making and strategic MIS are required to stimulate occasional directional change in strategic management. Figure 15.7 also emphasises how strategy formulation techniques and strategic MIS must be interdependent and interactive.

There are four essential strategic management tasks: (1) giving strategic direction; (2) creating a strategic culture; (3) designing a strategic organisation; and (4) developing strategic managers.

STRATEGIC DIRECTION

Strategic direction entails defining the organisation's current strategy and role, describing the strategic issues and how they are to be dealt with, and

FIGURE 15.7. A strategic planning system

telling managers how they are expected to contribute. From this set of statements is derived the strategic profile database.

Strategic direction is particularly important in ensuring that MIS development is in tune with the organisation's needs. In Chapter 3 we saw how experience up to now suggests that MIS frequently have been designed to meet the designers' goals rather than the objectives of the organisation or the needs of the users. In other words, there is a strong case for strategic planning of MIS. A model of this process, by King,[27] is reproduced in Figure 15.8. Given strategic direction, the organisational strategy set will exist in the form of the strategic profile database. Otherwise it must be explicated by the MIS professionals and validated by top management. Once derived, it is transformed by a process of strategy inferences and interpretation by the MIS specialists into the MIS strategy set, again being validated by top management. The outputs of MIS strategic planning then become the inputs to the subsequent systems development process, so that all MIS are closely related to the organisation, its strategy and its capabilities. Of course, since MIS—especially strategic information systems—affect strategic thinking and ultimately strategy-making, the process is in reality circular. However, strategic planning for MIS ensures that the consequent systems are not obsolete at the outset.

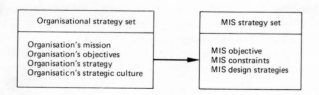

FIGURE 15.8. MIS strategic planning process

STRATEGIC CULTURE

Clearly strategic direction helps create a strategic culture. Other conditions, however, are required. Managers must be motivated to contribute to strategy-making; so resources must be made available and effort be rewarded. In particular, performance measurement and reward systems should encourage entrepreneurship, creativity and problem-seeking. Then a planning attitude in all managerial activities can be encouraged, and an appreciation that change is normal and inevitable can be fostered. Participative strategic management is another means of creating a strategic culture.

Indeed participation is perhaps essential, for it emphasises that strategic planning is a management, not a specialist, responsibility. Of course, professional planners are needed to devise and understand strategic techniques, to administer the strategic database and to ensure that strategy-making is given its due priority. However, they are initiators, facilitators, consultants and evaluators rather than strategic decision-takers. As such they are key components of strategic MIS, but they must not be seen as the end user.

It is because specialists can be naive, impressionistic and opinionated, because they often lack a sense of relevance and experience, and because they do not have a monopoly on creativity, that participative strategic management is commonly advocated. Also, it has been found that participation by those who have to implement the strategy is beneficial, for often it seems easier to devise strategies than to carry them out. There is often a gap between the authors of strategic decisions and those who prepare and execute the operating plans. Implementers not only bring different perspectives and make critical practical contributions, but also may be motivated to ensure that implementation is successful. Finally, broad-based participation also helps foster strategic thinking at an early stage and establishes the idea that strategy-making depends on all management, and not just those at the top. Clearly, these arguments for participation apply just as much to the strategic MIS design process—and the participants are identical.

STRATEGIC ORGANISATION

Design of an organisation which facilitates strategic planning is a question of both structure and process. Structure is required to coordinate and focus strategic thinking and strategic information processing. Processes are required to enhance responsiveness, encourage flexibility and ensure adaptation. Wilensky[28] has suggested that intelligence failures are built into complex organisations. To avoid such failures, it would seem that the organisation should be able to:

(1) Collect and assemble unrelated data into strategically meaningful information sets. Organisation structures have evolved to meet this need. Examples include the General Electric concept of the 'strategic business unit' outlined in Chapter 13, matrix structures to aid integration and coordination, project management structures to enable boundaries to be crossed, and various forms of 'the corporate office'.

(2) See the strategic message of information once it is collected and assembled. Parochialism of managerial experience, of functional disciplines and of departmental boundaries often prevents or frustrates this. Investment in processes may be a solution, examples being job rotation, management education courses, value-exposing experiencing, interdepartmental activities and participative experiments.

(3) Use any intelligence which may be available. Here investment in processing may be required to break down the mechanistic and routine thinking that reliance on structures can bring. This process orientation may require acceptance that irregular procedures are sometimes required, that external specialists may have a role, and that cultivation of contacts, networks and similar unofficial intelligence can be valuable.

STRATEGIC MANAGERS

Finally the need for management development is perhaps a recognition that to succeed in the learning process that is strategic planning, we first must plan how to learn. An emphasis probably should be laid on learning by doing, as it seems that there is no substitute for experience. Strategic thinking is best cultivated by exposure to strategy-making. The more that strategic planning is cultivated, the higher will be the quality of strategic MIS and strategic decisions. Equally, the more that managers are developed into change agents and change seekers, the more that change will be accepted as inevitable and the better we will manage change.

One vehicle for management development, which in turn contributes to achievement of the other three tasks of strategic management, is participative development of the strategic profile database. Involvement of developing managers from different functions in the team which defines this database may not only cultivate strategic thinking but help ensure that use of strategic MIS becomes an essential part of the strategic planning process.[29]

The more that organisations seek to plan, the more they find themselves dependent upon the outcomes of other agencies, both public and private, and the more they become aware of the complex interrelationships of the economic, social and political environments in which they operate.[30] Faced with such complexity, it is easy for organisations to internalise too passive a frame of reference for understanding the environment. The most important task of strategic management, and the most fruitful form of management development, could be to extend strategic horizons and open up these frames of reference by encouraging involvement in inter-organisational, national and international planning. We might then not only better understand, but also influence, our environments. The industry sector working parties of NEDO in the UK provide an example of this. Another instance is an experiment with a new MIS design technique called 'the expectations approach'.[31] Here managers from interacting organisations in a local region joined together to define their expectations of each other's roles, responsibilities and information needs. Congruences and inconsistencies were then analysed and explored in order to improve the organisations' interactions.

The vital role of management development provides an apposite conclusion to this chapter, and indeed to the entire book. The key to progress in strategic planning does not lie in developing more sophisticated strategy formulation techniques and 'advanced' information systems. The key is developing managers' environmental sensitivity and strategic thinking. Likewise progress in management information systems in general does not depend on developing more sophisticated information processing technologies and system design techniques. It depends, above all, on information management—which has been the theme of this book.

CHAPTER 15—PROJECTS

1. Management information systems which scan the business environment commonly focus only on economic variables. For one of the following activities, design a system for scanning political and social variables: (1) a joint stock bank; (2) a multinational chemical corporation; (3) a local government authority in a major metropolitan region; and suggest why such a system is necessary.

2. Devise a framework for measuring the performance of a strategic planning information system.

3. 'Management should apply operations research or systems analysis principles of mathematical analysis to complex strategic questions' (Smaller, D. J., and Ruggles, Jnr., R. L. 'Six Business Lessons from the Pentagon', *Harvard Business Review*, March–April 1966). Discuss this assertion.

4. 'Today's facts become tomorrow's misinformation' (Toffler in *Future Shock*). How relevant is this claim to strategic information system design?

5. For an organisation with which you are familiar, consider how you would develop a database system to serve the null strategy approach to strategic planning.

6. With the help of colleagues, develop a strategic profile database for your own organisation.

NOTES

1. Interview, 'Shortcomings of Strategic Planning', *International Management*, September 1976.
2. Aguilar, F., *Scanning the Business Environment*. New York: Macmillan, 1967.
3. Simon, H. A., *The New Science of Management Decision*. New York: Harper and Row, 1960.
4. Mintzberg, H., Raisinghani, D., and Theoret, A., 'The Structure of "Unstructured" Decision Processes', Montreal, McGill University, Faculty of Management Working Paper, 1973.
5. *Ibid.*
6. Thompson, J. D., and Tuden, A., 'Strategies, Structures and Processes of Organisational Decision', in Thompson, J. D., *et al.* (eds.), *Comparative Studies in Administration*. Pittsburgh, Pa.: University of Pittsburgh Press, 1959.
7. Toffler, A., *Future Shock*. London: The Bodley Head, 1970.
8. Rhenman, E., *Organization Theory for Long-Range Planning*. London: Wiley, 1972.
9. Bower, J. L., 'Managing the Resource Allocation Process: A Study of Corporate Planning and Investment', Division of Research, Graduate School of Business Administration, Harvard University, Boston, 1970.
10. Grinyer, P. H., and Norburn, D., 'Strategic Planning in 21 UK Companies', *Long-Range Planning*, August 1974.
11. Hedberg, B., and Jönsson, S., 'Designing Semi-confusing Information Systems for Organisations in Changing Environments', *Accounting, Organisations and Society*, 3, No. 1 (1978).
12. Aguilar, F. J., *Scanning the Business Environment*. New York: Macmillan, 1967.
13. King, W. R., and Cleland, D. I., 'Decision and Information Systems for Strategic Planning', *Business Horizons*, April 1973.

14. Grinyer, P. H., and Norburn, D., 'Strategic Planning in 21 UK Companies', *Long-Range Planning*, August 1974.
15. Aguilar, F. J., *op. cit.*
16. *Ibid.*
17. Cleland, D. I., and King, W. R., 'Competitive Business Intelligence Systems', *Business Horizons*, December 1975.
18. Zacharias, E. M., *Secret Missions: The Story of an Intelligence Officer*. New York: Putnam, 1946.
19. Wilensky, H., *Organisational Intelligence*. New York: Basic Books, 1967.
20. Derived from Cleland, D. I., and King, W. R., *Systems Analysis and Project Management*. New York: McGraw-Hill, 1975.
21. Rodriguez, J. I., and King, W. R., 'Strategic Issue Competitive Information Systems', University of Pittsburgh Graduate School of Business, Working paper 222.
22. For an example of mergers and acquisitions modelling, see McCosh, A. M., and Scott-Morton, M. S., *Management Decision Support Systems*. London: Macmillan, 1978, Chapter 7.
23. See, for example, Smaller, D. J., and Ruggles, Jr, R. L., 'Six Business Lessons from the Pentagon', *Harvard Business Review*, March–April 1966.
24. Weber, J. R., 'The Corporate Command Post', *Business Automation*, December 1968.
25. Beer, S., 'The Cybernetics of National Development', The Zaheer Lecture, 1976, Manchester Business School.
26. Lorange, D., 'A Framework for Strategic Planning in Multinational Corporations', *Long-Range Planning*, June 1976.
27. King ,W. R., 'Strategic Planning for MIS', *MIS Quarterly*, March 1978.
28. Wilensky, H., *Organisational Intelligence*. New York: Basic Books, 1967.
29. King, W. R., and Cleland, D. I., 'Information for more effective Strategic Planning', *Long-Range Planning*, February 1977.
30. Friend, J. K., *et al.*, *Public Planning: The Inter-corporate Dimension*. London: Tavistock, 1974.
31. Machin, J., 'The Expectations Approach', Working paper presented at the European Institute of Advanced Studies in Management, Brussels, September 1977.

BIBLIOGRAPHY

Aguilar, F. J., *Scanning the Business Environment*. New York: Macmillan, 1967.
Ansoff, H. I. (ed.), *Business Strategy*. Harmondsworth: Penguin, 1969.
Earl, M. J., and Hopwood, A. G., 'From Management Information to Information Management', in Lucas, H. (ed.), *The Information Systems Environment*. North-Holland, 1980.
Lorange, P., and Vancil, R. F., *Strategic Planning Systems*. Englewood Cliffs, N.J.: Prentice-Hall, 1977.
Taylor, B., and Sparkes, J. R., *Corporate Strategy and Planning*. London: Heinemann, 1977.
Toffler, A., *Future Shock*. London: The Bodley Head, 1970.
Wilensky, H., *Organizational Intelligence*. New York: Basic Books, 1967.

Index